Becoming an Emotionally Focused Couple Therapist

Becoming an Emotionally Focused Couple Therapist

The Workbook

Susan M. Johnson

Brent Bradley, Jim Furrow, Alison Lee,
Gail Palmer, Doug Tilley, Scott Woolley

Routledge
Taylor & Francis Group

NEW YORK   LONDON

Published in 2005 by
Routledge
Taylor & Francis Group
270 Madison Avenue
New York, NY 10016

Published in Great Britain by
Routledge
Taylor & Francis Group
2 Park Square
Milton Park, Abingdon
Oxon OX14 4RN

Printed in the United States of America on acid-free paper
10 9 8 7 6 5

International Standard Book Number-10: 0-415-94747-2 (Softcover)
International Standard Book Number-13: 978-0-415-94747-3 (Softcover)

Library of Congress Cataloging-in-Publication Data

Catalog record is available from the Library of Congress

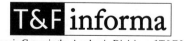

Taylor & Francis Group is the Academic Division of T&F Informa plc.

Visit the Taylor & Francis Web site at
http://www.taylorandfrancis.com
and the Routledge Web site at
http://www.routledge-ny.com

CONTENTS

PREFACE

This workbook is designed to help therapists and counselors use the emotionally focused perspective and interventions to transform couple and family relationships. It is based on two decades of practice, research, and writing. The book should be used in conjunction with the manual for EFT (*The Practice of Emotionally Focused Couple Therapy: Creating Connection*, 2nd ed., Brunner-Routledge, 2004) and other resources, including training videotapes, found on the EFT Web site (http://www.eft.ca). A list of EFT supervisors is also included on the website.

To feel confident in EFT and use it effectively with different kinds of couples, most therapists should read the manual and additional chapters and articles, attend training with an EFT trainer, and obtain clinical consultation/supervision. Such diligent training is required for any form of psychological intervention but especially one in which a therapist is intervening in an ongoing, multidimensional, and emotionally powerful interpersonal drama. Becoming fluent in EFT is like learning ballet—it is an ongoing process and cannot be learned by simply reading a book or watching an expert therapist. This book is designed by seven practicing EFT therapists—who still learn from every couple they see—to help the reader engage in that learning process. It is not designed to stand alone. Over the years, we have found that other modalities such as watching tapes of one's own sessions and belonging to a supportive peer supervision group are an invaluable part of this process.

Everyone who reads this book will likely have their own way of conducting EFT and will bring their own styles and strengths to the model. In the era of brief and briefer therapy, it is tempting to try to reduce interventions to four or five invariant quick fixes and to teach therapists in this way. We believe that you do not have to move to a simplistic level to be efficient and incisive in couple and family therapy. Instead, you must learn to create a safe, collaborative environment, know how to focus on what matters, and help people work with the powerful emotional dramas in which they are caught.

There are certain elements of EFT that are very difficult to learn from any printed page. For example, we find that students of EFT learn about key issues of pacing from watching their own videotapes of therapy. Often the difference between an experienced EFT therapist and a novice therapist is not the interventions used, but rather that the more experienced therapists go more slowly, repeat themselves, and circle again and again through the same territory until clients can hold a tangible new emotional reality in their hands. The more experienced therapist knows the emotional process that the couple is engaged in more intimately and can slice risks thin, structuring new responses again and again until powerful bonding events emerge.

In light of the above, an explicit structure exists to support those who wish to become registered as EFT couples' therapists. This structure, which is laid out on the EFT Web site, includes training, supervision, and case review. EFT is now taught in many graduate programs in North America and in many other parts of the world. We hope that those who teach these programs will also find this workbook useful and supportive.

You cannot practice EFT without also using it as a lens for your own relationships and as a path into your own attachment issues—we all have them. We hope that this book will help you use this lens in a positive way for your personal and your professional life. Most of all, we hope you find your journey through this book stimulating, powerful, and emotionally engaging.

This workbook is divided into three sections. Chapters 1 through 3 present a theoretical overview and summary of interventions. Chapters 4 through 8 describe the treatment process over the nine steps of EFT and include an ongoing case description. Chapters 9 through 11 address special issues, relationship traumas, and family interventions. The last chapter is a detailed case review.

SECTION I:

THEORETICAL OVERVIEW AND SUMMARY OF INTERVENTIONS

1

INTRODUCTION:
THE NATURE OF EFT

Emotionally focused couple therapy (EFT) is a short-term, systematic, and tested intervention to reduce distress in adult love relationships and create more secure attachment bonds. The approach is also used with families (EFFT). The title reflects the priority given to emotion as a key organizer of inner experiences and key interactions in love relationships. A focus on emotion is seen as the essential transforming element in effective couple therapy. The word "emotion" comes from the Latin word "to move." EFT uses the power of emotion to "move" partners and evoke new responses in recurring key interactions that make up a couple's relationship "dance." When we speak of being emotionally "moved" we are usually talking of being touched, stirred up, compelled to respond to a powerful cue that evokes action in us. Emotion pulls for and organizes key responses in close relationships.

If you were to watch an EFT couple therapist work, what would you see? You would see the therapist creating a safe, egalitarian relationship with the partners. You would see the therapist tracking and exploring how emotions direct the couple's dance and how the dance then shapes key emotions. You would see the therapist expanding emotional responses to include basic fears and needs and helping to create a new dance based on these expanded emotions. Constriction and rigidity is replaced by expansiveness and flexibility. The therapist shifts from questions like "What happens to you when your partner moves away, as he did just now?" to formulations such as "Your desperate anger scares your partner—and it is so hard for you to show the loneliness and longing underneath," to requests such as "Can you tell him 'Please, I need you to hold and reassure me.'"

This book is designed to help therapists and counselors learn the EFT model and apply it with confidence. A manual and an extensive literature base describe EFT interventions and should be used in conjunction with this book. Given the difficulty of learning any therapy approach simply from descriptions of ways to see problems and ways to intervene, this book offers examples and exercises to involve the reader and to bridge the gap between reading words on a page and being part of the evolving drama of a therapy session. The goal of this book is to take readers by the hand and walk them through the EFT model. We have attempted to present the model in small steps and to build those steps gradually to the point where readers will sense that they have a compass and a map to improving their clients' relationships and will know the road to take with clients at key moments in therapy. The model offers a coherent and researched theory of adult love relationships, an outline of the process of change and the steps in that process, and a clear outline of interventions.

EFT has evolved in the last decade from a marginalized and little recognized approach into a mainstream model that is accepted by the American Psychological Association as empirically validated. EFT is taught in numerous couple and family therapy, social work, counseling, and psychology graduate programs in North America and throughout the world. This model is also taught in many different cultural contexts and is used for many different kinds of clients. It is not difficult to see why EFT has become better known and widely accepted. Attitudes to and research on key elements of EFT, namely emotion and adult attachment, have changed and grown, as has the recognition of the need for empirical validation of interventions.

In the 1980s, when EFT was first formulated, actively working with emotion was not generally popular in the couple and family field. Emotion itself was most often seen as a troublesome intrapsychic variable that was not part of a systemic interpersonal perspective. Emotion was then viewed as part of the problem rather than as a potent part of the solution. Attachment theory, the model of adult love used in EFT, has also been more clearly articulated and researched in the last decade, and the need for a model of adult love as a map for couples' intervention has become more obvious. Part of the present popularity of EFT rests with the greater recognition of the positive power of working with emotion, and that adult attachment has generated a large following and a vibrant body of associated research and literature. In addition, with the advent of managed care in North America, the need for a treatment model to be able to demonstrate positive outcomes has become more and more compelling. The outcomes on EFT can be seen as the most positive and promising in the field of couple therapy (Johnson, Hunsley, Greenberg, & Schindler, 1999).

EFT reflects the priorities and recent foci of the present couples' therapy context in the following 10 ways:

1. It is a brief treatment focused on key factors in relationship distress and so it can be used in a managed care environment.

2. It has been systematically described and rigorously tested and found to be effective. A recent meta-analysis of the best studies found 70–73% of couples to be recovered from marital distress and 90% of couples to have significantly improved.

3. Relapse is a significant concern in the couple therapy field. Research with high-risk couples suggests that relapse is not a significant issue with EFT.

4. The need for studies of how change occurs and exactly how therapists should intervene at key times is an ongoing issue in this field. Process research exists that supports the clinical wisdom of EFT and elaborates on how change occurs, specific processes, and change events in therapy.

5. EFT fits with recent research on the nature of marital distress and satisfaction within the developing science of personal relationships. The findings of Gottman and colleagues have emphasized the significant role of emotional communication in the development of relationship distress. For example, research suggests that rather than help couples resolve content issues, therapy should help couples develop soothing interactions and maintain emotional engagement during disagreements. The process of change in EFT mirrors this research in that it structures small steps toward safe emotional engagement so that partners can soothe, comfort, and reassure each other.

6. There is an increasing focus in couple therapy on issues of diversity. EFT is used with many different kinds of couples, with couples of different social classes, with different kinds of problems (for example, partners facing depression or chronic illness), and across cultural groups. The therapeutic alliance in EFT is collaborative and egalitarian. The experiential roots of EFT generally promote a therapeutic stance of respect for differences and an openness to learning from clients what is meaningful for them and how they view intimate relationships. Every individual and every

couple system is a culture unto itself, and the therapist must learn about and adapt interventions to this unique culture. But EFT also assumes that there is a certain universality that tends to cut across differences of culture, race, and class. For example, Tomkins (1962) lists what appears to be a small set of universal basic emotions: interest/excitement, joy, surprise, distress/anguish, disgust/contempt, anger/rage, shame, and fear/terror. Considerable evidence also suggests that attachment needs and responses are universal.

7. EFT shares a number of characteristics with gender-oriented and feminist approaches to couple therapy. The EFT attachment perspective on relationships parallels the work of feminist writers (Jordan, Kaplan, Miller, Stiver, & Surrey, 1991) who depathologize dependency. EFT and other feminist-informed therapies examine the impact of gender-based constraints and work to increase personal agency and to develop egalitarian relationships where reciprocity, intimacy, and interdependency can flourish.

8. EFT has also followed the move toward integration of interventions across models by combining systemic and experiential perspectives and attachment theory as a theory of love. It also integrates recent research on marital distress with these elements.

9. EFT fits with the present climate of couple and family therapy in that it takes a postmodern stance, promoting a collaborative alliance where clients are the "experts" on their reality, and therapists discover with their clients how inner and outer realities are constructed. This stance parallels the humanistic perspective of Carl Rogers (1961), whose main concern was to honor his clients' constructions of reality. EFT can be thought of as a postmodern therapy in that EFT therapists help clients deconstruct problems and responses by bringing marginalized aspects of reality into focus, probing for the not-yet spoken, and integrating elements of a couple's reality that have gone un-storied. They also help couples create integrated narratives about their cycles, their problems, and the process of change. But EFT does not fit with the more extreme postmodern position that there are no common existential conditions or processes, that reality is arbitrary and random, and that problems generally exist only in language and can therefore be "dis-solved" in language.

10. Last, but not least, the growth of the EFT model reflects the increasing pressure for clinicians to find empirical support for their conceptualizations of key variables and to document the impact of these variables on relationship problems and repair processes. The attachment theory of adult love used in EFT has a substantial and growing research base (Johnson & Whiffen, 1999; Johnson, 2003; Cassidy & Shaver, 1999). In fact, all of the elements of EFT—the EFT perspective on relationship distress, the way of treating this distress, the process of change, and the explanatory attachment framework—have research support.

This workbook is designed not to stand alone, but to be used in conjunction with other EFT resources (see Appendix A).

Some of the answers to the questions asked in the exercises, especially in the first few chapters, will be found in the EFT literature rather than in the text of this book. We assume that readers will allow themselves to guess at answers—to play—to follow hunches and then discover how accurate their hunches were from the answers given in the back of the book, especially if their exposure to the EFT literature is only preliminary. We hope this engagement in the process of discovery will allow the EFT model to come alive. As in the model itself, the point is not to focus on performance (on getting the right answer), but on presence (on engaging in the process of discovery that occurs when you consider options or, in later chapters, draft your own responses).

EFT references and resources can be found on the EFT Web site (http://www.eft.ca). The main resources are the following:

1. The manual for intervention, first published in 1996 and revised in 2004, *Creating Connection: The Practice of Emotionally Focused Couples Therapy.*

2. The EFT training tapes (available from the Ottawa Couple and Family Institute).

3. Supervision/consultation from EFT therapists, some of whom are listed on the EFT website.

4. General reading on EFT—articles, chapters, and books listed on the Web site and in Appendix A of this book. Most chapters have transcripts of therapy, which can help the less experienced EFT therapist understand how the process of therapy unfolds.

5. General reading on topics such as emotion, experiential and systemic models, and attachment theory, and research on marital distress and satisfaction. Key resources on each of these topics are listed at the end of this book. Suggestions for learning EFT for couples are given in Appendix B.

EXERCISES: THE ESSENTIAL NATURE OF EFT

Check correct answer or answers from options offered below. As with all the exercises, the answer key is in the back of this book. Often more than one of the possible answers given will be correct.

Exercise 1:

1. The theoretical basis of EFT can best be described as:
    a. A Bowenian view of close relationships and a solution-focused approach to intervention in therapy. ＿＿＿
    b. An attachment view of close relationships and a traditional insight-driven psychodynamic approach to intervention. ＿＿＿
    c. A behavioral/exchange theory view of close relationships and a skill-building approach to intervention. ＿＿＿
    d. A pragmatic, nontheoretical view of close relationships (love as friendship) and a solution-focused approach to intervention. ＿＿＿
    e. An attachment view of close relationships and a humanistic/experiential approach to intervention. ✓
    f. A differentiation of self-focused view of close relationships and a cognitive narrative approach to intervention. ＿＿＿

2. Which of the following is not a goal of EFT?
    a. To expand and reprocess the key emotional responses that make up the "music" of the dance between intimates.
    b. To create a more secure bond between partners.
    c. To restructure interactions toward accessibility, responsiveness, and engagement.
    d. To de-escalate arguments so that the couple are effective negotiators.

3. A prototypical scene/slice from EFT in process would look like: (two correct answers)
    a. The therapist linking clients' present responses to childhood conflicts. _____
    (b.) The therapist encapsulating a key emotional response with a client and asking this client in turn to share this with the other partner in a congruent, open way. _____
    c. The therapist suggesting another, more skilled way to express anger and helping partners practice this in the session. _____
    (d.) The therapist tracking and validating emotional responses and putting them in the frame of patterned cycles of interaction and attachment needs and fears. _____

4. EFT fits with the present context of couple and family therapy in the following ways except:
    a. It is brief and constructionist. _____
    b. It is integrative (integrating systems and experiential approaches). _____
    c. It is empirically validated. _____
    d. The alliance in EFT is collaborative and egalitarian. _____
    e. It is used with many different kinds of clients and to address different kinds of problems. _____
    f. Its reliance on the process of change has been systematically studied and outlined. _____
    g. Its focus fits with recent research on the nature of marital distress and satisfaction. _____
    (h.) It echoes extreme postmodern positions that view all realities as arbitrary and random. _____

5. The EFT perspective fits very well with the recent body of research on the nature of marital distress and satisfaction and predictors of divorce. The most obvious points of convergence are: (check all correct answers)
    a. The expression and regulation of emotion are noted as key factors in the definition of close relationships: e.g., fear and contempt on the face of partners predicts divorce according to Gottman's (1994) research, and attachment fears are a primary focus in EFT. _____
    b. Conflict is not seen as the best predictor of dissolution. Emotional disengagement is noted as being more dangerous for close relationships. _____
    c. Rigid, patterned interactions, such as criticize/complain or defend/distance that preclude safe emotional engagement are toxic for close relationships. _____
    d. The power of soothing emotionally connected interactions to define relationships is considerable. _____
    e. Elements such as give–get equity or problem-solving skills do not seem as crucial as the ability to create safe emotional engagement. _____

6. In terms of empirical validation, the status of EFT is: (four correct answers)
    a. EFT has only a few promising but very preliminary studies. _____
    b. A solid and rigorous empirical basis for the effectiveness of EFT exists. _____
    c. EFT for couples is accepted by APA as empirically validated. _____
    d. Process studies have outlined EFT change events and key interventions. _____

    e.   Empirical validation is considered unnecessary in a postmodern world and by EFT therapists. _____

    f.   Only weak studies of EFT (studies without control groups) exist. _____

    g.   The percentage of clients who recover from marital distress (70–73%) and who significantly improve (90%) found in the meta-analysis of the best EFT studies are impressive in terms of psychotherapy outcomes generally and for couple therapy in particular. ✓

7. Which of the following is not an essential role of the EFT therapist?

    a.   Process consultant. _____

    b.   Creator of a safe haven and secure base in each session. _____

    c.   Surrogate processor of emerging experience. _____

    d.   Supportive, collaborative partner in the change process. _____

    e.   Choreographer of key change events in therapy. _____

    f.   Coach in the practice of specific new communication skills. ✓

8. The naming of EFT: (four correct answers)

    a.   The title EFT arose out of the originators, respect for catharsis and distrust of emotional repression. _____

    b.   The title EFT was assigned to reflect the originators' understanding of the key importance of emotional signals in the drama of close attachments. ✓

    c.   The title was assigned to stress emotion as a key agent of change in a field that was focused mostly on cognition and behavior. ✓

    d.   The title reflected the humanistic experiential perspective of the originators of EFT and their recognition of the role of emotion in the creation of meaning. ✓

    e.   The title is a statement of the usefulness of ventilation as a way out of repression and inhibition. _____

    f.   The title reflects a view of emotion as an adaptive rapid response system that has a unique power to "move" people into new ways of seeing and acting. ✓

9. In EFT, emotions are not viewed as:

    a.   Adaptive responses, providing a rapid and compelling response system that organizes behavior in the interests of security, survival, and the fulfillment of needs. _____

    b.   A powerful focusing and orienting force; a compass that directs attention to needs and specific environmental cues. _____

    c.   A major element in the creation of meaning, especially in social interactions where many responses tend to be ambiguous and we have to "fill in the blanks." _____

    d.   A prime "mover" and organizer of responses in attachment relationships. _____

    e.   An activator of key cognitions concerning the nature of the self and others. _____

    f.   Arising from the more primitive part of the brain that is ruled by cognition in mature adults. ✓

    g.   The primary signaling system in interactions with key others (the music of the dance of intimacy). _____

10. Which of the following are primary tasks of EFT? (three correct answers)

    a.   To prevent all occurrences of negative cycles, such as blame/defend. _____

    b.   To reprocess and expand clients' key emotional responses. ✓

    c. To structure and shape new kinds of interactions—accessible and responsive interactions. _____

    d. To foster secure emotional bonds between partners. _____

    e. To help partners choose marriage over divorce. _____

11. Change occurs in EFT primarily through which two ways?

    a. New corrective emotional experiences. Core attachment responses then take on a new shape and color. _____

    b. New emotional moves create new relational events that redefine the security of the bond between partners. _____

    c. Revision of the dominant story of a distressed relationship and the externalizing of problems. _____

    d. Creating new problem-solving and communications skill sequences. _____

    e. Insight into past childhood dynamics and unconscious wishes. _____

12. The three stages of EFT are:

    a. De-escalation of conflict; the step of clarifying underlying feelings; promotion of positive narratives. _____

    b. De-escalation of negative interactions; changing/restructuring interactional positions; consolidation and integration. _____

    c. Position restructuring; emotional engagement; consolidation. _____

    d. Alliance creation; behavioral contracting; the change event entitled blamer softening. _____

13. Pick three contraindications for EFT:

    a. Ongoing abusiveness/violence in a relationship, especially if the "victim" expresses fear and/or the "perpetrator" does not take responsibility. _____

    b. Discordant goals; for example, where one partner has already disengaged and exited from the relationship and the other desires reconnection. _____

    c. The inability to create any kind of collaborative alliance. _____

    d. Depression or posttraumatic stress in one partner. _____

    e. An "inexpressive" style in the male partner. _____

    f. Less education and lower socioeconomic status of clients. _____

14. Check the following statements to see if you can identify the two best predictors of success in EFT. This information is not included in the brief information on EFT given at the beginning of this workbook. If you have not read the literature in detail, see which ones make the most sense to you and then compare your answer to the ones given in the back of the book.

    a. Initial relationship distress level accounts for almost 50% of the variance in behavioral couple therapy outcome. As might be expected, this is also the best predictor of success in EFT. _____

    b. The traditionality of the couple predicts success in EFT: It is hard to get traditional couples to talk about feelings. _____

    c. The faith of the female partner that her partner still cares for her is the best identified predictor of success in EFT. _____

    d. Higher income and length of marriage predicts success in EFT. _____

    e. The quality of the alliance with the therapist is a significant predictor of success in EFT. _✓_

15. Of the three elements of the therapeutic alliance—bond with the therapist, agreement about goals of therapy, and the perceived relevance of therapy tasks—the element of the therapeutic relationship found to be the most predictive of outcome in EFT is:

    a. The bond aspect of the alliance between each partner and the therapist. _____

    b. The goal agreement aspect of the alliance between each partner and the therapist. _____

    c. The task aspect of the alliance: how relevant processes and tasks feel in the sessions. _0✓_

16. The usual number of sessions in EFT studies and in EFT clinical practice are: (two correct answers). (Again, if you are just beginning to read the literature, go with your hunch about the answer and see how it compares with the one we give in the back of the book.)

    a. In studies and in practice the usual number of sessions is 15. _____

    b. In studies the usual number has been 10 to 12, whereas in practice it is 10 to 20. _____

    c. In studies the usual number of sessions is 20, whereas in practice it is 30. _____

    d. In practice with clients suffering from PTSD the average number of sessions is 30 to 35. _____

17. In EFT, the focus is on the present process: the unfolding of inner and interpersonal dramas and how they evolve from moment to moment. The many Ps of EFT can be encapsulated as: (four correct answers)

    a. A focus on what is most present and poignant in the session. _____

    b. A focus on primary core emotion, after naming and validating secondary reactive emotions, such as irritation. _____

    c. A focus on the process of shaping inner worlds and outer dances. _____

    d. A focus on the positions partners take in the dance and the recurring patterns that define this dance. _____

    e. A focus on the pathology of particular ways of responding and how they pull for negative reactions. _____

18. In EFT the main way a focus on the past is used is to:

    a. Explain the developmental delays of the clients and their need for reeducation. _____

    b. Make unconscious desires and conflicts conscious. _____

    c. Validate and empathize with each client's present ways of seeing and dealing with distress and insecurity in the relationship. _____

    d. Contrast past negative responses with the unique positive responses of the present. _____

19. Which of the following is not a core assumption of EFT?

    a. Emotion is the music of the couple's dance. Rigid, constricted, or "stuck" emotions evoke constricted patterns of responses/interactions. _____

    b. Narrow patterns of interpersonal responses then evoke narrow, self-perpetuating emotional states. _____

0 ✓ c. The alliance and the safety it provides is the most significant change ingredient in EFT—it is sufficient to create change in and of itself. _____

d. Partners are stuck in ways of dealing with emotional needs and fears and in negative interactions. _____

✗ e. In key defining interactions, emotion often has control precedence. It can then easily undermine possible shifts in direction, or it can be a potent force promoting such change. _____

f. Change involves new attachment experiences and new relationship events. _____

g. Effective couples' therapy addresses the security of the bond between spouses. _____

h. Secure attachment is a major resource and a potent source of individual growth, positive identity, and resilience in the face of stress. _____

20. In each session, an EFT therapist might be expected to: (more than one correct answer)

✓ a. Monitor and check the collaborative alliance with each client. _____

✓ b. Discover/distill with each client new elements of his/her emotional experience or responses. _____

✓ c. Track and reflect on the sequence/patterns of interactions in the session and in narratives told in the session. _____

✓ d. Place emotions in the context of the cycles dominating the relationship, and place each partner's moves in the cycle in the context of primary attachment emotions. _____

✓ e. Generally frame responses in terms of attachment needs and fears. _____

✓ f. Unfold specific emotional responses and create an enactment where partners share these responses with each other. _____

✓ g. Reflect on each partner's strengths and validate responses. _____

✓ h. After the clients have left, the therapist notes the present stage and step of therapy, the current blocks to engagement with experience or with the other, and key themes and emotions to follow in upcoming sessions. _____

This chapter has offered a general overview of EFT and its place in couple therapy interventions. The next chapter will review the theoretical basis of EFT in more detail. A key reference for a recent general overview of EFT is the chapter by Johnson and Denton (2002) in the *Clinical Handbook of Couple Therapy*, 3rd ed. (Alan Gurman and Neil Jacobson, Eds., pp. 221–250, New York: Guilford Press).

2

THEORETICAL BACKGROUND TO EFT

Emotionally focused therapy integrates humanistic and systemic perspectives on human functioning and change. More specifically, it reflects the viewpoints of humanists such as Carl Rogers (1961; Johnson & Boisvert, 2002; Bradley & Johnson, in press), and general systemic theorists such Bertalanffy (1956) as well as clinicians who apply systemic theory in family therapy, such as Minuchin and Fishman (1981). A basic understanding of these perspectives, as exemplified by these two authors, is necessary to become a competent EFT therapist. The basic humanistic perspective on how to create change in therapy has been augmented by more specific recent writings on emotion and how to use emotion in this change process by authors such as Greenberg, Rice, and Elliott (1993) and Fosha (2000).

The essence of any brief therapy intervention is focus. The integration of the experiential and systemic perspectives provides a focus for each therapy session and a guide to effective intervention in these relationships.

EFT espouses a specific theory of close relationships—attachment theory (Bowlby, 1969, 1988)—as applied to adults by social psychologists such as Phil Shaver and Cindy Hazan (1993). This way of understanding close relationships offers a map to the change process in couple and family therapy (Johnson & Whiffen, 2003). The EFT therapist must then understand attachment theory as a guide to the territory of adult love and be able to use this map as a reference point in therapy. Attachment theory provides an overarching meaning to the framework that makes sense of emotional realities and signals sent to the partner and interactional patterns in distressed relationships.

The EFT therapist also attempts to integrate the above perspectives on therapeutic intervention and the nature of adult love with general writings in the couple and family field on gender and cross-cultural issues.

The following overview provides a brief synopsis of the systemic, humanistic experiential, and attachment concepts underlying EFT and emotionally focused family therapy (EFFT). Imagine that Carl Rogers, Ludwig von Bertalanffy, and John Bowlby, with comments from emotion theorists and culture and gender theorists, have come to visit and offer their perspective on the task of being a couple therapist.

ATTACHMENT THEORY

The central tenets of attachment theory are

- Attachment is an innate and primary motivating force: Seeking and maintaining contact with significant others is essential for human beings across the life span. This sustained connection is seen as a survival imperative laid out by the process of evolution. Dependency, often pathologized in our culture, is an innate part of being human. It is not a childhood trait that we need to outgrow.

- Secure dependence is a sign of health and complements autonomy: Secure dependence fosters autonomy and self-confidence. Secure dependence and autonomy are then two sides of the same coin, rather than dichotomies. The more securely connected we are, the more separate and different we can be. Health in this model means maintaining a palpable or felt sense of interdependency, rather than being "self-sufficient."

- Attachment offers a safe haven: Contact with attachment figures is an innate survival mechanism. The presence of a positive attachment figure provides comfort and security, whereas the perceived inaccessibility of such figures creates distress. Proximity to a loved one is the natural antidote to anxiety and vulnerability. Positive attachments create a safe haven and an optimal context for the continuing development of the personality.

- Attachment offers a secure base: Secure attachment also provides a secure base from which individuals can explore and most adaptively respond to their universe. The presence of such a base encourages exploration and openness to new information. It promotes the confidence necessary to risk, to learn, and to continually update models of self, others, and the world. When relationships offer a sense of felt security, individuals can reach out to others and deal with conflict and stress positively. These relationships tend then to be more stable and more satisfying.

- Accessibility and responsiveness build secure, healthy bonds: The building blocks of secure bonds are emotional accessibility and responsiveness. An attachment figure can be physically present but emotionally absent. Separation distress results from the appraisal that an attachment figure is inaccessible. It is emotional engagement that is crucial and the trust that this presence—this engagement—will be there when needed. Our strongest emotions arise in attachment relationships; this is where they seem to have the most impact. Emotions tell us, as well as communicating to others, what our motivations and needs are; they are the music of the attachment dance (Johnson, 1996).

- Attachment strategies were first identified in experimental separations and reunions with mothers and infants. These prototypical situations offer us a clear image of secure attachment, both in children and in adults. Secure attachment is characterized by confidence in the connection with the loved one, resulting in the ability to modulate distress on separation; to acknowledge and give clear, unambiguous signals about attachment needs and to reach for and make reassuring contact with an attachment figure; and then, once reassured, to return to exploration of the environment. This theory gives us a clear definition of a positive secure bond (Roberts & Greenberg, 2002) and tells us that this is the optimal outcome of couple therapy. It gives a direction and destination for the couple therapy journey.

- Anxious attachment, on the other hand, manifests as extreme distress on separation and clinging, recurring expressions of angry protest to the loved one on reunion, with difficulty soothing attachment fears and feelings. Avoidant attachment manifests as physiological distress linked with suppressed displays of emotion at separation or reunion and a resolute focus on tasks and activities. Individuals can have different "styles" or ways of engaging different attachment figures. The stances distressed partners take with each other in negative patterns of interaction are seen in terms of these patterns of insecurity and ways of dealing with attachment emotions.

- Fear and uncertainty activate attachment needs: Powerful emotions arise when an individual is threatened, either by traumatic events; by the negative aspects of everyday life, such as illness; or by any assault on the security of key attachment bonds, such as the one between adult partners. Attachment needs for comfort and connection then become compelling, and attachment behaviors, such as proximity seeking, are activated. A sense of connection with a loved one is a primary inbuilt emotional regulation device.

- The process of separation distress is predictable: If attachment behaviors, such as bids for attention and reassurance, fail to evoke comforting responsiveness and contact from attachment figures, a prototypical process of angry protest, clinging, depression, and despair occurs, culminating eventually in detachment. Depression is a natural response to loss of connection. In secure relationships, protest at inaccessibility is recognized and accepted. Separation distress is seen as the underlying plot in the drama of significant marital distress.

- A finite number of insecure forms of engagement can be identified: The number of ways that human beings have to deal with a negative response to the question "Can I depend on you when I need you?" are finite. As mentioned above, attachment responses seem to be organized along two dimensions: anxiety and avoidance. When the connection with an irreplaceable other is threatened but not yet severed, the attachment system may become hyperactivated; this is called anxious attachment. Anxious clinging, pursuit, and even aggressive attempts to obtain a response from the loved one escalate. Hyperactivated attachment might sound like "He'll let me down. They always do. Why can't he just be more attentive—then I wouldn't get so mad." The second strategy for dealing with the lack of safe emotional engagement is to deactivate the attachment system and suppress attachment needs; this is called avoidant attachment. Individuals focus then on tasks, avoiding distressing attempts at engaging attachment figures. Deactivated attachment might sound like "I am a bit of an island; nothing touches me. I just shut down when things get too much." These two strategies—anxious preoccupied clinging and detached avoidance—can develop into habitual styles of engagement with intimate others. A third insecure strategy has been identified that combines seeking closeness with fearful avoidance of closeness when it is offered. This strategy is usually referred to as "disorganized" in the child literature and "fearful avoidant" in the adult literature. It is associated with traumatic attachments where others are, at one time, both the source of and the solution to fear. It might sound like "I want him close. I need him so. But then, I don't trust him so I end up saying 'Come close but no touching.'"

- These ways of engaging significant others are self-maintaining patterns of social interaction and emotion-regulation strategies. They can be modified in new relationships, but they can also mold these relationships, thereby becoming self-perpetuating. These habitual forms of engagement, sometimes called styles or strategies, are best thought of as continuous, not absolute (one can be more secure or less secure). They will also play out differently depending on the attachment characteristics of a partner. Individuals with insecurely attached partners report lower satisfaction. Couples where both partners are securely attached report better adjustment than couples in which either or both partners are insecurely attached. Attachment theory is a systemic theory concerned with viewing people in a relational context and with recurring patterns of interaction that both create and reflect a person's relational reality—their experience of a close relationship.

- Attachment involves inner cognitive working models of self and other: As stated above, attachment strategies reflect ways of processing and dealing with emotion. Some spouses catastrophize and complain when they feel rejected; some become silent for days. Cognitive representations of self and other are inherent in these responses. Secure attachment creates confidence in the self and in relationships. It is characterized by a working model of self as worthy of love and care. The self is seen as lovable and competent and loved ones are seen as dependable and trustworthy. These models of self and other, distilled out of a thousand interactions, become relationship expectations and procedural scripts for how to create relatedness. These models involve goals, beliefs, and strategies and they are heavily infused with emotion. Working models are formed, elaborated, maintained, and, most important for the couple and family therapist, changed through emotional communication.

- Isolation and loss are inherently traumatizing: It is important to recognize that attachment theory is essentially a theory about the trauma of isolation and loss. It began with the study of maternal deprivation and separation and its effects on children. Attachment theory describes and explains the trauma of deprivation, rejection, and abandonment by those we need the most. These are traumatic stressors that influence both general personality formation and a person's ability to deal with fear and stress. The stress of deprivation and separation is seen as the core of the ongoing drama of "ordinary" marital distress.

- Attachment is an integrative theory. It deals with within and between aspects of partner's relationships. It is able to integrate a focus on universal patterns of close connection with others and individual differences that evolve in specific relationship contexts. Attachment theory focuses on patterns of communication with key others and how these patterns construct inner realities and organize the regulation of emotion. It integrates a focus on self and on relational context and how each continually defines the other. This theory integrates different kinds of responses, such as bonding, caretaking, and sexual responses, in a coherent whole. It is consonant with feminist perspectives (Fishbane, 2001); with scientific data on marital distress; and with constructivist, moderate postmodern thought (Johnson & Denton, 2002).

- In the last 10 years, research on adult attachment has demonstrated that secure relationships show higher levels of intimacy, trust, and satisfaction (Johnson & Whiffen, 1999). Research tells us that secure partners are more assertive and collaborative and use rejection less, whereas avoidant dismissing partners, for example, are distant and unresponsive precisely when they or their partner is anxious and vulnerable.

EXERCISES: THE EFT THEORY OF ADULT LOVE—ATTACHMENT THEORY

Exercise 1:

1. Theorists of adult attachment espouse the idea that: (more than one correct answer)
   a. The need to connect with and depend on key others is wired in by evolution. ____ ✓
   b. Attachment is a universal, primary survival motivation in human beings across cultures. ____ ✓
   c. Recent understandings of attachment are that it involves not just bonding but caretaking and sexuality; these are not separate systems. ____
   d. Attachment is only applicable to mother–child relationships. ____
   e. Attachment is a systemic theory: it deals with key patterns of interaction between intimates. ____ ✓
   f. Attachment is also an intrapsychic theory: It deals with affect regulation and inner models of self and other. ____ ✓

2. The attachment view of dependency is: (more than one correct answer)
   a. Dependency on a few key others is a lifelong adaptive survival mechanism and promotes adaptation and growth. ____ ✓
   b. Dependency is adaptive in childhood, but adults should be self-sufficient. ____
   c. The more securely interdependent we can be, the more separate and different we can be. ____ ✓
   d. Dependency and autonomy are dichotomous: They are opposite ends of a continuum. ____

3. A positive secure attachment relationship has two basic elements: (more than one correct answer)
   a. A set of procedures to minimize conflict. ____
   b. A safe haven—an antidote to fear and helplessness. ____ ✓
   c. A secure base from which to explore the universe with confidence. ____ ✓
   d. A caretaking contract in the case of need. ____

4. When distressed, in the relationship or in life, a securely attached adult is likely to deal with his/her emotions by: (more than one correct answer)
   a. Reaching for the comfort and caring of a significant other. ____ ✓
   b. Using the representation of an attachment figure to soothe the self. ____ ✓
   c. Asserting needs for care in a way that invites responsiveness. ____ ✓
   d. Being optimistic about others' willingness/ability to respond. ____ ✓
   e. Protesting any upsetting distance in hopeful, constructive ways. ____ ✓
   f. Numbing and focusing on tasks, thereby increasing feelings of control and competence. ____
   g. Being able to resist flooding with negative emotions, thereby being more able to reciprocate responsiveness. ____

5. What element would you not typically see in a secure attachment relationship?
    a. Both partners can reach for the other when vulnerable. _____
    b. Both express needs for closeness, reassurance. _____
    c. Both use the comfort offered to soothe the self. _____
    d. Both feel wary of dependency needs and wish to put them aside. ✓____
    e. Both find it rewarding to be able to calm and reassure the other. _____
    f. Both feel basically safe and engaged and can then play and explore the relationship.
        _____

6. To increase a person's sense of attachment security the partner must become: (more than one correct answer)
    a. More accessible, especially when the other is stressed, fearful, or uncertain. ✓___
    b. More responsive on an emotional level to attachment requests, fears, needs. ✓___
    c. Less dependent on this person. _____
    d. More morally committed to staying in the relationship. _____
    e. More consistently reflective rather than emotional during difficult times. _____
    f. More able to stay emotionally engaged when the less secure person protests distance or disconnection. ✓___
    g. More comfortable with offering reassurance. _____

7. When a person cannot get an attachment figure to respond/engage, separation distress occurs. The first two steps in this distress are:
    a. Sulking followed by depression if sulking is not effective in getting a response from an attachment figure. _____
    b. Rage, contempt, and criticism, followed by defensive distancing. _____
    c. Protest, often in the form of anger, and clinging or seeking closeness and connection.
        ✓___
    d. Distancing and denial of attachment needs. ___

8. In couples' therapy these two steps—protest and seeking connection—show up as/look like the following: (more than one correct answer)
    a. Criticism and complaining. ✓___
    b. Clear, logical negotiations as to exactly how the spouse should change. ✓___ ✗
    c. Expressions of emotional anguish/hurt and fear for the relationship. ✓___
    d. Descriptions of grief, isolation, and loss, as in "I am alone." ✓___
    e. Calm and caring discussions about how problems can be solved. _____

9. If there is still no emotional response from the partner, the last two steps of separation distress outlined in attachment theory are: (more than one correct answer)
    a. Problem-solving as to how each partner can be more independent. _____
    b. Spiraling into depression and despair. ✓___
    c. Logically discussing and moving to friendly problem-solving. _____
    d. Grief beginning to evolve into detachment and true separateness. ✓___

10. In couples' therapy, in which ways do these last two steps of separation distress show up?
    a. Expressions of grief and hopelessness/helplessness. _✓_
    b. Brief flares of angry contempt, as in "I will make you respond to me." _✓_
    c. Calm acceptance of the relationship as it is. _____
    d. Eventually a letting go and a growing detachment from the relationship. _✓_

11. Attachment concerns move to front and center and become compelling at particular times. In what way can these times be summarized?
    a. Stressful conditions in the environment or life transitions/challenges, such as parenthood, that increase attachment needs. _✓_
    b. Conditions/shifts that appear to threaten the future—the status of the attachment relationship. _✓_
    c. Conditions that increase personal fear and vulnerability, such as illness. _✓_
    d. Unconscious projective identifications from the past are aroused and the partner is maneuvered into playing them out. _____

12. As well as universal elements, attachment theory focuses on individual differences in attachment responses. The two basic dimensions of attachment insecurity that vary among individuals are:
    a. Anxiety _✓_
    b. Disorganization _____
    c. Avoidance _✓_
    d. Self-sufficiency _____

13. These dimensions have resulted in three categories of insecure adult attachment responses (check the correct three categories below).
    a. Anxious attachment (where people are preoccupied with bonds and are vigilant for any threat to them). _✓_
    b. Dismissing avoidant attachment (where people deny attachment needs and fears, especially when they are vulnerable). _✓_
    c. Fearful avoidant attachment (where people are anxiously vigilant but also do not trust closeness and turn away when it is offered). _✓_
    d. Disorganized chaotic attachment (where no pattern can be seen). _____
    e. Detachment (where people become so mature that they do not need others). _____

Exercise 2:

See if you can identify a person in your own life that could often be described as engaging with you or others in one of the ways described above.

_____C. is looking for evidence of attachment failure_____

_____

Exercise 3:

Aspects of anxious attachment may be accurately described in the following terms: (check accurate statements)

a. Attachment emotions/concerns go into hyperactivation/overdrive in anxious attachment. _✓_
b. Clinging, pursuit, and frequent bids for reassurance are the order of the day. _✓_
c. People become vigilant for threat; for example, more jealous and distrustful. _✓_
d. Bids for attention often escalate into angry blaming and coercive demands. _✓_
e. Ambiguous cues about the other's dependability are likely to be taken negatively. _✓_
f. Anxiety can become an absorbing state and can disrupt the ability to empathize with the other partner. _✓_
g. Anxious partners often become very reactive and less than coherent in their presentation of the problem and the relationship. _✓_
h. Anxious partners use rejection less and soft evocative requests for caring more. _____
i. Anxious partners tend to see themselves as flawed and unlovable. _✓_
j. Anxious partners actively worry about abandonment. _✓_

Exercise 4:

See if you can think of a client who might be described as anxiously attached and check whether the descriptions above might fit his or her responses. _____

Exercise 5:

Aspects of avoidant attachment may most accurately be described in the following terms: (more than one correct answer)

a. Attachment emotions and concerns are generally deactivated and suppressed. _✓_
b. Deactivation is particularly employed when avoidant partners or their partners become in any way vulnerable or needy. _✓_
c. Avoidant partners prefer to focus on objects and instrumental tasks, away from attachment cues and issues. _✓_
d. In avoidant partners, arousal is high but awareness and expression of emotions is blunted and masked. _✓_
e. Avoidant partners are more likely to somatize, to become hostile, and to engage in promiscuous sexuality. _✓_
f. Avoidant partners often make disparaging remarks about dependency; e.g., "This is weakness." They tend to disown vulnerability. _✓_
g. Avoidant partners see others as unreliable and untrustworthy. _X_
h. Avoidant partners often state the goal of "just wanting the arguments to stop," rather than a change in the relationship, closeness, or caring. _✓_
i. This way of engaging others has been called "closed," "diversionary," and "fragile" in that it does not deal with or really diminish distress. _X_

Exercise 6:

See if you can think of a client who might be described as avoidantly attached and see if these descriptions might fit his or her responses. _____

Exercise 7:

Fearful avoidant attachment is not associated with:

a. Past trauma and violations by attachment figures. _____
b. A tendency to view one's self negatively, as unlovable or shameful. _____
c. A tendency to desire and pursue closeness, but also to fear and distrust it. _____
d. A paradoxical view of others as both the source of and solution to fear. _____
e. The ability to openly trust and accept caring and reassurance when it is offered. ___✓___

Exercise 8:

In the face of a relationship threat—perhaps a sexy, ambiguous phone message from the husband's new secretary—write out what a securely attached, anxiously attached, and avoidantly attached wife might say to this husband about the phone call when he came home.

The securely attached wife might say: _____ *I'd like reassurance in response to what was*
The anxiously attached wife might say: _____ *Where you home so often*
The avoidantly attached wife might say: _____ *It doesn't bother me. I don't care*

Exercise 9:

How will the husband be most likely to respond in the moment to each one?

Exercise 10:

1. The kinds of attachment—secure, anxious, avoidant, and fearful avoidant—are best thought of as: (check all that you think might apply. If attachment theory is new for you, check the answers that make most sense to you and see how they fit with the answers in the back of the book.)
    a. Labels for set personality types/traits; people are the same across time and different relationships. _____
    b. Habitual but changeable forms of engagement in close relationships. ___✓___
    c. Strategies for managing dependency in close relationships. __✓__
    d. Scripts or default options for emotion regulation in close relationships. __✓__
    e. Forms of engagement or strategies or scripts that can be different in different relationships and at different times in the same relationship. __✓__

    f. Models that can be coherent, elaborated, and open to revision or relatively inaccessible, undifferentiated, and closed. ___✓___

    g. Strategies that are kept stable by confirmation processes in a relationship, rather than just as existing models that always bias perception. ___✓___

2. In terms of dealing with their emotions in a distressed attachment relationship, more securely attached partners will tend to: (more than one correct answer)

    a. Ask openly and clearly for comfort and support. ___✓___

    b. Stay curious and open to new evidence and cues even when distressed. ___✓___

    c. Tolerate uncertainty and see whole cycles of interaction from a metaperspective. ___✓___

    d. Discuss emotions and emotional events in a coherent, integrated way. ___✓___

    e. Empathize with and respond to their partner's disclosures. ___✓___

    f. Own needs and fears and ask for needs to be met in a congruent way that pulls for a compassionate response. ___✓___

    g. Be unable to turn easily and trustingly to friends and other resources for comfort when partners are unavailable. _____

3. An anxiously attached person will most often tend to:

    a. Amplify and become absorbed in the different elements of their own anxiety: cues, body sensations, negative meanings/attributions, actions. ___✗___

    b. Become reactively angry and desperate, critically pursuing the other. ___✓___

    c. Recall and obsessively recount specific incidents, but be unable to articulate a coherent overall picture of their relationship. ___✓___

    d. Be difficult to soothe in that responsiveness or caring is not necessarily trusted. ___✓___

    e. Turn easily to inner representations of the spouses to calm the self down and regulate distress. _____

    f. Speak of past attachment figures as being inconsistent and unpredictable. ___✓___

    g. Experience unpredictable, large, and rapid swings in attachment-related emotions. ___✓___

4. A dismissingly attached person will most often tend to:

    a. Deny distress and focus on tasks—external events. ___✓___

    b. Speak in vague general abstract terms or idealized images. ___✓___

    c. Have difficulty focusing on their own or their partner's emotional signals. ___✓___

    d. Shut down, defend, and distance emotionally and physically when anxiety increases or the other partner protests. ___✓___

    e. Problem-solve in a distant, detached manner when the partner becomes upset. ___✓___

    f. Express "incompetence" or "inadequacy" in relation to emotional closeness or responses. ___✓___

    g. Express cold, general hostility. ___✓___

5. A fearful avoidantly attached person will most often tend to:

    a. Demand reassurance, emphasizing their need and that the other is the only solution to their pain. ___✗___

b. Refuse engagement when offered, stating that they cannot trust the other and that he/she is the source of their pain. __X__

c. Become disorganized as many emotions—anger, shame, fear, and grief—arise together and become overwhelming. __X__

d. Be unable to assert emotional needs, becoming caught in a sense of shame and unworthiness. __X__

e. Flip between anxious pursuit and numb distancing and defense. __✓__

Exercise 11:

In terms of acknowledging distress and needs, engaging with a partner, and seeking connection and support, read the following interactions/scenarios and label the pattern of responses as typical of secure, anxious, dismissing, or fearful attachment.

1. Wife to husband: "I don't care what you say. You are never around, never there for me. I just never feel really sure of this relationship, how much I matter to you. I might as well not be married. All you want is sex anyway. Even last week, on my birthday, when you promised…." She bursts into tears. She turns in her chair and her voice then becomes very biting, "But then, as you point out, I get 'unreasonable,' so how can you stay home with me! All I am is a maid. I am so alone." _anxious_

2. Husband to wife: "I refuse to speak with you when you get like this—there is no point. I don't know what gets into you when you get like this. I try to talk about our issues and come up with some solutions, but you just go off the deep end all the time. I think our marriage is fine—if you could just be more reasonable." _avoidant_

3. Wife to husband: "I'd like you to talk to me more, to show me I am important to you (stares into the distance). Sometimes I think I am just too difficult to love—too difficult. I want more connection between us." Husband: "Maybe we can be closer. I liked holding you last night." He reaches and tries to take her hand, but she sighs and moves away. Wife: "Don't. I feel sick. Last night was too much for me. It got so I felt I couldn't breathe, you were looking at me all the time." _fearful avoidant_

4. Husband to wife in the eighth session of EFT: "Yes, you are right. I do shut you out. I get kind of paralyzed. I don't know what to do. I get so scared that I am going to disappoint you again. So I kind of freeze up. But, you know, I do want to be close and I miss the easy closeness we used to have. Maybe I just need to say, well…I need you to give me a chance, I need to know you still want to be with me. I do want that connection too. So, put your tally sheet down and dance with me a little, huh?" This man is moving out of _avoidant_ into _secure_ .

5. Husband to wife: "It was last night, and I sat down beside you and tried to chat. And I moved my leg next to yours and it touched yours—just a little touch. And, wham. Wham! You just got all cold, all huffy." (He starts to tear). "My depression is coming up again. (Wipes his eyes, then says in a soft voice) "It was just a little touch. But I never get it right with you. And then I tried to talk about it and you said to wait till the therapy session." (He throws up his hands) "That is the way it always is. This relationship is a minefield." (He turns and bangs his hand into the table) "Sometimes I just wonder what it is with you, what you expect of me." _anxious_

6. Wife to therapist: "And it felt so different. We just held each other all night. And in the morning...I just told him how safe I felt. I felt precious to him. Like we were going to be okay, even if we fight sometimes. And now—since then—it just feels like I can count on him. I can reach out and bring him close. I don't think I have ever felt this, even when we were first together." *secure*

Exercise 12:

These patterns occur as the result of and are maintained by: (more than one correct answer)

   a. Past relationship history and the sensitivities it creates. ___✓___
   b. Present relationship interactions: the confirming or disconfirming responses of the partner. ___✓___
   c. Models/beliefs/expectations about others and relationships. ___✓___
   d. Negative or positive cycles of attachment responses in the present relationship. ___✓___
   e. How attachment-related emotions are regulated and dealt with and communicated in the present relationship. ___✓___
   f. The process of projective identification where expectations are projected onto the partner in such a way as to confirm the worst fears. ___✓___

Exercise 13:

Attachment involves not only affect regulation but also cognitive models—expectations, needs, biases. Connect up the main models of self and other usually found in each kind of attachment style (fill in the blanks with the correct style).

1. The self is seen as lovable and competent. The other is basically dependable and trustworthy. This is a description of a *secure style* person.
2. The self is seen as lovable but others are basically untrustworthy. *avoidant*
3. The self is often seen as undeserving of care and the other is mostly idealized and seen as lovable and desirable. *ambivalent anxious*
4. The self is seen as defective or deficient and the other is seen as unreliable or dangerous. *fearful anxious*

Exercise 14:

1. As a whole, attachment theory can be described as: (more than one correct answer)
   a. A systemic theory that focuses on patterns of interaction and their impact. ___✓___
   b. A theory of affect regulation. ___✓___
   c. A theory of trauma—the trauma of isolation. ___✓___
   d. A constructivist theory, focusing on the construction of inner and interpersonal attachment realities. ___✓___

    e. A theory of how the wounds of childhood are inevitably projected onto our partner. _____

    f. A theory that offers a map of the defining elements in our closest relationships; childhood bonds predict adult bonds._____

    g. The most comprehensive and well-researched theory of adult love. _____

2. In a couple therapy session, EFT therapists find that attachment theory offers: (more than one correct answer)

    a. A language; a frame; a way of making sense of the intense emotional drama of relationship distress. _____

    b. A guide through many content issues and secondary reactions to the deep emotional longings, needs, and fears—the music of the dance of adult love. _____

    c. A compass in the territory of adult love, directing the therapist to pivotal defining moments and moves. _____

    d. A vision that tells the therapist what to target; what will make a difference; what the steps are on the route from distress to secure connection. _____

3. Once partners become more accessible and responsive and thus feel more securely attached, the theory suggests that they will be able to: (more than one correct answer)

    a. Be more open, less defensive. _____

    b. Be curious and explore new information and to problem-solve more effectively with their partners. _____

    c. Trust that the other partner will be there for them, to turn to their partner for comfort and support. _____

    d. Be separate and different from key others without anxiety. _____

    e. Be able to see the big picture and talk about patterns of interaction rather than getting stuck in proving points or sorting emotions. To metacommunicate and subsequently be able to unlatch from patterns like criticize/withdraw. _____

    f. Name and explore fears and doubts that arise in the relationship rather than assuming the worst (e.g., Is he distant because I don't matter, or is he just tired?). _____

    g. Have deeper specific insights into past relationships and to link this insight into present responses. _____ ✗

    h. Listen to their own emotional needs for comfort and caring and clearly articulate them. _____

    i. Consider the other partner's perspective and to tune in and to respond empathically. _____

    j. Prevent all fights and negative cycles such as demand/defend. _____ ✗

    k. Be more intimate, if intimacy is trusting self-disclosure and empathic responsiveness (Wynne & Wynne, 1986). _____

    l. Protest, to assert one's needs without using rejection or threat. _____

    m. Hold a positive sense of self and feel entitled to care. _____

    n. Be more resilient in the face of depression and anxiety (stress) since they are not alone but connected to a loved one. _____

4. From an attachment point of view, love relationships are primarily defined by: (more than one correct answer)

   a. Equity of giving and getting, so that each profits rather than loses. ___ ✗

   b. The ability to negotiate and problem-solve concrete issues together. ___

   c. The companionship and friendship between partners. ___

   d. Moments of emotional responsiveness when key attachment needs and fears arise and are responded to or not. ___

   e. Times when one partner provides emotional and/or psychological "proximity" to the other, or the other feels abandoned, rejected, alone. ___

   f. Key moments when people are able to be independent and differentiated, preventing fusion and allowing each person to go their own way. ___ ✗

note this ⟵ {

Exercise 15:

Here are the key moments of an experiment to assess attachment security between mother and child, called the "strange situation." In a securely attached child, the drama unfolds as follows:

1. The child is in a "strange," that is, a stressful, situation, in an unfamiliar room with a stranger and the mother has exited. But the child can handle her inevitable distress, believing the mother will return and come close to her.

2. When the mother returns, the child is able to ask, clearly and assertively, for comfort and reassurance, most often desiring physical touch.

3. When the mother responds, the child takes in the comfort and allows herself to be calmed and soothed.

4. The child can then, feeling connected to the mother and trusting in her responsiveness if needed, turn and explore the environment.

Take the above four moves and write them out as they would likely occur between a securely attached couple when the man comes home after a very difficult day at work and meets his wife.

1. ___ he looks forward to getting home ___

2. ___ asks for hug + comfort if needed. ___

3. ___ wife hugs him, turns off stove & sits ___

4. ___ ready to move on, went more? ___

Example:

A wife goes to a party with her husband. She knows no one there and they have a fight on the way to the party. At the party, she finds him engrossed in a conversation with a beautiful new colleague. She feels small and unimportant and remembers their fight on the way to the party. Her emotions explode. She feels anguish and then, after a few moments, rage. She storms up to her spouse and taps him on the shoulder, insisting that he speak to her. She finds it difficult to be coherent but she accuses him of flirting and then asks to be taken home. He becomes very cold and distant and refuses to talk about what is happening. He attempts to change the subject while implying that she has had too much to drink and should be more polite. When she asks, he refuses to introduce her to his colleague. He then points out that colleagues are often easier to talk to than "paranoid" spouses. She then insists on going home and harangues him for his "inappropriateness" all the way home. She cannot concentrate on anything on the way home and goes to sleep in another room.

Exercise 16:

In the contrasting scenario above, which involves a distressed adult relationship, identify who is the anxiously attached, critical blamer and who is the avoidantly attached, distancing withdrawer.

1. Who is anxiously attached? _wife_ Who is avoidantly attached? _husband_

2. Write out what the wife might have been able to say to her partner if she had been in a happy stage in their relationship and had been securely attached; that is, had trusted that he would listen and respond to any vulnerabilities she might express.

> *I'm feeling small and vulnerable watching you are having a good time with that beautiful woman. I need to know you love me and will include me in this party. I'm lonely & out of place here*

Example 1:

Husband: "You say I just want sex, but it's not true. I just feel like giving up when you say that, like we are doomed. How can it ever work?"

Wife: (in a calm flat voice) "I really don't know. But if you would just calm down and be less demanding. I just move away to stop the fights. I just think it is better if we don't get caught in these arguments…the relationship is easier—calmer—that way."

Husband: "How can things be 'easy' when we never make love, when you are never close to me? Tell me that. It's like everything else comes first with you, but my feelings…they never count. You just focus on the event, like all I want is an orgasm. But that is not all I want. I want to feel close to you—desired—like I am important to you. But first comes the kids, then the house, then your job, and then—maybe—if there is time left—maybe us. Sometimes I think if I were dying you would tell me to hold on till you were less busy. You wouldn't be there for me. I might as well live alone."

Wife: "I just get that whatever I do will never be good enough for you, I am a big disappointment…so I just give up, I just shut down. It just doesn't feel safe in our house anymore. I am not sexy enough for you, not warm enough—not enough."

Example 2: (the same couple at the end of session 10 of EFT)

Wife: "I am starting to feel a lot safer here. Like I am not on trial all the time, being tested. I just give up when I feel that, I just shut down and go numb. I am starting to get that we both get scared and insecure and then we don't know how to reassure each other." (To spouse) "I do want this relationship and you are important to me—very important. I feel lonely too, you know. I just want to be held sometimes, and talked to, paid attention to—not always asked to make love. Then I just feel like I am just a route to an orgasm, not like you want me." (She cries) "When we were first together you made me feel like I was so special—so precious. I miss that—I do. But now you seem so mad at me all the time."

Husband: "I know. I get desperate—feel like I am losing you—so I guess I come on all furious and pushy. But really it's just because I am so unsure of us—of you. And it's pretty risky to tell you this—guess it's easier to demand to make love."

Exercise 17:

Take the above pieces of interaction and underline the attachment language that the couple uses. This language often reflects the following themes:

1. Abandonment, loss, and aloneness: fears of finding the other unavailable and unresponsive.
2. Rejection and being unvalued or seen as inadequate by the other: feeling unworthy or unlovable.
3. Lack of safety and support: doubting that one would come first, that one can count on one's partner, and therefore being overwhelmed by stress.
4. Feeling that you do not exist in the mind of the other—that one is peripheral and dispensable—and how this impacts one's sense of self.
5. The risks involved in reaching out: fears of asking for attention and admitting need.

THE EFT THEORY OF CHANGE—HUMANISTIC AND SYSTEMIC

EFT is an integration of the experiential/humanistic and systemic approaches to therapeutic change. It is a constructivist approach in that it focuses on the ongoing construction of present experience (particularly experience that is emotionally charged), and it is a systemic approach in that it also focuses on the organization and construction of patterns of interaction with intimate others. The EFT therapist's focus is constantly on patterns of experiencing, especially affect regulation and expression, and patterns of responses in interactions with intimate partners. These patterns define how the self, other, and relationship are experienced at any point in time.

The Basic Elements of the Experiential/Humanistic Model

1. Alliance is key. The experiential/humanistic perspective focuses on emotional responses and uses them in the process of therapeutic change. But to deal with emotions, a sense of safety is crucial. Therefore, humanistic therapies feature a strong

focus on the quality of the therapeutic alliance. EFT follows two basic premises: (a) that the therapeutic alliance creates a safety that is to a certain extent healing in and of itself and that should be as egalitarian and collaborative as possible, and (b) that the acceptance and validation of the client's experience is a key element in therapy. Empathic responding is then perhaps the most basic building block of EFT. In couple therapy, this involves an active commitment to validating each person's experience of the relationship without invalidating the experience of the other. The therapist's empathy and acceptance allows each client's innate self-healing and growth tendencies to flourish. To be seen and heard allows people to reorganize and make new sense of their experience. The scaffold of safety in each session is fostered by the authenticity, presence, and transparency of the therapist.

In general, experiential approaches take the position that we are formed and transformed by our relationships with others. Feminist writers, such as the Stone Centre group (Jordan, Kaplan, Miller, Stiver, & Surrey, 1991), and attachment theorists also focus on how identity is constantly formulated in interactions with others.

2. An optimistic, nonpathologizing stance is essential. The essence of the humanistic perspective is a belief in the ability of human beings to grow and make creative, healthy choices if given the opportunity. This approach is essentially nonpathologizing. The focus is the person not the problem—the process of growth, not the symptom per se or the offering of solutions by the therapist. As in systems theory, people are seen as stuck rather than as innately dysfunctional. The therapist helps to articulate the key moments when choices are made in a relationship drama and supports clients to formulate new responses. A humanistic therapist assumes that we find ways to survive and cope in dire circumstances when choices are few, but then later find those ways limiting and inadequate for creating fulfilling relationships and lifestyles. Bowlby and Rogers would agree that all ways of responding to the world can be adaptive, but problems arise when those ways become rigid and cannot evolve in response to new contexts. Therefore, a therapist must first accept where each partner starts from—the nature of his or her experience—and understand how each has done his or her best to create a positive relationship.

3. Health is openness and engagement. The humanistic model of health for individuals and relationships is one that stresses openness to experience and engagement with others. As in attachment theory and in systems theory, health is flexibility and the ability to learn from experience and adapt to new situations. Health is also seen as an inherent acceptance and prizing of self and others and a sense of responsibility for our construction of experience and our responses. The fostering of the above is then the ultimate goal of therapy.

4. Sessions focus on moment-to-moment process, in the present. Experiential therapies encourage an examination of how inner and outer realities define each other. The therapist is a process consultant who follows this moment-to-moment shaping of these realities the way a dancer follows music. The inner construction of experience evokes interactional responses that organize the world in a particular way. These patterns of interaction then reflect back and, in turn, shape inner experience. The EFT therapist moves between helping partners recognize and reorganize their inner world and their interactional dance. The focus of sessions is on the here and now rather than on the past or future. In emotional moments, the therapist may use the past to validate present responses and emotion may also bring past events alive in the session.

5. There is a privileging of emotion. Humanistic therapists encourage the integration of affect, cognition, and behavioral responses. But they tend to privilege emotions as sources of information about needs, goals, motivation, and key meanings. They help clients change emotions, especially anxiety and fear, that constrict information processing and also use emotions to create change events. Emotion is seen as intelligent and as a primary mover and organizer of action. Emotion is discussed further in the next chapter.

6. Significant change requires a new corrective emotional experience. Experiential approaches attempt to foster new corrective emotional experiences for clients that emerge as part of personal encounters in the here and now of the therapy session. Cognitive insight or superficial behavior change is generally not viewed as optimal or as having sufficient impact. New choices arise out of new emotional experiences.

The Systemic Model

The other half of the EFT synthesis is the contribution from family systems theory. In systems theory, the focus is on the circular feedback loops that occur between members of a relational system, therefore organizing this system, giving it stability. The hallmark of all family systems therapies is that they interrupt negative repetitive cycles of interaction that include problem/symptomatic behavior.

EFT draws on Minuchin's structural systemic approach with its focus on the enactment of "new" patterns of interaction. In terms of systemic therapies, the unique contribution of EFT is the use of emotion in breaking destructive cycles of interaction and creating new patterns. Systemic therapies have also traditionally focused on certain elements, such as power hierarchies and boundaries, whereas EFT focuses more on nurturance and connection. Consonant with systems theory, the EFT therapist helps the couple to develop new responses to each other and a different, more relational "frame" on the nature of their problems.

EFT follows the basic premises of systems theory including:

• Causality is circular, so that it cannot be said that action A "caused" action B. In distressed couples, demanding by one partner creates and maintains withdrawal in the other, and vice versa. Both partners' responses are shaped by a feedback loop, a cycle of interaction.

• We must consider behavior in context. In order to understand the behavior of one partner, the therapist must always consider this behavior in the context of the behavior of the other partner. The system as it is organized, not the behavior of any one partner, is the problem.

• The elements of a system have a predictable and patterned relationship with each other. These patterns have a life of their own and tend to remain stable. Couples' relationships are characterized by the presence of regular, repeating cycles of interaction. The more narrow and rigid these cycles, the more likely the relationship is to be distressed.

• All behavior has a communicative aspect. What is said and how it is said defines the role of the speaker and the listener. Turning away and saying nothing is a communication.

• The task of the systems therapist is to interrupt negative cycles of interaction so that new, more adaptive patterns can begin to emerge and offer alternative ways to relate to others.

The Experiential/Systemic Synthesis in EFT

The experiential and systemic approaches to therapy share important commonalities. Both focus on present experience rather than historical events. Both view people as process rather than product, as fluid rather than as possessing a rigid core or character structure that is inevitably resistant to change.

The two approaches also bring something to each other. Experiential approaches have focused within the person to the exclusion of a consideration of external relationships. The systemic therapies, on the other hand, traditionally focus on the interactions between people to the exclusion of a consideration of the emotional responses and associated meanings that organize such interactions.

To summarize the experiential/systemic synthesis of EFT, there is a focus in both the circular cycles of interaction between people as well as the emotional experiences of each partner during the different steps of the cycle. The word "emotion" comes from the Latin word meaning "to move." As mentioned earlier, emotion moves the individual and communicates to others, thereby organizing the dance between intimates. In EFT, emotions are identified and expressed as a way to help partners move into new stances in their relationship dance, stances that they then integrate into their sense of self and their definition of their relationship. This results in a new, more satisfying cycle of interaction that does not include the presenting problem and, more than this, promotes secure bonding.

EXERCISES: THE HUMANISTIC NATURE OF EFT

Exercise 18:

1. The therapist in EFT is best thought of in the following terms: (more than one correct answer)
   a. As a skills coach. _____
   b. As an expert who can offer unique insight and direction. _____
   c. As a creator of safety—a secure base—in the therapy session. ✓
   d. As a process consultant for inner and interpersonal processes. ✓
   e. As a collaborative consultant who learns from and with the clients. ✓

2. The EFT therapist strives to be: (more than one correct answer)
   a. Attuned to and emotionally engaged with both partners. ✓
   b. Active; e.g., choreographing interactions and promoting safety. ✓
   c. Nonjudgmental: accepting and validating partner's experience. ✓
   d. Genuine and transparent. ✓
   e. Primarily a teacher and coach about skills and the nature of relationships. _____
   f. Emotionally present. ✓
   g. Approving and endorsing all responses. _____

3. The most basic building block of EFT, and one that reflects its humanistic perspective, is:
   a. Empathic reflecting on each client's emotions. _____
   b. Validating each partner's experience. ✓

   c. Structuring new interactions to teach communication skills. _____
   d. Promoting catharsis. _____
   e. Allowing for the safe ventilation of emotions. _____

4. The therapist's empathy, in which imagination plays a key role, allows people to: (more than one correct answer)
   a. As Rogers said, explore and discover "the order in experience." _✓_
   b. Place defensiveness, vigilance, and the need to avoid aside. _✓_
   c. Regulate difficult and sometimes overwhelming emotions. _✓_
   d. Focus on, and thereby distill, the complex meanings—the whole—from the parts in their experience. _✓_
   e. Accept and integrate elements of their experience that they judge themselves for or find difficult to deal with. _✓_
   f. Tolerate ambiguity and uncertainty. _✓_
   g. Take responsibility for how they construct their experience and their responses. _✓_

5. Which of the following is not an essential humanistic stance?
   a. People have good reasons for their ways of seeing and responding and, if supported, can grow and learn. _____
   b. Emotion colors perception and plays a key role in the formation of meaning. _____
   c. The task of therapy is to enhance awareness, thereby creating an expanded sense of agency. _____
   d. All the therapist needs to do is create a good alliance, empathize, and validate. _✓_
   e. Adaptive defenses become chronic and begin to constrict awareness—experience—and, therefore, choices. _____

6. Health, in humanistic, systemic, and attachment theories, is essentially: (more than one correct answer)
   a. The ability to be open to experience and adapt to new contexts with flexibility. _✓_
   b. Acceptance of self and the ability to take responsibility for perceptions, actions, and impact on others. _✓_
   c. The ability to process experience and form coherent and integrated wholes where meanings and needs/goals are clear. _____
   d. The ability to engage with others in an open, flexible manner. _✓_

7. The focus of the humanistic EFT therapist is: (two correct answers)
   a. On the present, and the past as it becomes present. _✓_
   b. On past events and how they defined the individual client. _____
   c. On the structure of personality and psychodynamic understandings. _____
   d. On present process and the ongoing construction of reality and interaction patterns. _✓_

8. In what way is emotion not viewed in humanistic interventions?
    a. Providing the organism with rapid, compelling, and vital information about what matters (what is important in terms of key issues) such as survival and answering basic needs. Alerting people to the significance of events for their well-being.

    _____

    b. Focusing attention and priming and organizing appropriate action responses.

    _____

    c. Playing a crucial role in the construction of meaning. _____
    d. Communicating with others: emotional expression is the primary signaling system between primates and pulls for specific responses. _____
    e. Needing to be ventilated without reflection, thereby discharging tension. ___✓

EXERCISES: THE SYSTEMIC NATURE OF EFT

Exercise 19:

1. EFT adds to/departs from the usual structural systemic approaches in that it: (more than one correct answer)
    a. Focuses on emotion, not just behavior and cognition, as a key organizing factor in relational systems. ___✓
    b. Focuses on nurturance and vulnerability, not only on power, hierarchy, and boundary issues. ___✓
    c. Focuses on change in a particular direction, toward a secure bond, not just change in itself. ___✓
    d. Focuses on patterns of interaction and the self-reinforcing circular nature of these patterns. ___✓
2. EFT is systemic (fits with the original formulation of systems theory) in the following ways: (more than one correct answer)
    a. Reality is seen as a circular feedback loop, rather than in terms of linear cause and effect. ___✓
    b. It is the organization of the interpersonal system (patterns of interaction) that are the focus of therapy rather than simply intrapsychic change. ___✓
    c. Each partner's behavior is continually seen in the context of the other's responses.

    ___✓

    d. Emotions are seen as being what Bertalanffy (the father of systems theory) called "leading" or organizing elements in a relationship. ___✓
    e. Dysfunction is seen in systemic terms as narrow, stuck patterns that cannot be revised and updated. ___✓

Exercise 20:

Identify the following interventions as systemic or as not fitting with a systemic orientation. See if you can say why each one is systemic or not systemic.

1. The therapist says, "So I can really see here how the more distant you see your partner as being, the more you naturally begin to push to get his attention. And then he begins to see you as pressuring him and tends to move away. Is that it?"

    Is this systemic? (Yes/No) _____ How is it systemic? _interaction_

2. The therapist says, "So you are both caught in this cycle of demand and defend. It has taken over your relationship."

    Is this systemic? (Yes/No) _____ How is it systemic? _cycle and linear_

3. The therapist says, "Can we just hold off on the details of this issue for a moment? Rather than focusing on all the content issues, I was noticing how, once again, you, Mary, were taking your 'I will make you listen to me' stance, and Will, you were getting into what you call your 'Can't get me, I'll put up a wall' stance. Is that right?"

    Is this systemic? (Yes/No) _____ How is it systemic? _interaction_

4. The therapist says, "Can you put down your wall for a moment, Will? Can you do what you just spoke about, and come out and meet your wife? Can you tell her 'I want to let you in'?"

    Is this systemic? (Yes/No) _____ How is it systemic? _restructuring_

5. The therapist says, "So, you see yourself as quite retiring and naturally withdrawn, Will, but when your wife becomes soft and shows you her softness and how she needs you, as she did just now, you really come out of your shell and take her hand and show yourself. You are right out there."

    Is this systemic? (Yes/No) _____ How is it systemic? _interaction_

LINKING EXPERIENTIAL AND SYSTEMIC PERSPECTIVES

John Bowlby (in his book *Separation*, 1973, p. 180) spoke of inner and outer rings of a system. The inner ring (processes within a person's skin) and the outer ring (relationship interactions with others) complement each other and maintain each other in a homeostatic way. Experiential approaches have tended to focus on inner processes (the construction of inner experiences). Systemic approaches have focused on interpersonal processes (the construction of relational patterns). The EFT therapist puts them both together.

EXERCISES: LINKING EXPERIENTIAL AND SYSTEMIC PERSPECTIVES

Exercise 21:

Experiential and systemic approaches both: (more than one correct answer)

a. Focus on process, inner and outer. Inner and interpersonal realities are fluid systems constantly in the process of being constructed, not fixed entities. _____

b. Both focus on the present more than on how the past determines the present. _____

c. Both view people and systems as stuck rather than deficient or sick. _____

d. Both espouse joining with clients in a respectful, collaborative alliance. _____

e. Both focus on triangulation and hierarchies. _____

Exercise 22:

Write out in the space below, in your own words, what experiential and systemic approaches add to each other that helps the EFT therapist.

combining the inner emotional with the outer interactional

Exercise 23:

In summary, when experiential and systemic perspectives are put together, the primary theoretical assumptions of EFT are: (more than one correct answer)

a. All relationship behavior is about attachment. Secure attachment will ensure that no difficult conflicts occur in a relationship. _____

b. Emotion is key in organizing inner relational experience and interactions with loved ones, making it an essential target of intervention. _✓_

c. Working with emotional communication also offers the most powerful route to significant change in love relationships. _____

d. Attachment theory offers the couple therapist a much needed, coherent, and in-depth map to the territory of adult love. _✓_

e. People's needs and desires are essentially healthy and adaptive. It is the disowning and constriction of these needs that becomes problematic. _✓_

f. Change involves new emotional experience and new attachment-oriented interactions. _✓_

g. The most powerful route to change is through catharsis, insight, or negotiation skills. _____

h. An accepting and nonpathologizing stance is most productive in therapy, and all three of the forerunners of EFT—Rogers, Bertalanffy (or his clinical translator, Minuchin), and Bowlby—actively promoted this. _✓_

Exercise 24:

To stress the nonpathologizing nature of EFT, please link up the following quotes to the forerunners of EFT. Are these the statements of Rogers, the father of experiential approaches; Minuchin and colleagues, systemic therapists; or John Bowlby, the father of attachment theory? Link each statement with a person.

1. Most often, even negative attachment models, where the self is seen as unlovable and/or others are seen as untrustworthy are not neurotic "projections" but "perfectly reasonable constructions" that are adaptive in a particular context. Hopefully they are then updated and revised. Who said this? *Bowlby*

2. If the therapist is accepting and empathic then the client finds that he is "daring to become himself." This results in clients becoming "more self-directing and more self-confident" and open to emotion that leads to the "discovery of unknown elements of the self." Who said this? *Rogers*

3. "Different contexts call forth different facets of self....Expanding contexts allows for new possibilities to emerge." Changing people's "position" in a system changes their subjective experience. Who said this? _Minuchin_

4. "When I accept myself as I am, then I change." Who said this? _Rogers_

Exercise 25:

In terms of theory construction and how EFT theory links with empirical evidence, identify and check the correct answers.

a. In terms of descriptions of marital distress and satisfaction, the experiential foci of EFT—emotions and interactional patterns, such as criticize/distance—fit with recent research. _✓_

b. In terms of predictions of relationship change, especially how to improve distressed relationships, empirical evidence is strong for EFT interventions being on target and powerful. _✓_

c. In terms of explanation, the attachment perspective on adult love has considerable and growing empirical support. _✓_

d. Empirical evidence is not necessary for our ways of seeing relationships, predicting change, and understanding relationships to have a basis in empirical research. All realities are relative and arbitrarily constructed. _____

We have now reviewed the basic theory base of EFT. The next chapter is a synopsis of the basic EFT therapeutic tasks and interventions. A brief list of the references given in the chapter can be found in the back of the book under Theory References.

If you wish to take the theory and make it more personal to your own life, the exercises below are offered to help you begin to do that. The model does demand a lot from the therapist. It demands a certain flexibility in that it asks the therapist to focus within and between, to work evocatively with emotion and to be able to be quite proscriptive when working with interactions, when creating enactments; for example, the therapist is specific and directive. EFT also requires that you are willing to really be present and engaged with the client. It is hoped that the exercises in this book will help you take the EFT model and make it your own.

EXERCISES:

Exercise 26:

List the points of theory that make the most sense to you, or most capture your imagination, from experiential, systemic, or attachment theory. Then list any points that puzzle you or that do not make sense to you.

It relates attachment & self-differentiation

Exercise 27:

How does the style and focus of the experiential therapist fit with your personality and preferences? More specifically, see if you can rate yourself on the following.

I am able to put aside my own judgments and concerns, place myself in another's shoes, and empathize:

Most of the time _____
Some of the time _____
With difficulty _____

Exercise 28:

For most of us there are specific issues/times when it is difficult for us to resonate and empathize with another—certain behaviors that we find very upsetting. If this is true for you, see if you can identify, perhaps by thinking of a client or a friend or loved one whose behavior you found it hard to accept or understand, any responses or issues that make empathy hard for you. (Note: certain behaviors like abusive name-calling or violence are, of course, not to be empathized with in and of themselves, although we can sometimes empathize with the person, if not with his or her behavior.) Write out a brief description of the times that acceptance and empathy might be hard for you:

_____

_____

Most less experienced couple therapists find that working with couples involves a refinement of their sense of empathy. The challenge is empathizing with both clients at the same time when they take opposing positions. The EFT therapist needs to see through difficult and sometimes alienating or oppositional behaviors to the attachment hurt and fears underneath. Empathy becomes easier as we know the territory better (we know what to expect) and as we give ourselves permission not to "know" but to discover the shape of experience with our clients. Our clients have to teach us about their inner world and their relationship dance. In EFT, self-disclosure by the therapist—for example, disclosing confusion or even upset or sadness—is part of the model (see Johnson, 2004).

Exercise 29:

How does the style and focus of the systems therapist fit for you? For example, can you begin to identify patterns in the dance of clients or patterns that operate in your personal relationships? It is sometimes hard to empathize with withdrawers if you are struggling with a withdrawer in your own relationship. If you think of a couple you are seeing, what is their dominant negative pattern? Who pursues and who criticizes and complains? Who demands and who resists or distances? Who distances and defends or withdraws? Who tries to control the dance and who just goes along? Who turns up the emotional heat and who shuts down? How does each partner's behavior keep the others in place? See if you can now describe the pattern.

_____

_____

Exercise 30:

See now if you can describe a negative pattern in one of your own relationships and the impact it has on you. Keep the description to very simple moves/responses (e.g.; he pushes, and I shut down then I keep my distance even more).

_____

_____

Exercise 31:

1. Does attachment theory speak to you personally? Is it easy for you to connect with your own attachment needs and fears? _____

2. Can you identify one part of the theory that particularly resonates with you? _____

3. Can you identify times in your daily life when your own attachment needs become compelling? _____

4. Whom did you feel you had a secure attachment with when you were growing up? _____ If there was no secure attachment, how did you manage? _____

_____

5. Can you identify your default responses when you do not feel responded to by a present loved one? For example, do you usually avoid or anxiously protest? _____

Exercise 32:

How comfortable are you with strong emotion?

Very comfortable _____
Not so comfortable _____
Quite uneasy _____

Exercise 33:

Do any of these responses fit for you?

1. Strong emotion will get out of hand, take over, and make everything worse between the couple. _____

2. As a therapist, I will not know how to contain and structure strong emotion and I will feel helpless and incompetent. _____

3. Clients may hurt themselves further or respond impulsively. _____

4. If strong emotions get going, the session will dissolve into chaos. I will not be able to take charge. _____

5. I am just not quite sure what to do with strong emotion, so I have tended to avoid it in sessions. _____

As you work through this workbook, you will become clearer and more comfortable about the theories presented above and how they translate into effective interventions with distressed couples. You will become more confident about working with clients' emotional experience and using this experience as a compass and a guide, and about working with patterns of interactions to create new steps in a couples dance. I hope you will appreciate the relevance of attachment theory as a map to the terrain of adult love.

Many resources—books, articles, chapters, research studies and videos—can be found in Appendix A. These will help you access the theory, research and practical interventions that are the basis of EFT.

3

INTERVENTION IN EFT

This chapter reviews the basic practices of the EFT therapist. The three primary tasks of the EFT approach are described and the interventions used to accomplish these tasks are reviewed. Exercises help the reader both distinguish the different interventions and practice their use with case material. Gaining a detailed understanding of these interventions is an important step in understanding how the EFT process unfolds. Mastery of these in-session practices enables the therapist to effectively engage couples through the nine steps of EFT.

SUMMARY OF THE THREE TASKS OF EFT

Task 1. Creating and maintaining a therapeutic alliance. EFT is effective when the therapist's rapport with a couple is characterized by accessibility and responsiveness. This secure base allows couples to explore interactional processes and the emotions underlying them. The early stages of therapy require therapists to foster a secure connection, and the therapist continues to monitor the alliance throughout the EFT process assuring the constancy of trust and support through a secure therapeutic alliance.

Task 2. Accessing and reformulating emotion. A therapist's ability to access and engage a couple's emotional experience is essential to promoting change in a couple's relationship. The therapist must learn to facilitate the expression of new or expanded emotional experience that, in turn, forms the basis for transforming the couple's problematic pattern. Couples find new opportunities to respond to one another as they encounter these new emotional experiences. A therapist must be skilled in helping clients identify, express, and experience these emotions in session.

Task 3. Restructuring key interactions. The restructuring of a couple's interaction pattern is a primary treatment goal in the EFT approach. The therapist uses a number of interventions to set the stage for facilitating a change in problematic patterns. These skills include tracking the pattern and helping partners understand their actions in the light of unexpressed attachment fears and needs. The use of therapeutic enactments highlights problematic patterns and leads to more positive, loving responses. The completion of this task results in prototypical bonding events that form a new basis for security in the relationship.

TASK 1 INTERVENTIONS: CREATING AND MAINTAINING A THERAPEUTIC ALLIANCE

The first task in EFT requires the therapist to adopt a therapeutic stance that emphasizes empathy, genuineness, respect, empathic attunement, along with a focus on monitoring and joining the interactional system. The therapist actively promotes the security of the treatment relationship through careful attention to the changing responses that constitute the therapeutic alliance.

True to humanistic approaches, empathy is at the heart of the therapeutic alliance in EFT. A cornerstone of the alliance, empathy creates the safety needed to foster a client's emotional engagement in the treatment process. Empathy promotes engagement through:

- Reaffirming and clarifying the client's experience.
- Modeling acceptance of both partners' experience.
- Slowing down the session, enabling clients to process their experience.
- Organizing different aspects of client's experience into a whole.
- Comforting a client in response to a difficult emotional experience.
- Exploring the meaning of important and often powerful human experiences.

The therapist's empathic responses strengthen a client's ability to "make sense" of his or her experience. Together, the therapist and each partner explore and "discover" a couple's individual and shared experience. The therapist immerses herself in each client's world and uses this experience as a reference point, facilitating her ability to attune to and resonate with each client's experience.

Therapeutic Alliance: Stance and Practices

The formation of a therapeutic alliance relies less on a set of particular interventions and more on a therapist way of "being" with the client. This way of sitting with a client is characterized by five qualities. These qualities include:

1. Empathic attunement. A therapist uses words, phrases, and nonverbal responses that enable the therapist to connect with a client's experience. Typically focusing on what a client has said as well as what a client may express through nonverbal cues, the therapist uses imagination and personal reflection to empathically connect to a client's experience. Therapists may find this level of attunement difficult with some clients and may have to "fight" for this attunement by actively imagining what a client's experience may be when it is not obvious in the therapy process.

2. Acceptance. The EFT therapist takes a nonpathologizing stance and actively resists the tendency to see her clients as deficient or defective. This leads the therapist to differentiate between a person's problematic behavior and the emotional reality underlying that behavior. The therapist is not likely to describe the client in the fixed terms of character disorders, such as narcissist or borderline. Instead, she seeks to understand how the client's problematic behaviors may make sense in the context in which those actions occur. This emphasis promotes an acceptance that enables the therapist to validate a client's experience and action as a potentially adaptive and "reasonable" response to an unmet need or fear. The therapist assumes that at some level a client's problematic behavior makes perfect sense in the context of the client's reality and their need for connection.

3. Genuineness. A therapist's openness to being impacted by the client and sharing this impact through self-disclosure extends the felt sense of security a client experiences through his or her alliance with the therapist. The therapist is available for a real human encounter with the client, which may include the therapist admitting

missteps and privileging the client's experience over the therapist's interpretation. A therapist's genuineness is evidence of the accessibility and responsiveness of the therapist to the client.

4. Continuous active alliance monitoring. A therapist takes active steps to monitor his or her engagement with each partner. This involves tracking the couple's responses to interventions and probing to make sure that the therapist is still in tune with the each partner's experience. The therapist invites direct responses from the couple about their experience in the session or in treatment as a whole. Active monitoring underscores the value of each partner's experience and the therapist's conscious attention to pacing with the couple. Monitoring enables the therapist to empathically respond to possible ruptures in the therapeutic alliance.

The EFT therapist not only engages in a relationship with each partner but with the couple's relationship as a whole. Focusing on the unique experience of each partner and the all encompassing couple's problem creates a metaperspective that the therapist uses to help the couple engage their personal reactions to the problem they together share. Joining the system enables the therapist to highlight and validate each partner's experience and how it is related to the couple's stuck pattern. For example, a therapist can join with the experience of one partner who is worn thin from pursuing another who withdraws from his efforts to connect. Joining the system, the therapist can validate the pursuer's frustration as well as the impact of their behavior on the withdrawn partner. In engaging the system, the therapist is able to help the couple see how their actions make sense in the context of their relationship.

Examples:

"I know we worked hard today, and really pushed. I was wondering what that was like for you? Do you have any concerns about how things went?"

"It seems like this is very difficult for you. Is there a way I can be of greater support?"

"John, I am wondering what is going on for you now; I seemed to have lost you. Was that too strong or off the mark for you?"

"So that was too much for you and it felt like I was pushing too hard. Like it was more my agenda than yours, was that it?"

EXERCISES FOR TASK 1: CREATING AND MAINTAINING A THERAPEUTIC ALLIANCE

Exercise 1:

1. Which of the following promotes empathic attunement?
   a. Therapist maintains eye contact. _____
   b. Therapist asks couple about a recent argument. _____
   c. Therapist explains couple's problem in light of their interaction pattern. _____
   d. Therapist trains couple in a communication model. _____

2. Bob turns away from Marie, crossing his arms and legs in a tight fashion, saying, "You just don't understand." Which of the following would most powerfully promote empathic attunement?

   a. So she doesn't understand you? _____

   b. Bob, I think you are withdrawing from her because you are scared. _____

   c. So you don't think she understands you, and you think it is pointless to try. _____

   (d.) Yes, it's difficult, you feel like you are not getting through, like even your body is closing off. _____

Exercise 2:

List two comments you might make that could show a client you are connecting with his experience as the client closes off his body posture and turns away from his partner saying, "You just shut me out."

1. _You feel shut out and you need to turn away it hurts, so much to try_

2. _when you feel shut out, you turn away & close off_

Exercise 3:

1. A client's eyes well with tears as she describes the frustration she has in trying to reach out to her partner. What could a therapist do to promote empathic attunement?

   a. Note the discrepancy between her tears and her spoken frustration. _____

   b. Notice the tears and ask about her experience. _✓_

   c. Identify with her pain and frustration through self-disclosure. _____

   d. Focus on a time when she felt less frustrated. _____

2. The therapist infers that a husband is afraid of the intimacy that his wife is seeking, noting that he seems curious but proves hesitant when his wife pursues him. The husband withdraws in silence and pulls back from being involved in the session. How might the therapist respond in monitoring this change in the therapeutic relationship? What would you say?

   a. "If you were to put words to your silence what would they say?" _____

   b. "I wonder if that fits for you, I am not sure if my comment about your fears is really what you experience. What's it like when you hear me talk about this fear of intimacy?" _____

   c. "Many husbands that I work with have similar fears." _____

   d. "I wonder if it is safer for you to hold onto your thoughts and feelings than to share them." _____

3. If the therapist offended the client, the therapist could respond to the client to minimize the rupture by saying:

   a. "So it seems like I jumped to a conclusion. Fear and vulnerability are strong words that really don't fit what you are going through. Do you think you can help me better understand what it is like for you?" _✓_

   b. "It seems like it is difficult for you to see this intimacy issue in your relationship."

   _____

c. "Could you tell me when intimacy was less of a problem for you than it is now?"

_____

d. "What is it like for you when I raise these questions about closeness and intimacy?"

_____

TASK 2 INTERVENTIONS: ACCESSING AND REFORMULATING EMOTION

Assumptions: Working with Emotions

The focus on the expression and expansion of emotional experience in EFT is pivotal to the restructuring of interactional patterns among couples. The case of Tom and Susan provides one example of the important role of emotion in shaping a couple's experience.

Tom and Susan have grown increasingly dissatisfied with their relationship. Susan believes that Tom is no longer willing to work on their relationship, and she believes his frequent silence and withdrawal are evidence of his rejection of her and their relationship. Tom doesn't understand why Susan doesn't believe he is committed to their relationship. He explains his occasional distance as a coping response to her incessant nagging. The EFT therapist can use a number of interventions to help this couple access the emotions that inform the meaning that they are making about this relationship.

Accessing primary emotions enables a person to:

- Bring new meaning to understanding a partner's behavior. As Tom is able to talk about his fear of rejection, Susan sees Tom's withdrawal from her not as his rejection of her, but as his own fear of being found inadequate.

- Process the experience and underlying emotions that may be outside of awareness. Tom is able, through focusing on the loneliness that results from his withdrawing actions, to identify his fear of not being good enough for Susan.

- Challenge long-held perceptions of their partner, enabling new responses toward the other. Susan begins to see Tom's withdrawal as a sign that he might be feeling threatened by her response to him. Rather than challenging him, she offers him space and an invitation to talk about his concerns when he is ready.

Basic Principles of Working with Emotions in EFT

A number of basic or universal emotions are common to human experience. They are recognizable by common patterns of verbal and nonverbal expressions. EFT therapists recognize the following list as key universal emotions:[1]

- Anger/rage
- Joy/elation
- Sadness/despair
- Fear/anxiety
- Shame/disgust
- Surprise/curiosity

_____

[1] Note: Some attachment theorists regard love as a basic emotion. In this model, love is understood as a complex set of emotion, and not on the same basic level. Contempt may also be described as a universal emotion but we describe expressions of contempt as a response of reactive anger to the emotions of sadness and despair.

Exercise 4:

Match the following statements to one of the following universal emotions (anger/rage, joy/elation, sadness/despair, fear/anxiety, shame/disgust, surprise/curiosity):

1. "My world falls apart when I hear you talking about leaving." _sadness/despair_
2. "I could care less about talking to you after you fail to take my needs seriously." _anger/rage_
3. "I can't talk about this. No, I don't want to even look at him. I don't want him to see me like this." _shame/disgust_
4. "So you get shaky when I am angry? I've never seen it, is that really true?" _surprise/curiosity_
5. "It's too much. I can't do it. I feel so fragile." _fear/anxiety_
6. "Yeah, I say those things just to get a response out of you. I know you can't handle it. You're emotionally dead." _anger/rage_
7. "I am so lonely, and we used to be so close. Some days it is just too much for me." _sadness/despair_
8. "I know it's my fault. I try my best, but it's really not good enough. It's not what she is looking for." _shame/disgust_
9. "It just felt so good – to have him come down and ask me for a hug. It felt like we really turned a corner last night." _joy/elation_
10. "Sometimes I feel so alone, and I can't stand it, like what if she never comes back or never opens up to me again." _fear/anxiety_

Fostering an emotion focus.

Therapists who are learning the "emotion-focused" approach are reminded of the powerful role emotional experience has in shaping a couple's relationship. Emotion motivates and signals key moves in the dance between spouses. The word emotion comes from the Latin form emovere meaning, literally, "to move." Johnson (2004) describes how emotions are conceptualized in the EFT approach.

Emotions are viewed as action tendencies that arise from automatic appraisals of the relevance of situations to a person's basic concerns and needs (Frijda, 1986; Johnson & Greenberg, 1994). It is anything but a primitive, irrational response. It is a high-level information processing system that integrates innate biological and emotional needs with past experience, present perceptions of the environment, and anticipated interpersonal consequences (Frijda, 1986).

Emotions can be understood in terms of a process that unfolds in a series of steps described by Arnold (1960). These steps include:

1. Appraisal: a rapid assessment of stimulus involving limbic system of brain, indicating warning of a potential danger or threat
2. Arousal: physiological activation, preparing to respond
3. Reappraisal: reevaluation of initial assessment of stimuli involving more cognitive processes
4. Action tendency: behavioral response to stimuli

These steps are illustrated in the following example of a typical couple interaction. A wife's emotional process is cued when her busband becomes silent in a discussion about her concerns regarding the time they spend together as a couple. Her internal response or appraisal is a global assessment indicating a warning of possible danger or distress. As a result, her response at a physiological level is to go hot – the pace of her breathing increasing, and her face flushes. In her reappraisal of the situation, she interprets his silence as indifference and responds by getting his attention by lashing out with criticism and complaints. The following exercise focuses on the elements of the unfolding process just described.

Exercise 5:

Track the underlying process of emotion through each of these scenarios.

Jack tells his wife that he does not want to comfort her. She stiffens in her chair and flushes red as she gestures by wringing her hands. The therapist reflects her stiffening and her hand gesture and asks what is happening for her. She looks down and says, "I can't hear that—I just can't bear it." She stares out the window and sighs.

1. Identify the emotion she maybe experiencing: *fear*
2. Now label the steps leading from her appraisal to her action.

Cue: He refuses to comfort her.

Appraisal: _____ *danger* _____

Arousal: _____ *Flush, wringing hands* _____

Reappraisal: _____ *Can't cope* _____

Action Tendency: _____ *withdraw stare out window* _____

Marcy becomes very still and presses her lips together as her depressed and withdrawn partner expresses that she has become "difficult and demanding" and says that he is no longer willing to put up with her criticism. She moves forward raising her voice and, with a challenging tone says, "Oh, so it's my problem, I am the bad guy? This has nothing to do with your affairs! You're just trying to shift the responsibility away from your lies. You blame me when it's your weakness that you can't handle. I will not stand for this. Do you hear me?"

3. Identify the emotions she may be experiencing: *anger fear*
4. Now label the steps leading from her appraisal to her action.

Cue: His criticism and labeling her "difficult and demanding."

Appraisal: _danger, blamed_

Arousal: _pressed lips, tighten body_

Reappraisal: _It is not fair to blame me_

Action Tendency: _blame & attack_

Kim embraces Larry after he returns from a weekend away. Larry's body stiffens and is rigid in response. He looks toward the ground and she asked him three times in a fast paced anxious tone how his trip went. She backs away. Larry responds in a guarded fashion reassuring her that everything was fine. He walks into the other room and she follows, inviting him to tell her what is on his mind when he is ready.

5. Identify the emotion she is experiencing: _worried / fear_
6. Now label the steps leading from her appraisal to her action.

Cue: His response to her hug is to become rigid.

Appraisal: _Danger, something is wrong_

Arousal: _back away, quick interrogation_

Reappraisal: _Something is bothering him_

Action Tendency: _invite when ready_

Later that evening, Larry kisses Kim good night hoping that she will respond to what he views as a sexual invitation. She responds but then turns away closing her eyes. He feels tense and slides away from her in an aggressive manner saying good night in frustration. Kim moves toward him but Larry is now keeping his distance.

7. Identify the emotion he is experiencing: _Frustration_
8. Now label the steps leading from her appraisal to her action.

Cue: Her turning away.

Appraisal: _Danger_

Arousal: _tense, slides away_

Reappraisal: _she doesn't care about me_

Action Tendency: _rejection_

Emotions as "action tendencies" prompt certain responses. Therapists can anticipate that certain emotions will prompt certain behaviors.

Exercise 6:

Think over the last month or so and reflect on the times when you experienced each of the following emotions. Then match the emotion to the actions in the lettered listed below. Note: The emotions can elicit more than one emotional response.

Ex. When I felt afraid that he was mad at me, I pulled away.

Emotion: fear; action: withdrawal

Emotion

1. Anger _____
2. Shame _c b_
3. Fear _____
4. Surprise _e a_
5. Joy _____
6. Sadness _____

Action

a. Explore/approach
b. Assertion/attack
c. Flee/escape/avoid
d. Mourn/shut down/evoke help
e. Hide/retreat
f. Engage/connect

Exercise 7:

Now apply these emotions and action tendencies to the following situation:

1. When a couple gets in an argument that is heated the husband withdraws from the argument by disengaging from the intensifying escalation. What feeling would typically lead to this action? _anger/rage, fear_
2. As his wife finds him less and less responsive to her complaints, her anger escalates, as she is less able to sense that she is getting through to him. How will anger typically prompt him to respond? _withdraw_

Emotions inform the actions partners take in response to one another in their relationship. They function like a compass guiding personal responses to others and the larger social world. Emotions serve an important role in organizing adaptive responses to a person's environment and this can be seen in many ways in a close relationship.

Exercise 8:

Which of the following assumptions is "true" regarding the adaptive role of emotions in close relationships? Mark the statement as T for True or F for False.

1. Emotions focus attention on interpersonal needs. __T__
2. Emotions color perceptions and meaning. __T__
3. Emotions prime and organize key responses to others (e.g., attachment-related behaviors). __T__
4. Emotions are basically secondary responses to cognitive processes. __F__
5. Emotions enable communication with others. __T__

Primary, secondary, and instrumental emotions.

Primary emotions are direct responses to a present situation. Common primary emotions include: fear in response to a threat from another, anger in response to a violation, or hurt in response a loss.

> *Ex. A husband feels hurt in response to his wife's critical statement. (He has lost esteem or respect in her eyes.)*

Secondary emotions are secondary reactive responses to the primary emotion that enable the person to cope with these primary responses. These responses typically obscure the initial emotional response that a person has to a given situation. Anger may be masked by depression or fear; and hostility may cover over a sense of shame.

> *Ex. The husband, reluctant to express his anger, becomes numb and disconnects in order to avoid an escalation of hostility.*

Instrumental emotions are an emotional expression used to influence others. In relationships, a person may learn that expressing certain emotions may move others to action. For example, a person may find that expressing anger in an aggressive fashion leads to others backing down from their opposition.

> *Ex. The father yelled at his son to get him to clean up his room.*

Exercise 9:

Identify the type of emotion illustrated in each sentence below (primary, secondary, or instrumental):

1. She said she was afraid, hoping that he would hold her and be protective of her. __I__
2. When he told her that he did not want to make love, she flew into a rage and began to list all of his mistakes and shortcomings. __S__
3. As he saw her smiling at his friend, he felt sick and a sense of dread and hopelessness overcame him. __P__
4. She cried continually in the session watching and hoping that her husband would feel bad and change his behavior. __I__

5. As she made her demands clear, he seemed to recoil and get smaller. He shut down and said he felt fine about her comments. _S_

6. He says in a soft voice, "When you talk that way, it really hurts me." _P_

Exercise 10:

Identify the primary emotions underlying each of the following client statements.

1. "I numb out, it just feels better than listening to you tell me that I can't do anything right." Then quietly, "I know I am not perfect, not what you need." *Sadness*

2. "It's beyond frustration. I get exasperated when he just sits there. Not reacting. Not responding. It is like no one is home. I think to myself, I can get him to respond. Then I show my anger." *fear, desperation*

3. "I get so upset. He says I don't parent the children right. And when I try to talk about it with him, he will just lecture me. I never get it right. So I just pull away and don't try. Silence is better than his disapproval." *fear/shame*

4. "You went cold on me, so cold that I just said to myself that I was not going to take this any longer. So I just walked out." *fear of rejection, grief*

5. "I feel kind of trapped, like my efforts are futile. When I try to open up to her it doesn't work. I just don't know how to talk about how I feel." *hopeless, fear*

6. "If I didn't talk then nobody would in this relationship. Silence would be all you hear and I can't handle it. I get angry when he doesn't seem to care." *fear of abandonment*

7. "Sure I get angry when she points out how her father handles a situation. It's like she is saying I am not man enough, and she has to tell me how to be like her old man." *shame, fear of inadequacy*

8. "Sometimes this relationship seems like too much work. I am just exhausted and when he doesn't give any effort, I think why should I try. My efforts don't make a difference anyway. Nothing is going to change." *hopelessness   sadness/grief*

Couples are often stuck in cycles of conflict because they are caught in a spiral of negative emotions and behaviors. This results from a lack of awareness and expression of emotions that signal unmet needs and desires in the relationship. The EFT therapist tracks and responds to the couple's presenting pattern and works with the couple to attend to and differentiate the primary emotions underlying the couple's escalating conflict. The therapeutic process promotes the processing, regulation, and expression of difficult emotions that define and inform the couple's problematic behavior. The therapist leads the couple to new levels of emotional engagement through working with the couple in the experience and expression of their primary emotions.

Three Key Issues in Focusing on Emotion

1. Involvement: Working with emotions requires the direct engagement and experience of those emotions. The therapist uses simple, concrete words and images that help a person connect to their experience. The therapist helps the client work at a "safe distance" from their emotion. A partner can talk about the rejection they experience from the withdrawal of their partner without having to contemplate the totality of

what it means to be rejected or becoming overwhelmed with the feelings of rejection. The therapist works with the concrete experience of the relationship to provide a safe working distance from a potentially overwhelming emotion.

2. Exploration: The therapist leads the couple in a process of emotional discovery based on their personal experience and their experience of the other. Emotions are tied to specific interactions and each partner's emotional experience of that interaction. Exploration includes helping clients "unpack" an emotion enabling them to name a variety of emotional experiences that have come to be represented by one emotional label; e.g., frustration.

3. New emotion: The second task of EFT involves the discovery and expansion of previously unrecognized or unformulated emotional experience. Here the focus is on supporting a couple's engagement with primary emotions, which will enable the couple to respond with a new level of engagement that changes the couple's pattern or dance.

Summary.

In observing the EFT therapist at focusing on emotion, the following would be seen:

1. The therapist would access and evoke emotions that inform an understanding of individual's needs and fears and how the couple interacts.

2. The therapist helps partners shift their habitual ways of processing and regulating their emotions in interactions with their partner. This may include helping partners see how they are expressing anger indirectly through criticism and hiding softer emotions such as fear.

3. The therapist works to unfold and restructure key emotional experiences that may be marginalized in a person's awareness, such as the experience of loss and abandonment that fuels expressions of apathy or numbness.

4. The therapist also uses primary "soft" attachment emotions to shape new responses—responses that are crucial to secure attachment, such as the ability to express needs or ask for comfort and caring.

5. The EFT therapist assumes that it is not simply reframing negative emotions or naming emotions that is crucial for change, but a new experience of emotion that then organizes new interactional responses.

Guidelines for Focusing on Emotions in EFT

- Focus on the most poignant or vivid aspect of experience: nonverbal expression of emotions
- Focus on emotions that are most salient to attachment needs and fears
- Sadness and grief are related to sense of loss and helplessness
- Anger is often a reaction to a perceived or actual nonresponsive attachment figure
- Shame may be indicative of a partner's lack of entitlement to share his or her needs or longing for closeness and a fear that sharing those needs will lead to rejection
- Fear and vulnerability are core elements in human attachment and evoke a partner's longing for closeness and secure connection
- Focus on emotions that play a role in organizing negative interactions: therapist explores and expands emotions that are present in the couple's problematic pattern

The process of engaging emotional experience begins with the therapist drawing out and acknowledging the secondary emotions expressed by the couple. As the couple shares emotions such as frustration and contempt, the therapist is gradually able to begin to touch on the underlying fears and insecurities that spark these reactive emotions and place them in an attachment context. Even while the therapist may be aware of underlying primary emotions, she works with the client couple in clarifying and expressing their emotions at the secondary level, rather than pursuing underlying primary emotions immediately. The therapist joins each client where she stands and only gradually leads each person forward into a new reality. For a client who habitually blames the other, the admission and clarification of anger, although a secondary emotion, is the first step forward. Only gradually can this person also begin to access the pain and longing underlying this anger. So a client's numbness and lack of feeling will also be explored, named, and placed in the context of negative cyclical interactions and attachment dilemmas, but gradually the EFT therapist will also reach for the hopelessness that may underlie such numbness.

The therapist's goal in Task 2 of EFT is then to explicate, expand, and reformulate key attachment emotions, use newly formulated emotions to expand meaning frames, use emotion to "move" clients into new responses, and use expanded emotion to enhance the ways couples are able to engage each other.

SKILLS AND INTERVENTIONS FOR EMOTIONAL ENGAGEMENT

This section reviews the primary skills used to facilitate emotional engagement in the therapy session. These skills include: RISSSC, reflecting primary and secondary emotions, validation, heightening, evocative responding, and empathic conjecture.

R-I-S-S-S-C

The decision about which intervention to use at varying points in the therapy process is vital; however, the congruence between the therapist's nonverbal and verbal messages is of supreme importance. RISSSC, an acronym that represents the core, nonverbal practices of the EFT therapist, enables the therapist to hold and keep a client in the present moment with the therapist's own voice. These therapeutic responses invite the client into a deeper engagement with his or her emotional experience.

R: The therapist intentionally REPEATS key words and phrases for emphasis.

Ex. "So it's painful to stay here, to feel the hurt, sadness, the pain is just too much to handle."

Note: Each repetition invites a client to further engage with and process an emotional experience.

I: The therapist uses IMAGES or word pictures that evoke emotions more than abstract labels tend to do.

Ex. "He shuts you out, and you are on the other side of the door. Knocking, hoping he will come out, but only getting silence in return. As you say reaching for him is like 'jumping off a cliff,' what is that like when you face 'jumping off a cliff'?"

S: The therapist frames responses to clients in SIMPLE and concise phrases.

Ex. A therapist who wants to help a client understand her experience within the context of an attachment frame would frame a client's need for responsiveness: "So part of you just wants him to be there for you." The therapist does not explain the attachment concepts, just simply reflects the concept in the everyday language of the client.

S: The therapist will SLOW the process of the session and the pace of her speech to enable a client's deepening of emotional experience.

Ex. "So it's quiet and lonely there (pause), you're alone (pause), all alone."

S: The therapist will use a SOFT and soothing tone of voice to encourage a client to deepen his or her experience.

Ex. The therapist softens her voice and responds to the client's tears and his underlying fears. "It hurts and this is hard. (pause) Hard to sit with this, not knowing whether she will really be there for you."

C: The therapist uses CLIENT words and phrases in a supportive and validating way.

Ex. The client characterizes his partner's anxious pursuit as "nagging and critical." He states: "She is never happy with a thing I do." The therapist later in the session provides the following reflection based on his telling of a recent experience of her criticism. "So it almost sounds like that was one of those 'She's not happy with what I do' experiences, is that it?"

Note: These key phrases can be recorded by the therapist and used from session to session to evoke emotions and create continuity.

RISSSC is important to performing many EFT interventions effectively. Use the following exercises to practice a combination of verbal and nonverbal responses to hold and highlight another person's experience.

Exercise 11:

This exercise requires two additional participants. One participant will act as the observer, one will role-play a client, and the third will act as a therapist. The goal of this exercise is for the therapist to practice each of the RISSSC elements in a role-play interview with a fictitious client. The person playing the client will identify a relational experience that he or she can describe in emotional terms. The experience may be either positive or negative. The goal for the observer is to identify each of the six RISSSC characteristics used in the interview. The goal for the therapist is to engage the client being portrayed and to elicit and support the client's experience using all six aspects of the RISSSC. The role-play should last about 10 minutes. The therapist may begin the exercise by asking what the "client" would like to talk about, later following with the question "What was this experience like for you?" As the client tells her story, rate the number of times each RISSSC response was used to enhance the conversation. You may also use this exercise to review a recent video or audiotape of your work with a client couple. Choose a 10-minute segment and rate your use of each of the RISSSC responses.

Reflecting Emotional Experience

The therapist follows the emotional process of the couple by tracking and responding to each partner's emotional experience. In doing so, the therapist keeps the focus on the essential aspects of the client's experience; this helps the therapist focus the therapy process, build the therapeutic alliance, and clarify the relationship of emotional experience to attachment needs and interaction patterns. The therapist reflects the emotional experience of the couple at two levels, one focusing on secondary responses and the other highlighting primary or underlying emotions.

Main function of the intervention.

1. Focuses the therapy process
2. Builds and maintains the therapeutic alliance
3. Clarifies emotional responses underlying interactional positions

Examples:

"So then you back away, John, going flat and numb, it's when you see her anger. It is about the anger, and it is too much to handle."

Here the therapist reflects to John that his secondary response or emotion is to withdraw because when he sees her anger, it is too much for him to manage.

"As you say that, John, it seems like you are overwhelmed, by her anger, but also by not knowing how to respond. It is like you are suddenly lost, vulnerable, and exposed?"

Here the therapist reflects John's secondary response but also expands on this emotion including the suggestion that in being overwhelmed he is experiencing a sense of vulnerability and exposure.

Exercise 12:

The following exercises will help you develop your recognition of secondary emotions and will provide you with practice exercises in reflecting secondary emotional responses.

1. Which of the following is typically a secondary emotion in a distressed relationship?
   a. Loneliness _____
   b. Anger _____
   c. Fear _____
   d. Shame _____
2. Which of the following is typically a secondary emotion?
   a. Sense of frustration _____
   b. "Black hole in my stomach" _____
   c. Sadness _____
   d. Guilt _____

3. Which of the following descriptions is typically not a secondary reactive response?
    a. I get so mad at you. _____
    b. I can't stand being blamed. _____
    c. I hate it when you shut me out. _____
    d. I am not sure that you care about me. _____

Example:

"I can't take it anymore. He raises his voice and demands an answer, and I don't have one. It drives me nuts! I get so angry at him. I just launch right back into him."

Exercise 13:

List the secondary emotions stated or described in the example above.

_____

In forming a reflection the therapist combines both the secondary emotion with the couple's cycle or pattern of interaction. The reflection links that partner's experience to the couple's pattern.

Example:

"So you he gets angry and demands an answer. Then you don't have an answer so you respond back with anger, pushing him away."

Exercise 14:

Now from the example above create a brief reflection of secondary emotion within the context of the cycle.[2]

_____

_____

Example:

"She just doesn't care. She could hurt me and just walk away, not thinking about it again. She hurls these accusations at me and I just tune them out. I've heard it all before. At that point I just shrug it off, like, 'Yeah. Whatever.'"

---

[2] Note: It's not sufficient to simply "name" or "label" emotions in EFT. It's vital to reflect them within the interactional context and narrative from which they occur. The EFT therapist takes the time to "paint" pictures as she reflects. This often also serves the purpose of slowing things down in-session, which allows for more experiential processing.

Exercise 15:

Choose the reflection that best fits the secondary emotion within the couple's cycle described in the example above.

a. So she does not care and this is clear from her accusations, so why listen?

b. I can understand that. It makes sense to me that you'd see her that way.

c. When she is angry and attacks you, you tune her out. It's like, 'Whatever. You can't get to me." Is that how it goes?

d. What's it like for you to feel attacked, all the while believing that she doesn't care? What happens inside when the battle rages hot?

Example:

He just gets too irritable. I can feel it coming. I get tense…like I prepare for the onslaught. I fear that I won't be able to appease him. I won't measure up to his demands of me. I don't know what to do; it's awful. I try to respond, and he just gets more irritable. So I try again, and he gets angrier. I keep trying to explain, but at some point there's just no use. I can only take so much, so I end up either going cold, shutting down, or going off alone.

Exercise 16:

1. What are the apparent secondary emotional responses for the male in the example above?

   _____

2. What are the apparent secondary emotional responses for the female?

   _____

3. Create your own reflection of secondary emotion within the context of the cycle.

   _____

   _____

   _____

4. Choose the best reflection of secondary emotion within the context of the cycle:

   a. You try to explain, but it just doesn't work. _____

   b. His anger sends you packing. You just can't win. This leaves you all alone. _____

   c. Are there ever times when you don't respond like this? _____

   d. Let me see if I am getting this: Tom, you get irritable, like you want more from Betsy. Betsy, you sense this, and you begin trying to explain, trying to keep the battle at bay. But your answers are not sufficient, and Tom you get angrier in your questions, while Betsy, you get more frustrated in your attempts to derail the fight? _____

Exercise 17:

The following exercises will help you clarify your understanding of primary emotions and will provide you with practice exercises in reflecting primary or underlying emotional responses.

1. Primary emotions are:
   a. The emotions most often or primarily witnessed in couple's interactions.
   b. The primarily reactive emotions.
   c. The primary, most infantile emotions.
   d. Direct core emotional responses to external stimuli.
2. EFT therapists focus on primary emotion related to:
   a. Blocks to effective communication skills.
   b. Individuation.
   c. Attachment bonds.
   d. Unresolved hurts from the past.
3. Primary emotions in distressed relationships are often:
   a. Disorienting
   b. Pushed out of awareness
   c. Unconscious
   d. Here and now
4. Which of the following best describe common primary emotions:
   a. Frustration, bitterness, fear, guilt.
   b. Guilt, forgiveness, shame, anger.
   c. Sadness, bitterness, shame, frustration.
   d. Anger, sadness, fear, joy, shame.

Example:

"I have fifteen years of anger built up. It's very hard for me talk about my fear because the anger just comes so quickly."

Exercise 18:

In the statement above, the secondary emotion is most likely _____ while the primary emotion is most likely _____.

Example:

Therapist: "Let me see if I am on track here guys. Grace, you see him coming and think 'What have I done now?' Right? You immediately notice this expression on his face, and initially you kind of freeze in fear. It's like, 'Here we go again; he's pissed off about something. I once again don't measure up.' You then quickly move into defending or lashing out."

Exercise 19:

Respond to the statement above using the questions below.

1. What is the primary emotion noted in the context of the cycle?

   _____

2. What action is associated with this primary emotion?

   _____

3. What is the key attachment-related client descriptor associated with primary emotion reflected above?
   a. What have I done now?
   b. Here we go again.
   c. He's pissed about something.
   d. I once again don't measure up.

4. How did the couple respond at a secondary level to their primary emotions above?

   _____

   _____

Example:

Therapist: "And Don, you come toward her wanting an explanation, right? In your mind she has once again 'dropped the ball' as you say, which you initially take as an expression of how she doesn't really care about your wishes. You've said that this initially hits you 'like tearing a hole in my heart,' and you question her love for you, which brings on all kinds of fear, panic, and sadness. But these emotions are extremely painful, and they quickly move to intense anger in you. And in that anger you go 'let her have it.' Is this how it goes?"

Exercise 20:

Respond to the statement above using the questions below.

1. What are possible primary emotions underlying this cycle? _____

   _____

   _____

2. Name one attachment-related theme associated with the primary emotion being described.

_____

_____

3. What is the secondary, more reactive emotion in the cycle described above? _____

4. Name one client phrase/theme that is associated with a secondary emotion in the cycle being described. _____

Example:

Therapist: "This cycle hits, and you guys fall in line, don't you? You really march to the beat of this cycle. It's a beat you both know all too well. You go at each other, eventually going into your separate corners, both of you very alone... and afraid. Is this how it goes?"

Exercise 21:

Respond to the statement above using the question below.

What are the attachment-related primary emotions resulting from the couple's cycle that ends in separation and emotional disconnection? _____

_____

Validation

As a primary intervention in EFT, validation is used to communicate acceptance and to recognize the legitimacy of a client's emotional experience. These responses promote the therapeutic alliance and encourage further client exploration. The clients experience support and begin to feel entitled to their experience of the relationship and attachment needs and fears. Validation promotes the client's acceptance of his or her experience by normalizing his or her perceptions and underscoring the legitimacy of their experience. This helps the client to reduce the notion that he or she "should" or "should not" have a particular feeling. This increases a person's entitlement to experience and encourages the person to both engage with and develop their emotional experience.

The therapist validates client's emotions and his or her experience of the relationship. Example: "So it is really hard to say that. To feel that you're hurt, when all along you are supposed to be strong, show no weakness. Yet you find yourself angry and hurt. Hurt like you are so alone, so missing her. Is that it?"

Two forms of validation are used by the EFT therapist:

1. The therapist may use validation to respond to a partner's description of their present experience. A client Janet may express her frustration with Bob's passivity when confronting an important issue. Imagine that the therapist in the early stages of therapy hears Janet complain: "I just don't get it. After we have been over this so many

times in the past, I raise my concerns and Bob does nothing. He just ignores me." The therapist validates Janet's experience by reflecting her experience and acknowledging the validity of her response. The therapist responds: "Yes, and that makes sense why you would become frustrated when you don't see that your words seem to have an impact on Bob. It is frustrating that it seems like your voice is not heard."

2. The therapist may use validation to respond to a client's newly experienced emerging emotion. The therapist responds to the client's sharing of primary emotions providing affirmation, which acts to promote acceptance of this experience in session and interrupt the patterns of disqualification and self-protection that are present in distressed couples, especially as more vulnerable concerns and needs are expressed. Later in the session with Janet and Bob, the therapist notices tears in Janet's eyes as Janet describes the isolation she feels in the relationship. As the therapist reflects Janet's primary emotion Janet's tears turn to sobs, and patiently the therapist responds: "So, it's really tough to not get a response, not only because it makes you angry, but also because you feel alone in this relationship, like there is no one here for you. Yes and when you get nothing back from him it's like you don't exist."

Main functions of the intervention.

- Builds and maintains the therapeutic alliance
- Legitimizes client responses and experience
- Supports further exploration of client's experience

Framing a validation statement.

The following phrases provide a way of framing your response to a client that begins by affirming their experience or understanding. It is important in validation for the therapist to affirm the client's unique experience (which may be very different from the other partner's intention or experience).

- "Yes, I hear what you are saying...."
- "That makes sense to me that you feel...."
- "Okay from your point of view...."
- "Yes I can see how..."

Exercise 22: Review Questions

1. Validation of a partner's responses is most effective when:
   a. The therapist validates the underlying or primary emotion
   b. The therapist's validation is communicated indirectly versus directly
   c. Both partners' responses are validated
   d. Partners are taught to validate one another

2. Validation and reflection are intended to:
   a. Reduce anxiety and decrease self-protection in the interactions of distressed couples
   b. Help couples through the therapist modeling empathic understanding
   c. Teach couples the reasons certain emotional responses are appropriate
   d. Encourage appropriate dependency of a client on a therapist

Exercise 23: Practice Forming Validation Statements

After Leo's affair, Lisa found it difficult to not check up on Leo if he was late in returning home. In Lisa's words: "I feel better calling him, even if it annoys him. But I just can't stand not knowing if he is where he said he would be."

1. Now form a statement to validate Lisa's experience.

    _____

    _____

Later in the session, Leo responds: "I know I have to earn her trust, but her calls get me so frustrated. I start thinking about why she has to call me, like all this effort I put in to show her that things are okay and she can count on me, and it just seems like the trust just disappears."

2. Now form a statement to validate Leo's experience.

    _____

    _____

Review the two statements you composed. Does your statement include a reflection of each partner's experience? Does your statement include a statement validating her/his experience?

In the session Leo moves from the sense of futility he has felt in rebuilding trust in the relationship to his fears that the relationship may not make it. He wonders if the relationship is broken beyond repair and fears that he has lost Lisa. He shares that he has always been hopeful that things would get better, and now he is afraid that he has ruined their relationship.

3. Form a validation statement responding to Leo's new experience of his underlying emotions. [Keep in mind his initial frustration. Validate his response to her defensiveness. Help him see how his response makes sense given the interaction.]

Often in the early stages of therapy, we could expect Lisa to respond to Leo's vulnerability with a dismissive or defensive comment. For example, the therapist might turn to Lisa and ask her what it was like for her to hear Leo share these fears and Lisa might respond: "Well, I don't know. I mean I just can't say everything will be better. I can't make promises; he is the one who broke his." The EFT therapist could use validation to respond to Lisa's present response by saying:

Therapist: "Right, Lisa, it's like you can't reassure him right now. You can't respond to his fear and say everything will be okay, because that would take trust that is still uncertain. And it makes sense that you would want to back away from his fear, not knowing what to say."

Now imagine Leo responds to Lisa's defensive response with one of his own. He pulls back and folds his arms, saying "See why it's hard to want to try, when she doesn't even give things a chance. She doesn't give me a chance."

4. Now form a validating response to her defensiveness. Help him see how her response makes sense given the interaction.

_____

_____

This exercise illustrates how validation is an effective intervention for containing the anxiety and defensive responses common to distressed couples. The therapist works to communicate both empathy and understanding of the emotional responses of partners who are often locked into a cycle that prompts responses which invalidate their emotional experience. The therapist enhances the security of the therapeutic alliance by demonstrating an awareness of their experience and recognizes that each partner is entitled to his or her emotional experience. At times a therapist may find it difficult to validate a client's experience. This may occur when:

- The therapist believes that the client should not have this response to the particular situation.
- The therapist fears that by validating the client's response the therapist will be encouraging or condoning a problematic behavior.
- The therapist sees that validating may lead to a negative impact on the partner.

5. In which of these situations would you have the most difficult time validating the response of a client?

In these situations, it is important to recognize Fosha's (2000) observation that validation of a client's defensive responses is more likely to lead the client to lessen his or her use of this defense. The therapist can effectively challenge a client's problematic actions by using the past to validate the present response.

Consider the husband who avoids any discussion of his wife's concerns about their relationship by withdrawing in silence. The therapist can respond to his problematic behavior by validating this action as a coping response that makes sense in an attachment frame.

Therapist: "So it's too much to talk about these issues, and your family was never comfortable with any level of conflict or intimacy. So it makes sense to pull away to protect your relationship. It is better to take the blame for the problems of the relationship, than fight it out and risk losing what is important to you."

Or another response focuses on a stuck coping response.

Therapist: "So you learned to withdraw in your family to stay connected when the conflict was flying between your parents. And it makes sense that when conflict is building in your relationship that you withdraw, because it's the only thing you have known. It worked in the past and it seems like the only thing you know to do. Does that fit for you?"

Exercise 24:

Keeping these things in mind, construct a validation statement for the following partner who is a "chronic criticizer." She wants a more intimate relationship with her partner and her common approach to issues of concern in her relationship is to point out areas that he could change. When he challenges her, she redoubles her criticism until he backs down. You also learned from her in an earlier session that using harsh words was the only way she was heard in her hostile family of origin.

_____

_____

_____

Evocative Responding

Evocative responding involves the use of questions and prompts to call up emotions into the conversation. These questions expand the emotional experience of partners as they share about their relationship. They are used to identify and intensify emotions that are often marginal to the partner's everyday experience. These prompts invite the couple to further explore and engage their emotional responses. The therapist may use evocative responding to help clients express emotions that are being communicated nonverbally through somatic indications or physical cues.

Examples:

"So what is it like for you when Mark turns away and won't give you eye contact?"

After a period of silence the therapist asks the silent partner, "What is going on for you now?"

In response to a withdrawn partner now engaging their pursuing partner, "What is it like for you to have him respond this way?"

"Phil, how does it feel when your wife says to you that she's afraid she's not special enough? That she's going to be too much trouble. That she thinks you are going to get fed up. What do you feel when she says that?"

"What is going on for you right now, as you look at him and see his sadness?"

"You say you are open to discussing this fight, but when I look at you, your legs and arms are crossed and you are looking away. So I wonder what is going on for you now as you think about this last fight?"

A client says: "I just don't need anything from this relationship." The therapist responds: "How are you able to do that? There is nothing you need from your wife?"

The therapist always presents an evocative response in a tentative manner. The use of imagery helps the client experience the emotion that is being elicited by the response. Evocative responding works to direct the client to the "leading edge" (Wile, 1994) of their experience. The therapist's response, often through a question, will invite the client to explore and process a newly formulated emotional experience.

Main functions of the intervention.

- Expands elements of emotional experience
- Helps to formulate unclear aspects of emotional experience
- Encourages exploration and engagement of emotional experience

Framing an evocative response.

The therapist will use questions to explore the emotional experience of a client often building from a non-verbal emotional expression, bodily cue, new experience, or information shared in the session. The therapist will focus on the how, what, and where of a person's experience. The use of a "why" question is not an evocative response in that it usually calls forth more abstract cognitive responses.

- Ask a question: "What is it like for you when...."
- Ask about the impact of an event: "What is happening for you as you hear him say that?..."
- Focus on personal response: "What happens inside of you when she turns away?"
- Ask about different parts of the person's experience: "So when you hear him say that, part of you acts as if it doesn't matter, but another part is wounded?"
- Focus on level of arousal: "So is the tightness you feel in your shoulders when he talks about his affair an anxious tightness or an angry tightness?" "As you were sharing that, I thought I heard a sigh. Like it hurts to go over this again?"
- Evoke the voice or speak as an attachment figure: "So you said your aunt was there for you. You felt safe with her. What would she say to you now? What would she say to your fear?"
- Ask a client to repeat a poignant phrase: "Can you say that again Paul, how lost you feel that she has pulled away?"

Exercise 25: Review Questions

1. Evocative responding guides the client to the _____ of their experience and _____ the client to explore and reprocess their experience making it more specific and tangible.
   a. Unresolved aspects, instructs
   b. Leading edge, invites
   c. Underlying assumptions, coaches
   d. Hidden aspects, teaches
2. Giving an evocative response, the therapist gives direct attention to:
   a. The general comments a client makes.
   b. Irrational or unrealistic assumptions.
   c. Conflicting elements of a client's response.
   d. Bodily cues indicative of affect.

3. Important to forming any evocative response is the use of:
   a. The couple's cycle.
   b. A partner's primary emotions.
   c. Tentative and speculative phrasing.
   d. Attachment theory.

Exercise 26:

Form an evocative response to the following client situations.

1. Your client has a pained expression on his face when describing what happens when he tries to talk with his partner about the way he makes financial decisions.

   _____

2. Shannon has just heard how Bob withdraws from their conflicts because he doesn't know how to respond to her criticism. He is afraid to hurt her and fears that she may be losing interest in him. What might a therapist say to explore Shannon's experience of hearing Bob's fear?

   _____

3. Felicia has tears in her eyes as she describes her angry pursuit of Hosea when he ignores her, preferring to talk to his friends rather than her.

   _____

4. Jane looks at Steven after explaining the couple's most recent fight. Steven glares back at her and rolls his eyes. The therapist seeing a pained response on Jane's face uses evocative responding to explore this emotional reaction. How would you phrase an evocative response to Jane?

   _____

5. Now form an evocative response for Steve.

   _____

6. Russell seems to withdraw from Ceslie as she, in tears, laments the state of their relationship. How might you evocatively respond to Russell's sudden withdrawal?

   _____

The therapist may also respond to bodily cues that are indicative of an unexpressed emotional experience. If a client shares that he feels bad or uncomfortable, the therapist may deepen that client's experience by asking a question that references the client's bodily experience.

Example:

"How do you feel that in your body?" Or "I noticed that you really tensed up as you heard her say those words?"

Exercise 27:

Consider how you might use an evocative response to draw out a client's experience.

1. "I feel sick when she talks about leaving me."
2. "After our fight, I had to go and lay down. I was exhausted."
3. Sheri stumbles struggling to find words to describe her sadness when she hears Paul talk about leaving the relationship.
4. Shawn describes his grandfather as the one person in his life he has always trusted and turned for support. How might the therapist form an evocative response to address Shawn's fears of inadequacy in his relationship with Karen? Form an evocative response speaking as the grandfather to help Shawn with his fear.
5. Shawn grips his chair as tears stream down his face, while he shares the words of reassurance from his grandfather. How might the therapist expand on Shawn's experience using an evocative response?

Heightening

Heightening intensifies a client's emotional experience creating a more vivid emotional engagement with this experience. The therapist's response crystallizes and deepens key elements of this emotional experience. It is out of this heightened engagement that the therapist will facilitate new patterns of interaction in the relationship. Heightening can take many forms including the use of repetition, metaphors, images, and enactments. The therapist often intensifies her comments by leaning forward, slowing the pace of her words, and softening her voice as the heightening builds.

- Repetition: "So you're saying to Phil, 'I'm scared and I find it hard to believe that you really, really want to be with me. I'm so afraid; I am scared to let you in, to rest in your arms.'"
- Presentation: The therapist can heighten emotion by how they respond to the client. The therapist can intensify the experience by leaning forward and matching the pace and volume to the emotion being heightened: A slow and soft voice for more vulnerable emotions or a louder, more abrupt voice for assertive responses.
- Metaphors and images: "And I'm scared to let you in. I start to doubt that if I open the door and start to count on him, how do I know that he won't find me too scared... or too depressed... or too 'sick'?"
- Sharing intrapersonal experiences with their partner (most common in enactments and heightening): "Can you tell her that? Can you say that to her again? Can you say, 'I am so alone, I can't find you.' Can you turn to her and say that?"
- Focusing: Therapist maintains the emotional intensity of the session by keeping the couple repeatedly focused on the emotional experience in the room.

Functions of the intervention.

- Highlight the key experiences that organize actions in the relationship
- Highlight key experiences that lead to new formulation of experience
- Highlight key experiences that will reorganize the couple's interaction

Common metaphors and images.

The following list summarizes common metaphors and images used by EFT therapists to symbolize emotional experience. Often the most powerful images are found in the client's own description of her or his experience.

- Edge of cliff
- Alarm going off
- Door—come out from behind, closed
- Dragon/fear in facing
- Little child/boy/girl
- Paralyzed/numbing
- Bomb is ticking or may go off
- Hot/cold/freezing/frozen
- Military—foxhole, fire, run for cover
- Light, darkness
- Desert—dying of thirst, parched
- Dance
- Water—deep, shallow, drowning, flooding
- Passing the test, litmus test, on trial, condemned

Example:

A withdrawer is frustrated by the constant pursuit of his or her partner.

Possible response:

"It's like there is no place to hide, no way to get away, and you feel trapped in this frustration."

Exercise 28:

Use an image or a metaphor to form a heightening statement in response to the following situations.

1. A withdrawer's loneliness at her partner's disengagement in the relationship.

   _____

2. A pursuer's fear that his partner will never respond to his needs.

   _____

3. A pursuer's frustration about not getting a meaningful response from her partner.

   _____

4. A partner's hope with the changes that have taken place in her relationship.

_____

5. A partner's surprise at the support he experiences from his previously distant spouse.

_____

Exercise 29:

Select the therapist response that would most likely heighten the partner's affect.

1. I guess I just find it hard to keep trying to reach him after years of no response.
   a. So you protect yourself from his distance by staying away?
   b. That makes sense that this is a challenge, he hasn't been there for you.
   c. It's hard to know where to start, where to begin. Should I risk? Should I put myself out again? It's hard to keep dancing when your partner seems to be listening to different music.
   d. So you fear what it might be like to be close.

2. There is no pleasing her. Why should I try? She will always find some way I don't measure up.
   a. So you fear that you will never be good enough.
   b. It's hard to believe that one day you would pass her test. Hard to believe you are not a failure in her eyes, that she could treasure you?
   c. So she sees you as a constant failure and you are tired of trying to prove different.
   d. Can you tell her what its like to hear her criticism?

3. I can't believe that. He says he wants to be with me, but he's afraid. I don't get it. Most of the time it seems like he doesn't care.
   a. It's too hard to believe, to hold on to the hope he cares, that he really, really wants you?
   b. It's hard to believe him when he says one thing and acts just the opposite.
   c. Can you tell him you find it hard to believe his fear?
   d. So can you see that he's hiding, can you see his fear? And he wants more than anything to be close?

4. Sometimes, though we are together, he could be miles away. I am so alone.
   a. So you feel more and more lonely.
   b. So can you tell him? Can you say to him that there are times when you are together and he feels miles away and you are alone, so desperately alone?
   c. Does he know how alone you feel at these times?
   d. And you are often alone in this relationship even if you are together, is that it?

5. It was so good. He started to back away and then it was like he stopped. Turned to me and I could tell he was there for me.
   a. So he showed you he was really there for you.
   b. Yes, and that is your secure bond at work. It makes you both feel safe.

    c. Can you tell him how much you appreciate his being there for you?

    d. Wow! That's amazing! How did you do that? See that pattern and resist it? You really showed her you were there for her.

6. I don't see what difference it makes. Why does she need to know how I feel about that?

    a. So you close that part of your world off. Shut the door. It is private. For you alone?

    b. It's safer to hide than to show her how you feel?

    c. What's that like for you to keep this to yourself?

    d. Can you tell her that she does not need to worry about you and your feelings?

7. How many times do I have to tell him? He just doesn't care. He's in his own world. I could be dying out here and he wouldn't know. He wouldn't care!

    a. So he hides from you and you are left alone both angry and hurt.

    b. He builds a wall to protect himself from you and your anger toward him.

    c. Perhaps there are times when his wall comes down and you are less alone.

    d. You feel alone. Abandoned. Like he is not there for you. And you are dying from it?

8. It is so hard. I don't think I could tell him that. I am just not sure.

    a. Yes, it makes sense that you do not trust him yet, after what you have been through.

    b. What's it like for you to not be able to open this door to him?

    c. It's safer to keep the wall up but a part of you wants to connect.

    d. You are on a cliff; you're at the edge. And I am saying jump, he will catch you, but it seems too far, too dangerous, too hard, and too scary.

9. I don't want to spend our lives like this. I want to be close. I want to know her, to really know her.

    a. So part of you has not given up. You still hope for change.

    b. Can you tell her that? That you want that closeness, and you want to know her? Can you share that with her, now? How much you long to know, touch, reach, and dance with your wife?

    c. This is important. She needs to hear this from you. She doesn't believe you. Can you tell her?

    d. You are in pain and you want her to know that this pain is because you love her, right?

10. Jane shares with Tim her lack of desire to be with him sexually. Tim's eye's well with tears as he says "I don't understand."

    a. Yes and it makes sense that you would feel this hurt, most people would find this painful.

    b. It is painful, yes, so difficult to hear these words, like a rejection, like a wound being opened?

    c. Her lack of interest is her coping response to her own fear of being close to you.

    d. What's that like for you to hear these words Tim?

Exercise 30:

Look for the example below where the therapist is heightening a client's positive sense of self.

a. It is amazing to see the progress you have made in trusting your partner.
b. What's it like for you to see your growth in these areas?
c. It makes sense that you would feel proud of all that you have accomplished.
d. Though you didn't know what it would look like, you have shown great courage, strength, and bravery in fighting and risking being who you are in this relationship.

Exercise 31:

Now form a heightening response of your own using the following client statements.[3]

1. James is afraid to tell his partner that underlying his withdrawal is a fear of not being good enough.

    _____

2. Kris describes feeling safe with Richard for the first time in months.

    _____

3. Paul expresses his irritation at being interrupted with his wife's personal calls while he is at work. (Use an enactment to heighten this response.)

    _____

4. Leslie fears that she is not good enough for Manuel and hides her desires to be close to him.

    _____

5. Shannon shares how much better she feels about herself when she is immersed in work compared to the insecurity she feels in her relationship with Chris.

    _____

6. Peter describes his pattern of attacking Marcia when she presses him about his feelings. Peter complains: "She gives me no space, so I make space. I push her away. It is the only thing I know to do."

    _____

---

[3] Note: While these exercises help you to construct heightening statements, it is important to remember the effect of heightening is determined by how it is said as much as what is said. RISSSC is essential to the heightening of emotional experience.

Empathic Conjecture and Interpretation

The therapist draws on experience of couple cycle, empathic immersion in client's position and experience in this cycle, and understanding of adult love based on attachment theory, to make inferences that promote a more intense emotional experience. The therapist uses these inferences to facilitate the engagement of emotions that a partner may not be able to formulate. The goal is to promote a more intense awareness and experience of emotion. These interventions may draw attention to defensive strategies a partner is using that are informed by fears of engulfment, rejection, and abandonment. Care is given to offer these conjectures in a tentative manner that is open to correction or dismissal by the client. They are also ideally close to the client's experience, just one step further than the client's formulations.

Assumptions about conjectures/interpretation (these terms are used interchangeably):

- Interpretations are exploratory responses to enhance client's emotional experience.
- They are not cognitive labels to give new information to clients.
- The goal is to help client more intensely focus on their experience.
- They are based on the therapist's empathic immersion in client's world of experience.
- Often they are based on therapist's knowledge of attachment processes in couple relationships.

Main functions of the intervention.

1. Clarifies and formulates new meaning related to interaction positions, emotional experience, and resulting behaviors and patterns.
2. Clarifies and formulates new meanings related to the strategies that prevent emotional engagement with partner and self.

This section reviews the different types of empathic conjecture/interpretation interventions. While both simple and complex conjecture serve the same purpose, the formulation of these therapist statements are based on different levels of engagement with the client couple.

Simple empathic conjectures.

The following examples include simple empathic conjectures based on the therapist's immersion in the client's emotional experience.

- Conjecture about experience beyond client's awareness. The therapist takes one step beyond the client's stated experience. Here the client has described his or her experience and the therapist conjectures about emotions that may underlie what the client has described.

Therapist: "As I listen to you I hear you saying you're angry about his lack of concern for you, but I see the tears in your eyes and I wonder if you are also saying that you are hurt by his lack of concern. Does that seem to fit?"

- Conjecture about experience that the client has not yet formulated. Here the therapist is clarifying the client's experience and introducing a formulation of this experience. Often this conjecture is used when a therapist observes nonverbal responses of a partner that have not been articulated in relation to his or her emotional experience.

Therapist: "So it sounds like when things heat up in a conflict, that you, Jim, check out of the conflict, but you stay in the room with her. You are still present with her. It's like your conversation is saying I am not going to argue with you, but your body is saying this is important and I am still here."

- Conjecture about experience that a client does not yet own.

Therapist: "What's it like to hear that she is angry because what she really wants is to be close to you?"

Client: "I don't know. It is hard to say."

Therapist: "Perhaps there is a part of you that is drawn to being close but another that wants no part of her angry attack. Does that fit?"

Complex empathic conjectures.

A more complex form of empathic conjecture interpretation draws upon the therapist's engagement with the couple's interaction pattern and individual experience. The therapist's conjecture and interpretation is formed based on assumptions of attachment theory and couple bonds. The therapist will use the attachment related themes found in the couple's interaction to propose an interpretation of the couple's experience that points them toward a new pattern of interaction. The focus of these conjectures can take one of three directions:

1. Defensive strategies: the need for self-protection from partner.
2. Attachment longings: the longing for connection and comfort.
3. Attachment fears and fantasies: the fear that the partner will be rejected by their partner or abandoned by partner.

Example: Empathic Conjecture for Defensive Strategy[4]

"So it seems like you hear her words and they say to you that you are a 'failure.' Like there is something wrong with you, and you will never measure up. That, this is about you being not worthy, not lovable? Hmm? So you pull away more and more. Yet at the same time there is a part of you saying, 'I don't deserve this, all this rejection. I don't have to constantly prove myself to you. Like that is not all of who I am.' Is that it?"

Example: Empathic Conjecture for Attachment Longings

"You are telling me that it is lonely and the loneliness is overwhelming like a complete rejection and you respond with an attack, because it hurts. And I hear that it hurts, but a part of me wonders if that hurt is not just the loneliness, the rejection, but the hurt is about a desire to connect, to make a connection and to be held and comforted. So it's not just about your loneliness, but a part of you longs to be with him, to make that connection, to be with him, really with him. Does that fit for you?"

Example: Empathic Conjecture for Fears and Fantasies

"So you are angry with him even though he has opened up to you. He says he wants to be with you, but that is confusing because he hasn't been like this before. I am not

---

[4] Note: This conjecture underscores the partner's need to keep some distance to protect himself.

sure if this fits for you, but it seems like there is a part of you that wants to embrace this openness because it is what you have always wanted, but there is this other part that doesn't trust it. So if you reach out to meet him, he might change his mind and pull away, because, maybe you do not really matter to him."

Seeding attachment.

A variation of empathic conjecture builds on a therapist's skill to validate and heighten a partner's emotional engagement. This intervention is used to bring to light the attachment related needs and longings that are being blocked by client fears. The intervention helps the couple see beyond the fears to the needs that ultimately underlie their stuck pattern of interaction. Seeding attachment opens up new possibilities for the couple's connection as the therapist helps them see beyond the fear to a more secure interaction.

Framing the seeding attachment intervention:

1. The intervention sequence begins with the phrase: "So you could never..."

"So you could never turn to her and say, I need you and I need to come first. I want to be important."

2. Then the therapist addresses the fear that keeps the client from a more engaged stance with his or her partner. "So you could never..." (disclose attachment-related fear or need)

"So you could never turn to him and tell him that the criticism hurts you too much, and it makes you question your worth. What you really want is a chance to be close."

Disquisition.

A disquisition is a special type of empathic conjecture most often used when partners are reluctant or resistant to explore their emotional experience. It is used when other evocative strategies are not effective in promoting emotional experiencing. It is a non-threatening intervention that promotes the couple's identification with their own pattern and emotions through the story about another couple or couples in general. The therapist often prepares the disquisition in advance rather than responding in session on the spur of the moment.

A disquisition includes:

1. A general story about a couple's problem
2. The story is similar or relevant to the issues of the client couple in therapy
3. The story includes a description of couple's pattern including details on underlying emotions associated with the pattern
4. The story relates the couple's actions to their underlying emotions

A disquisition may be used:

1. To help a client engage an emotional experience that he or she does not own
2. To enable a therapist to reflect on negative experience of a couple's cycle without making these specific to the couple
3. To normalize the negative response of a blaming partner to the new experience and behaviors taken by their partner

Example:

The therapist is working with a remarried couple that has difficulties being unified in their approach to the children. Loyalty binds exist between the biological and stepparents. The therapist uses a disquisition to get them to consider their own stuck relationship in light of another couple.

Sometimes couples get locked into a pattern that is difficult for them to understand. I have been thinking about a couple I know that gets stuck around holiday celebrations. They can even see it coming, but they just feel helpless once the issues get going. She has a close relationship to her family and wants to be part of her family's gatherings at the holidays. He sees this as her family's control over her. At any rate, he tends to challenge her desire to hang out with her family as a sign of her lack of commitment to their marriage. She resents his judgmental attitude and is angered by his critical comments about her family. He then backs off and becomes passive and sulks. She is furious at his behavior and sees him as overly demanding and immature. He played the victim, explaining that things would be different if he had better relationships with his family, which she sees as his problem not hers. Funny thing is that they both want this "family dance" out of their relationship. He wanted reassurance that he was important to her, as family holidays tended to be painful times for him, and he felt rejection in the face of her excitement of spending time with her family. While she understood how painful holidays were for him, she felt criticized and controlled by the "Solomon's choice" he would demand. Her anger got stronger as she feared she had no choice in the situation. She didn't get that he wanted reassurance and support, and he didn't see that she wanted to be there for him but couldn't because she would have felt too controlled. I wonder sometimes if this couple could identify with what it is like for you both when dealing with family expectations.

Exercise 32:

1. Empathic conjecture is:
    a. A cognitive restatement of emotional experience
    b. An objective summary of personal emotional experience
    c. An intervention that gives insight to the self and other
    d. Just one step ahead of the client's articulated experience

2. Many empathic conjectures focus on:
    a. A client's experience of fear or shame in the context of the relationship bond.
    b. A client's experience of pursuit and withdraw in the context of the relationship.
    c. Educating the client about the role of attachment bonds in their relationship.
    d. Directing partners to share their relationship fears with one another.

3. This intervention is used to bring to light attachment-related needs and longings that are blocked by a client's fears.
    a. Evocative responding
    b. Validation
    c. Disquisition
    d. Seeding attachment

4. This intervention is used when a partner or a couple is extremely resistant to exploring their emotional experience.

    a. Evocative responding

    b. Validation

    c. Disquisition

    d. Seeding attachment

Exercise 33:

Identify the therapist statement that is an empathic conjecture:

1. Cherise and Samuel have a long-standing pursuit-and-demand cycle that organizes around Cherise's chronic dissatisfaction with Samuel's "commitment" to her. The couple says this frequent fight dates back to Samuel's lack of support following the death of her father. Which of the following would help Cherise reflect on the hurt she has that underlies her anger?

    a. "This anger you feel is often the result of an attachment injury you experienced with Samuel's lack of accessibility."

    b. "Your anger is a secondary emotion, do you think you might really be grieving that he was not there for you."

    c. "As you say that, I hear your anger and frustration, and I wonder if you also want him to see the hurt this situation causes you?"

    d. "I know you are angry at Samuel, but can you tell him what hurts you as well?"

2. Later Samuel is asked about his experience in hearing Cherise recount how abandoned she felt when Samuel does not respond to her pain. Samuel talks about his confusion, of not knowing how to respond to her feelings. He admits that it's sometimes safer if he just "takes it in" rather than trying to respond it. Which of the following statements would a therapist select as an empathic conjecture that would lead Samuel to the leading edge of his experience?

    a. "So you see her emotions and back away, because it is not safe. Is that it?"

    b. "It makes sense that you are uncertain how to respond to her emotions, because her feelings are strong and you have not done what she wanted in the past."

    c. "Can you ask her to tell you what she would like from you?"

    d. "So it's confusing, and you hold back, almost like something bad will happen if you show your concern, it's scary to not know if your offer will be received or rejected."

3. The therapist asks Samuel what it's like for him to sit in the room while Cherise expresses her disgust regarding his concern for her. Samuel describes the sense of sinking in his chair and getting smaller and smaller.

    a. "So she sees you stone-faced, a stoic man, but inside you're shrinking like a little boy, not knowing what to do, just afraid, afraid that she will not want what you have to give her? So you hide from her not knowing what to say or do, just hoping to disappear."

    b. "So she shows contempt and you withdraw. Your defend yourself and she goes on the attack. That must be difficult."

c. "How does she know the difference between your fear and your indifference?"

d. "You avoid—it seems the best response in the circumstances."

4. After exploring his fear of being seen as inadequate in Cherise's eyes and his concern about losing her, Cherise finds it hard to believe Samuel really cares underneath all of his silence. The therapist explores her experience and returns to the pain she feels. Choose an empathic conjecture the therapist could use to help Cherise expand her experience of Samuel and her pattern of demanding in the face of his silence.

a. "You never really saw men caring for you in your family growing up and it's hard to really trust Samuel when he says he cares and really wants to be with you but doesn't show it?"

b. "It makes sense that you would find all this talk about Samuel's care and concern difficult to believe, when most of what you have known is his silence."

c. "It's hard to believe he cares, and it's like it's hard to hope he cares, especially when he is quiet. One part of you wants to believe him, but the other is saying don't believe it, it's not true. Those are just words. So you want to keep pushing/checking if he will respond."

d. "He has wounded you and you need to protect yourself. It is hard to see his vulnerability because of your own hurts."

5. As treatment progresses, it becomes clear that Cherise's doubts and fears about her trust of Samuel also reflect her underlying feelings of shame and questions of personal worth. Choose an empathic conjecture that will invite Cherise to explore this further.

a. "Sounds like you are afraid that Samuel won't be there for you, but I also hear that you are afraid you are not worthy of his care."

b. "I think anyone would question whether she can trust given what you have been through, but I wonder if you have trouble trusting him because you wonder if you really are lovable."

c. "So it's like this fear keeps you apart, and it's hard to trust to open up to him, but it also seems, and I may not have this right, but it seems like a part of you is afraid. Afraid to risk being open / seen / not sure if he will really want you/if you are really enough?"

d. "And it seems like it is really, really hard to show him the soft, tender, vulnerable place in you that wants to connect, is that it?"

6. The therapist works to further expand this vulnerable moment for the couple by seeding attachment. Select the intervention below which best fits this intervention and this scenario.

a. "So you could never say to him, 'I am too scared to let you in.' I am scared that I will disappoint you, and I want to be there for you, but if I reach and you turn away....It would be too hard to say, 'I am too scared to let you in.' Right?"

b. "So you could never say to him, 'I can't tell you what I really feel because of the messages I had from my family that I was not good enough.'"

c. "So you could never say to him, 'It is not just about you. I have insecurities, too.'"

d. So you could never say to him, that you really mattered and that your needs were important.

Exercise 34:

You are working with Mark, who frequently attacks his partner, Julie, when she asks him about his feelings toward her. He reveals that he feels out of control in these conversations.

1. Form an empathic conjecture that will draw him to the leading edge of the loss of control feeling.
2. Now write an empathic conjecture that will help this partner explore the ways in which his anger functions as a defensive strategy.
3. Form an empathic conjecture that will help Julie connect her anxious pursuit of Mark to her questions about Mark's feelings regarding the relationship.
4. Form an empathic conjecture that connects Julie's need for reassurance to an attachment-related fear or fantasy.
5. Mark later explores his own pattern of attack followed by withdrawal in the relationship. He touches on the loneliness and frustration he feels when he comes up against an impasse and is unable to comfort her after an argument. Form an empathic conjecture that will help Mark connect his loneliness to an attachment-related theme.
6. Now take the attachment-related theme you used for Mark and write a seeding attachment conjecture.

Exercise 35:

Imagine you have a couple that has begun to make changes. The withdrawn partner is reengaging the relationship and has been more forthcoming with his needs and hopes for the relationship. At the same time, his wife, who is now getting what she said she wanted from him, now shifts between receiving this new attention and distrustful rejection of his attempts. She concludes: "How do I know he is really sincere?" Compose a disquisition that includes:

1. Acknowledgment of the client's difficulty in trusting these new changes.
2. A description about how other clients have had similar struggle.
3. Either describe a particular client's experience or describe the general experience of pursuers to the engagement of a withdrawer.
4. Be sure to include reference to emotions underlying the distrust of this change.

_____

_____

_____

_____

_____

SELF-DISCLOSURE

On occasion the EFT therapist will use self-disclosure in a session to strengthen the alliance with a couple. The therapist's disclosure can be effective in validating client responses by normalizing the client's experience as something that the therapist herself can relate to. A self-disclosure may also facilitate further emotional exploration, but great care should be taken to maintain the focus on the client's experience rather than the therapist's personal experience. As a rule, self-disclosures are brief and focused on identifying with the client's experience or validating the client's experience to further both their entitlement to and experience of his or her emotional experience.

Exercise 36:

Which of the following therapist's statements is an appropriate self-disclosure for the therapist who is seeking to intensify the validation of the client's emotional experience?

1. Select the most appropriate response:
   a. I hear what you're saying. I used to struggle to stay in touch with my anger, but I was able to work through it, just like you are doing here.
   b. It has been my experience that many couples get stuck right where you are and I just want to encourage you to recognize that sharing your feelings is part of working through this stuck place you are in.
   c. When I hear you talk about being stuck, and I see one of you reaching out and the other holding back, it seems sad to me. I feel this sadness in the room right now.
   d. I know what you mean. My wife and I had the same argument last week and I can identify with the blamer role because she tends to withdraw when we talk about sex.

2. Select the most appropriate response to help a client who is cut off from his anger move closer to experiencing this feeling:
   a. I have seen many men in your situation and they tend to withdraw rather than express their anger in order to protect their wives.
   b. I know exactly how you feel. There are times in my relationship where I just can't put words to my feelings, and I just shut down.
   c. Men and women are different when it comes to conflict and many men have difficulty expressing their feelings directly.
   d. Yes, I can see the position you are in, and why you say you need to pull away. So when I try to put myself in your shoes, a part of me understands how the distance is a solution but another part still feels the frustration and anger.

TASK 3 RESTRUCTURING INTERACTIONS:

The third task in EFT involves the therapist restructuring the couple's interactions. Although EFT is probably best known for its interventions to reprocess emotional experience, the model assumes that change does not come simply from new emotional experience but rather from the new contact and interactions that arise from that new emotional experience.

For this reason it is extremely important that the EFT therapist be comfortable and proficient in using restructuring interventions. Also in this discussion, therapists should keep in mind that in EFT, interventions aimed at restructuring interactions and reprocessing emotional experience are always intertwined. However, for the sake of clarity they are presented separately and here the focus is on restructuring interaction. There are three basic interventions used in EFT to restructure interactions:

1. Tracking and reflecting patterns and cycles of interactions.
2. Framing and reframing problems in terms of negative cycles and attachment responses.
3. Using enactments to shape interactions, i.e., choreographing new events to modify, step by step, each partner's interactional position.

Assumptions about the Nature of Negative Interaction and Distress

Before considering the question of how to restructure interactions, let's examine how the EFT therapist views the systemic nature of a couple's relationship. Some of the assumptions the EFT therapist holds while observing and working with distressed couple's interactions are:

1. Each partner's responses cue the other's responses (e.g., criticism cues distancing.)
2. The couple's behavior is organized into reoccurring cycles of interaction.
3. The negative cycles of behavior are driven by secondary emotion such as anger and blaming, which are reactive to more primary emotions such as fear of abandonment or a longing for contact and connection.
4. The negative cycles become self-reinforcing and are difficult to exit from.
5. The negative cycles both cause distress and maintain attachment insecurity.

Tracking and reflecting interaction.

The EFT therapist starts "where people are," by tracking and reflecting the couple's present interactions. The therapist tracks the couple's response patterns by observing and noting the sequences—the steps in the couple's interactions—and then reflects the couple's response pattern back to them; e.g., "As you point out problems and lean forward, Mary, you, John, turn away and say, 'There is nothing I can do.'" Through this process the therapist pieces together reoccurring sequences, makes them explicit, and identifies the couple's basic patterns and positions. As the therapist tracks and reflects the couple's patterns over time, the ways in which each partner pulls for a particular response from the other becomes tangible and clear. The identification of these patterns provides a metaperspective for the couple, helping the partners stand outside themselves and view their own interactions. Tracking and reflecting also provides an opportunity for the couple to experience themselves "within" and "doing" the interaction. This helps partners expand their sense of both who they are in the relationship and the nature of their relationship interaction. Each partner begins to see how he or she creates this negative cycle and how each is a victim of it.

Tracking and reflecting interaction is akin to and intertwined with reflecting emotional experience (discussed earlier in this chapter). As with reflecting emotional experience, the therapist's collaboration with the client and immersion in the client's experience makes the intervention powerful and gives it meaning. Through tracking and reflecting, the therapist eventually constructs a frame for understanding the couple's distress in the context of the negative cycle. Also through tracking and reflecting, the therapist accesses secondary and then underlying emotional experience.

What interactions should the therapist focus on? The EFT therapist will often find it useful to track and reflect the interactional sequences that occur during:

1. Recent incidents

"What happened during the fight last night?" "What did the fight look like?" "When he said 'I'm so frustrated with your ignoring me,' how did you react?"

2. Recurring patterns

"When you are not getting along and are feeling distant, what do you do?" "What does he do?"

3. In-session moments of interaction

"Help me understand. What just happened there? She just said she is swamped and overwhelmed and I noticed that you then looked down."

In addition, therapists should pay particular attention to those key moments of interaction that involve attachment-significant contact such as: greeting, parting, keeping in touch, connecting, fighting, moments of physical and emotional vulnerability; as well as moments of needing comfort, support, reassurance, physical touch, or intimate contact. All these moments are likely to reflect the partners' sense of attachment security and to evoke positive or negative cycles of interaction.

Examples:

"I feel I walk in the door and you couldn't care less." (greeting)

"I was afraid and then pissed when you didn't call." (needing to make contact)

"I was overwhelmed and confused, and needed someone to talk to." (needing reassurance)

"After mom died it felt so good that you held me." (needing support, physical touch)

"When we don't make love, I start to build a wall." (intimate contact)

"I wish when you left in the morning you would say good bye. A kiss would be nice." (parting)

How to track and reflect interaction and experience.
Tracking and reflecting often begins by observing and reflecting simple actions and then becomes more complex by reflecting perceptions, cued reactions, underlying emotional experience, cycles of interaction, and attachment consequences. These reflections may then later be incorporated into reframings. The following are some of the components of interaction and experience that the therapist will commonly reflect.

1. Reflecting simple actions

"She doesn't speak to you"; "You move away."

2. Reflecting perceptions

"You see him as...." "She seems to you so...."

3. Reflecting the impact of each on the other

"When he does _____ you react by _____."

4. Reflecting secondary emotion cued by perception of other and other's actions

"You're saying that when he won't talk you see him as not caring and then you get angry?"

5. Reflecting the primary feelings and attachment needs cued by perception of other and other's actions

"You're saying when he won't talk you feel isolated and scared?"

6. Reflecting the cycles of interactions: how each cues the other

"So you get caught in these cycles of interactions where you pursue him to talk and he shuts down?"

7. Reflecting the attachment consequences of the cycle

"You are both so alone as you are caught in this negative dance."

Reflections are always offered tentatively and collaboratively. If, when offered by the therapist, reflections don't fit with the client's experience, the therapist must explore further and amend the reflections to better fit the client's experience.

Exercise 37: Tracking and Reflecting

This exercise is designed to help you learn to track and reflect interaction. Notice that the excerpt below contains both a recent event and an in-session moment. Below you will see that the therapist's reflections of Nick's interactions and experience are filled in. As the therapist, fill in the blanks reflecting Nora's interactions and experience:

Nick: "Yeah, I'll tell you how this goes between us. Last night was a good example. I came home. I walk in the door, and she doesn't look up. She ignores me." (To wife) "Yeah, and then you were pissed off because I wasn't all cheerful."

Nora: (wife jumps in) "You don't really get this at all. When you came home, I was working with your son trying to help him with his homework. You didn't offer to help. You went straight to your office. I can't ever count on you. I used to get up and give you a kiss but you seem to walk right past me, and I don't see you for the rest of the night, so I quit. You are hardly a part of my life anymore. Why don't you make the family a priority in your life?" (Nora gives Nick a stern look.)

Nick: "Of course I went to my office, because you give me that attitude every day. Who wouldn't leave and go be alone?" (Nick looks down and away.) "If I try to come in and help, you just get angry and we start fighting. It doesn't matter what I do. I can't get it right with you."

Therapist: "Wait a minute, let's slow this down. Let me get what's going on here. This sounds important to me."

Reflect Nick's simple actions:

Therapist: "Nick, You're saying you walk in, you walk past Nora, you go to your office."

1. Reflect Nora's simple actions:

Therapist: _____

Reflect Nick's perceptions of Nora's actions:

Therapist: "Nick, you see her as ignoring you, that she doesn't care, that she is pissed off, it seems to you that it doesn't matter what you do, you can't get it right."

2. Reflect Nora's perceptions of Nick's actions:

Therapist: _____

Reflect how Nick's perceptions cue his actions:

Therapist: "It seems to you that she is mad and that it doesn't matter what you do because no matter what you do it is wrong, so you distance yourself."

3. Reflect how Nora's perceptions cue her actions:

Therapist: _____

Reflect Nick's secondary emotion evoked by the interaction:

Therapist: "You perceive that she is not interested in you and so you put up your guard and get defensive."

4. Reflect Nora's secondary emotion evoked by the interaction:

Therapist: _____

Reflect Nick's primary underlying emotion:

Therapist: "You experience her as not interested and you feel hurt, lonely, rejected."

5. Reflect Nora's primary underlying emotion:

Therapist: _____

Summarize Nick's experience in a reflection

Therapist: "So, Nick, tell me if I'm getting it right. Your experience is that when you come home Nora doesn't look up, she ignores you, and you get that she is pissed off and has an attitude. You feel it doesn't matter what you do; it's never right. So you walk past her and leave and don't feel there is any use in coming back. And you end up feeling alone and isolated. There is a kind of cycle that happens here where you feel she doesn't care and you walk by and don't say anything to her. She reacts by getting mad and critical and you then shut down. And, of course, the more you shut down, the more she experiences you as not there and the more upset and critical she gets. Yeah? Is that how you see it?"

6. Summarize Nora's experience in a reflection

Therapist: "And Nora... _____

_____

Exercise 38: Tracking and Reflecting

Using the following scenario, you will be asked to create your own reflections.

Therapist: "Can you both tell me what happens when you fight? What do the fights look like?"

Ilsa: "He is demanding and tries to control me. He makes his point and I don't get a say. It's pointless to say anything."

Therapist: "It's pointless? So what do you do when you feel it's pointless to say anything?"

Ilsa: "I'll shut up and I'll hold it in for days and won't talk to him. He knows how to argue. He went to college and I didn't. I feel like nothing when we argue. I feel alone and by myself after the fights. It takes a long time before I'm ready to talk again."

Rick: (interjects) "She won't let me in close when she is mad. I try to talk to her to explain my point but she either shuts down or gets mean. She gets that mean face and I react very calmly and try to help her out and do things around the house. When I can't stand it any longer I'll snap and get angry. I feel isolated in the relationship. She won't let me in."

Create a reflection of their sequences of interaction and internal experience. Include simple actions, how each perceives the other, how each cues the other's responses, and the resulting cycle of interaction.

1. Reflect Ilsa's experience and actions:

    _____

    _____

2. Reflect Rick's experience and actions:

    _____

    _____

3. Reflect the couple's cycle of interaction:

    _____

    _____

Exercise 39: Review Questions

1. The therapist helps to make the negative cycle of interaction more explicit and helps the couple to stand outside and view themselves by which of the following:

   a. Reframing _____

   b. Tracking and reflecting _____

   c. Restructuring interactions _____

2. The therapist finds it especially useful to track and reflect key moments with attachment significance. While almost any contact between partners has the potential to have attachment significance, which of the behaviors below are most likely to do so? (more than one correct answer):

   a. Greeting and parting _____

   b. Performing household chores together _____

   c. Fighting _____

   d. Moments of needing support or physical comfort _____

   e. Making a grocery list together _____

Framing and reframing interactions.

As the therapist tracks and reflects the couple's interactions, she frames their experience to give meaning to their distressing dance and to create a context for the process of therapy. There are three perspectives that inform how the EFT therapist frames a couple's interactional pattern.

Systems perspective: Each partner's responses are cued by the other and in turn cue the other, creating self-reinforcing and cyclical patterns of negative interaction—each partner unwittingly helps create and is a victim of the other's behavior.

Emotion perspective: The negative cycles are driven by powerful negative emotions. Secondary emotions such as anger and fear are reactive to and obscure more primary underlying and attachment-related emotional experience.

Attachment perspective: The negative cycles and powerful negative emotional experiences arise out of attachment fears and insecurities. The negative cycles interfere with the partners making safe, responsive contact, thus cuing attachment fears and vulnerabilities. Reciprocally, attachment fears cue the negative cycles of interaction.

Through the lenses of these perspectives, the therapist frames and reframes a couple's experiences. While there are many possible "reframes," this section reviews several key reframes essential to the treatment process.

KEY EFT REFRAMES

"Fighting against the Enemy of the Negative Cycle"

A basic reframe in EFT involves tying each partner's subjective experience of distress to the couple's negative cycles of interaction. The therapist reframes each partner's behavior in the context of the cycle. The cycle of interaction is labeled the "enemy," shifting the focus away from the partner's personal deficiencies. This reframe externalizes the problem, essentially saying to the couple, "the cycle is an enemy in your relationship which keeps you from having a safe, responsive connection." This reframe provides a context for the couple to come together against this common enemy that victimizes both of them. The therapist will return again and again to this reframe as more information is gathered from the couple, making the reframe more elaborate and vivid.

Example:

Therapist: "We've been talking here about this cycle in which the two of you are caught. John, you experience Carla as not being available to talk and as shutting down. You get afraid that you will lose her if you don't do something. So, you push her to talk but she just gets more silent. And, Carla, you experience John as pushy and angry and you try to defend yourself the only way you know how, which is by shutting down and pulling away. Of course, your shutting down just cues John to try even harder to get you to talk. The more you try to protect yourself by shutting down, the more John pushes. And, John, the more she shuts down the more you get afraid of losing her and the more you push her to talk. The two of you are caught in this never-ending vicious circle which has become an enemy in your relationship and has you both feeling distant and alone."

"Fighting for Secure Attachment"

The negative cycle causes each partner to experience attachment insecurities and distress and, in turn, to react in negative ways, causing more distress in an endless, vicious cycle of negative behavior and attachment distress. By reframing the cycle in terms of attachment fears and insecurity, and as preventing safe, responsive contact, the therapist reframes the couple's distress not only as a struggle against the enemy of the negative cycle but as a struggle for secure attachment. Each partner's behavior is placed in the context of romantic attachment processes. Responses are framed in terms of underlying attachment vulnerabilities and the attachment process.

An attachment frame is inherently a positive, nonpathologizing frame and is generally accepted by the couple. Viewing through the attachment lens, the therapist sees reactive behavior by one partner as a "normal" reaction to a perceived threat to attachment security, not as "overly dependent" or "maladaptive" behavior.

The two most common reactive behaviors in distressed couples are critical pursuing and withdrawn stonewalling.

Withdrawal and Stonewalling—"Protecting the Relationship"

Withdrawal or "stonewalling[5]" as described by Gottman (1994), is not a passive state of partner avoidance as may be assumed by their partners. Instead, withdrawing partners are generally responding with high levels of physiological arousal indicative of emotional distress. From an attachment perspective, stonewalling can be understood as an attempt to regulate intense attachment fears and to protect the relationship from further negative escalation.

Example:

Therapist: "You withdraw when you are confronted by her anger because it's hard to bear the feelings that you've done it wrong. And you know that fighting back is not an

---

[5] Note: Often critical pursuit or stonewalling comes in the form of what observers might consider as "extreme reactions." These extreme reactions can be seen as a partner's attachment sensitivities or "sore places" resulting from their experience in previous interactions in the relationship or from previous attachment relationships.

option. That to fight back is to risk a massive meltdown, to risk getting out of control and to risk hurting her and that's not an option. So you withdraw to protect yourself, Julie, and the relationship. Right?"

Criticism and Pursuing—"Fighting for Connection"

The angry, critical behavior of a pursuing spouse can be difficult to understand, manage, and frame for the beginning couples therapist. However, when viewed from an attachment perspective, these behaviors are adaptive and make sense. In attachment terms, critical pursuing behavior is understood as attachment protest, a reaction to the unavailability of the other, and an attempt to regain responsive contact and to pull the other close by fighting for the relationship.

Example:

Therapist: "It is because you love her so much that you feel so much urgency to know where she is and to call her so frequently, which ironically has the effect of pushing her away."

Example:

Therapist: "You have these 'sore places' from the loss of your first husband to cancer. You want to be able to trust again but it's so hard. When he is quiet, you can't bear the longing and being uncertain about whether you're important to him, so you get angry and fight to get a response or you leave to protect yourself."

"Painting a Picture" and "Implying the Possibility" of Secure Attachment

Most EFT therapists are very familiar with how to frame the couple's negative cycle as precluding safe attachment, but beginning therapists often pay too little attention to creating a positive frame that both provides an image of secure attachment and also implies the possibility of making safe, responsive contact.

In a secure relationship, attached partners are able to turn to the other to seek safety in the midst of danger, and comfort in times of distress. Secure attachment provides a secure base from which partners can move about in the world. Securely attached partners are able to ask for what they need in a way that pulls their partner toward them. As the therapist frames the couple's experience, she paints pictures for the couple of what secure attachment looks like. Some couples who are distressed have had a secure attachment earlier in the relationship and so already have an image to build on. Other couples have had few secure relationships and will need repeated exposure to images of secure attachment to make the frame meaningful for them.

EFT employs three methods to "imply possibilities" of safe attachment:

1. Validating their negative view while implying the possibility of safe attachment.

"You're not sure that now you could turn to him and ask for what you need."

2. Highlighting exceptions to the problem that point toward safe attachment.

"It seems that you were able to confide in her here today in a way you aren't usually able to do. Is that right? So maybe you can do it. You just need more practice and to feel safe."

3. Implying possibilities by giving them an image of safe attachment.

"So if you were able to go to her for support and to share with her when you were feeling overwhelmed like this, that would be different? It would be like being in a foreign country?"

Example: "Painting a Picture of Safe Attachment"

Therapist: "I think what you are both telling me is that in a way this fight was about wanting to come home to a safe haven where both of you could have a moment to connect and feel supported by the other. Marcus, you walked in the door tired and discouraged about the bad day at work and wanting to see a kind, accepting smile on Linda's face, wanting a moment to connect and to feel that someone was on your side. But instead you bumped up against Linda being irritated and unavailable and you felt hurt and got defensive. And, Linda, you were feeling swamped and depleted, struggling all day with the children and you were 'drowning,' wanting someone to throw you a life raft. Instead of feeling that you are together in the boat battling the storm together, you feel alone. Is that it? Am I getting it? And I think what we are working on here and what is hard to imagine is that sometimes the relationship could be a resource or a safe haven where you could turn to each other for a moment of contact or support. That when one of you falls out of the boat the other can help pull you back in. And if both fall out you can work together to save yourselves. I think that is what you both are fighting for but having trouble creating."

Exercise 40:

Fill in the blanks:

1. The therapist reframes the problematic cycle as an enemy in the couple's relationship that keeps them from being close. The reframe shifts the couple's focus of the problem from their partner to their _____. (Hint: a process element.)
2. The therapist helps the couple view the negative behaviors of critical pursuit and stonewalling as serving a positive function by framing their struggle as a _____.
3. Looking through the lens of attachment, the EFT therapist frames critical pursuing as: _____.
4. Looking through the lens of attachment, the EFT therapist frames withdrawal and stonewalling as: _____.

Case Example: Reflecting and Reframing Interactional Experience

Gina and Tim are in their 40s, married for 10 years and have three children. Tim moved out to a room in a friend's house for a month but came back to the house. They came for therapy agreeing that he wouldn't pursue finding an apartment, and she would stop legal proceedings. Below are some of the statements each made in the first interview. In the exercise below, use some intuition and imagination to reflect Gina and Tim's experience and then create a framing for their interactions and experience.

What Gina said:

"When I confront him on things, everything blows up and then he pulls away."

"There is a lack of responsibility on his part. He gets frustrated and leaves."

"When he left, I felt abandoned. I feel like chasing him down the street."

"We used to get along but now when there isn't any conflict it seems like we are just roommates, separate."

"When he shuts down and turns away I feel anxious, panicky, unimportant, alone, invalidated. No matter how hard I try, he won't talk." "I want him to need me."

What Tim said:

"I can't stand confrontation and when I leave to avoid confrontation it has always been a problem to her."

"She pushes to get to the bottom of things. It sets me off. She blames me. I feel guilty for getting angry."

"I get defensive and attack back. I feel like it is always my fault. She doesn't take any of the blame."

"I feel sad and guilty when we aren't getting along. I'm always under the microscope."

"When I complain, she attacks back. I can't ever win."

"I feel stressed from work. I don't like to complain. I let things build up."

"She hasn't seen a lot of my 'insides.'"

Exercise 41:

Reflect how Tim's behavior cues Gina's responses:

Sample answer: Therapist: "Gina, when you try to confront him, he shuts down, and you want to "chase" him. You try to get him to talk but he won't, but you keep trying."

1. Reflect how Gina's behavior cues Tim's responses:

Therapist: "Tim..._____

_____ ."

Reflect your sense of Tim's behavior in terms of his underlying emotional experience and attachment needs.

Sample answer: Therapist: "Tim, you're saying, 'We get in a confrontation, I start feeling guilt like it's my fault and I can't stand feeling I've upset her. So I leave. I keep things inside. She doesn't know my insides. I leave and end up feeling isolated. So it feels like I can't win, like it's hopeless and like I'll never make it with her.'"

2. Reflect your sense of Gina's behavior in terms of her underlying emotional experience and attachment needs.

    *Therapist: "Gina, you're saying...*_____

    _____."

3. Create a framing that includes reflections of Gina and Tim's experience and frames their negative cycle as an "enemy" in their relationship.

    Therapist: "What I'm hearing... _____

    _____

    _____."

4. Create a framing of Gina and Tim's experience that "seeds possibilities" of safe attachment.

    Therapist: "I think that it must be difficult to imagine... _____

    _____

    _____."

RESTRUCTURING INTERACTIONS USING ENACTMENTS

EFT uses enactments to shape and restructure interactions. This section presents a general model for using enactments and three of the most common uses for enactments:

1. Enacting present positions.
2. Turning new emotional experience into new interactions.
3. Highlighting rarely occurring responses.

In an enactment, the therapist typically asks one partner to talk to the other and gives that partner specific directions. The therapist monitors the contact and then helps the partners process their experience of the interaction. These directives often stimulate a conversation. The therapist monitors the resulting interaction and discussion. When using enactments, the therapist generally encourages attachment-productive conversations and blocks and redirects negative escalations and detours. Enactments provide the therapist with a flexible and process-oriented intervention that allows the therapist to be attuned and responsive to each partner as the partners confront new experiences within themselves and new behaviors and reactions from their partner.

Enactments are focused and choreographed, allowing the couple little room for failure. When partners cannot follow the directives, the difficult moment is processed not as a failure or a violation of the rules of conversation, but as an opportunity to further explore and understand their experience in that moment. Throughout the course of therapy, the therapist will likely create numerous enactments. These create "bite-size" amounts of interaction allowing each partner to "digest" small moments of contact. By creating many small moments of successful contact, the therapist gradually moves the process each time one step closer to shaping more secure bonding interactions.

The goal of enactments and how to use them differs from one stage of therapy to another. For example, an enactment in Step 3 to turn new experience into new interactions will likely have less emotional intensity than an enactment in Step 7 where one partner is being asked to risk and ask for his or her needs to be met. This section pays more attention to enactments in their generic form and how they are created and used. Later in Section 2 of this book you will find various examples of enactments as they occur across the model.

How to Create an Enactment

In an enactment, the therapist makes simple requests for one partner to make some kind of direct contact with the other.

> Therapist: "Daryl, you said you've put up this curtain between you? Can you tell Ronda what it is like for you to be separated by the curtain?"

Setting the Stage for an Enactment

Before actually initiating an enactment by asking one partner to make contact with the other, the therapist should consider the following questions:

- Have I created a clear context for the enactment?
- Have I created sufficient emotional intensity to move the enactment?
- Do I need to help the partners anticipate the contact?

Creating a context.

The therapist must provide a frame, or context, for the new interaction before he asks partners to make contact or take risks. The frame may include the couple's ongoing cycles, their negative cycles of interaction, the emerging underlying emotional experience, and their attachment concerns. The frame also can be used to refocus partners when they detour from the process. In the following example, the therapist frames the couple's cycle of negative interaction and attachment concerns as an introduction to an enactment.

Example:

> Therapist: "What happened just then, Daryl? Ronda turned to you and said, 'I can't ever count on you,' and you looked down." (present interaction) "I think what you have been telling me is that you experience Ronda as being critical, and then you shut down." (negative cycle of interaction) "And you say that when you shut down you feel you have disappointed her again, let her down, and failed" (underlying emotional experience) "and you feel isolated and alone." (attachment concerns) "Can you tell her right now what that is like for you to feel like you're always disappointing her in the relationship?"

Building intensity.

Emotional intensity is usually a requirement for an enactment to be successful. Enactments that are emotionally "cool" are not likely to have the power to affect or change interactions. Intensity within an enactment is created by the emotion that is brought into the enactment and it is created by the encounter itself. Sometimes the therapist uses emotion that has spontaneously emerged in the session, but often the therapist has deliberately laid the groundwork by accessing and heightening underlying emotional experience that is then utilized to fuel the enactment.

Example:

Continuing with the above example, the therapist explores Daryl's sense of being criticized, which is expanded into feeling he has let Ronda down and disappointed her. The therapist validates and heightens these feelings. In a soft and quiet voice, the therapist says, "Daryl that must be so hard for you...continually feeling that you let her down. (pause) That's hard..." (pause; Therapist sees Daryl look down and his face sadden.) "Could you tell Ronda what that is like for you to feel like you are always letting her down?"

Anticipating contact.

The therapist may tentatively introduce and hypothetically "walk through" the idea of an enactment by "wondering" or "imagining" what it would be like for the partner to do it. This gives partners a chance to anticipate the enactment directives without immediately responding to them. Also, this gives partners an opportunity to "warm up" and to express fears associated with the anticipated contact.

Example:

Continuing with the above example: "Daryl, just now when Ronda said, 'I can't ever count on you,' you looked down. I think you have been telling me that when you hear her being negative, you feel you let her down again and you feel you can't ever please her, and that is very hard for you. Right? So, Daryl, have you ever wondered what it would be like to tell Ronda how it feels when you think you have disappointed her? To say to her 'Ronda, when you are critical, I feel like I've failed, and I feel like you don't want any part of me.' What would that be like to say that?" (Here the therapist helps Daryl anticipate or "walk through" the idea of the enactment before asking him to actually do it.)

Not all enactments are set up as deliberately. Sometimes the context and intensity are already present in the interaction and the therapist jumps right into making the request for contact. But always the therapist should consider these three questions when approaching an enactment: is the context clear; is there sufficient emotional intensity; and do I need to help the couple anticipate the contact?

A Model for Enactments with Three Phases

The therapist creates enactments through a three-phase process:

1. Making the request
2. Maintaining the focus
3. Processing responses

The therapist must consider each phase in creating and using enactments. Therapists don't need to overtly develop and direct each phase of the process when some phases are already present or arise spontaneously in the ongoing interactions.

Phase 1: Making the request to make contact.

This phase is the most obvious part of an enactment. The therapist gives simple, specific, well-timed directives for one partner to make contact with the other. Most typically the therapist asks one partner to share some aspect of that partner's experience with the other. These requests are generally made in simple, straightforward language: "Could you help him understand what happens for you when…?", "Tell him what it is like for you when…?", or "Could you tell him, 'I can't…'?"

These directives are the most proscriptive part of EFT. <u>The art of creating enactments is to make them evocative and to build them on the heightening of emotion.</u> The therapist facilitates the initial request in an enactment by softening her voice, leaning forward, and gesturing for one partner to talk to the other. These changes focus attention and alert the partners that a transition is happening. The directives should be unobtrusive and subtle. They are more easily accepted and most meaningful when performed with a "naturalistic," conversational, and personal tone and not in an instructional or rule-based mode. In this phase, the therapist creates actual contact between partners with the focus on the moment of contact and on their experience of this new contact.

Example:

The therapist gestures with a hand motion for Daryl to turn to Ronda. Lowering voice, with a gentle tone, therapist says: "Could you tell Ronda now what that is like for you to feel like you are always letting her down?"

It is important that the therapist, on the one hand, conveys the conviction that the partner can do it while, on the other hand, allowing the partner to balk and express his fears related to the anticipated contact.

Phase 2: Maintaining the focus, blocking detours, and containing and framing escalations.

The therapist must be ready for the enacting partner to try to exit the enactment at any point. The success of these interventions rests on the therapist's ability to gently block exits and to refocus the enactment after detours. The following are examples of possible detours that Daryl could create:

"Ronda, I wish we could just get along. After all, we are two rational people." (evasive or abstract)

"There is no sense in telling her anything. I don't believe she will hear me." (directing comments to the therapist)

"Ronda, you're never satisfied. Saturday you got that disgusted look on your face after I couldn't balance the checkbook. Well, I hate doing the checkbook. Why don't you just do it yourself? I give up." (attacking/clamming up)

"Daryl, if you don't like doing the checkbook you can just do the dishes every night!" (counterattacking)

There are three primary ways in which an EFT therapist maintains the focus of an enactment:

1. Block exits and redirect after detours: When the therapist makes a request like the one above and the partners ignore, evade, or fall into old familiar patterns of attack and defend, the most usual way for the therapist to interrupt a detour and to refocus the enactment is simply to restate the request.

Example:

Therapist: (interrupting the detour, the therapist responds) "I noticed you were caught in talking about the checkbook, would you come back to what it is like for you to feel like you are always letting her down? Could you try again? Could you tell her now, 'Ronda, I feel so defeated. I constantly feel like I've let you down'? Could you tell her now?"

2. Contain and frame escalations: When an escalation occurs, the therapist must be ready to gently refocus the enactment and, if necessary, to actively block the escalation. It is often useful to frame the escalation as part of the couple's negative cycle and their attachment insecurities and then to redirect the enactment.

Example:

When the therapist asks Daryl to share the feelings of hurt and failure, Ronda reacts defensively saying, "Of course you feel like you are disappointing me because you are basically there only in body, your mind is somewhere else." Then Daryl responds by also being defensive and attacking back, saying, "Ronda, this is why I never talk to you—you never listen," and he falls silent. The therapist immediately interrupts, blocking the escalation and framing it and redirecting the enactment. "Hold it a second guys. Let's slow this down. I think you just got caught in the old cycle. Ronda, you heard what Daryl said as critical which hurt and then you reacted and attacked. Then, Daryl, you heard that you are a disappointment and then you attacked back and turned away and became quiet. I think that is part of the old cycle. Can we go back? Can we stay with this a minute? Daryl, can you tell Ronda what it is like to always feel that you are letting her down."

3. Refocus by doing another "walk through": After a detour, the therapist often sets up the request again by doing another "walk through." But keep in mind that when partners balk at the request to do an enactment, it is often useful for the therapist to process the partner's response, "walking through" the request again.

Example:

Therapist: "Daryl, could you please come back to this for a minute. I think what you were telling me here was very important, and I just want you to stay with it for a minute. Is that all right? I think what you were telling me, Daryl, is that when you hear Ronda being negative, you feel you let her down again and you feel you can't ever please her—and that is very hard for you. Is that it? So Daryl, I wonder if it was hard a moment ago when I asked you if you could tell Ronda how it feels when you think you have disappointed her? Was that scary? (Therapist could explore Daryl's fears here).

Could you come back and tell her now, 'Ronda, I feel so defeated, I constantly feel like I've let you down?' Could you tell her now?"

Phase 3: Processing each partner's experience of the enactment.

The anticipation and the execution of an enactment both act as stimuli for evoking underlying emotional experience and an opportunity to work with that experience. The therapist must monitor the interaction and reactions of the partners through the whole process. At any point in doing an enactment the therapist can pause and process the experience, especially the fears of contact that are evoked in partners. However, the therapist usually processes the partners' reactions after partners have made actual contact. Therapists use reflection, validation, evocative responding, empathic conjecture, tracking and reflecting, and framing to explore and process the emotional experience evoked by an enactment. How the therapist helps each partner process their experience varies according to the type of enactment and the stage of therapy.

A variety of enactments are presented in this book. Therapists may process enactments in many different ways, but it is always important to help the partners process their experience. Below are four common themes in processing the partners' experience of the enactment:

1. Validating reactions: It is fundamental to EFT that all reactions of both partners are an understandable reaction to the negative cycle and to their attachment issues. When the therapist initiates an enactment, partners can react positively, negatively, or ambivalently. The therapist must be prepared to respond to any reaction presented by accepting, validating, and putting it in the context of the cycle and of attachment needs.

Example:

Therapist: "Daryl, of course it's hard to take a risk to tell Ronda about your sense of always disappointing her. Why wouldn't it be? The two of you have never felt safe enough in this relationship to open up and talk about your fears. And when you have tried to talk, you experience Ronda as uninterested or critical, so you shut down."

2. Processing "blocks" and "fears" elicited by the enactment: Partners may experience fears and balk at a request to make contact. This becomes an excellent opportunity for the therapist to explore, expand, heighten, and process the underlying fears elicited from the contact, and then to help the couple re-engage in a new way. The method with which the therapist helps process these blocks will differ depending on the particular step of the model. Notice how the following enactment from Step 5 has evoked underlying feelings and views of self and other.

Example:

Therapist: "Daryl, could you tell Ronda, 'I feel so defeated. I always feel like I'm letting you down'?"

Daryl: "I'm not sure I want to. I'm not sure there is any use in telling her. She never seems interested" (view of other) *"and anyway that would feel weak and pathetic to me."* (view of self)

As Daryl's fears and views of self and other are evoked, the therapist may use validation, empathic conjecture, and reflection to process his experience. Also here, the therapist may shift and use an enactment to enact Daryl's present position (discussed in more detail in the next section) as in the following:

Therapist: "So can you tell her, 'It's too hard to tell you this. It might backfire—I might feel small'?"

3. Facilitating acceptance of the observing partner: In general with enactments and especially in Step 6 of EFT, the therapist works to facilitate each partner accepting the other partner's experience. The observing partner must be helped and given some time to digest and process what the experiencing partner has said. See Chapter 6 and the section on Step 6 for a more detailed discussion on ways to facilitate acceptance and to work with non-accepting responses.

Example:

Therapist: "Ronda, what is it like to hear Daryl talk this way? To say he wants to open up but is tired of feeling weak and pathetic, and he needs you to be less critical?"

Ronda: "I'll try to be less critical. I've wanted him to talk to me more. It means a lot to hear him open up."

Therapist: "Can you tell what it means to you for Daryl to open up?"

From here the therapist can further help process each partner's experience using: reflection, validation, evocative responding, empathic conjecture, tracking and reflecting, reframing, and enactments.

4. Reinforcing and consolidating new attachment-significant experience and new interaction: Whenever an enactment creates successful attachment-significant contact between partners, the therapist helps to reinforce and integrate the new experiences and interactions into a new sense of self and relationship.

Example:

Therapist: "Hey, guys. I think you were able to talk here and hear each other just then. That seems different to me. I think you both were able to step out of the old cycle a bit and open up a little. How was that for you both?"

Exercise 42: Review Questions

1. Prior to an enactment, which question is <u>not</u> important for the EFT therapist to consider?
   a. Have I created a context in which the enactment will make sense?
   b. Have I elaborated on and defined the rules for their conversation?
   c. Have I created sufficient emotional intensity to begin?
   d. Do I need to help the partners anticipate the contact?

2. Which of the following would be the best directive for an EFT enactment?

   a. Using an "I" statement, could you tell Jim how you feel?

   b. This money issue has been hard for the two of you to manage, could you talk together so I can get an idea of how you solve problems?

   c. I think we agree that the anger you express is a reaction to feeling alone in the relationship. Could you explain to Tom what you are talking about?

   d. You're saying this feeling of shame is hard to bear, and it's so hard to look at her. Is that it? Could you tell Jane now how hard it is to feel the shame and how hard it is to look at her?

3. The three stages of an enactment are: (a) _____; (b) _____; (c) _____.

4. The therapist can help a partner "anticipate" contact by doing a hypothetical walk through which is: _____.

5. What is the most usual way for the therapist to refocus after a detour? _____

Three Types of Enactments[6]

Enacting present positions so that they may be directly experienced and expanded.

By enacting present positions the therapist highlights and makes more explicit the key interactions that serve to maintain the structure of the relationship. For instance, in a situation when one partner wants to be forgiven for a transgression and the other is hostile and shut down, the therapist may ask the hostile partner (using that client's own words) to say to the other, "I can't. I can't let you in and forgive you. It is too painful and risky. Right now I want you to hurt and feel helpless." This allows the partners to view their own experience and behavior from a new and different vantage point. Change can begin with partners enacting their positions and moving from a passive, stuck position to actively taking on and "owning" the position. They can thus integrate this new experience into their sense of self and relationship.

The purpose is not to create paradox by having the couple do what they are already doing and so have them rebel into different behavior. But rather, to partners expand their experience and so be able to more actively own and choose their own behavior and more actively engage with their emotional experience.

There are two instances in the therapy process when an EFT therapist would likely ask partners to enact their present positions:

1. In the beginning of therapy to make the negative cycle more clear and to help partners "see" and "own" their positions. (See examples in the chapters on Steps 1–4.)

2. Later in therapy, especially in change events, when the couple is "blocked," or "stuck" and unable to take a risk toward making contact. (See examples in the chapter on Step 7.)

In the following vignette of a couple early in therapy (Step 3), read the dialogue and continue the therapist's response by creating an enactment designed to enact their present positions.

George: "Amy, I've been trying and working at this with you but I don't get any feeling from you that you see my efforts. Do you see anything positive in what I am doing?

---

[6] Note: EFT enactments are occasionally used in other ways. In the beginning of therapy, for example, the therapist may use an enactment as a diagnostic "probe" to assess the couple's readiness, flexibility, and responsiveness in turning toward each other and making contact. But most enactments in EFT are variations of the three types illustrated above.

I wish you would give me a little credit and say I'm doing something right. Is there anything I am doing that is good?"

Amy: "I'm here, aren't I, George? You basically ignored my needs and acted like I wasn't there for years and now you want me to bounce back. I don't think so. It's not that easy."

Therapist: "Amy, you're saying that you are afraid to trust again, that when you were drowning and calling for help he wasn't answering you. You were left on your own. You were hurt and the hurt became anger. The anger says 'not so fast,' 'step back, George.' So now, when positive things happen now it is hard to even acknowledge them because there is still part of you that you have to hold back saying, 'Don't expose yourself—protect yourself, or you'll get hurt again.'"

Exercise 43:

Which of the following would be a typical EFT directive for enacting present positions? (more than one correct answer)

a. "Can you tell George, 'I can't let down my guard. I won't let down my guard. I won't be hurt again.' Could you say that to him now?" _____

b. "I wonder, Amy, have you ever thought of telling George that you don't want to let down your guard? It's too scary to trust. You were on your own for so long and now you have to protect yourself. Can you tell him?" _____

c. "It is important for you to tell George how you feel directly. Can you tell him the reasons you feel defensive?" _____

Turning new emotional experience into a specific new response to the partner that challenges old patterns.

Enactments that turn new emotional experience into a specific new response to the other partner that challenges the old patterns, in many respects embody the essence of EFT. These enactments utilize what is probably the single most potent change factor in EFT: using new emotional experience to create new interaction. In this type of enactment, following one partner's intense engagement in his/her own underlying emotional experience, the enactment is created to help that partner take a risk in sharing his/her experience with the other partner. This is a first step toward creating a new kind of positive dialogue and modifying partners' positions.

The purpose of this type of enactment is to build bridges between the inner world of experience and the outer world of interaction. These enactments can help create an in-the-room experience that is a counterpoint to the partners' experience of each other while caught in their usual negative cycle. They can be an antidote to the toxic interactions that the couple normally experiences. They can create true moments of I–Thou contact (Buber) and often produce the most intensely personal, poignant, and therapeutically powerful moments in therapy. This type of enactment is used throughout the therapy process and generally becomes more intense as therapy progresses.

The following exercise illustrates how an enactment can be used to turn new emotional experience into a specific new response to the partner, one that challenges old patterns. The enactment is broken into the three-phase process. The therapist will go through the three phrases as she helps Sylvia express her fears to Sam and helps both of them process the experience.

Case Example:

A wife and husband, Sylvia and Sam, came for treatment reporting that they have intense fights which result in their not talking for days. During conflict, Sylvia aggressively pursues to talk and Sam withdraws. As Sylvia continues to pursue, Sam lashes out verbally and Sylvia feels threatened and intimidated, and then shuts down. Following the fights, the couple may not talk for several days. Sylvia says, "When Sam is angry and I see that look on his face, I get afraid and intimidated and then furious." The couple reports that there has been no physical violence. In a previous enactment, Sylvia told Sam that she could not feel close to him if he continued with his "mean" looks. Sam was able to hear and was receptive. The therapist has further explored Sylvia's experience of intimidation, and the underlying experience of fear and vulnerability. In this session, the therapist is now ready to create an enactment to introduce this new emotional experience into a new interactional experience. The enactment is aimed at creating an experience where Sylvia can reveal her fears instead of getting angry and shutting down, which in turn has the possibility of drawing a different kind of response, one of understanding or reassurance, from her husband.

Sylvia: "When I see that angry look on his face, my stomach tightens. I felt the same sick feeling in my stomach when my 'crazy' brother would fly into rages. I know Sam won't hurt me but I get so afraid and feel so vulnerable. I have to shut down and my feelings turn into anger."

Creating contact, building intensity, and anticipating contact

Before asking Sylvia to risk, the therapist may put the request in context of their negative cycles and attachment experience, thus creating a frame for the enactment. As part of creating the context the therapist could offer the following frame:

Therapist: "I think what you have been telling me, Sylvia, is that when you see that look on Sam's face you get afraid and then put up your guard and get mad. You remember your 'crazy' brother who picked on you, was abusive to you, and frightened you. When Sam gets mad and has 'a mad look on his face' you get afraid and then angry and then shut down and you can't say anything and you end up feeling alone for days. Is that it?"

Leading into the enactment, the therapist may build intensity by heightening Sylvia's experience:

Therapist: (slowing down the pace and lowering voice) "That's hard. Could you just stay with that a minute and tell me what that's like for you to be alone all that time, disconnected from Sam?"

The therapist may help Sylvia anticipate the enactment by doing a hypothetical "walk through" and exploring fears that she may have about doing the enactment. When the therapist thinks the client may balk at or be fearful of making contact, it is often useful to help the client anticipate the contact. Here is an example:

Therapist: "I wonder what it would be like for you to turn to Sam and tell him how hard that is for you? What would it be like for you to say to him that you get afraid, then mad and then shut down and you feel alone for days? I guess I imagine that might be hard, maybe scary. What would that be like?"

The therapist may have to help Sylvia process fears she may have about making contact. The therapist may explore and expand these fears with the client and may spend a considerable amount of time before initiating the enactment.

Sylvia: "Yes, it's scary. I get this tight feeling in my stomach. I know Sam wouldn't hurt me but I get afraid."

Therapist: "That scary feeling says 'It's dangerous, it's not safe, watch out, he'll hurt you.' But another part of you says, 'It's OK, Sam won't hurt you.' Is that right? Am I getting it?"

Sylvia: "Yes, that's it."

Making the request for one partner to make contact with the other:

Exercise 44:

In the space below write a statement asking Sylvia to make contact by sharing her experience of Sam when he gets that "mean look" on his face:

_____

_____

Maintaining focus and blocking detours:

Exercise 45:

Sylvia detours by deflecting to another topic and saying to Sam, "You scare me sometimes. That's why I went to your sister's last year after that fight. But you know, she's no piece of cake either. I mean, I like her but she's not always easy to get along with." Write a therapist response to help her refocus.

_____

_____

Processing both partners' experience of the enactment:

Exercise 46:

Write a therapist response helping to process each partner's experience of the enactment.

   1. Therapist: "Sylvia... _____

   _____

   2. Therapist: "Sam... _____

   _____

Heightening new or rarely occurring responses, that have the potential to modify a partner's position:

Enactments in which the therapist heightens new or rarely occurring responses are some of the easiest to perform, are often very powerful, but are most often forgotten by the beginning therapist. When partners either report or demonstrate a new response, one in opposition to old patterns, the therapist can highlight and amplify it through the use of enactments. For instance, a husband reports that it was meaningful when his wife contacted him after a difficult job interview. The therapist asks the husband to turn and tell his wife what that meant to him. In doing so, the report is turned into a meaningful encounter. The often-distant husband is now engaging his wife in a positive way. Of course, amplifying positive exchanges is rewarding and creates a counterbalance to the sometimes difficult emotional work in EFT.

Example 1:

Tom: "I'm really trying to make contact with Chris. She means so much to me and I'm often at a loss about how to do that."

Chris: "Well I don't see what the big trouble is. I don't think I'm that difficult."

Therapist: "Hold it a second. Tom, you just said something important. You just said that Chris means so much to you. Yeah?"

Tom: "Yeah. She really does."

Therapist: "Could you say that to her again, a little slower? I'm not sure she heard you."

Tom: "Sure." (to Chris) "Chris you mean so much to me—you are so important." (Tom reaches for Chris's hand)

Therapist: "Chris, what's it like to hear that from Tom?"

Chris: (tearing and face flushing and directing comments to Tom) "That's really nice."

Tom: "That means a lot."

Therapist: "Wow! That's cool. How did you guys miss that a moment ago? I'm impressed with how close and genuine your contact can be."

Chris: "Well I guess I was expecting a 'but' and then something negative."

Therapist: "Yes, it is easy to skip right over the good stuff and fall into that old cycle. By slowing things down, I think you were able to appreciate the moment."

Example 2:

Therapist: "Sam, just then you said to Linda that you want to be able to be there for her but that she is going to have to stop being critical of the way you do it. That seemed really different to me. I've never seen you speak up like that before. Can you tell her again that you want to be there for her but that you want her to stop being critical of the way you do it?"

Example 3:

Mary teared up as she talked about her recent miscarriage. John, observing, tentatively reaches for Mary but stops short of touching her. Therapist notices and says:

Therapist: "John, you were reaching for Mary. Could you reach for her again and tell her what you are feeling?"

Exercise 47:

Write a therapist response that initiates an enactment to highlight and/or reinforce the positive interaction in the following situation.

Mary tells the therapist how pleased she is that John supported her after she had a dispute with her mother.

Therapist: _____

_____

If you have worked your way through this entire chapter on interventions, you have become familiar with the basic interventions used in the therapeutic process of EFT. These interventions will be used repeatedly in the chapters that follow and you will be more and more at home with them.

Couple therapy can be overwhelming, especially if you are just beginning to see couples. In addition to a theoretical map and a set of interventions, it is useful to have a way of focusing just before a session. A checklist is offered for this purpose in Appendix C.

SECTION II:

THE TREATMENT PROCESS

The next five chapters will describe the steps of EFT and the treatment process and interventions used in these steps. In addition, we will follow EFT therapist Jane as she works with Inez and Fernando, a couple who progress through the steps of EFT.

The process features three stages and nine steps:

Stage 1: Cycle de-escalation.
   Step 1. Identify the relational conflict issues between the partners.
   Step 2. Identify the negative interaction cycle where these issues are expressed.
   Step 3. Access the unacknowledged emotions underlying the interactional position each partner takes in this cycle.
   Step 4. Reframe the problem in terms of the cycle, accompanying underlying emotions, and attachment needs. The goal, by the end of Step 4, is for the couple to have a metaperspective on their interactions. They are framed as unwittingly creating, but also being victimized by, the cycle of interaction that characterizes their relationship. The therapist and the couple shape an expanded version of the couple's problems that validates each person's reality and encourages partners to stand together against the common enemy of the cycle. A new cycle that promotes attachment security must then be initiated.

Stage 2: Changing interactional positions.
   Step 5. Promote identification with disowned attachment emotions, needs, and aspects of self. These emotions often involve fear, shame, and grief; attachment needs most often include the need for reassurance, comfort, and connection. Aspects of self that are explored may include a sense of shame or unworthiness.
   Step 6. Promote acceptance by each partner of the other partner's experience. As one partner said to another, "I used to be married to a devil, but now...you are a stranger—and I don't know how to deal with that."
   Step 7. Facilitate the expression of needs and wants to restructure the interaction based on the new understandings and create bonding events. The goal by the end of Step 7 is to have withdrawn partners reengaged in the relationship and actively stating the

terms of this reengagement. The goal is also to have more blaming partners "soften" and ask for their attachment needs to be met from a position of vulnerability. This "softening" has the effect of pulling for responsiveness from the partner. This latter event has been found to be associated with recovery from relationship distress in EFT (Johnson & Greenberg, 1988). When both partners have completed Step 7, a new form of emotional engagement is possible and bonding events can occur. Partners are then able to confide in and seek comfort from each other, becoming mutually accessible and responsive.

Stage 3: Consolidation and integration.
    Step 8. Facilitate the emergence of new solutions to old problems.
    Step 9. Consolidate new positions and cycles of attachment behaviors. The goal here is to consolidate new responses and cycles of interaction. The therapist can promote consolidation, for example, by reviewing the accomplishments of the partners in therapy and helping the couple create a narrative of their journey into and out of distress. The therapist also supports the couple in solving concrete problems that have damaged the relationship. As stated previously, this step often proves relatively easy since dialogues about these problems are no longer infused with overwhelming negative affect and issues of relationship definition.

In this process, the EFT therapist has three primary tasks. The first task, creating an alliance, will be considered in the following chapter. The second task is to facilitate the identification, expression, and restructuring of emotional responses. The third task is the restructuring of interactions and choreographing of new relationship events.

4

STEPS 1 AND 2:
ASSESSMENT AND CYCLES

This chapter discusses EFT couple assessment, which encompasses Steps 1 and 2 of the EFT process. An EFT assessment differs from other types of couple assessment. In EFT, the focus of the therapist is on gaining an understanding of clients' emotional experience of their partner and of their relationship. As the intake session progresses, the therapist tracks and delineates the negative interactive cycle that traps and distances the couple. The therapist then labels the cycle, validates the associated negative feelings, and frames the couple's distress in the context of this cycle. EFT therapists assume that therapy starts from the very beginning and that assessment is an ongoing process.

A good EFT first session consists of a compelling and intimate interview between a warm, empathic therapist and a couple who may begin as nervous or even skeptical. As the session progresses, the couple usually begin to feel safe enough to take the risk of sharing private fears, doubts, and hurts. If things go well, the therapist can help them discover that their negative reactions to each other, while understandable given their individual experiences, trap them in a compelling cycle that leads to conflict and distance. The couple leave the session feeling understood and hopeful that they have found somebody who can help their relationship.

To an observer watching an EFT initial assessment session, the therapist's work may seem effortless. However, the therapist is very clear about what needs to be accomplished and how this will be done.

OVERVIEW OF EFT ASSESSMENT (STEPS 1 AND 2)

- The therapist's first objective is to connect with both partners, building an alliance with the couple in which each partner feels safe, accepted, and understood by the therapist. The therapist is empathically attuned to the clients and takes a collaborative, accepting, and genuine stance with the couple.

- Using the therapeutic skills of reflection, validation, evocative responding, and some reframing, the therapist listens to their story, trying to understand how their relationship evolved and why they sought out therapy at this time.

- The therapist also assesses the clients' attachment history and begins to form hypotheses regarding vulnerabilities and attachment issues underlying each partner's position in the relationship. The therapist looks for blocks to secure attachment and emotional engagement within and between partners.

- As the couple's story unfolds, the therapist begins to enter the experience of each partner, discovering how each partner constructs his/her experience of this relationship. The therapist watches for specific focus points and intervenes as they occur.

- The therapist tracks and describes the typical and recurring sequences of interaction that perpetuate their distress (i.e., the cycle, dance, or pattern).

- The therapist also assesses the couple's responses to EFT interventions by asking them to interact or by trying to access primary emotion. The therapist also notes the strengths and positive elements in the relationship.

- As the session continues, the therapist assesses the nature of the problem and the relationship, including its suitability for couple therapy in general and for EFT in particular. This includes understanding the goals and agenda of each partner, to ascertain whether these goals are feasible and compatible, not only in terms of the partner's individual agendas but also with the therapist's own ethical considerations and skills.

- The therapist then creates a therapeutic agreement between the couple and the therapist, a consensus of therapeutic goals and how therapy will be conducted.

Case History: Inez and Fernando

Jane, the therapist, greets Inez and Fernando warmly in the waiting room. She brings them into the office, where chairs are placed so that the couple can easily face each other and the therapist. The EFT therapist sits with the clients and not behind a desk. This way the couple can begin to feel the collaborative nature of the interview and the therapist can easily observe the clients' body language.

Inez is short and plump with salt-and-pepper stylishly cut hair. When she smiles, dimples appear. Fernando is tall, tanned, and quite striking looking, with an abundance of white hair and brown eyes. Jane learns that the two are in their late 50s, and both are retired. For Fernando, retiring was a difficult process. Vice president of a high-tech company, he was offered a buyout package 3 years earlier and felt he had been forced out of the company that he had spent much of his working life building. Since retiring, he had embarked on several ambitious projects around the house but spent the majority of the time on the computer. "Not playing games," he added hastily, "but important research for the political party." Fernando previously had a long relationship with a psychiatrist, who helped him through considerable anxiety related to his work relationships and performance. He had also recently been struggling with symptoms of depression including weight gain, sleeplessness, irritability, and lack of energy and motivation.

Inez stayed out of the workforce to raise their three children. Approximately 2 years earlier, she was diagnosed with depression but had recently dropped out of treatment and stopped her antidepressant medication. She also currently experienced depressive symptoms including weight gain, difficulty sleeping, and lack of motivation to do much at home. She was, however, involved in many activities outside the home, including a cross-stitching group and volunteer work at a local food bank.

The couple reported that they had tried couple therapy 2 years earlier. Inez liked the counselor, but Fernando, who felt blamed by her, ended their sessions. Their children had all left home and were doing well. Their sons were both married and had good jobs, and their daughter was finishing university.

The couple were prompted to try therapy for a second time because they were not getting along with each other. "In fact," said Fernando, "I can hardly bear it, the way she talks to me. She treats me so badly I feel just awful, and I just won't take it anymore." Jane asked if they could help her to understand what happened at home that resulted in Inez treating him so. Inez merely shrugged and said that she had difficulty getting herself motivated to do much around the house.

The following transcript begins after this basic information is gathered, and as the therapist begins to track and understand the negative interactive cycle.

Inez: "Look at this morning for example. We were getting ready to come here to see you. He's throwing things round the kitchen and yelling at the dog—he kicked her actually."

Fernando: "And you come along and attack me!"

Inez: "I didn't. I just asked what's wrong. Maxie hadn't done anything wrong and you kicked her."

Fernando: "I didn't kick her, I pushed her out of the way with my foot. I was worried we'd be late for our appointment."

Therapist: "Sounds like you get a bit worried and tense. Is that it, Fernando?"

Reflecting the "worry" (tracking Fernando's emotional experience).

Fernando: "Yes, I get anxious inside, and then she's in my face, you know? She wants to know exactly what's going on."

Therapist: "And what's that like for you?"

Goal here is to understand his experience and get a sense of the cycle.

Fernando: "I just want her to back off. Back off!"

Therapist: "You want her to give you some space?"

Reflecting; mild reframe.

Fernando: "Yes."

Therapist: "So what happens then?"

Tracking cycle.

Inez: "He snaps at me." (Inez looks sad; she looks down at her fingers)

Therapist: "That's hard for you, eh Inez?"

Empathic reflection.

Inez: (tightens her mouth) "It's always been that way. I just do my thing. I should be used to it by now."

Therapist: "So you kind of suck it up, is that right?"

Tracking cycle.

Fernando: "No it's not! She lays right into me. My heart goes thump, thump in my chest. I feel attacked and disrespected. It hurts. Boy, I see a side in her that I don't like to see! When she gets angry, I see an ugly woman inside. Hatred! It consumes her face. Over the last five years she has been enraged at me."

Therapist: "So, let me get this…a situation comes up where you feel anxious, Fernando, and you get…tense and edgy, and Inez, you approach him to find out what's up. That's when you try to get her to…to leave you alone, Fernando? And sounds like you get a bit…short with her, and from your perspective that's when she gets really mad?"

Therapist stays with process; attempts to begin to describe cycle.

Fernando: "She attacks me!"

Therapist: "And then you get all upset on the inside, and what do you do then?"

Tracking cycle.

Fernando: "I get out of there. I go off to the computer."

Therapist: "So you go off on your own then?"

Tracking cycle.

Fernando: "Yes, that's my only option."

Therapist: "That feels like that's the only thing you can do. Get out of there, and go off to the computer. And so, Inez, what's that like for you?"

Reflection; tracking cycle.

Inez: (sighs heavily) "What else is new? What else is new? I'm on my own."

Therapist: "When he leaves, then you feel like you're on your own?"

Reflection of Inez' experience.

Inez: (looks down at her fingers, which are tightly woven together) "That's how it always is."

Therapist: "You feel on your own a lot, Inez?"

Empathic question.

Inez: (nods, keeps looking down at her fingers)

Therapist: "Sounds like that's hard for you, Inez, yes? Makes you feel real mad sometimes?"

Empathic reflection; empathic conjecture based on Inez' body language.

Inez: (nods again and sighs)

Therapist: "That's a heavy sigh, Inez. Sounds like this is really hard. Hard for you to talk about?"

Reflects nonverbal; empathic question.

Inez: (small voice) "Yes." (long pause follows)

Therapist: "So it sounds to me like you are both left feeling really low after one of these things." (both partners nod glumly) "It seems like there's a sort of pattern here that you are both getting stuck in, yes? I'm not sure exactly what triggers it, but it seems to get going when you see him scowling and uptight, is that right Inez? That's when you go to him and try to get him to tell you what's up? To let you know what's wrong?"

Attempt to delineate cycle.

Inez: (nods) "Yes, I want to settle him down."

Therapist: "You want to settle him down. It makes you feel uncomfortable when he…"

Reflection. Attempt to explore experience.

Inez: "There's no need for it. It's ugly! Why be like that? Why not be nice to people?"

Therapist: "Right, for you it's difficult…"

Attempt to enter Inez' experience.

Inez: "It hurts me. It hurts me to see him in a horrible mood. Why? Why all the time?"

Therapist: (softly) "It hurts you when he's in a mood?"

Empathic reflection, evocative responding.

Inez: (begins to tear) "I feel like he hates me. He hates me, hates the dog—he hates us all."

Therapist: "That must be really painful for you. To get that feeling. To feel like he hates you, Inez."

Empathic reflection, based on her tears.

Inez: (nods; reaches for a Kleenex) "That's when I yell at him."

Therapist: "Aha I get it, hmmm...no wonder, if you get the feeling he hates you, yes I can understand you 'attack' him."

Validation (also acceptance).

Inez: "I blow up like a puffer fish. And I yell at him."

Therapist: "A puffer fish! Like you get twice as big?"

Reflection.

Inez: "And four times as angry."

Therapist: "And for you, Fernando, that's when you feel that you need to get away?"

Tracking cycle.

Fernando: "Well that's ridiculous! Of course I don't hate her. What a stupid thing to say. I just need for her to cut me some slack."

Therapist: "So off you go to your computer?"

Tracking cycle.

Fernando: "Well it's safe there."

Therapist: "So, yes, it seems there's this pattern you get into here... this sort of bickering pattern where Fernando you get tense, Inez tries to settle you down, and you feel crowded. So you try to get her to 'back off.' And, Inez that's where you get hurt, get that awful feeling he hates you. And that's where you puff up and turn up the volume and Fernando, here's where you get hurt, disrespected...and you withdraw to the safety of the computer. Is this how it is?"

Again attempts to delineate cycle.

Inez: "Yes. Anything can start it off."

Therapist: "So what happens next?"

Tracking.

Inez: "We each do our own thing. He's on the computer all day."

Fernando: "And you do cross-stitching all day. Or you're never there."

Therapist: "Sounds like it's very lonely. How do you get close again?"

Empathic conjecture; tracking.

Inez and Fernando: "We don't."

Fernando: "That's why we're here."

Therapist: "You're here because you don't like the pattern and because you'd like to get close?"

Reflection that emphasizes attachment needs.

Fernando: (nods)

Inez: (shrugs, looking down at her fingers)

Therapist: "I see you shrugging, Inez. Does that fit for you?"

Reflection of non-verbal communication; clarifying.

Inez: "I tried for years for us to get close and now I'm tired."

Therapist: (low, soft voice) "You've been trying to be close to Fernando for a long time, and now you are tired. But you're here, Inez, so perhaps there's a part of you that is still hoping?"

In this transcript, the therapist listened empathically to Fernando and Inez, trying to help each partner feel understood and accepted. As she listened to their story, she began to track and describe the sequences of interaction that perpetuate the couple's distress. She also began to enter the experience of the partners in an effort to find out how each constructed his/her experience of their relationship. She learned that Fernando becomes anxious inside, and this generates a need for space. He then snaps at Inez, and then feels attacked when she responds to his snapping. Inez feels hurt and rebuffed by his snapping and responds by puffing up in anger. The couple then withdraw from each other and appear to have no way of regaining the closeness.

CREATING A THERAPEUTIC ALLIANCE—A SAFE HAVEN IN THERAPY

Creating a therapeutic alliance is the therapist's prime objective in the initial stage of therapy. If clients feel safe, supported, understood, and accepted by their therapist and confident in her skills, then couple sessions can provide a safe haven where partners can risk exploring both their relationship and their own primary attachment-related emotions.

Thus, the EFT therapist deliberately sets out to create a collaborative alliance with the couple, and, throughout the therapy process, continually monitors this alliance to ensure it remains intact. If the therapist believes the alliance is in any way threatened or ruptured, she will take active steps to repair it. Repair of a ruptured alliance is fully addressed in a later chapter.

Therapists can promote the therapeutic alliance by obvious actions like being on time for appointments and sitting with clients rather than behind a desk. In order to foster the alliance, the EFT therapist also takes a therapeutic stance that involves being empathically attuned. Being empathically attuned allows the therapist to be genuine and accepting of what the clients say. These aspects of the therapeutic stance are discussed below.

Empathic Attunement

Simply put, empathic attunement is the therapist's ability to tune into the client. As the client describes his/her experience, the therapist metaphorically allows herself to step across into the client's world. By doing this, and by using her imagination, her personal experience, and/or her present feelings, the therapist can connect with the client's experience. The therapist can hear, for example, a wife berate her husband for the long hours he works and the weeks he spends away on business and knows even before the client voices it that this woman is lonely.

Empathic attunement permits the therapist to "be with" the client in a way that engenders a sense of "feeling connectedness," signifying to the client: "you are not alone, you are making sense to me" (Stern, 1985; p. 157). The empathically attuned therapist creates with the client a shared experience whereby the therapist mirrors and echoes the client. By tracking and attuning to emotion, the therapist signals to the client, by use of verbal and nonverbal responses, the following important messages:

- I hear you; I am with you.
- I am understanding you.
- I support you.
- I am not judging you.

Non-verbal therapist communications:

- Makes eye contact, leans forward, open posture
- Nods
- Echoes/mirrors the client's affect. The therapist looks concerned when the client is sad, laughs when the client laughs.
- Offers a tissue when the client weeps.

Verbal therapist communications:

- Joins with the client, using the client's words and images.
- Says "hmm," "aha" to indicate attention.
- Reflects to clarify and deepen understanding.

If the therapist is accurately following the client, understanding and accepting, the client then is:

- Reassured: "My feelings actually make sense to this person."
- Comforted: The client can maintain a working distance from the emotion and not become overwhelmed.
- Safer: Reduced need to defend against difficult emotions as they are accessed.
- Open: Explores his/her own experience more deeply.

Example: Empathic Attunement

Let's take another look at Jane's session with Fernando and Inez.

Fernando: "I just want her to back off. Back off!"

Therapist: "You want her to give you some space?"

Fernando: "Yes."

Therapist: "So what happens then?"

Inez: "He snaps at me." (Inez looks sad; she looks down at her fingers.)

Therapist: "That's hard for you, eh, Inez?"

Inez: (tightens her mouth) "It's always been that way. I just do my thing. I should be used to it by now."

This is an example of Jane being empathically attuned to Inez. Jane puts together the harshness of Fernando's tone as he says "back off" and the sad look on Inez' face as well as the tightening of her mouth as Inez looks down at her fingers. If Jane's partner snapped at her, it would certainly be painful for her. It might also make her angry. Jane's response to Inez stems from her awareness of all these factors and her ability to step across into Inez' world to connect with her experience.

In the small excerpt above, the therapist might equally well have stayed "in tune with" Fernando's experience and explored his need to have his wife "back off."

Exercise 1:

In which of the following responses does the therapist demonstrate her empathic attunement with Fernando?

a. "Can you see, Fernando, how that leads to distance between you?" _____
b. "Yes, but you sound rather harsh when you say, 'Back off.'" _____
c. "If only you could tell her how anxious you get." _____
d. "It's hard for you then; sometimes you just need some space?" _____

Acceptance

The therapeutic stance of acceptance means the therapist does not judge the way a client responds, but rather understands responses in light of the client's experience. Notice that the example above is also an example of the therapist simply accepting Fernando's need for space rather than frowning on the response. The therapist might then move into exploring and understanding his need for space.

Example: Acceptance

In the following example, the therapist accepts—and even validates—an angry response from Inez by understanding her response in the context of her experience.

Inez: (nods; reaches for a Kleenex) "That's when I yell at him."

Therapist: "Aha, I get it, hmmm…no wonder, if you get the feeling he hates you, yes I can understand you 'attacking' him."

Exercise 2:

As the therapist tracks the cycle she says to Fernando:

Therapist: "So you go off on your own, then?"

Fernando: "Yes, that is my only option."

Choose the therapist response that best demonstrates acceptance:

a. "I can understand why you do that, Fernando, but do you think it is helpful?" _____
b. "Inez, do you see how your attacking leaves him feeling like he has no choices?" _____
c. "Yes, I can understand that it feels like all you can do." _____
d. "Inez leaves you with no choices." _____

Genuineness

As the therapist steps into the client's world, she is genuine in her reactions to what she hears from the clients. She is available for a real human encounter with the clients. When clients perceive the therapist as real, accessible, and responsive in a very genuine way, they are more able to trust the therapeutic alliance and thus the therapeutic process. The EFT therapist will try to answer frankly and honestly within her own comfort zone any questions the clients may ask her, including about her own life. If a client is confrontational with the therapist, the therapist will endeavor to understand the interaction between them, including her own part in it that led to this response.

Example: Genuineness

The therapist mistakenly refers to the couple's oldest child as Sarah. Fernando curtly reminds her that Sarah is their youngest child.

Fernando: (sharply to therapist) "Were you not listening?"

Jane: " Sorry, Fernando, yes, I was confused there."

Exercise 3:

At the end of the session Fernando turns to Jane and asks her if she ever fights with her husband. Pick the response from Jane that best demonstrates the therapeutic stance of genuineness.

a. "No we are very happily married."
b. "My personal life is not the issue here."
c. "Yes of course we fight sometimes, everybody does. We usually find a way to sort things out afterwards."
d. "You have concerns about my relationship?"

EXERCISES: CREATING THE THERAPEUTIC ALLIANCE

Exercise 4:

1. The prime objective of steps 1 and 2 is:
    a. To identify the negative interactive cycle. _____
    b. To discover the attachment style of each partner. _____
    c. To create a therapeutic alliance with each partner. _____
    d. To take a relationship history. _____
2. Which of the following is not necessary to develop the therapeutic alliance?
    a. Making eye contact. _____
    b. Mirroring and echoing the client. _____
    c. Accurate empathic reflections. _____
    d. Going over time in the sessions. _____

The next questions are about Gerald and Barbara, who have the following exchange in their initial session:

Example:

Gerald: "We seem to be getting on just fine and then suddenly we're not. Barbara launches into a tirade. It comes right out of the blue! She ambushes me! Before we know where we are, she's telling me she wants a divorce. Me,– I'm like a turtle. I withdraw into my shell where no one can hurt me…" (a tear begins to trickle down his cheek) "We haven't even had a hug in years."

Barbara: "We aren't getting on fine! You come home every night and switch on the TV and there you stay for the night. You never even see me. I don't exist for you. That's why we never hug. I'm too busy sucking up my anger. I suck it up and suck it up, and then I can't take it anymore—I blow!"

Exercise 5:

1. Which response is not an example of empathic attunement to Gerald?
    a. "It sounds like it's all very confusing for you. One minute things are fine, the next minute there's the threat of divorce." _____
    b. "So how do you get out of the shell?" _____
    c. "Right! You withdraw into your shell where it's safe." _____
    d. "It seems like it's safe in that shell, but terribly lonely." _____
2. Which response is not an example of empathic attunement to Barbara?
    a. That must be painful, to feel like you don't even exist for him. _____
    b. You're feeling continually so far away from him that hugs are out of the question. _____
    c. Can you talk about your anger with him? _____
    d. I can understand why you blow now and then, if you're always sucking up your anger. _____

3. Try to step across into Gerald's world. What do you guess is his experience? Pick the answer that best captures his probable experience.

    a. Angry, irritated, and distant. _____

    b. Lonely, puzzled, sad, and possibly angry. _____

    c. Attacked, defensive, and angry. _____

    d. Stonewalling and blaming. _____

4. Now try to step across into Barbara's world. What is her experience? Pick the answer that best captures her probable experience.

    a. Angry, irritated, and disengaged. _____

    b. Lonely, puzzled, sad, and possibly angry. _____

    c. Attacked, defensive, and angry. _____

    d. Angry, hurt, and rejected. _____

Exercise 6:

1. Write your own empathic response that signals to Gerald that you have understood him.

_____

2. Write your own empathic response that signals to Barbara that you also understand her.

_____

THERAPY SKILLS USED IN ASSESSMENT

In this section the EFT skills most frequently used are described and exercises are provided for practice. The skills we will discuss are as follows:

- Reflection
- Validation
- Reframing and catching the bullet

Reflection

Beginning EFT therapists are often surprised at how much reflection is used in EFT, particularly in the early stages of the process. As in other therapeutic approaches, the clients' words are reflected, especially in the beginning of the session. Reflection of content signifies to the client that the therapist is listening and grasping what they are trying to convey. It also helps clarify the therapist's own understanding of the content presented.

In the initial session of EFT, the therapist also reflects the client's experience, secondary (reactive) emotion, and also primary emotion. (In some cases, especially in first sessions, primary emotions can only be guessed at. Some clients may not be aware of their primary emotions, or may not be ready to acknowledge them). The therapist may also reflect incongruence between a client's verbal and nonverbal communication. Finally, the therapist may reflect and comment on interactions between partners (for example, significant look is exchanged, or one partner may reach to comfort the other). This is discussed in a later section, Key Moves in the Process.

Reflecting client's experience.

Reflecting a client's experience slows the pace of the session and helps the therapist to keep the focus on the clients' experience of their relationship. Such reflections can open a gateway to exploring and deepening the experience. A good reflection can better organize the client's experience, metaphorically providing a platform he or she can stand on to go to another level.

Example: Reflecting Client's Experience

Fernando describes the process whereby he lost his job and finishes his description with the following exchange:

Fernando: "Finally, I had no choice, and I accepted a buyout package. But it was rough—I was one of the main founders of that company."

Therapist: "Sounds like retirement was an extremely painful experience for you, Fernando."

Fernando: (looks pained and upset) "Yes, yes it was a hard time. I felt so pushed out, like I was no longer any use."

This led the therapist into further exploring his experience around losing his job, and asking if he had shared these feelings with Inez.

Example:

Emily: "Charles was having a crisis at work when I had my surgery, and he wasn't there for me at all."

Exercise 7:

Choose the therapist response that provides a reflection of her experience:

a. "What was your surgery for?" _____
b. "I can imagine you must have been furious about that." _____
c. "So you were both stressed out at the same time." _____
d. "You felt like he wasn't there for you." _____

Reflecting nonverbal communication.

The therapist will also notice and reflect clients' nonverbal communication. These may include signs of strong affect (e.g., weeping, reaching for tissues, eyes becoming red, looking down at hands, flushing, clenching fists), or of efforts to dispel feelings (e.g., swallowing hard, looking away, biting lips). Alternatively, one client may give the other a hostile look, or roll his/her eyes or reach to comfort the other. The therapist may choose to just silently be aware of these nonverbals, or, depending on the therapist's sense of the developing alliance and of the client's willingness to respond, she may choose to reflect them to the client.

Example: Reflecting Nonverbal Communication

In the transcript with Fernando and Inez, the following exchange between the therapist and Inez occurred:

Inez: (sighs heavily) "What else is new? What else is new? I'm on my own."

Therapist: "When he leaves, then you feel like you're on your own?"

In this example the therapist reflected Inez' experience (when he leaves I am on my own). She might equally well have reflected Inez' nonverbal communication as follows:

Inez: (sighs heavily) "What else is new? What else is new? I'm on my own."

Therapist: "You give a heavy sigh there, Inez, as you say 'I'm on my own.'"

Example:

Therapist says to Emily: "That must have been a difficult time for you."

Emily: (long pause; Emily tears, and then reaches for a tissue.)

Exercise 8:

Pick the therapist response below that best illustrates reflecting nonverbal communication:

a. "You get tearful as you think of this." _____
b. "Take your time, Emily." _____
c. "Perhaps you have never talked about this before?" _____
d. "Let's move on to something that is easier to talk about." _____

Verbal and nonverbal communication incongruence.

Reflecting of incongruence between what is said verbally and what is said nonverbally can be done very respectfully and gently.

Example: Reflecting Incongruence

Therapist: "Yes, Fernando, I hear you say that this doesn't bother you when it happens, but I also see how tearful you look, and that gives me the impression that at one level you might get quite upset by this?"

Example:

Charles: (grinning) "Yes, she's been mad at me for a long time."

Exercise 9:

Pick the therapist response below that best illustrates reflecting the incongruence between what Charles says and what the therapist observes.

   a.   "What's funny about her being mad at you?" _____

   b.   "I notice you smile as you say that, Charles, but I wonder if there aren't some pretty painful feelings associated with knowing she's mad at you." _____

   c.   "Sometimes, Charles, we smile when we have other feelings that we are not comfortable with sharing." _____

   d.   "So what do you do, Charles, to make her mad at you?" _____

Validation

Validation is used extensively in EFT assessment. The therapist's goal is to affirm the client's experience, to convey to each partner that his/her emotions and responses are legitimate and understandable in the context of their experience.

Being validated is a positive experience for clients and this helps to build the alliance. Equally important, when the clients feel validated they can risk saying more about their experience. Further, validation helps clients to feel entitled to their feelings, and as their feelings and responses are validated and normalized, clients are better able to regulate feelings of shame and self-judgment.

Validating client's experience.

The therapist may use validation to respond to a client's description of past experience or their present here-and-now experience in the session. This includes secondary (reactive) emotion, which usually involves either anger or denial of any feelings. The therapist always places secondary emotion in the context of the client's experience (and also in the context of the cycle) and validates it.

Example: Validating Client's Experience

Sonia: "Trouble is, he won't speak to me for days after we fight."

Therapist: "And what's that like for you?"

Sonia: "I feel...it makes me feel desperate, afraid. It's like I feel, well—that's it, you know? It's over."

Therapist: "So after one of these fights then, for you it's like you lose him. And you feel desperate, afraid that he's gone forever?" (empathic reflection)

Sonia: (begins to cry) "Yes, I feel certain he won't ever speak to me again. I must be such a baby to get so scared."

Therapist: "Well, I can easily understand how afraid you get. He's very precious to you, right?" (Affirms and legitimizes her experience; places it in context)

Example:

Julia: "Things are so tense when he comes home from work. The kids stop playing—God! Even the dog hides under the chesterfield sometimes! He's just really grumpy and anything sets him off. It makes me feel very nervous."

Exercise 10:

Pick the therapist response that best validates Julia's experience:

a. "It sounds like the two of you fall into some kind of angry cycle at the end of the day."
b. "Yes, Julia, I'm getting that he's very tightly wound and that certainly isn't acceptable."
c. "Yes, if it seems like anything will set him off, I can understand you might feel nervous."
d. "Yes, I can understand you must feel very angry with him."

Careful validation.

The therapist takes care that her validation of one client does not invalidate or alienate the other. This is especially so when the couple appeal to the therapist for her perspective on their story. (At these times it is far safer to comment on their process, than on the content they are describing).

Example:

Jack: "Take this morning. He was beating an egg and he spilt it on the counter. He just went for me...screaming, yelling, like, anyone would think I spilled the dam' egg not him! I felt completely attacked and beaten up."

Frank: "What did I yell? What did I yell? There's your answer! I yelled that an egg only costs 10 cents and it's not worth YOU starting World War III over it like you usually do."

Therapist: "So I get from your perspective, Jack, it feels like he gets on the offensive easily and you feel beaten up on, and that's really hard for you. And on your side, Frank, I can also get there is history between you both that leaves you feeling the best defense is a good offense."

Example:

Brian: "I'm doing it fine! You're out of line! You're always trying to get in there and correct me and do it better. It's infuriating!"

Marjorie: "Well then we're at an impasse. I'm sick of not being part of this. We're not a partnership and I'm not going to let myself be treated like that anymore."

Exercise 11:

Your new couple are very angry with each other as they discuss their finances. Marjorie is adamant that she should take over paying the bills and controlling the budget. Brian insists he's doing a good job and she needs to back off. Pick the therapist response below that validates each client's position.

a. "So for you, Brian, it feels like it's about her doing it better than you do, and I can understand that makes you mad. But for you Marjorie, there's something here about not feeling included, not a partner, and I get that this is the part that's difficult for you, yes??" _____

b. "Yes, Brian, I understand it must be hard for you to get the message that you don't do it right. Can you see where he's coming from Marjorie?" _____

c. "Why don't you compromise…say, take it in turns?" _____

d. "So Marjorie this is about not feeling included and not a partner with him. That must be really painful to not feel included, yes? Can you let him know, can you tell him how hard that is for you?" _____

Reframing

EFT therapists use reframing in initial sessions on a superficial level. The therapist needs to have some understanding of the intrapsychic issues that the clients are struggling with (e.g., fear of conflict, a need to protect the self from the other, a longing for closeness.) Care must be taken not to rush reframing and invalidate the client.

Example: Reframing

Angela: "Too right. I'm angry. He spent last weekend fishing with his buddies and then stayed at the bar three nights last week. Once again, I'm on my own. Anyone would give him hell when he got home."

Therapist: "Right. For you it's about wanting time with him, and giving him hell is about letting him know you want to be important to him, too."

Example:

Kevin: "We were at the meeting and I was so proud to be with her. Her speech was awesome. And then at coffee time she completely ignored me. I thought 'What am I? Chopped liver?' I was livid! Yes, I know I went for her on the way home."

Exercise 12:

Pick the therapist answer that is the best example of a reframe.

a. "But I can understand that you felt really left out and abandoned, and that must have been very painful for you." _____

b. "Yes, well I can understand that, I might have reacted just that way if I were in your shoes." _____

c. "You can see now that she didn't mean to ignore you or let you down, and I'll bet you've already apologized for your behavior." _____

d. "Your anger was about your longing to be there at her side because she is so important to you, right?" _____

Catching the Bullet

At the beginning of the initial session, the therapist may notice that spouses direct hurtful comments at the other. As the session progresses, the therapist gains some understanding of these comments and where they are originating, She will interrupt such comments and bypass the aggression, focusing instead on the underlying pain. By "catching the bullet," the therapist takes the sting out of the comments and helps to create safety in the session.

Example:

Husband: (angrily to wife) "Why don't you just call your lawyer and get the divorce rolling—you're always threatening it anyway."

Therapist: "I think what I am hearing from you right now is that it's too painful for you. It's so painful and difficult for you to hear her criticizing, that some part of you moves to shut her down and end it."

Example:

Wife tearfully describes how her husband didn't understand her sadness following her third miscarriage. Her husband's response is swift and angry.

Husband: "If I had a dollar for every time you weren't there for me I'd be a rich man."

Exercise 13:

Pick the therapist response that best exemplifies "catching the bullet."

a. "What I'm hearing is that this is so hard for you, so painful, because you know she has let you down, too." _____
b. "Can you just listen to her, right now? She needs for you to understand this." _____
c. "What I'm getting is that it's truly hard for you to hear her disappointment, so hard that somehow you move in to stop her." _____
d. "You sound really defensive as you say this to your wife." _____

Exercise 14: Therapist Skills Used in Assessment

Answer True or False:

1. Reflections help maintain the focus of the session. _____
2. When the therapist validates a client, it helps the client to regulate feelings of shame and self-judgment. _____
3. A validating statement affirms and reframes a client's experience. _____
4. The intervention called "catching the bullet" is a kind of reframe where the therapist bypasses the aggression and focuses instead on the underlying pain. _____
5. The EFT therapist only uses reflection in the early stages of assessment. _____

Example:

As the initial session unfolds, you learn that Aaron's first wife Rachael was killed in an automobile accident. Aaron's relationship with his former mother-in-law Ruth is now the subject of many of Aaron and Sarah's fights. As the couple discuss Aaron's recent lunch engagement with Ruth, you hear the rage in Sarah's voice as she attacks her husband.

Aaron: "This is all in the past. I only wanted to honor Rachael's mother for what we had together and what we all lost."

Sarah: "You say it's in the past, but it isn't. Even last night you defended Ruth! You said, let's agree to disagree. Are you for her? Or for me?"

Aaron: (weeping) "My caring for Ruth is different. Actually, sometimes I don't even like her very much. But she's the mother of my first wife and the grandmother of my son. I just never wanted to ride roughshod over her feelings."

Sarah: "There it is again! You care for her feelings – you ride over mine. Who is in your heart? Her? Or me?"

Exercise 15:

1. What is Sarah's secondary (reactive) emotion?
    a. Anger _____
    b. Loneliness _____
    c. Numb denial _____
    d. Fear _____

2. The therapist says: "Sounds like it's really hard for you, Sarah, when he spends time with Ruth?" This therapist response in an example of:
    a. Reframing _____
    b. Reflection _____
    c. Catching the bullet _____
    d. Validation _____

The following exchange then occurs between the therapist and Sarah:

Sarah: "Yes, of course it's hard for me."

Therapist: "Can you help me to understand, Sarah, what it means for you when Aaron spends time with Ruth?"

3. In this exchange the therapist is trying to:
    a. Validate Sarah _____
    b. Understand Sarah's experience _____
    c. Reframe her anger _____
    d. Catch the bullet _____

Exercise 16:

Write a statement that validates each partner without invalidating the other.

_____

_____

KEY MOVES IN THE ASSESSMENT PROCESS—FOCUS POINTS

- Process goal: Begin to enter the experience of each partner: How does each construct his/her experience of this relationship?

As the couple's story unfolds, the EFT therapist is trying to understand each client's experience of their partner and of their relationship. How does each partner construct his/her reality in this relationship? How do they perceive themselves in relation to their partner? How do they process their experience of their partner? What does their partner's reaction or behavior mean to them?

Example:

Inez feels that Fernando is often mean and snappy. This makes her angry, and she yells at him at which point he withdraws to his computer. She believes that he dislikes—even hates—her: "Why else would someone treat me like this?"

Jane the therapist asks Inez: "What's that like for you, Inez?"

The question elicits the response that with Fernando, she feels "on her own." This is a glimpse into her experience of this relationship.

Here are some questions that help you to enter or stay with the client's experience:

"So what's that like for you?"

"How do you feel about that?"

"What does that mean for you?"

"What happens for you when..."

"Can you help me to understand how it is for you when..."

The therapist reflects and acknowledges the emotional experience of each client. As the session progresses, the therapist begins to discover and differentiate secondary emotions from primary emotions. Secondary emotions are made explicit in the here and now and then placed in the context of the problematic pattern and validated (e.g., the anger and the attack from Inez as she feels pushed away and unimportant to her husband). Primary emotions may or may not be discovered in the first session. With Fernando and Inez, the therapist was able to see in the session when Inez did not acknowledge primary emotion (perhaps sad, lonely, rejected, unimportant), but instead "puffed up" into anger, her secondary emotion.

How does the therapist know what to focus on, how and when to intervene? The EFT therapist watches for the following focus points that signal what to notice and when to intervene.

Client's Narrative is Interrupted by Strong Affect

What the therapist sees:

As one partner tells his or her story, the narrative is interrupted by a strong emotional response. When a client is experiencing strong affect the therapist sees signs such as crying, flushing red, biting the lips, turning away, or perhaps clenching the fists. The client is usually unable to continue speaking.

Example:

Maria tells the therapist that if she tries to share problems and difficulties with Tony he seems angry and withdraws from her. "I feel so...so..." she stops speaking because at this point she is flooded with strong emotion.

What the therapist does:

- Focus on this response, giving the message that it is safe and appropriate to share this experience in the session. The therapist says gently to Maria: "I can see this is hard to say, Maria. Take your time, it's okay." Maria reaches for a tissue and the therapist helps her to talk about her hurt and her sadness.

Affect Is Conspicuous by Its Absence

What the therapist sees:

Sometimes, as one partner tells his/her story the lack of emotion is striking. Perhaps the client is describing a dramatic, traumatic, or clearly painful experience from a detached position that is not congruent with the content presented.

Example:

Pierre says things have been really difficult with Louise since their 2-year-old son died 2 years ago from a head injury following a fall. The therapist said to him: "This must have been so very hard for you both." Pierre shrugs and replies almost nonchalantly: "That's life, shit happens."

What the therapist does:

- Explore the lack of engagement in the personal experience being related.
- Discover its significance in terms of the couple's engagement in and definition of their relationship.
- The therapist says: "You say that lightly, Pierre. Perhaps that kind of helps you to keep the pain at bay?" Pierre swallows hard and nods. The therapist does not push Pierre further because they have not yet established a good alliance and instead moves into exploring if the couple have shared their mutual pain and given support to each other.

Personal Landmark

What the therapist sees:

A story that a partner cannot seem to forget or resolve. Such stories open the door into the client's experience of the relationship and the client's sense of self in relation to the partner. The partner often may not really understand the significance of the story, and may be exasperated that the other is still focusing on it.

Example:

Hélène tells how, when recovering from surgery, she asked Serge to go to the corner store to buy her some bottled water before he went to work. Serge refused, saying that it would make him late for work. He reminded her that she could use the water filter. Serge could never understand why Hélène kept bringing up this incident.

What the therapist does:

- Focus on and explore story.
- Uncover the meaning of the story from client's perspective.
- Ask if the partner understands the client's experience.
- Label story as unresolved issue for couple and validate associated primary or secondary emotion.
- The therapist says to Hélène: "It sounds like this was an important moment for you Hélène. Can you help me to understand what this meant for you?" The therapist learns that this was the second incident during Hélène's recovery where she came to believe that she could not count on Serge when she really needed him. This stood in sharp contrast to the care she had lavished on Serge when he had broken his leg one year previously.

From the bottled water incident, Hélène concluded that she wasn't important enough for Serge to go out of his way for her when she needed him. Thus, this relatively small incident had a very important meaning for her. The therapist then asked Serge how he felt as he listened to his wife's story.

Interactional Landmark

What the therapist sees:

An interaction between a couple suggesting possible interactional positions of the couple. The interaction might indicate the availability for contact or support in the relationship (e.g., one partner cries, the other partner looks away). Alternatively, the interaction might suggest a power or dominant position.

Example:

Following the suicide of her brother 3 years earlier, Edith had become severely alcoholic. She had recently finished a recovery program and in the initial session she described her rapid and successful recovery with great pride. When the therapist asked Harry, her husband, what her drinking period had been like, Harry replied that it had indeed been very painful. Immediately Edith whirled around and glared at him, saying: "You didn't suffer!" Harry gulped, and told the therapist that things were now going very well.

What the therapist does:

- Observe this interaction.
- If alliance is developing well, refer to interaction in this session.
- Otherwise, simply take note of the interaction.

In this case the therapist decided to explore it. First, she referred to the interaction: "I noticed that was a tricky moment for you both when Harry said your drinking was painful." Then the therapist made an empathic conjecture and asked Edith: "Tell me if I'm wrong, but my guess is it's incredibly hard for you to hear that he was hurt by your drinking." This led to Edith beginning to weep and talk about how difficult it was to hear his experience around her drinking.

Position Markers

What the therapist sees:

The therapist observes comments or responses that seem to define power/control or closeness/distance as partners talk to each other, to the therapist, or tell stories about their relationship.

Example:

Alex says: "Well, I'd love to go back to Greece for a holiday, but I would never make a decision like that. The only kind of decision I'm allowed to make is when to change the kitty litter!" His wife replies: "That's fair. Why should we go somewhere I don't want to go, when I'm the one who earns most of the money?"

What the therapist does:

- Get a clear picture of the position each partner takes in response to the other.
- Ask how each partner perceives and feels about such positions.
- The therapist says, "It feels like the only decision you can make is when to change the kitty litter?" Alex nods his head. Therapist asks then: "And how is that for you?" Alex pauses for a long time, then he bites his lips and shifts uncomfortably in his chair. Here, the therapist says: "I see you biting your lip and looking uncomfortable Alex, and I'm wondering what is happening for you?" The process then moves into exploring the power dynamics of the relationship.

Responses to Positive Contact

What the therapist sees:

The therapist notices how couples interact when there is opportunity for positive contact, as when one partner moves to physically comfort the other. In particular, it is noted how such gestures are received—is the partner open to receiving comfort and, if not, how does this partner exit from contact?

Example:

As Tina begins to cry, her husband reaches over and takes her hand. Tina pulls her hand sharply away.

What the therapist does:

- Explore the exit from the contact
- Acknowledge attempts to comfort and ability to receive comfort as a strength of the relationship.
- Therapist says to Tina: "You're not feeling open to receiving comfort from him right now?" Had Tina accepted his comfort, the therapist might have said, "I notice you reached and took her hand there—that was to comfort her?" The husband nods. The therapist then says, "This is one of the good aspects of your relationship, then. You can comfort her, and you, Tina, can accept for him to do that."
- Alternatively, as a wife cries, the partner may turn and look out of the window. Here the therapist might say: "I see you turning away as you hear her distress and I am wondering what is happening for you right now?"
- Negative cycle markers denote the partners' role in the negative interactive cycle.

What the therapist sees:

- The therapist observes how partners react to each other as they get into conflict
- What the therapist does
- The therapist tracks and elucidates the cycle so that it can be framed to the couple in a way that is relevant and true to their experience.

In the next section, this is explained in more detail.

IDENTIFYING AND DELINEATING THE NEGATIVE INTERACTIVE CYCLE

In EFT, all negative interactive cycles are seen in terms of separation protest and attachment insecurity. Cycles are understood as being scripted by unmet attachment needs and attachment fears. All cycles have a control and closeness dimension. (Pursuing spouses feel controlled by their withdrawing partner, while withdrawn partners feel controlled by their nagging spouses.) The partner's position in the cycle reflects his/her experience in the relationship. For example, a wife may feel lonely and unimportant to her husband who, feeling a sense of inadequacy, withdraws. This makes her angry and she nags, criticizes, and demands. Her husband, who hears confirmation that he is inadequate, withdraws further. Thus, a partner's position in the cycle not only reflects the person's experience but also creates it.

Example:

Patty often feels lonely and unloved in her relationship. Her husband, Peter, has some feelings of inadequacy and frequently withdraws. Patty's typical stance is to take a critical, angry position, saying to Peter: "You are never there for me. I can't count on you because you are only interested in yourself." For Peter, this is confirmation of his feelings of inadequacy. He withdraws further.

Distressed couples interact with only a limited number of basic interactional patterns, cycles, and positions. Therapists should be skilled at identifying and empathically exploring these patterns, as they are, in large part, the plot of the couple's distressing attachment drama. Over time, distressed couples become caught in a "dance" of repetitive interactional patterns. Each partner cues the other in what becomes a cyclical pattern of negative interactions. Partners may have their own ways of describing cycles, and if they do, the therapist can use the clients' own words. For example, a spouse might say, "He shuts me out so I just try to bash the door down," or "I just build a wall—and then she pushes and pushes."

The Basic Negative Cycles and Interactive Positions

Pursue/withdraw.

The most common cycle is a demanding spouse interacting with a withdrawing or distancing partner. In this pattern, the distancing or "stonewalling" position is in a shutdown, nonresponse mode that often cues panic or aggression in the other partner as in "I will make you respond to me." Most other patterns can be seen as variants of the basic pursue/withdraw pattern. When trying to identify the couple's negative pattern keep in mind that the positions are "default" options: they are what the partners do when they feel threatened or vulnerable. A common mistake of beginning EFT therapists is to be confused by a withdrawing husband who pursues for sex in a single incident, but who generally takes a withdrawn position, especially when confronted or vulnerable. This cycle has been described by different clinicians in a variety of ways including: demand/distance, criticize/stonewall, complain/placate. There tends to be a gender assignation to these roles, with a female most often in the position of pursuer and a male in the position of withdrawer. A male pursuer will tend to appear different from a female pursuer because of the often coercive element to male pursuit. The therapist needs to take note of this, particularly when assessing for abuse. Same-sex couples will also present in pursue/withdraw patterns.

Withdraw/withdraw.

Sometimes the therapist will observe couples whose interactions appear to be a withdraw/withdraw pattern. In this pattern, both partners are reluctant to engage emotionally and, in the face of conflict, both will further withdraw. While this may be the couple's basic pattern, it is more likely that a pursue/withdraw pattern underlies it. The withdraw/withdraw cycle is frequently the product of pursue/withdraw pattern, where the pursuer gave up reaching for the partner. The withdrawal of the "burnt out" pursuer sometimes represents the beginning of grieving and detaching from the relationship. In other cases, the pursuer may be a "soft" pursuer who is hard to recognize because he or she does not show the overwhelming anxious energy seen in many pursuers and because he or she gives up the pursuit rather easily. These cycles are difficult for a couple to maintain over time. This cycle is also described as numb distancing/refusal to engage.

Attack/attack.

Therapists often observe attack/attack sequences and escalations in couple interactions. Most often these escalations are deviations in an otherwise pursue/withdraw pattern in which the withdrawer turns, erupts into anger, and fights when provoked. After the fight, the withdrawer usually reverts back to the withdrawn position until sufficiently provoked again.

Complex cycles.

These cycles are multimove cycles that often occur in trauma-survivor couples where both anxiety and avoidance are high, resulting in more complicated sequences of steps. In one example of a complex cycle, the husband makes coercive demands for compliance and attention. The wife withdraws, the husband then escalates his demands, and the wife attacks in self-defense. Both partners then withdraw, and the wife becomes depressed for a period of three days or so. The husband then begins pursuit, and the wife slowly responds and a brief period of loving sexuality ensues. Then the cycle repeats.

Reactive pursue/withdraw cycle.

These cycles evolve over time from long-term cycles. For example, a pursuing wife gradually gives up trying to get close to her husband and begins to limit her investment in the relationship. Her distancing, work-obsessed spouse does not notice. The children leave home, an important transition, and then the wife announces she is leaving. The couple come into therapy with a reactive cycle, where the husband is frantically pursuing his wife in order to prevent a separation, and the wife is cautious and withdrawn, refusing to commit herself to the relationship. This cycle is, of course, the reversal of their original pattern where she pursued, and he withdrew. In the case of a reactive cycle, the therapist works with the cycle presented in the session, but the fact that the pattern is recent and evolved from a far different long-term cycle provides an important part of the client's history and must be kept in mind by the therapist. Fernando and Inez are an example of a reactive cycle.

Identifying the Cycle

When does the therapist begin to track and identify the cycle the couple typically engage in that leads to their distress? It depends on the therapist's own judgment as well as the couple's eagerness to get to the heart of their problems. Ideally, the therapist will try to get some background information to provide context for the conflict or difficulty the couple is experiencing.

Look for the predominant pattern.

Therapists working with distressed couples will frequently notice that both partners complain about and criticize the other; both may even escalate to verbally attacking, or to withdrawing or stonewalling (Gottman, 1989). When identifying the negative interactive cycle, the EFT therapist is looking for the overall predominant pattern that most typifies the couple's interaction. The couple will fall into this pattern when they are vulnerable.

The cycle can be identified the following ways:

- Ask a couple what happens between them when they fight.
- Learn about their history.
- Watch their interaction in the session.

The therapeutic task is to track the couple's interactions around closeness and distance. The therapist will ask the couple to describe their interaction by asking leading questions. Questions such as the following elicit the information you need:

"What happens when you have a fight?"

"How do the two of you feel close?"

"Pretend that I am a fly on the wall of your kitchen; tell me what would I see if the two of you were having a fight?"

"Play me the video..."

"What do you do then?"

"So what happens next?"

"What do you do when you see 'the look' on her face?"

These questions help to focus the discussion around delineating the cycle. As the pattern emerges, the therapist labels the position that each partner relies on in times of vulnerability, when attachment needs are activated. The cycle is identified as those predictable behaviors that make up a couple's default position when they feel threatened or vulnerable.

The therapist listens for statements that describe the behaviors (the moves) that each partner displays in their cycle as well as the emotion-laden statements (the music) that each partner may use to describe his or her relationship. Clients often use descriptive phrases or metaphors describing their own position in the relationship (e.g., "Me, I'm like a turtle. I climb into my shell where it's safe."). A list of statements common to withdrawers and pursuers is provided below.

Withdrawers often say...	Pursuers often say...
"You never come near me or touch me."	"My heart is breaking." "I am going to die."
"I never get it right or satisfy her."	"He is never there. He is always at work."
"I don't bother—what's the point?"	"He never looks at me when I talk to him. He just watches TV."
"I am amazed that she can take something so small and blow it out of proportion."	"There are birthdays that are forgotten, or Mother's Day when nobody gives me a card."
"I don't know what I feel. I'm lost."	"I do it by myself and just take care of things on my own."
"She gives me that look and I'm paralyzed."	"I am way down on his list—after his work, the kids, his family, and then maybe me."
"She never initiates sex—it's always up to me."	"He's not there—no one has ever been there."
"I can never get it right, or to her standards. It's like she has a scorecard and I always come up short. That's all I hear, anyway, is what I do wrong, never what is going right."	"He won't listen. He never listens. It doesn't matter how long I talk to him or how many examples I give him or how hard I try—I can never get through to him."
"I feel like she's got me dangling from the end of a rope that is going to fray at any minute and it's going to be all over."	"It's like we are roommates or brother and sister. Any hope for passion or romance is futile—he just doesn't want it."
"I don't feel anything—nothing at all."	"Other couples seem to have lives that are full, and they enjoy each other. We don't have anything."

Delineating the Cycle

The therapist outlines (a) the moves that each partner makes in the cycle and (b) the emotional music that primes these moves. The therapist then combines the moves and the music, showing how they prime and maintain each other. The therapist also outlines and elaborates on how each partner suffers from being caught in this cycle. The therapist explicitly paints the cycle as the enemy that isolates the partners.

1. The moves: Let us return to Fernando and Inez. The moves Inez makes are (a) to "puff up and be angry" with Fernando and then (b) to withdraw to her cross-stitching or her outside activities. The moves that Fernando makes are (a) to be snappy and irritable when he is anxious, (b) to respond angrily to his wife's attack, and (c) to withdraw to his computer. In a later session, Fernando provides a metaphor for (b) and (c), as: "I fire off a round and I run for cover."

2. The emotional music: From our transcript, let us try to discover the emotional music that primes the moves of Fernando and Inez. Fernando gets anxious around being on time and then feels "attacked" by his wife when she tries to "settle him down." This makes him feel disrespected, which results in anxiety, "makes his heart go thump in his chest." He then goes to the safety of his computer. Perhaps Fernando's moves are primed by feeling anxious or put down, not precious to his wife or perhaps he feels he is failing in this relationship. Her attacks seem to confirm that she disrespects him; that he is not enough for her; if this is indeed his experience, then this would be hurtful or even scary (primary emotion). The anger he shows when she attacks him is the secondary or reactive emotion. Hypothesis: underlying attachment fear: "I am not adequate"?

Inez, on the other hand, feels hurt by her husband's way of interacting when he gets tense and upset, and because this is a long standing pattern, she sees it as indicative that he dislikes—even hates—her. Understandably, this hurts her (primary emotion) and makes her angry (secondary or reactive emotion). Hypothesis: underlying attachment fear: "I am not loved"? Even "I am unlovable"?

3. Putting it together: The therapist will then paint the picture for the couple and if necessary explore and expand it until there is a good understanding of the pattern and the emotions that prime each partner's moves. The therapist may not achieve a complete understanding in the first session. When the couple do understand the cycle and the emotions that drive the cycle, they are ready to see the cycle as the enemy and begin de-escalating. In the next chapter cycles and de-escalation are addressed more extensively.

Delineating the cycle of Fernando and Inez.

Fernando gets tense and edgy and Inez tries to settle him down, causing him to feel distressed. He responds with anger, which reinforces for Inez the painful feeling that he dislikes or even hates her. Inez used to turn up the volume and get angry but now she more often stays away and finds other things in her life to occupy her. Fernando withdraws to the safety of the computer. Each partner is then left feeling alone and unsupported, not important to the other. Neither partner reaches out to contact the other or to regain closeness. Instead, they each spend time apart, soothing themselves with other activities. The cycle has the couple trapped, and leaves each partner feeling sad and alone. The predominant pattern for this couple is, then, mutual withdrawal. As the couple move into therapy, Fernando begins to pursue his wife. The cycle becomes a reactive pursue/withdraw cycle with Fernando pursuing Inez.

Exercise 17: Identifying the Negative Interactive Cycle

Answer True or False:

1. When identifying the negative cycle, the therapist looks for the overall predominant pattern that occurs when partners are vulnerable (for example needy or anxious). _____

2. There are only a limited number of basic patterns that couples get into when they fight. _____

3. When one partner has been traumatized, cycles are always simple to understand. _____

4. A person's position in the cycle not only reflects his/her experience but also creates it. _____

5. In EFT, all negative interactive cycles are seen as tension reduction activities. _____

6. All cycles have a control and closeness dimension. _____

7. The most common cycle is an insecure appeasing spouse interacting with a withdrawing or distancing partner. _____

8. The criticize/stonewall pattern is another name for the attack/attack cycle. _____

9. When a "burnt out" pursuer begins to withdraw, this may represent the beginning of grieving and detaching from the relationship. _____

10. The three ways a therapist can identify a couple's cycle include asking leading questions, learning about their history, and observing their interaction in the session. _____

Exercise 18:

Wendy states that Barry always seems to put other things ahead of her. She feels she is at the bottom of his list, and this hurts. She fears that she is not very important to him, and tries to talk to him, to get him to understand how unhappy she feels about this. Ultimately, the only time he turns to her, she says, is when he wants sex. This makes her angry, and she is critical of Barry, often escalating to shouting at him. Barry gets the message from Wendy that he is a disappointment to her. He feels he must be failing her. He feels insecure, inadequate, but he also becomes quite resentful of her criticism. He begins to avoid her, working long hours and often stopping at the bar on the way home. Sometimes he approaches Wendy for sex, but recently she almost always refuses him.

1. The negative cycle of Wendy and Barry is:
    a. Complex cycle _____
    b. Attack/attack _____
    c. Pursue/withdraw _____
    d. Withdraw/withdraw _____

2. In this cycle:
    a. Barry pursues, Wendy withdraws. _____
    b. Barry attacks and Wendy pursues. _____
    c. Wendy attacks and Barry pursues. _____
    d. Wendy pursues and Barry withdraws. _____

3. Wendy's secondary (reactive) emotion is:
    a. Hurt _____
    b. Fear _____
    c. Anger _____
    d. Shame _____

4. Barry's secondary (reactive) emotion is:
    a. Hurt _____
    b. Fear _____
    c. Anger _____
    d. Blame _____

Homework assignments that can help couples understand their cycle and the emotions in this cycle are set out in Appendices D1 and D2.

TAKING THE HISTORY OF THE RELATIONSHIP

- Process goal: Hear and understand the story of this couple: How did their relationship evolve and why did they come for therapy at this time?

Clients have a need to tell their own story and the EFT therapist listens to each partner empathically. The therapist wants to know who these people are and how their relationship evolved. Generic couple therapy information is gathered. Here are some sample questions:

- How long they have been together? What attracted them to each other?
- Do they live together? Who else lives with them? How old are their children? What is their relationship with extended family?
- What was it like when things were good between them? Were they satisfied with their sexual relationship?
- When they fight/argue, do they feel they resolve issues? How do they make up? Who initiates closeness and sex?
- What was their relationship like at the beginning? Were they once able to confide in each other? How/when did this change?
- What prompted them to come for therapy at this time? Whose idea was it that they seek therapy? What changes would each like to see happen?

Attachment injuries.

The EFT therapist also notices if there has been an attachment injury in the relationship. An attachment injury is a critical incident where one partner learns they cannot count on the other and often pulls away. Attachment injuries, their diagnosis and management, are discussed in chapter 10. Attachment injuries may emerge as the history of the couple's relationship is gathered or in the individual sessions.

ASSESSING ATTACHMENT STYLE

- Process goal: Begin to hypothesize as to the blocks to secure attachment and emotional engagement within and between partners, and to explore these.
- Process goal: Begin to make hypotheses as to the vulnerabilities and attachment issues underlying each partner's position in the relationship.

Simply put, an individual's attachment style is the manner in which the client has learned to manage the response he/she expects to the question: "Can I depend on you when I really need you?" Attachment styles are currently understood as organizing around two continuous dimensions, avoidance and anxiety (Fraley and Waller, 1998), and resulting in four attachment styles: secure, preoccupied (anxious), dismissing avoidant, and fearful avoidant. These styles are habitual ways of engaging partners and regulating emotion (See chapter 5). For further readings on attachment styles readers are referred to *Attachment Processes in Couple and Family Therapy* (Johnson & Whiffin, 2003).

We stress that the EFT therapist does not intend to pigeonhole clients into categories. The goal is rather to gain impressions of how the clients typically respond to each other during times of need or stress. This provides context for understanding partners' emotions and defensive moves in relation to each other and helps the therapist to formulate hypotheses regarding underlying primary emotion.

Attachment style can be assessed in three ways: (a) from the attachment history of each partner, (b) by understanding the interaction between partners, and (c) by using self-report questionnaires.

Assessing Attachment History

In addition to generic history taking, the EFT therapist explores the attachment history of each client. The goal is to determine whether they have ever experienced a secure attachment relationship, and if not, how they have managed their need for soothing and connection. This is also explored in the individual sessions. The therapist will ask each couple about their family of origin and previous significant adult relationships.

- What was their model of attachment relationships like? Did the client's parents seem close? Were they openly affectionate? Did they fight? Did they resolve arguments and become close again? How did the client experience any fights and arguments that occurred in the home?
- Did the clients have a secure relationship with a dependable parental figure? Who was available for comfort, confiding, and soothing? Does either partner have a history of loss or of abuse? How did he/she deal with this?
- To whom does each partner turn for comfort and confiding now?

Assessing Partners' Interactions

Information regarding attachment styles is also gathered by (a) observing the couple as they interact in the session and (b) asking how each typically responds to the other. Who seeks closeness? Do they seek support from each other? What does each partner do when the other is distressed? The EFT therapist listens for indices of secure attachment, heightened fear of abandonment, or intimacy avoidance.

- A client with a secure attachment style tends to:
  - Be able and willing to openly express positive and negative emotions.
  - Be able to give the partner the benefit of the doubt.
  - Seek out the partner for support when distressed.
  - Be available to comfort and support partner when partner is needy.
- A client with an avoidant attachment style tends to:
  - Not seek support from partner.
  - Find it difficult to provide support especially when partner is anxious or needy, and withdraw precisely when their partner needs him/her.
  - Dismiss or minimize threats and hurts to self.
  - Intellectualize and exhibit restricted emotionality, focusing instead on tasks and activities.

- A client with an anxious attachment style tends to:
  - Have an intense need for support and affection from partner.
  - Catastrophize and exaggerate threats and hurts to self.
  - Be vigilant and readily interpret partner's behaviors as a threat.
  - Be demanding on partner for time and attention.
  - Exhibit intense emotionality.

- A client with a fearful avoidant style tends to:
- Manage fears by avoiding intimacy and have difficulty being emotionally and physically close.
- Hold in emotions and be reluctant to self-disclose.
- Have difficulty believing that their partners care about them.
- Not seek support from their partners, or to seek it only to withdraw when it is offered.
- Behave in a passive manner.
- Have often been violated in love relationships.

Self-report questionnaires.

EFT therapists may also administer a self-report attachment style questionnaire such as the Experiences in Close Relationships Scale (Brennen, Clark, & Shaver, 1998). For a general assessment of the relationship, the Dyadic Adjustment Scale (Spanier, 1976) can be administered. A score of 70 is typical of divorcing couples and a score of 114 is typical of happy North American couples.

Individual sessions.

Following the first one or two meetings with the couple, the EFT therapist usually meets with each partner individually. This provides the therapist the opportunity to continue to foster the therapeutic alliance by listening and focusing on the individual's concerns and to obtain a history of previous adult relationships including an understanding of their conclusion.

Individual sessions enable the therapist to observe and interact with each client in a different context (i.e., without the spouse). Clients can frequently be more candid about problems with their spouse when the spouse is not present. The therapist can use individual sessions to explore information that is difficult to obtain in the presence of the spouse. Here, for example the therapist may ask about violence and other forms of abuse. Asking the individual whom he/she confides in can ease the therapist into asking about competing relationships, whether there is another partner or perhaps an Internet relationship.

The therapist also uses individual sessions to explore previous attachment relationships. Family of origin may be explored in further detail, and the therapist also asks questions about previous significant adult intimate relationships. The therapist will also assess for personal attachment traumas that may have impact on the present relationship. This permits the therapist to further understand the client's model of intimate relationships, and to discuss with the client the underlying feelings and attachment issues that might affect the present relationship.

The question of secrets.

Conducting individual sessions leads to the question of secrets. Will an EFT therapist agree to keep information learned in an individual session from the spouse? This issue may be raised at the beginning of an individual session. The therapist may advise the client that, although they have a right to individual privacy, holding secrets between the couple can interfere with the process of EFT. The therapist would encourage and support a partner to share secrets with the spouse regarding, for example, ongoing affairs in a conjoint session. Other information for example, a past abortion never talked about or a brief affair that ended years ago would not be considered necessary to bring into the current couple therapy process. If a client did tell the therapist that he/she was having an ongoing extramarital affair, and the client did not wish to share this information with the spouse, then the EFT therapist would tell the client that she was unable to work with them because this secret would inevitably undermine the process of relationship change. The condition to at least place the other relationship on hold and be open about it in therapy is necessary to proceed with therapy.

CONTRAINDICATIONS TO EFT

Different Agendas

EFT is not appropriate for couples who present with different agendas. For example, one partner's goal may be to marry the other while the second partner's goal is to remain single; one partner's objective may be to persuade the other to engage in outside sexual relationships, while the other clearly does not wish to do so. In such cases the therapist will clarify the impasse and present it clearly to the couple.

Separating Couples

When it is clear that one partner has emotionally left the relationship and the couple will be separating, EFT should not be offered. Occasionally one spouse will initiate couple sessions in the hope of securing support for the other as he/she lets the partner know about the plan to move on. Partners may then be offered sessions to help them with pragmatic aspects to separation. The therapist may also work individually with the second partner or refer him/her for support/grief work with another therapist.

Abusive Relationships

EFT is also not used in clearly abusive relationships (see Johnson, 2004). EFT involves encouraging partners to be vulnerable with each other; in abusive relationships such vulnerability could be dysfunctional, putting the abused partner more at risk.

However, one abusive incident does not necessarily mean an abusive relationship, and, conversely, some relationships have no history of physical violence but verbal abuse is present in the form of threats, denigrating comments, and deliberate moves to hurt or intimidate the other. For example, a wife may confide in her individual session: "He has never hit me...but I am afraid of him." The EFT therapist will listen for fear, and if one partner is afraid of the other, will not proceed with EFT. A violent partner may be asked instead to participate in therapy that is directed at appropriate expression of anger.

An in-depth analysis and discussion of abusive relationships is outside the scope of our workbook. The reader is referred to several excellent sources (e.g., Bograd & Mederos, 1999; JMFT 1999 Edition on Violence). In addition, therapists may want to seek supervision or consultation when deciding how to proceed with abusive relationships.

Substance Abuse

Alcohol or drug dependence does not necessarily preclude EFT, as long as couples can participate in sessions while sober. However, the EFT therapist does require that addicted partners (both if necessary) are able to acknowledge the problem and attend some form of individual or group treatment for the addiction. In this case, the therapist will explore the substance use and understand it in the context of the couple's negative interactive cycle. For example, the therapist will explore how the substance use affects the relationship as well as how the relationship impacts the substance use.

Depression and Other Psychiatric Illness

It is not unusual for partners experiencing marital distress to be depressed, and EFT can have a positive impact in alleviating depression. However, if a partner has significant impairment and is untreated, the client may be referred for assessment and concurrent individual therapy. Depending on the therapist's confidence in his/her own skills, the same is true for most other psychiatric disorders.

CREATING A THERAPEUTIC AGREEMENT

The EFT therapist briefly describes how EFT is conducted and invites clients to ask questions or express fears or concerns. For example, the therapist may say:

"We find that distressed couples tend to get stuck in a pattern—we also call this a 'cycle' or 'dance'—that leaves them feeling perhaps unhappy, alone, angry or hurt and far apart from each other. What I will do is to try to understand your pattern, and also to understand the feelings that you each have in relation to each other. I will try to help you to understand each other and relate to each in a deeper and more satisfying way."

The couple are invited to ask questions (e.g., how long does therapy usually take?) and to express fears and concerns about the process, which are then addressed. Most EFT therapists predict therapy will take 10 to 20 sessions.

Exercise 19:

1. A client tells you her partner hit her during a recent fight. You:
    a. Tell her you will need to break confidentiality if she reports this again. _____
    b. Tell her you will not be able to work with them in couple therapy. _____
    c. Decide to use only a cognitive-behavioral approach. _____
    d. Explore the history of violence and determine if she is afraid of her partner. _____

2. In an individual session your client tells you that his partner is drinking to excess, and he is worried that she may be alcoholic. Your best response would be to:
    a. Tell him that his partner needs to join a twelve-step program. _____
    b. Ask him if he has discussed his concerns with his partner. _____
    c. Decide this is not a suitable couple for EFT. _____
    d. Suggest he join Alanon. _____

3. EFT is contraindicated if:
    a. There is ongoing intimidation and violence. _____
    b. There is ongoing substance abuse. _____
    c. One partner is severely chronically ill. _____
    d. One partner has bipolar disorder. _____

Exercise 20:

Match the following attachment styles to the examples given below:

Attachment style:

1. Dismissive/avoidant attachment style.
2. Fearful/avoidant attachment style.
3. Preoccupied (anxious).
4. Secure attachment style.

a. Husband asks wife for support and comfort when he is laid off from his job. _____
b. Wife is extremely angry because husband is late from work as he tries to meet important deadline. _____
c. Husband looks out of the window as wife tearfully describes her recent miscarriage. _____
d. As wife lights candles for their anniversary dinner, the wife berates husband because he has only completed four of five tasks she asked him to do for her. _____

Exercise 21:

Answer True or False:

1. EFT can be used where one partner has a substance-use problem. _____
2. In the individual session, the therapist agrees to keep the secret when the wife reports an ongoing affair. _____
3. The EFT assessment process involves exploring attachment history, assessing the suitability of the couple for EFT, and identifying the partner(s) with dysfunctional communication skills. _____
4. In EFT assessment the therapist will ask the couple who initiates closeness and sex. _____

Following the individual session and by the beginning of the second or third couple session, the therapist should have developed a basic alliance with both partners and gained a sense of the history of the relationship. The therapist should now know whether the couple ever knew a happy, secure bond and should have a sense of the problematic cycle and how it impacts the emotional realities of each partner. The therapist should also have a sense of each partner's pain in this relationship as well as an understanding of how each attempts to deal with it. At this point also, the couple should have the beginning of a sense of trust in and ease with the therapist and a new perspective on their problem/cycle. Each partner should also have seen glimpses of the underlying emotions in their partner, and both should have some hope for the future of the relationship.

An assessment form to aid in EFT assessment sessions can be found in Appendix E.

5

STEPS 3 AND 4: DE-ESCALATION

After the assessment process of Steps 1 and 2, the EFT therapist moves into Steps 3 and 4. In Step 3, the therapist will access the unacknowledged emotions underlying interactional positions. In Step 4, the therapist reframes the problem in terms of underlying emotions and attachment needs. The cycle is framed as the common enemy and the source of partner's emotional distress.

After the first two conjoint sessions, Inez and Fernando began to see the cycle of negative interactions that was taking over their relationship. Inez experienced Fernando as irritable, unhelpful, and withdrawn while Fernando found her bossy and "in his face," and he pushed her away. Efforts to connect with one another seemed to lead to bickering, with Inez "puffing up" and shouting at him. Inez had shut down physically and spent more and more time away from the home. The couple was settling into separate lives, and since his retirement, Fernando had begun to realize that his wife was not there for him anymore. Although the cycle had been identified and the couple was able to see it, they presented in the following session, session 5, in full-blown cycle mode.

Inez had been feeling ill for 3 weeks. Her eyes were red and scratchy and she had a cough and frequent headaches. She wondered if she was developing allergies, and decided that she would shampoo the rug in the living room and completely dust the house. Fernando, who was beginning to understand that she was unhappy because he wasn't giving her more help with the household tasks, went to the store to rent the carpet shampoo machine and made a list of all jobs that needed to be accomplished that day.

As the couple worked together on the carpet cleaning, their daughter Angela arrived. Inez was unaware that Fernando had arranged with his daughter by email to help her with her income taxes. Fernando went off to his study with Angela leaving Inez to struggle with the carpet on her own. Inez silently worked alone, becoming more and more angry. Later that day Fernando was again called away by their son Chris, who was having car trouble and needed a ride. Soon after Fernando returned home, and an argument erupted between the partners.

Inez: "All I did was ask him when supper would be ready."

Fernando: "Well for God's sake! I hadn't had a moment all day. I was at everyone's beck and call. Inez – for God's sake I'm trying."

Inez: "All I did was ask when supper would be ready. You gave me "the look" then you went for me. And you haven't spoken to me since."

Fernando: "Well, look at the day I had. And I started out by helping you. I got the machine; I did the heavy work..."

Therapist: "You said you're really trying, Fernando?"

Fernando: "Yes, I'm trying to stop this cycle. I'm doing things for her, trying to make things work better, but she nags and I can't stand it."

Therapist: "That's a real hot button for you, Fernando, the nagging, the bossing—what happens for you when you feel she's bossing you?"

Fernando: (sounds angry) "It's total disrespect. I feel like she thinks I'm subservient... nothing."

Therapist: "You feel like she thinks you're nothing? Yes, I can understand. That makes you feel angry." (validating secondary emotion.)

Fernando: "She doesn't value anything I do; it's like she sets the standards, I have to meet them. And I won't do it!"

Therapist: "So what happens for you when you get that feeling, like she thinks you're nothing?" (evocative response)

Fernando: "That upsets me. So I give out clear signals. Then I shoot and duck."

Therapist: "You shoot and duck?"

Fernando: "Yes. I lash out and then isolate myself to stop getting hurt."

Therapist: "So what I'm getting is, when you feel 'bossed' by Inez you get a painful feeling like she's talking down to you, like she thinks you're nothing, and that really hurts you, yes? That's when you give out your signal to her—is that 'the look'?"

Fernando: (nods) "Yes."

Therapist: "So then when you yell and go off to the computer or down to your tool room—that's about protecting yourself from getting hurt?"

Fernando: "That's right. I get cranky. I get scarce."

Therapist: "This is where the cycle takes over, yes? You get the feeling of being disrespected, and suddenly you are caught in your anger. You want to be close, to make her feel you're there for her, but then you get that feeling of disrespect that hurts you, so you "fire away" and then you withdraw to avoid further hurt?" (tracking the cycle)

Fernando: "Yes. It's like I put my armor on and disappear."

Therapist: "You put on your armor so that you won't get hurt."

Inez: (angrily) "Well, I'm the one that wasn't well yesterday. I needed your help and you dropped everything and went off with Angela. To heck with me! I'm on my own! No wonder I yell at you."

Therapist: "That's what happened for you yesterday, Inez. You got that feeling again, like you're on your own."

Inez: "Yes! I don't count. I'm on my own, even in my own family."

Therapist: (RISSSC manner) "That must be a very painful place to be, Inez. On your own in your own family."

Inez: (swallows and pauses) "I've...I've been there for a long, long time. On my own. Even in my own home."

Therapist: (RISSSC manner) "For a long time you've felt unsupported and on your own, even in your own home. And that's been very hard, very painful?" (heightening)

Inez: (looks down at her hands; tears well up in her eyes and she sniffs) "I feel unimportant and I get resentful. (She straightens up) I'm fed up with it. It makes me mad."

Therapist: "Yes, I can understand that. I notice Inez as you said that you looked really sad for a moment, I could feel the sadness, then you kinda sat up tall and said 'I'm fed up with it.' Is that where the puffer fish comes in? You puff up and get mad."

Inez: (nods) "That's right. I get angry..."

Therapist: "But on the inside, there's all these tender feelings..."

Inez: (looks down at her entwined fingers, pauses, and nods again)

Therapist: "It's hard for you to talk about the sadness on the inside?"

Inez: (nods again)

Therapist: "Mmm, so here's where the cycle kicks in, and you both are left far away from each other with all these emotions the other doesn't know about."

(Fernando and Inez are now calmer. Fernando reaches out and touches Inez' knee.) Fernando: "I'm sorry Inez. I'm sorry I didn't tell you Marie was coming over. I clean forgot about it, to be honest with you."

OVERVIEW OF STEPS 3 AND 4

In the case of Fernando and Inez, the therapist focuses on their cycle as an enemy invader that takes over the couple's relationship. The therapist carefully tracks and punctuates the negative pattern, noting the impact of each partner's actions on the other. Even more important to the EFT therapist is the attention given to each partner's emotional experience at different points of the cycle. The therapist works with each partner to acknowledge and experience these emotions and bring them into the session. Secondary emotions are noted and primary emotions are evoked as the therapist works to frame the couple's awareness of the cycle. Note that the couple is able to refer to the cycle as external to their relationship and the therapist emphasizes the negative impact of the cycle on the couple by highlighting the distance that occurs as a result.

The essential goals in Steps 3 and 4 include:

- The therapist helps partners to access the primary emotions that are typically outside the awareness of each partner and their interactions as a couple. The therapist goal is to help the couple tune in to the music of the dance by listening to their primary emotions.

- The therapist helps the couple expand their understanding of the problem as a reoccurring pattern or cycle that is influenced by each partner's emotional response and attachment needs in the relationship. The couple develops an understanding of their relationship as distinct from the problem cycle that defines the couple's experience.

KEY MOVES IN THE PROCESS

As the therapy process unfolds the therapist tracks key shifts in the couple's interaction. In Steps 3 and 4 the therapist responds to the couple's increasing awareness of their cycle and emotional experience by addressing these changes. The following section identifies several of these key moves in the process and how the therapist responds.

As partners increasingly express their secondary emotions, the therapist focuses on acknowledging and validating these secondary responses. At the same time the therapist draws out the experience of the partners as they become more aware of their partner's secondary emotions. For example, while focusing on the numb experience of a withdrawn husband, the therapist will explore the experience of his wife as she learns more about this numbing. She begins to see her spouse as numb or "frozen" rather than distant and unfeeling.

A second shift includes the expression of intense or incongruent nonverbal behaviors as the couple moves further into their emotional experience. This may be seen when a partner responds with intense crying or displaying laughing in the face of a partner's blame. As the therapist encounters these non-verbal expressions, the therapy process is slowed as the therapist works to connect nonverbal cues with the client's verbalizing of their emotional experience. RISSSC is used to address intense and incongruous nonverbal responses.

A third key move in the process is seen as partners encounter new primary emotional experience and their partners react to this experience by exiting the interaction or discounting the partner's new emotional experience. As the therapist evokes the underlying emotional experience of a partner, the other partner may react to this new awareness by dismissing the other's experience or may simply close off or shut down in response to this information. Therapists respond to this shift by redirecting the session back to exploring the emotional experience of both partners.

A final shift that is common in Steps 3 and 4 occurs when partners identify the specific pattern of interaction that defines their cycle and negatively impacts their relationship. Here the therapist actively focuses on each partner's position in the cycle and how this cycle functions to defeat even the couple's best attempts to connect.

THERAPIST TASKS

There are two primary therapeutic tasks in the process of cycle de-escalation. First the therapist works to help each partner access unacknowledged feelings that underlie a partner's position in the problematic cycle. The therapist heightens the emotional experience in the present in order to illicit and name these "new" emotional experiences. Second, the therapist reframes the couple's problem in light of their problematic cycle, underlying feelings, and attachment sensitivities and needs. The therapist then helps the couple reframe their problem cycle as the enemy.

Task 1: Identify the Cycle

The first therapeutic task in the de-escalation process is to identify the cycle with the couple (This is Step 2 of EFT but continues all through Stage 1 of EFT). Identifying the cycle requires the therapist to track the couple's interactions around closeness/distance. The therapist will ask the couple to describe their interaction by asking leading questions. Some common questions include:

"What happens when you have a fight?"

"How do the two of you feel close?"

"Pretend that I am a fly on the wall of your kitchen, tell me what I would see if the two of you were having a fight or being calm at a typical meal together, like supper?"

"How do you reconnect after a fight?"

These questions help the therapist focus the discussion on delineating the cycle. Identifying the cycle requires that you label the pattern that the partner relies on in times of vulnerability and when their attachment needs are activated. A woman may feel lonely and unloved but her typical stance is to take a critical, angry position, stating, "You are never there for me. I can't count on you because you are only interested in yourself." On the other hand other partners may feel lonely and unloved but their stance is a withdrawn, silent position, demonstrating sullen behavior but reporting that there is "nothing wrong." The cycle is identified by naming the predictable behaviors that make up each partner's default position in the context of a couple's common conflict or distance patterns.

The therapist listens for statements that describe the behaviors of each partner in their problematic interactions and arguments, and attends to the emotion-laden statements each partner may use to describe his or her relationship. Clients often use descriptive phrases and metaphors to describe their position in the relationship. The therapist reflects these statements and the emotions that they convey. Table 5.1 is a list of statements common to withdrawers and pursuers.

Negative cycles and interactional positions.

Distressed couples interact with only a limited number of basic patterns, cycles, and positions. It is important for therapists to be skilled at identifying and empathically exploring these patterns, as they are often the plot of the couple's distressing attachment drama. Over time, distressed couples become caught in a dance of repetitive interactional patterns. Each partner's behavior cue the other's, in what becomes a negative cyclical pattern of interaction. The most typical cycle is the pursue/withdraw (or demand/distance) pattern. There are five basic negative positions that partners take in distressed relationships and that EFT therapists should recognize:

Table 5.1

Common Phrases Used by Withdrawing and Pursuing Partners

Withdrawers often say:	Pursuers often say:
"You never come near me or even touch me."	"My heart is breaking." "I am going to die."
"I never get it right or satisfy her."	"He is never there. He's always at work."
"I don't bother—what's the point."	"He never looks at me when I talk to him. He just watches TV. The only time he comes to me is when he wants sex."
"I am amazed that she can take something so small and build it so way out of proportion."	"There are birthdays that are forgotten or Mother's Day when nobody gives me a card."
"I don't know what I feel. I am lost."	"I do it by myself and just take care of things on my own."
"She gives me that look and I am paralyzed."	"I am way down on his list, after the kids, work, his family, and then maybe me."
"She never initiates sex. It is always up to me."	"He's not there—no one has ever been there."
"I can never get it right or to her standards. It's like she has a scorecard and I always come up short. That's all I hear anyway is what I do wrong never what is going right."	"He won't listen! He never listens. It doesn't matter how long I talk to him or how many examples I give him or how hard I try—I can never get through to him."
"I feel like she's got me dangling from the end of a rope that is going to fray at any minute and it's going to be all over."	"It's like we are roommates or brother and sister. Any hope for passion or romance is futile—he just doesn't want it."
"I don't feel anything—nothing at all."	"Other couples seem to have lives that are full, and they enjoy each other. We don't have anything."

1. Pursue/withdraw: The most common cycle is a demanding spouse interacting with a withdrawing or distancing partner. In this pattern, the distancing or "stonewalling" position is a shutdown, non-response mode that often cues panic or aggression in the other partner as in, "I will make you respond to me." As can be seen from the description of the other patterns below, most other patterns can be understood as variants of the basic pursue/withdraw pattern. When trying to identify the couple's negative pattern, keep in mind that the positions are "default" options: they are what the partners do when they feel threatened or vulnerable. A common mistake of beginning therapists is to be confused by a withdrawing husband who pursues for sex in a single incident but who generally takes a withdrawn position especially when confronted or vulnerable. This cycle has been described in a variety of ways including: demand/distance, complain/placate, and criticize/stonewall. Common sex roles find the female in the position of the pursuer and a male in the position of a withdrawer. A male pursuer will tend to look different from a female pursuer. There is often a coercive element to a male pursuer, which the therapist needs to take note, particularly when assessing for abuse. Same-sex couples will also present in pursue/withdraw patterns.

2. Withdraw/withdraw: Sometimes the therapist will observe couples whose interactions appear to be a withdraw/withdraw pattern. In this pattern both partners are hesitant to engage emotionally and, in the face of conflict, both will further withdraw. While this may appear to be the couple's basic pattern, it is more likely that a pursue/withdraw pattern underlies it. In these cases, the pursuer may be a "soft" pursuer who is hard to recognize because he or she does not show the overwhelming anxious energy seen in a lot of pursuers and who, despite being a pursuer, gives up easily. The other possibility, which is more common, involves a "burnt out" pursuer who has now

given up reaching for the other partner. Withdrawal then can be the beginning of grieving and detaching from the relationship.

3. Attack/attack: Therapists often observe attack/attack sequences and escalations in couple interactions. Typically these escalations are deviations from a pursue/withdraw pattern where the withdrawer feeling provoked turns and fights, erupting in anger at specific moments. Here, after the fight, the withdrawer is likely to soon revert back to withdrawing until he or she feels provoked again.

4. Complex cycles: These cycles are multi-move cycles and often occur in trauma survivor couples where both anxiety and avoidance are high, resulting in more complicated sequences of interactions. An example would be: the husband makes coercive demands for compliance and attention, the wife withdraws, the husband escalates demands, the wife withdraws and then attacks in self-defense, both withdraw, the wife becomes depressed (for 3 days or so), the husband then pursues, the wife slowly responds, the couple has a short period of loving sexuality, and the cycle begins again.

5. Reactive pursue/withdraw cycle: These cycles occur when the couple reverses a previous long-standing pattern. For example, a pursuing wife gradually gives up and limits her investment in the relationship. Her distancing, work-obsessed spouse does not notice. The children leave home—an important transition—and she announces she is leaving. The couple then comes into therapy with a reactive cycle where the husband is now frantically pursuing to prevent a separation and the wife is cautious and withdrawn, refusing to commit to the relationship. The present negative cycle where the husband is aggressively pursuing and the wife has given up is a reversal of their previous long-standing pattern of her pursuing and his withdrawing.

While this chapter emphasizes negative cycles of interactions, the therapist is also keenly interested in positive cycles of interaction: interactions where partners are responsive to each other's needs. Whenever they occur, the therapist should highlight and reinforce these interactions and be an active champion of the positive cycle.

Task 2: Identify Partner Feelings

The second task in cycle de-escalation requires the therapist to identify each partner's secondary and primary feelings.[1] Typically the therapist will use the partner's position in the problematic cycle to draw an inference about the client's inner experience. The interpersonal positions of withdraw and pursue are associated with a number of emotional states. Table 5.2 includes a list of possible emotional experiences associated with a withdrawer or pursuer position.

Task 3: Frame Key Emotions in Context of Cycle

In Step 3 of EFT the therapist frames the emotional experience underlying each partner's position in attachment-related terms. The use of Attachment Theory provides a powerful frame for understanding a "connecting purpose" for the problematic interaction cycle. The negative cycles marked by patterns of blame/pursuit and withdrawal/distance can be understood in the context of a couple's search for connection and ways of managing disconnection. These

---

[1] Some assume mistakenly that EFT does not work well for clients who have difficulty expressing their emotions. EFT therapists assume that while an inexpressive client may not be able to talk about their emotions he or she is able to talk about his or her experience. It is then the therapist's job to elicit this experience and help the client connect this experience to their secondary and primary emotions. The therapist works with the inexpressive partner to identify feelings at the secondary and primary level by helping that partner identify with the emotional experience of another person, and then make a connection to the inexpressive partner's unarticulated experience.

Table 5.2
Common Underlying Emotions of the Withdrawers and Pursuers

Withdrawers often feel:	Pursuers often feel:
Rejected	Hurt
Inadequate	Alone
Afraid of failure	Not wanted
Overwhelmed	Invisible
Numb – frozen	Isolated
Afraid – scared	Not important
Not wanted or desired	Abandoned
Judged, criticized	Desperate
Shame	Disconnected
Empty	Deprived

patterns result in a reduction in responsiveness, accessibility, and a reduction of felt security in the relationship. As this occurs a couple's behavior in this cycle becomes automatic and compelling bringing more attention to the impact of these behaviors and less to the underlying reasons for these actions. The power of de-escalation is helping couples uncover the underlying intent of the responses that make up these powerful negative cycles, if only to help couples at this early stage to see that their cycle is evidence of a problematic attempt to connect.

The therapist can reframe the more anxious and preoccupied partner's pursuit and attacks as attempts to close the distance they experience in the relationship and at the same time note the ways these reactions tend to drive away their partner, providing evidence to that partner that it is not safe to be close. The therapist can reframe the withdrawal of the more avoidant or ambivalent spouse as a response to help regulate the intensity of the emotional experience and calm the relationship down. Expression of emotion is then blunted, and positive and negative affect is reduced, which only tends to escalate the anxious pursuer's efforts to promote an emotional response to her or his concerns. The therapist's use of an attachment perspective provides a logical frame for the couple's cycle and its relationship to both their desire to connect and the negative experience that results when they cannot.

The therapist may use one of the following themes to reframe the partner's position in the negative interaction cycle. These include:

- "Fighting Against the Enemy": The therapist frames the cycle as the enemy who intrudes into the couple's relationship and takes over, keeping the couple from the closeness the couple seeks.

- "Fighting for the Connection": The therapist frames the cycle as a struggle to find a safe place in the relationship. Attachment needs are validated as the therapist paints a picture of the couple's cycle as a response to each partner's attempts to close the distance in their relationship. The therapist may use a separate frame for the pursuing partner and a different frame for the withdrawing partner.

- "Protecting the Relationship": The therapist frames the response of the withdrawing partner as an effort to protect the relationship from potentially damaging emotions or emotions that would overwhelm the relationship. The withdrawal is recognized as a protective response to a situation that may increasingly feel "out of control" emotionally.

- "Protesting the Loss of Connection": The therapist frames the response of the pursuing or attacking partner as a protest to the loss of connection and the perceived unavailability of the other. The intensity of the pursuit or attack becomes a way of getting the partner's attention, or demanding a response. In attachment terms any response is better than none. No response translates into the sense that one does not matter to the other and that cannot impact the other. Loss and isolation then become tangible realities.

By the end of Steps 3 and 4, each partner will identify the habitual position that he or she takes in the relationship. Each will have also touched some of their inner world underlying this position and begun to understand their relationship in attachment terms. The negative cycle is framed as the enemy and block to partners connecting with each other in an intimate way.

The EFT therapist facilitates a shift from the couple's focus on problems to a focus on the cycle of interaction by attending to the following actions. Through carefully tracking and reflecting the couple's problematic pattern of interaction the therapist creates a non-blaming description of the couple's cycle. Using simple and straightforward descriptions the therapist will frame this pattern in the language of the clients. The therapist reflects the perception of the partners (e.g., "You see him as not really trying or even wanting to change.") as well as the impact of each partner's actions on the other (e.g., "And when she does not respond, it is like she doesn't care or she's scary to you.") As the therapist maps the different moves in the couple's pattern, she will clarify the cycle by first working with one partner and then shifting to the other's experience. The cycle is framed as the enemy that takes over the couple's relationship, reducing the security of the relationship. Identifying the cycle helps the couple recognize the self-reinforcing pattern which provides a basis for engaging the primary emotions underlying this patterned behavior and placing it into an attachment frame. These interventions help the couple to externalize the problem so that the cycle becomes the focus rather than either partner. The couple experiences more safety in their relationship as a result. The process of cycle de-escalation is described in the following case illustration.

Case Illustration: Withdraw/Withdraw Couple

Cycle de-escalation with a couple that is in a withdraw/withdraw cycle can look different from the more typical pursue/withdraw cycle. The quality of the interaction is different in that fights are less frequent and less intense; there may be less lovemaking, as there is an emotional disengagement. This relationship is characterized by conflict avoidance behaviors on part of both partners. The couple frequently have developed a reliance on recourses outside of the relationship to provide emotional sustenance, for example, children, friends, extended family or hobbies, and work. A variation on the withdraw/withdraw cycle is a "burnt-out pursuer," which can occur in long-term marriages where one partner has been a pursuer but has given up that position and has come to rely on a more withdrawn stance as well. This type of withdraw/withdraw is flavored with feelings of resignation, defeat, and hopelessness.

Tracy and Adam, a couple in their early 30s, were married for 10 years and did not have any children. They had successful careers in the same industry, which required a fair amount of travel. The presenting issue was that the couple had not had sexual relations since they had married and this was now an issue because Tracy wanted to have children.

In the first sessions, the therapist worked to establish an alliance with both partners and to alleviate some of the shame that they were both feeling about their problem by normalizing and placing the issue in the context of their cycle. Tracy and Adam were caught in a withdraw/withdraw pattern as both had avoided addressing their lack of sexuality but continued to function well together as housemates and colleagues, and within their family and social circle. They did not report any fights, but more that there might be some "tension" or silence between them that would wear off over time and after which they would be "good friends" again. At the point of therapy, Tracy was ambivalent about whether to stay in this relationship or pursue her goal of becoming a mother with another partner. Adam for his part wanted to save the marriage and was relieved that they were beginning to talk about their sex life, which had been so hard for them to talk about before.

Adam: "I think things are going a lot better. We have been able to talk about this subject, which was so hard for us to talk about before. It is great that it's now out in the open and we can do something about it."

Tracy: "I agree. Just coming here was so hard to do. I didn't think I could do it and never expected that Adam would either. Its like we have finally taken the skeleton out of the closet."

Therapist: "That was very difficult and it took a lot of courage to talk to each other and me and admit out loud with a witness that this was a problem. It is a very hard thing to do for most people." (validation)

Adam: "Well, I think it has helped a lot - we seem to be getting along better, talking more just about day-to-day stuff. Don't you think?" (looking to Tracy)

Tracy: "Yes, we are talking a bit more. We just couldn't do this before. We were just so busy with work. There was always more important things to attend to our house, our families. We did a lot in our time together—helping out my family and your mother and all our traveling. We lead very busy lives."

Therapist: "What's that like then to get this out in the open and to be able to talk more? How does that feel?" (evocative responding)

Tracy: "We have always got along fairly well. I know a lot of couples that all they do is fight. But that's not our style. We are very considerate of each other."

Adam: "We are good friends and we have a lot of friends. All my friends like Tracy, and the same goes for her friends. We never lack for things to do or people to hang out with. We keep busy."

Therapist: "One thing that we have talked about so far is how the two of you were stuck in a cycle where you would avoid talking about things that were painful or where you thought the other person might get hurt and that a strategy that you both took was to kind of close your eyes and hope that it would go away." (framing the problem in terms of the cycle)

Tracy: "But that is only part of our relationship. Sex isn't everything, and we have a lot of other things that are going well for us. We could never have got where we have if we had been arguing all the time."

Adam: "I know I don't like an argument and just found it so easy to get along with Tracy. We enjoy a lot of things together and have a lot of the same interests."

Therapist: "You have a lot of strengths as a couple and a bond that has kept you together for ten years. But, I had also understood that you were at a crossroad in your relationship that you needed to look at the lack of intimacy and how that was affecting you and how it was standing in the way of your future. Have I got that right or maybe I am off track?" *(framing the problem in terms of the cycle)*

Tracy: "No, you're right. It's just so hard to talk about it. I would rather just go on and ignore it sometimes. I am afraid I am not up to it—there is a lot of other stress in my life. There is a lot going on at work right now."

Therapist: "Maybe one thing the cycle has convinced you of is that it is hard to depend on your relationship to talk about things that are difficult. Yet they are things that are important to your relationship, the intimate things about sharing yourselves with each other. It's so tempting to rely on the old 'let's sweep it under the carpet' and see if it will all go away." *(framing the problem in terms of the cycle)*

Adam: "I know I did that. I kept thinking that this is just going to get better, or I wouldn't think about it at all. It was too hard."

Therapist: "It was hard to think that you were not making love to your wife and that this had gone on for a long time and it wasn't getting better?" *(empathic conjecture)*

Adam: "Yes. How could I do that? How could I let it go so long? I can't figure out what is wrong with me."

Therapist: "Sounds like you end up feeling bad about yourself." *(evocative reflection)*

Adam: "What else can I think? What other man would let this happen?"

Therapist: "It must be very hard then to think about or talk about when you end up feeling so bad about you. The feeling bad kept you stuck, stuck in the cycle." *(evocative responding)*

Adam: "There was lots of time I just never thought about it at all."

Therapist: "You had a way of putting it away in a compartment so it didn't penetrate and you could protect yourself from feeling bad that way." *(evocative responding)*

Tracy: "I wouldn't say that I ever saw him feeling bad. He sure didn't come off that way—we got along so well."

Therapist: "It's kind of a mystery to you Tracy to hear about these feelings when the cycle blocked the two of you from really talking about your feelings." *(validation)*

Tracy: "I never thought there was any point to talking about feelings. I knew it would just start an argument and why rock the boat. There was so much going well for us."

Therapist: "But to not have your husband hold you in his arms and for you to share with him your most special intimate self, how was that? It must have been hard, yes?" (heightening, empathic conjecture)

Tracy: "I got used to it. Actually it started to feel kind of strange to do anything different— I mean who wants to kiss their brother? I am sorry but that is how it came to feel."

Therapist: "It sounds like that part of you, that special intimate part kind of got lost and that you have lost touch with those feelings in relation to Adam. How is that for you to hear that Adam?" (empathic conjecture)

Adam: (quiet and downcast) "It's understandable. What else could you expect? It's been a long time."

Therapist: "You look so sad when you say that Adam, is that how you feel?" (empathic conjecture)

Adam: "Well, it is hard to hear that your wife doesn't feel anything for you. I haven't lost that feeling."

Therapist: "Can you look at Tracy and tell her that?" (restructuring interaction)

Adam: "You know I never stopped wanting you. I just didn't know how or what to do. After we stopped and then it seemed like you didn't want me, I didn't know how to get started again and the longer it went on the harder it got. I got so stuck there. I couldn't move."

Tracy: "I find that hard to believe. You haven't made any attempts to be close to me and I see how you look at other women—that certainly doesn't make me feel like you want me."

Therapist: "That's hard to believe that Adam actually feels that way towards you, that he wants to be close and that he really desires you. It just gets so scary to face the fears that you 'didn't want' him." (validation)

Tracy: "It's hard to believe and also kind of weird feeling. It's hard to imagine that we could be any other way than the way we are. This just is the way we are, and I just wonder if maybe I should just be satisfied with what I have and look at all the positives in my life."

Therapist: "Maybe it's even scary to imagine you in each other's arms. Maybe it seems awkward and weird and maybe even a little 'abnormal' now. The cycle has prevented you both from looking at this and talking about this sooner and the longer it went on the harder it became for both of you. For you Adam it seemed to be a kind of frozen paralysis—that you didn't know what to do or how to approach Tracy. For you Tracy the cycle kind of froze your feelings of desire for Adam. The longer it went on, the more stuck you got and the more distant the two of you became. It got to the point where it felt like you were more brother and sister than husband and wife. Is that how it feels?" (validation, tracking the pattern)

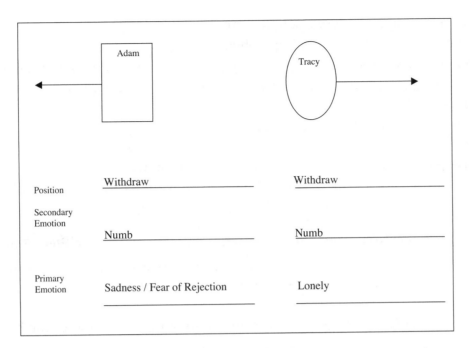

Figure 5.1   Diagramming the cycle.

The challenge to the therapist working with a couple that is in a withdraw/withdraw pattern is to block the couple's avoidance strategies without overwhelming them. The EFT therapist works with a strong alliance that provides the safety and the security for the couple to begin to explore the more difficult emotions that are threatening to their sense of equilibrium. The therapist's confidence that this is a process that can lead to greater intimacy for the couple helps the couple to take greater risks in moving away from the cycle of withdraw/withdraw to a more engaged and responsive relationship. Figure 5.1 illustrates the different elements that inform the withdraw/withdraw pattern of this couple.

Exercise 1:

1. In the case of Adam and Tracy the therapist facilitated cycle de-escalation by relating the couple's underlying emotions to:
    a. Secondary emotions _____
    b. Couple's presenting problem _____
    c. Position that each partner is taking in cycle _____
    d. Automatic thoughts of each partner _____
2. The process of accessing emotion in EFT does include:
    a. Labeling feelings to help partners change their behavior. _____
    b. Venting emotions to diminish their effect in the relationship. _____
    c. Interpreting quality of emotional experience and possible splitting. _____
    d. Active engagement of emotional experience in the here and now. _____
3. Cycle de-escalation represents a:
    a. First-order change _____
    b. Second-order change _____

    c. Positive connotation of a couple's problem _____

    d. Prescription of the presenting problem _____

4. The therapist will help each partner to expand his or her emotional experience to:

    a. Help the partner understand the different expectations they communicate in the relationship. _____

    b. Help each relate their experience in the relationship to primary and secondary emotions. _____

    c. Help the couple develop new communication skills. _____

    d. Help each partner understand how family patterns influence couple interactions. _____

Exercise 2: Identifying the Most Common Interventions Used in Steps 3 and 4

The five interventions used most often in cycle de-escalation are listed below. Match each of the interventions to the example below that best illustrates the intervention.

1. What's it like for you to be in this relationship, always waiting for the bomb to go off? _____

2. So when the conflict gets going, your pattern takes over, leaving both of you behind. Almost like you don't know what hit you. _____

3. So for you his silence is killing you. It makes sense that you need to do something to break through and find out what he is thinking. The silence leaves you fearing the worst. _____

4. So you feel cornered. Trapped. Like there is no place to go, no place to run. You want to hide. _____

5. And when you get angry to get his attention, it's like part of you is mad and the other part is sad hoping to connect to him. _____

    Validation _____

    Evocative responding _____

    Heightening _____

    Empathic conjecture _____

    Reframing problem in cycle _____

Exercise 3:

Read the following transcript of a cycle de-escalation event and identify the intervention used by the therapist throughout the session. Select the intervention(s) from the list below and enter the appropriate intervention in the space provided after each therapist's talk turn. Two spaces are provided when more than one intervention is used.

    Empathic conjecture

    Evocative responding

    Heightening

    Reframing

    Restructuring

Tracking the cycle
Validation

Example:

Ingrid: (high pitched, frantic voice) "I just found myself getting so angry and resentful over the weekend, all I could think about was what wasn't done and how she was away having a good time, and I was doing all of the work."

Therapist: "That was hard being alone all weekend with the work, and it was frustrating that there you were doing it all alone."

Ex. Validation

Ingrid: (high-pitched voice) "I wasn't lonely—I enjoyed being on my own. But she has come to expect me to do all the work and she can just sit back and that's not fair. I don't think she is going to change at all! All I see is more of the same—just more and more examples of things not changing. I don't know if she can really understand what I need or even cares."

Therapist: "It must have been especially frustrating. Here you are doing all the work and feeling like its just one more example of how things aren't changing. You are trying so hard and it feels like Frances is not doing anything."

1. _____

Ingrid: (irritated) "I just keep thinking that this is the way it's going to be—I am supposed to do everything and she doesn't do anything—she's lazy—she will do anything to avoid work. She's not changing—that's the way she wants it!"

Therapist: "That sounds like it is really frustrating and maybe even scary that maybe there was a part of you that was expecting, hoping that things will be different but then you are not seeing Frances change—and that begins to feel discouraging and hard to hold any hope."

2. _____

Ingrid: "I am not sure I am scared, but why should I change and she not change at all? She should be changing first! I am the one that supported her in her work—I gave a lot! I gave time, and have always been there. I don't see what she's giving—I can't give anymore."

Therapist: You gave a lot to help Frances. I would expect that you, like all of us when we join our lives with someone, had a lot of hopes of sharing your life with her and all kinds of dreams about building a future together with her, like working as a team."

3. _____

Ingrid: (voice starts to calm) "That's it. I don't feel like we are sharing. I am doing everything and she just goes along for the ride."

Therapist: "That is so hard because this is where the cycle takes over. You see yourself alone doing all the work and Frances is not there. The resentment starts to build and suddenly you are caught in your anger. You want to share with Frances but you really don't expect she'll be there, so you up the ante so that she will respond—to which Frances withdraws, shuts down, and she is even more unavailable. Is that how it is?"

4. _____

Ingrid: (starting to tear) "Yes, she is nowhere, I never know what is going on with her."

Therapist: (RISSSC manner) "That's very painful to you to have your partner but not be able to depend on her—that is a painful place."

5. _____

Ingrid: "I can't do everything. Frances just expects me to swallow it up and not say anything and just carry on like I always do."

Therapist: "Hmm…so on one hand you need to be with Frances and share with her. But on the other, it's like you are not supposed to speak or be able to say what you need and actually the cycle gets in the way of that really happening, getting your needs met. Once it takes hold you are off and running and you end up nowhere but frustrated, distant, and alone."

6. _____   _____

Ingrid: (crying, nodding)

Therapist: "What's that like for you? It looks like it hurts a lot."

7. _____

Ingrid: (calmer, softer) "It seems like she doesn't want to help. It's just my feeling— maybe it's just a perception." (looking directly at Frances)

Frances: (irritably) "That's not the way it is. I just came home. I wanted to relax. You can't expect me to start working the moment I open the door. I just felt like just walking out."

Therapist: "It's hard for you to hear what Ingrid is saying that she needs your help, needs to feel she can reach for you and get support. She gets scared when she can't, so she pushes. It hard to hear because you looked forward to seeing her and when you got home you saw her frustration, you just wanted to get away?"

8. _____   _____

Frances: "I don't know what she expects. I was going to get around to it but it doesn't matter what I do, it's wrong—so what's the use!"

Therapist: "This is a place that you go, Frances, when you are in the cycle, the place where you feel like there is no point. It seems like it doesn't matter what you do; it is wrong, that there is no point in trying. What's that like for you Frances when you are in this place? It sounds like an awful place for you."

9. _____   _____

Frances: "I just want to get as far away as possible. There is no point sticking around. It really doesn't matter if I am around, I will only get it wrong."

Therapist: "So the cycle takes over and when you see her frustration and disappointment, you just want to get as far away from that as possible, so you don't see it. It sounds like it really bothers you to see Ingrid's frustration, is that right?"

10. _____

Frances: "Yeah. I feel kind of useless—to her anyway."

Therapist: (RISSSC manner) "This is a really hard place for you Frances because when you see Ingrid's disappointment it has a huge effect on you and you end up feeling kind of useless like you'll never get it right."

11. _____

Frances: (starts to laugh, looking at Ingrid) "That pretty well sums it up, right, Ingrid? I am pretty useless."

Therapist: "So you move away because Ingrid's disappointment with you is so hard to bear, not because you don't care, is that right?"

12. _____

Ingrid: "You know I never said that. I just want you to help out more and see more of what I need."

Therapist: "The cycle has a huge impact on both of you. It gets in the way of you, Ingrid, being able to get your needs met and has you feeling alone. And you, Frances, end up feeling bad about yourself and feeling like the only thing you can do is get away."

13. _____

Frances: "I might as well. It seems like it would be better that way. It's the only thing I can do."

Therapist: "I am wondering, Frances, if you could try and talk to Ingrid about this now. I know it is hard because when we feel like we're kind of useless—we do want to go away, we want to hide to protect ourselves. It's hard to stay visible. But could you try and tell Ingrid what it is like for you? How it feels inside?"

14. _____   _____

Frances: (looking at Ingrid) "I don't know how it feels. There are some times that I just feel such hate and I just feel like leaving."

Ingrid: "Well if you feel hate, then we might as well just end it."

Therapist: "It is very hard to talk about feeling kind of useless especially in front of each other. It's easier lots of time to talk about hate—we feel bigger and stronger that way."

15. _____   _____

Frances: "It's not that I hate her. There is such a feeling of hate. I am not sure if she even wants me. She would be better off without me."

Therapist: "There is the overwhelming bad feeling that you can't please Ingrid and you end up feeling that Ingrid doesn't want you."

16. _____

Frances: (looking at Ingrid) "You never touch me. I go to you for hugs and cuddling and you never come to me."

Ingrid: "That part of me has just shut down. I can't be close physically when there is nothing happening anywhere else."

Therapist: "I know you need to protect yourself that way, Ingrid, but for you, Frances, it feels pretty painful not to be wanted or desired by your partner and maybe you end up feeling that it is you, that maybe you are not worth much or even kind of useless in Ingrid's eyes?"

17. _____   _____

Frances: (nodding, looking at Ingrid) "Do you even love me?"

Ingrid: "I don't know how I feel these days. I feel like you are just making an excuse— an excuse for not doing anything."

Therapist: "Frances, that takes a lot of strength and courage to ask how Ingrid feels and it seems like this is a painful place for you, not to feel the love and wanting coming from Ingrid, and it seems like it is very hard, Ingrid, for you to hear and take in what Frances is saying now, maybe because it is too hard to believe that Frances actually cares about being connected to you. Now what I have heard you saying is that you do want her, you actually want more of her, more of her to depend on, to count on and not to feel so alone."

18. _____   _____   _____

Ingrid: "But I am not sure she wants to do it. Maybe she's just not capable. She's never had any successful relationships."

Therapist: "It's hard to trust that she really wants to be there for you, that she really wants this relationship, this partnership, and that you are truly not alone."

19. _____

Ingrid: "I don't trust her. She has taught me not to trust her."

Therapist: "It is so hard to even begin to trust her—you have been so disappointed in the past, that has really hurt, yes? I wonder if Frances has any idea how hurt you feel. I would expect that she doesn't know."

20. _____   _____

Ingrid: "She doesn't want to know, she just shuts me down."

Therapist: "It's hard to think that she would even want to know how hurt you are, especially when the cycle takes over because all you see is Frances going away and not being there for you."

21. _____   _____

Ingrid: (starting to cry) "I can't depend on her. She's not there. I feel so alone."

Therapist: "What are you feeling, Frances? The look on your face looks like this bothers you to see Ingrid in such pain."

22. _____

Frances: "Well, it hurts. I don't want to see her so hurt."

Therapist: "Can you tell her that?"

23. _____

Frances: "I don't want you to feel so hurt. You've got to give me a chance. I am trying. I move away when I feel hopeless, like I'll never please you."

Ingrid: (looking intently at Frances) "I don't know if you can."

Therapist: "But Frances is here, and so are you, Ingrid, and you both are trying and struggling, the cycle pushes you apart and doesn't let you see each other but I get a sense that you both want the same thing, to be close and be there for each other—yes?"

24. _____

Frances: "I am trying. I will try."

Ingrid: "We have to make time for each other. I don't want you to feel useless."

Therapist: "Time is important, but it seems like the cycle convinces you that you really aren't there for each other. But what you did tonight with Ingrid sharing a bit of her hurt and Frances seeing that and Frances being more verbal about where she is at. All this helps you Ingrid know more what is going on with her. I would expect it helps you to be able to see a bit of what is happening for her. That was great guys; you really worked hard tonight and took some risks, which isn't easy."

25. _____   _____

Exercise 4:

Now take the example of Ingrid and Frances and diagram this couple's cycle. Name the position that each person typically takes in a conflict. Draw an arrow to indicate whether the person's position typically involves pursuit or withdraw. Then identify the secondary and primary emotions that relate to their experience.

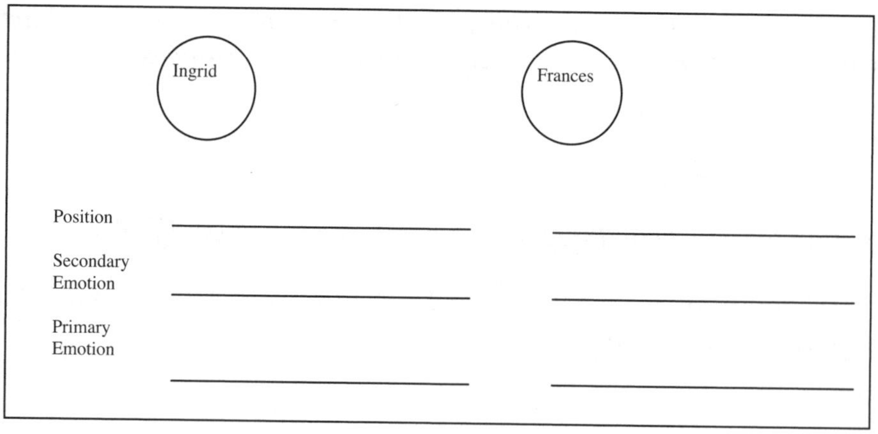

Figure 5.2   Exercise 4

Exercise 5:

Now imagine a couple that has a pursuit and withdraw pattern in their relationship. The pattern is often triggered by conflicts the couple has over leisure time. Sean experiences Lynn's efforts to arrange joint activities as controlling and invasive and Lynn finds his desire for personal time and solitude rejecting. Sean complains that she is dependent on him and Lynn claims that he is selfish and only interested in himself, not their relationship.

1. How does Sean see her as the problem in their relationship? Finish the following sentence using words that he might use. (See Table 5.1 for ideas.) "Things would be better between us if she would just..." _____

   _____

2. What secondary emotions might you expect Lynn to have in response? _____

   _____

3. Now match the secondary emotion to a possible underlying emotion Lynn might be experiencing, perhaps out of her awareness. (Refer to Table 5.2 for ideas.) _____

   _____

4. Is Lynn in the pursuer, attacker, or withdrawer position in this interaction? _____

   _____

5. Now ask, how does Lynn see Sean as the problem in their relationship? Finish the following sentence using words that she might use. (See Table 5.1 for ideas.) "Things would be better between us if he would just..." _____

   _____

6. What secondary emotions would you expect him to have? _____

   _____

7. Now match the secondary emotion to a possible underlying emotion Sean might be experiencing, perhaps out of his awareness. (See Table 5.2 for ideas.) _____

    _____

8. Is Sean in the pursuer, attacker, or withdrawer position in this interaction? _____

    _____

Exercise 6:

Bob and Sharon frequently argue about the couple's financial struggles. Both agreed that Sharon would manage the family finances. Bob is critical of Sharon's approach to handling the money and frequently challenges her decisions. Sharon experiences Bob as critical and hostile about finances, but otherwise disengaged in their relationship. The therapist has helped the couple identify a common pattern where Bob criticizes Sharon's financial decision making, and she responds with defensive silence and then later cross complains about his lack of commitment to the family. Then Bob backs away further and she escalates her efforts to get him to respond. He retaliates by blaming her for the family's financial problems, saying in the end that it is simply "All her fault, and she can't handle that." In replaying a recent argument Sharon said

"I just get so frustrated that he asks me to pay a bill and then he is relentless in checking to see if I have paid it. It doesn't matter if I say I will pay it, he is after me till I pay it. But if I ask him for help around the house, I am 'nagging' and 'insensitive to the demands of his work.' I am sick of him expecting me to do what he says, and him not caring a bit about what I want, or what I need. He can be a jerk sometimes."

Now as the therapist, follow the process of de-escalation. First reflect Sharon's secondary emotion and then validate Sharon's present experience.

1. As the therapist, write a statement using Sharon's comments above that will reflect her secondary emotion including a statement validating her experience within the cycle. _____

    _____

As the therapist engages Sharon's anger further she notices Bob turning away and closing off from the conversation. He folds his arms and looks at the floor.

2. Now as the therapist, how would you bring Bob's emotional experience into the room? Form an evocative question that will help Bob connect his withdrawn posture to his emotional experience in the couple's cycle. _____

    _____

Next, the therapist works to engage the underlying experience of each partner.

3. Using reflecting underlying emotions how would you invite Bob and Sharon to connect to their secondary emotions in the cycle? _____

_____

Now imagine Sharon responds: "Yeah, I just want him to stop. To look at me. To see me, not the checkbook. Why can't he see it? He just doesn't get it. His money is more important than me."

4. What is her underlying primary emotion? _____

5. Put into words how you would reflect her emotional experience focusing on her underlying emotion framing this reflection in the context of the cycle. _____

_____

Bob responds: "I just don't know what to do with all her anger. It is just too much and she seems to take all this so personally. Frankly, it confuses me why she responds this way and I don't know how to make it better, or to convince her otherwise."

6. What is Bob's underlying emotion? _____

_____

7. Put into words how you would reflect Bob's emotional experience focusing on his underlying emotion framing this reflection in the context of the cycle. _____

_____

Bob agrees and opens up further to his fear. As he talks he shifts the conversation from his fear in the relationship to his fear that Sharon will make poor financial decisions and that he can't rely on her at this point.

8. What would you say to Bob to help him refocus on his fear and vulnerability?

_____

9. What would you say to Sharon if she responded to Bob's vulnerability by dismissing his fear by saying: "Yes we have missed a few payments, but we have never been in real financial trouble." What would you say to Sharon to help her refocus on her hurt?

_____

Exercise 7:

Once the therapist refocuses the couple, the therapist returns to describe the couple's cycle and their positions in the cycle. Follow the therapist's framing of the cycle and then answer the questions.

Therapist: "So when this argument gets going, Bob, you raise concern about how Sharon is handling the money, and she hears you being critical, like you don't trust

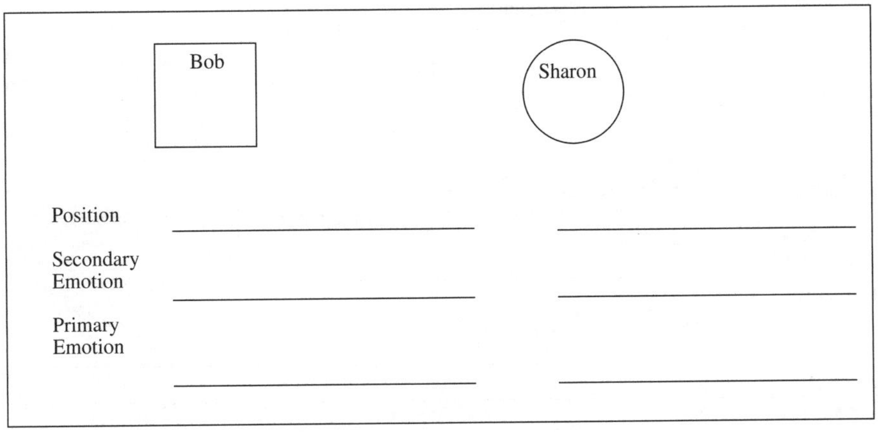

Figure 5.3   Exercise 7

her. And then Sharon you respond to his questions, by telling him that things are okay, and he need not worry. Bob, you hear her dismissing your concern and find ways to support your concern by bringing up past problems. Then Sharon feels attacked and responds by questioning whether you care more about her or the money. Bob, you then back away not knowing how to respond to her anger, and Sharon you find yourself even more upset because he doesn't seem to care because he is not responding and you use more anger and sharper words to get his attention. This goes on until Bob blows his silence, saying that he wants to give up because he doesn't know how to talk to you and Sharon you leave feeling like he has given up. Is that it?"

Bob: "Yeah, that's it, I mean I don't want it to go that way, but that is what happens."

Sharon: "Sometimes it just feels out of control, like we end up in the same place no matter how hard we try to avoid it."

Therapist: "So this cycle, this dance you get caught in pulls you both apart and leaves you confused, frustrated, and alone. And I get the sense that you both are looking for something else, someway to do this together, not alone, to not be divided by this cycle."

Use Figure 5.3 to identify the various elements of Bob and Sharon's cycle. Review the therapist's comments above to describe the couple's process. Name the position that each person typically takes in a conflict. Then identify the secondary and underlying emotions that relate to their experience.

Exercise 8:

Now return to the example of Inez and Fernando as they entered therapy, which is described in the previous chapter. Name the position that each person typically takes in a conflict and place into Figure 5.4. Draw an arrow to indicate whether the person's position typically involves pursuit or withdraw. Then identify the secondary and underlying emotions that relate to their experience.

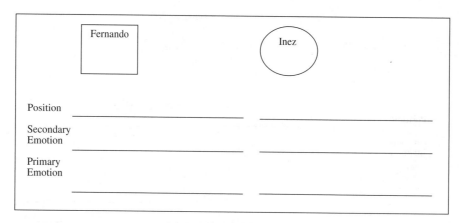

Figure 5.4   Exercise 8

Exercise 9:

Reviewing the couple in this chapter, at this stage in therapy, which of the following best describes their cycle?

a.   Fernando: withdraws; Inez: pursues/criticizes
b.   Fernando: pursues; Inez: pursues/criticizes
c.   Fernando: withdraws; Inez: withdraws
d.   Fernando: pursues; Inez: withdraws
e.   The couple's cycle is no longer evident at this stage of de-escalation.

Homework assignments for Steps 1 through 4, and also for Stage 2 of EFT, Steps 5 through 7, and Stage 3, Steps 8 and 9, can be found in Appendix F.

6

STEPS 5 AND 6:
EXPANDING AND
HEIGHTENING EMOTION

This chapter will present the first steps in Stage 2 of EFT, Step 5 and Step 6. Step 5 offers the most intensely intrapsychic step of EFT. The therapist will promote the engagement with unformulated or disowned attachment emotions—needs and fears—and help the couple express these emotions to each other. Step 6 consists of helping partners accept each other's "new" emotional experiences and so expand the way they see, define, and respond to the other. These two steps lead into the key change events that occur in Step 7, withdrawer reengagement and blamer softening, that will restructure the attachment bond between partners.

In the seventh session Inez related some incidents where Fernando had dismissed and hurt her (Inez, the more withdrawn partner, is becoming more engaged and opening up). When the therapist validated Inez' feelings of anger Fernando stood up to leave the session, saying: "This isn't working and I'm not going to sit here and listen to you two gang up on me." The therapist focused on process, and described how this was the point in the cycle in which Fernando felt hurt and typically withdrew. She asked Fernando if he could take the risk of staying and talking about the hurt. Fernando agreed to sit down and stay. He then began to take risks and the therapy process entered Step 5. With the therapist's help and support, he described his anxiety and owned feeling that he was inadequate, even as he compared himself with Inez whom he saw as immensely strong. He told her that he realized that he did indeed put her down, and this was because he felt so bad about himself. He then described the extreme difficulty he had at work. He explained that, when he brushed past Inez at the end of the day and went down to the basement, he went there to try to compose himself before facing his family. He would sit by his workbench and try to soothe himself, "putting back the armour that got stripped off that day at work."

Inez was amazed by this revelation. She had known that he was having a rough time at work, but never realized the extent of his distress. When Jane asked her how it was to hear this, she replied: "I always wanted to be there for him but he never let me in." The therapist processed with Inez (Step 6) how painful it had been for her to feel shut out for so long, and supported Inez to tell Fernando: "I'm too angry right now to hear the risk you are taking today." At the end of the session, Fernando nonetheless took Inez in his arms and hugged her and told he loved her.

In the next session, Fernando and Inez reported that day-to-day interactions were much calmer. They had started walking Max the dog together, and they were even going to bed at the same time. But, in session 9, Inez complained that Fernando had been really irritable all week. Jane explored this with Fernando.

STEP 5

Fernando: "Well I try things and they don't work. I put on a special supper for her on Thursday. Candles on the table—the whole nine yards, and she didn't show up. When she did come home she didn't even notice the candles."

Inez: (giggles) "Come on Fernando. I had no idea you were cooking that night. I stopped in at the drug store on my way home, and I took ages, that's all." (still giggling, to Jane) "I go into a trance in drug stores. Don't know why—I can spend hours in there looking at all the stuff."

Therapist: "Yes, I understand that one, it has happened to me. But it was very disappointing for you, Fernando?"

Fernando: "Well yes! Of course! I went to so much trouble; it was roast chicken and all the trimmings. I had it all ready, waiting and waiting. The food's overcooked and still she doesn't come home. I was livid."

Therapist: "Livid and disappointed, yes? So how did that go between you?"

Fernando: "Well it didn't go, did it? I spent the evening on my computer."

Inez: "And the rest of the week. I have hardly seen you, and when I do you've been irritable, snapping."

Therapist: "Sounds a bit like the old pattern happening here. That you've felt hurt, Fernando, and you've been withdrawn, protecting yourself?"

Fernando: "Well, I've really been trying to make this work. I'm helping her more, I cook special dinners. I ask her if she needs help, but it doesn't make a difference. She's still out all the time. Out with her friends, doing her bloody cross-stitching, off here off there…"

Inez: "Well, I do what I want to do. You should be happy for me."

Fernando: "But you're never home with me."

Inez: "Why should I when you're always on the computer?"

Fernando: "But Inez! I'm trying to change. I want you to change, too."

Inez: (Her forehead creases, and she looks down at her fingers, which are once again tightly entwined.) "I'm not doing very well these days. I'm still depressed."

Therapist: "What's happening for you right now, Inez? When Fernando said to you, 'I'm changing I want you to change'—what happens for you?"

Inez: "I feel depressed."

Therapist: "You feel depressed when he says he wants you to change? I don't understand."

Inez: (looks down at her hands, which are now clenched tightly together, and tightens her mouth)

Therapist: "I might be wrong here, Inez, but...your face looks really tight and you're clenching your hands so tightly...am I picking up some anger here?"

Inez: (long pause, compresses her lips) "No, it's just..." (sighs) "Yes, yes I am. I'm angry. I'm mad." (Turns to face Fernando) "I quit my choir because you retired and finally you had time for me in your life. So I quit. I loved that choir. But I quit for you. Pretty nice of me, considering. Pretty nice! So what happened? What did you do? You got involved in that convention and I didn't see you for six months. That's what happened."

Fernando: "But it's finished now."

Inez: "Exactly my point. Now you have nothing better in your life you want me. There have been years—years!—Fernando, that I've needed you to be there. Remember when Angela had her appendix out? I was so frightened. I needed you. You told me you had more important things to worry about. You told me not to bother you."

Therapist: "Sounds like that was a pivotal time for you, Inez, that you needed him."

Inez: "He wasn't there for me for years. I learned I am on my own. I have to do life alone. Make decisions, work through whatever crises come along. What I needed was never important. Now you are mad at me for being late for a meal. That's not fair! Why should I be there for you when you haven't been there for 20 years?"

(Inez begins to cry and Fernando, who is very pale, looks at Jane)

Therapist: (soothing manner; to Inez) "And that's been very painful for you?"

Inez: (nods) "I feel like I don't count. I'm not important."

Therapist: "Not important, even in your own family you don't count." (heightening primary emotion)

Inez: (sobs)

Therapist: "What's that like for you, Inez, so alone."

Inez: "It hurts. I felt very low...very sad." (Inez dabs at her eyes with a tissue) "The kids and I met him at the airport once, and he ran and hugged the kids...he...he never even said hello to me." (turns to Fernando) "You just ignored me like you always do!"

Therapist: "You sound angry again, now. That feels better than feeling the sadness?"

Inez: (smiles weakly) "Yes, I...I guess I turn into the puffer fish. It's safer than feeling so puny and sad."

Therapist: "And what happens to the sadness?"

Inez: "It's so pathetic."

Therapist: "It's pathetic to feel sad...What might happen if you let yourself feel the sadness?"

Inez: (begins to cry again) "What's wrong with me? I'm always the one on the outside. Even at home when I was a kid."

Therapist: (RISSSC manner) "All your life it's been like that. Never getting the message that you're precious and you count, wondering if there's something wrong with you." *(heightening)*

Inez: (nods, weeping; covers her face with her hands) "Feel like no one could ever love me."

The therapist then explores Inez' feelings of being unlovable and not important, both to her mother and in her relationship with Fernando. Together they describe how, to avoid her own fears and her sadness she "puffed" into anger and withdrew from Fernando. The therapist also validates Fernando for staying and listening to his wife's anger, noting he had threatened to leave in an earlier session when his wife voiced negative feelings about him.

STEP 6

Therapist: (turns to Fernando) "What's happening for you, Fernando, as Inez tells how sad she's been feeling inside?"

Fernando: (very small voice) "Right now, I want to go away and hide."

Therapist: "This is hard for you. What is it, Fernando, what is happening for you?"

Fernando: "I feel like a crumb. Like I failed. When she puts it like that, it sounds bad...sounds like...I was an ass. She is very precious to me."

Therapist: "Can you tell her that?"

Fernando: (looks at his wife) "I had no idea you felt like this. I just want to take you in my arms and hold you. (Inez raises her eyes and looks at her husband) It's amazing how alike we are. I—I never realized. Both so wounded. I always saw you as invincible. So strong you didn't really need me." *(He pauses, leans over and touches Inez' knee.)* "You are incredibly lovable to me. Now I can see a role for me here."

In the preceding transcript, you see both Inez, the person who usually takes the withdrawn position, and Fernando, the now more pursuing and critical partner, accessing, engaging with, and exploring primary emotions. This is usual in terms of the process of beginning Stage 2 in EFT. Inez accesses underlying anger and Fernando begins to access the fear and a sense of anxiety/shame that cues his critical responses to his wife. Inez is able to clearly crystallize her primary attachment emotion as rage at being "shut out for so long."

In the next session, Fernando describes trying to please his wife, being hurt and then withdrawing, since she does not respond to his attempts to "change" and be more engaged in the relationship. The therapist follows both partner's emotions but then stays with and expands Inez's responses. It is usual in EFT to emphasize bringing the more withdrawn partner out at the beginning of Stage 2. Inez moves from "depression" to anger/rage and then on to a sense of abandonment and a description of a possible attachment injury (namely that he was distant when their child was operated on), in which this sense of abandonment was particularly poignant. She then tells us her core conclusion regarding the security of the attachment bond to her partner. She says, "I don't count. I am not important." Bowlby might see Inez' words as her statement of her working model of other—her spouse is not to be relied on. She then expands this core emotion with the words, "alone" and "sad." The image of a "puffer fish" beautifully captures her attempts to cope with these vulnerable feelings. This image encapsulates her vulnerability and her coping response and can be used again and again by the therapist as a fast entry into her experience. The therapist then helps her reach even deeper to a sense of grief and fear that she may be unlovable. The core attachment emotions—that always include a statement about self and the model of self that is cued in close relationships—are now stated and experienced.

The therapist then focuses on helping Fernando hear his wife's emotion. He is quite open and responsive (which is not always the case at this point) and does not deny or dismiss her pain as some partners do. He is able then, at the therapist's prompting, to stay engaged and responsive and to tell her how he never grasped her vulnerability and that she is precious to him. The stage is now set for her to move into Step 7 where she can state the needs and wants in a way that maximizes Fernando's ability to respond to her.

This chapter focuses on the beginning of Stage 2 in EFT. The couple are de-escalated at this point and can cooperate and exit from their negative cycles of interaction. Now begins the task of deepening trust and building a more secure bond. Steps 5 and 6 involve the owning and integration of attachment needs and fears and promoting the acceptance of these needs and fears by the other spouse. This process then sets the stage for the key change events of Step 7 where withdrawers become reengaged and more blaming partners soften and ask for their attachment needs to be met, so that new bonding events can occur.

The focus of intervention, which up to this point has been on both partners, now shifts slightly so that interventions are directed more towards one partner than the other. The EFT therapist focuses on encouraging the more withdrawn partner to own attachment needs and fears more deeply, so to be able to move into Step 7. In this step he/she becomes more accessible and responsive, before the therapist then goes back and moves through this process again with the more blaming partner. It is a mistake to ask the more blaming partner to take the considerable emotional risk involved in asking for attachment needs to be met before the other partner has re-engaged and is likely to be accessible and responsive. If both partners are withdrawn, we usually go for the most accessible partner first. In relatively nondistressed couples who do have the elements of a secure bond, both partners tend to respond to intervention in a reciprocal manner so that this "withdrawer goes a few steps ahead on the dance floor" phenomenon is minimal.

Steps 5 and 6 are set out as sequential, in fact, like the other steps, they are a reciprocal circular process. In this process, one person touches an experience and shares a little of it; perhaps the other then blocks the shared message or even responds negatively, or struggles to accept it; the sharing spouse then elaborates more on his/her experience, while the other again struggles to let it in and integrate this new experience of their partner into their own world.

The essential goals of this part of EFT are:

- The therapist helps partners to increase awareness of, engagement with, and ownership of the attachment vulnerabilities, hurts, and fears that have been touched and named in Stage 1. <u>A new level of engagement in and delineation of these key emotions then sets the stage for a new level of engagement with the partner. This goal is called the "3 Ds": deepen, distill, disclose.</u>

- The therapist helps the other partner to hear and accept these fears and hurts. This often involves a considerable shift in perception. This goal is labeled as accept/acknowledge.

It is important to note that the therapist works to enable clients to maintain engagement with hurts and fears until they are tangible and clear enough to evoke a sense of need and "move" the client towards a new way of communicating these longings and needs in Step 7. As emotions deepen, longings and desires become more and more clear and compelling and can then, with the therapist's support, be asserted in a positive way that enables the other partner to respond.

Key Moves in the Process

How does the drama of Step 5 and 6 unfold? What does it look like? What are the key tasks that present themselves to the therapist?

The key moves in the drama might appear as follows:

1. There is more safety in relationship at this point, and both partners can pinpoint the underlying feelings identified in Step 3 and place them in the negative cycle that has taken over their relationship. Both can also begin to confide to the therapist about the attachment fears, hurts, and losses that result when the cycle is in full swing. The time has come to move into Stage 2, helping the couple move into deeper connection with their own emotions, needs, and with their partner.

   Main task: to ensure that de-escalation is in place and to begin deepening engagement with the emotions identified in Step 3 (unfolding underlying feelings) in both partners but with more initial focus on the withdrawn partner. At the risk of creating opposing metaphors, EFT speaks of the therapist heightening and developing underlying primary emotions in order to deepen each client's engagement with these emotions.

2. The partners, especially the more-withdrawn partner, begin to elaborate on their emotional reality in the relationship. The withdrawer gradually becomes more and more open to and immersed in his emotional experience. He is also able to begin to confide some of this experience to his partner in enactments, when asked to by the therapist. As emotions are elaborated and distilled, the associated cognitive models about the value of the self and the trustworthiness of the other become clear. The link between key attachment emotions and the key moves this client makes in the relationship dance also become clearer and clearer. Most often, the emotions that emerge here are fear, helplessness, despair, and shame—unworthiness of self.

   Main task: beginning to deepen emotional engagement and distilling attachment emotions. Integrating them with models of self and other and placing them in an attachment frame.

3. The more-withdrawn partner is able to distill the key emotional reality he or she lives with in the negative relationship dance. This reality crystallizes and "comes to the boil" as this person's engagement in it becomes intense. The experience is owned and its impact is felt. As emotional pain is clarified, its meaning becomes clear and concomitant needs begin to emerge. These can then be used to create enactments in the Step 7 change event, withdrawer reengagement.

   Main task: deepening active engagement with key emotions.

4. The other partner is able to hear and accept the more-withdrawn partner's "new" emotions, or actively resists and denies them. If acceptance is apparent, the therapist can validate this and explore its implications. If, as is more common, acceptance is difficult, then the therapist explores blocks and issues with this more-blaming client. Acceptance can be blocked by confusion, disorientation, anger, or fear.

> Main task: Tracking and blocking negative responses to the more engaged partner and facilitating acceptance and acknowledgment of other's emerging experience so that a Step 7 enactment is possible.

5. Once the withdrawer has moved into Step 7 and has become more accessible and responsive, the therapist then goes back and completes the Step 5 deepening and distilling of emotion with the other more-blaming client.

> Main task: as above.

6. The therapist assists the other once withdrawn spouse to stay engaged and responsive and aids the more-blaming spouse to own his/her key emotions and to become clear about needs and demands. These are then used to create enactments in Step 7 with this client.

> Main task: as above.

7. The therapist now supports the previously withdrawn spouse to accept the "new" emotions presented by this spouse. The second time through Step 6, with the previously withdrawn spouse, is usually easier than the first time. However, the therapist still works with any issues that block this spouse from taking in the new, more elaborated emotional responses of the other partner.

> Main task: as above.

The Client Process

If translated into key client statements to help you "see" the flow of the process, it might look like the following: (W stands for withdrawer, B stands for the more pursuing, blaming partner).

W: *"Seems like we are getting along better, and it feels a little safer between us."* (his wife nods her head in agreement) *"But it still feels like the deeper issues are kind of still there."* (de-escalation is apparent) *"I see how my shutting down leaves her alone—guess I just get scared. Can't stand to see that look."* (specifies cue for painful emotion) *"I go all hot* (specifies body response) *and I want to move away."* (action response cued by emotion) *"How can I tell you?"* (to wife)

B: *"I just want you to get how distant and difficult you have been for me."* (she stays with her anxiety to be heard; does not respond to his new message)

W: *"I put up a wall. I know I will hear how hopeless I am."* (emotional meaning frame for self and relationship becomes clearer) *"I never really understood why you married me. When I see that look on your face I get that I am a big fat zero to you, failed again. I just don't know how to do this. God, that hurts."* (weeps; intense engagement in emotional moment)

B: *"I never knew you felt that way— I didn't get it. I get so caught up in my own pain."* (begins to accept and process his new response and its attachment significance) *"I never knew my caring meant that much to you."*

W: "I feel lonely too, you know. I don't want to hide all the time, tired of feeling small but not sure I can ever ask." (new emotion begins to move him into a recognition of needs and sets up a move into Step 7)

B: "I never knew you struggled like this, that you were lonely too." (accepts and responds to new steps of spouse)

Exercise 1:

Place yourself in the role of the therapist in the above session, given that this is a synopsis of key statements and the process is seldom as clear, focused, and concise. It usually evolves with interruptions, stories, content issues, etc. How would you respond to some of these statements to keep the process moving forward? You can compare your response with the example in the answer section.

Key Interventions

Reflection and validation of inner and interpersonal responses are constants in EFT. In Steps 5 and 6, however, certain interventions are used more often or more intensely. The key aspect of Step 5 is the deepening engagement with and distilling of attachment hurts, fears, and longings. Evocative responding, heightening, and empathic conjecture/interpretation are particularly crucial here.

It is also essential that these interventions be conducted with RISSSC in mind. In Step 5, the therapist tries to use simple but vivid, concrete language—images and repetition to help clients not only step into but also stay with, explore, and live out of their experience rather than name it or discuss it from a distance. As clients' engagement in their experiences deepens, this experience evolves into new forms. In Step 5, experience is discovered as new rather than emerging fully formulated.

Exercise 2:

Both client's emotions and their interactions are always addressed in every EFT session, but in the beginning of Stage 2, the therapist first particularly emphasizes and helps to deepen engagement with which partner's underlying emotions?

Exercise 3:

1. Why is the manner (RISSSC) in which the therapist conducts interventions particularly important in Step 5?
    a. The client is risking more by engaging with difficult/unclear emotion—needs focus and safety. _____
    b. The therapist is encouraging deeper experiential engagement so needs slow pace, soft voice, repetition, etc. _____
    c. Research shows that focused low voice encourages emotional processing._____
    d. Research says that imagery elicits physiological responses when abstract words do not. _____

2. What are the emotions that usually emerge and deepen in Step 5?
   a. Attachment vulnerabilities, hurts, and fears. _____
   b. Grief/sadness and shame also can emerge. _____
   c. In trauma survivor's relationships, shame—a sense of contamination or unlovable-ness—nearly always emerges. _____
   d. Core primary emotions that involve existential issues such as aloneness and helplessness. _____
   e. Emotions concerning connection with the other—such as fears of loss and abandon-ment. _____
   f. Fears and shame about the nature of self. "I am lovable and acceptable"/ "I am inadequate/a failure." _____

Exercise 4:

Step 5 can be described as: (check the two correct answers)

a. The most intensely intrapsychic step in the EFT process. _____
b. A recap and intellectual synopsis of Step 3. _____
c. A time of discovery about one's own often unformulated attachment vulnerabilities.
   _____
d. An invitation into insight. _____

Example:

Client (stays distant, intellectual) "More general discussions are preferred. We try to put the disturbing emotion aside."

Therapist (uses concrete, vivid words) "You stay away. You don't let those feelings in?"

Exercise 5:

In the deepen, distill, and disclose phase, the therapist's language can mean the difference between intellectualizing and distancing or deeper experiencing. Language should be simple, concrete, and vivid, for example, "shut down," "shut out." Take the client words or phrases below and make them more vivid. Action words and images should be used whenever possible. Then compare your answers with those given in the answers section.

1. Client: "It is normal for me to be cautious, not disclose except when necessary. I think it is a natural, mature kind of tendency."

   Therapist: _____

2. Client: "I guess I do have a slight tendency to anticipate that she will criticize me, and perhaps I do expect the worst and try to attack first."

   Therapist: _____

3. Client: "Now he is interested!! After all this time. That is a little incongruous, don't you think? And now, after years of accommodating, I am to be the great communicator!!"

   Therapist: _____

4. Underline the phrases in the responses you gave above that might be more impactful if you used a soft, slow voice.

Exercise 6: Opening the Door to Stage 2 Primary Emotions

A very intellectual and withdrawn partner, Louis, who had asked for a divorce but has touched and named a sense of helplessness and failure in Step 3 and has, in Step 4, agreed that now he and his wife are friends. He adds that they are not close, and now begins in a calm distant manner:

"We have been together for so long. But things have eroded over the years. I am fond of her. I am perhaps uncertain of my commitment, so I cannot really talk about the future with any clarity. We have civil conversations now, but then there are moments when she seems difficult, so I am unsure as to my way here." (He rubs his hand furiously against his leg for a moment.) *"I have spoken before about always having to meet her demands and being tested. I feel quite detached. I'd feel more freedom perhaps if I did leave."*

Check the responses an EFT therapist might make to help this man begin the process of becoming more engaged with his emotional experience and distill the key parts of it. Check the responses that help to make his experience more concrete, specific, immediate, and tangible. If you wish you can also name the interventions that you check as appropriate:

a. "You are friends; you are civil. But you are still feeling quite 'detached' and 'uncertain.' How are you feeling as you say this, Louis? You seem a long way away." _____

b. "Yes, I remember you speaking of demands and feeling tested, with some pain, if I am remembering properly. How do you feel now as you talk about these things?" _____

c. "Could you help me understand 'difficult?' What does that look like? When did you see your partner that way this week? If I understand, these difficult moments bring up uncertainties in you, yes?" _____

d. "On a scale of 1 to 10, can you tell me how difficult you experience your spouse being this week?" _____

e. "Perhaps we can problem solve and see how you can feel more free with your wife." _____

f. "I notice as you speak in this detached way, Louis, especially as you speak of being 'unsure,' you rub your hand very hard against your leg. I was caught by that. The rubbing seemed very agitated, not so detached?" _____

g. "What happens in your body as you speak of being uncertain, unsure, tested?" _____

h. "Looking at the patterns in your family of origin, does this impact how you see this, do you think?" _____

Exercise 7:

These responses are also appropriate. Can you name them?

a. "What do you want to do when your wife gets 'difficult,' as you see it? What do you want to do when you feel uncertain as you seem to do right now?" (focus on action tendency) "Some part of you feels 'fond' and 'civil,' but some part of you says what? Better to stay away, keep your distance?" _____

b. "Could you help me? The word 'freedom' seems a little abstract. What would that feel like? Free from what?" _____

c. "The word 'detached' hits me. You seem to have become less and less detached over our sessions. You came in speaking of leaving the relationship. What does detached sound like? Is it like 'I have given up. Maybe it's safer to shut down and not want anything.' Or is it like 'She is too much for me. I can't make it with her, I am too hurt and afraid'? Not sure." (focus on reappraisal, meaning) _____

d. "It is so hard for you, Louis, to feel sure of yourself, not to begin to be worried about meeting her demands when, even if things have improved, there are moments when your partner seems 'difficult.'" (could also ask him to tell her this) _____

e. "Could you help me, Louis? I am remembering you talking briefly about a sense of failure in our last sessions. Is the 'uncertainty' about that? Is it like 'I will never make it with her, never pass her tests. It's hopeless, might as well give up.' Is it like that?" _____

Exercise 8: Deepening Engagement in Key Elements of Experience

In response to the above interventions, Louis agrees that he "detaches" (active-owned frame for this response; it does not happen to him) when he begins to feel "tested" and is "hypervigilant" for any sign of being judged. How might the therapist deepen and distill the attachment significance of this? Check the responses below that you think the therapist might use. If it is useful, you can also name the interventions.

Louis: "Well, it's test, test, test." (he jabs his hand into his other palm) "So, heh, I guess I get to—lets take stock here—not sure its good to walk back in. There is uncertainty, sure."

a. "Ah-ha. You have reservations. You find it so very painful to be 'tested' and not pass the tests?" (he nods) "Can you actually say that—speak it—that you find it painful to always be expecting to be tested and to 'know' that you will fail, you will not pass? It is hopeless, so you are helpless, yes?" _____

b. "What happens to you as you say 'test, test, test' and jab your hand? It almost seemed like an angry motion, is that right?" _____

c. "I think you said, 'It's not good to walk back in'…it's 'uncertain,' almost dangerous, is that it? Much too scary?" _____

d. "It must feel awful to begin to feel calmer and more civil and then to suddenly remember that there will be tests and you will not pass—that is very hard?" _____

e. "When you say that to yourself, 'Here we go again, another test,' and that sense of failure comes up, what happens? How do you deal with it?" _____

f. "Does it feel better—more powerful, less hopeless—to say to yourself, 'I don't have to stay'? It's the only way out of that pain and fear?" _____

g. "To be tested and to know for certain that you won't pass, you will fail, you will disappoint your wife—how does that feel for you? Can you let yourself feel what that is like for you?" _____

Exercise 9:

In response to the above interventions, Louis states that sometimes leaving seems best—and that he feels angry for a moment but mostly he feels "small" when he realizes that he will inevitably fail the test. Check the responses the EFT therapist might make to deepen his experience. It is useful to think of going over and over an experience to develop it, much as you put a photo into a tray of developing fluid over and over again until the picture becomes more defined.

a. (in soft, low voice) "You feel small—small—how do you say this—that in this relationship you are often suddenly 'small,' powerless?" _____

b. "Is that 'small' like 'not strong,' 'not competent,' kind of helpless/hopeless, kind of vulnerable?" _____

c. "You will fail—that must be so painful, you will never make it with your wife. So you detach, tell yourself you could leave? But in fact you are here working on the relationship, trying. What words would you give to that pain when you 'know,' once again, you try, but will be tested and fail?" _____

d. "Does this remind you of times when you were growing up, Louis? This is how you felt at home with those you needed, isn't it? This is a carryover from the past."

_____

Exercise 10:

Louis then says, with tears in his eyes: "It hurts—scary to fail." He uses a pushing-away motion with his hand. Check the most likely responses used to deepen his emotional experience further. (four correct responses)

a. "And when you feel that way—small, failed, hurt—that is scary—very scary. There is nothing you can do, nothing will work. Is that like: you have lost her already? You are helpless here?" _____

b. "Am I hearing: you get so hurt, you are afraid that you will never be 'good enough,' so you try to not want, to not care? Because it is so painful to try, to try to pass the test?" _____

c. "It's too scary to keep on trying to get her love, her caring, acceptance. Sometimes it feels better to give up, to shut down, to talk of leaving, yes?" _____

d. "Scary like you will never get her love, it's lost? Or perhaps scary like you are just not enough, not good enough, not lovable enough somehow? Is that it?" _____

e. "Do you see how your inability to stand up to her and tell her not to test you keeps you both in this impossible position?" _____

Exercise 11:

Louis: "I cannot bear to feel so small, so useless. I feel so worthless...can't make it with you. It seems easier to shut down and give up."

When Louis has been able to piece together his core emotional experience and how he now tries to deal with it (which ties into his stance in the marital cycle, his withdrawn detachment, and his threats to leave), and owns and experiences it, the therapist then moves to disclosure to the spouse. The EFT therapist might then say: (check the response that does NOT apply)

a. "So can you tell her, directly and assertively, 'It's too hard trying to pass the tests. If you cannot be less demanding, I will have to leave'?"

b. "Can you tell her, Louis, can you look at her and tell her, 'I get so despairing of ever doing it right, passing the test. I get so defeated and hopeless, feel like such a failure, that I can't bear it—the hurt, the hopelessness. So I try to let go, give up, not care so much.' Can you tell her?"

c. "So can you risk sharing with her, Louis? Can you tell her, 'I start to give up, not because I don't care but because I feel so defeated, so uncertain of ever being able to please you I can't bear it'?"

d. (If Louis cannot seem to risk, and so avoids this disclosure) "Can you tell her, 'It is too hard. I can't look at you and tell you these feelings. I am too unsure, uncertain'?"

Exercise 12:

The therapist in the above interventions goes on a voyage of discovery with the client and tracks, reflects and repeats, evokes and deepens attachment-related emotions. The essence of these emotions is distilled and synthesized into a statement that:

a. Organizes and captures the client's deeper emotions. _____

b. Recognizes the way of coping with these emotions that sets up this client's responses in the couple's negative cycle. _____

c. Meaning of these emotions for the client's sense of connection with the spouse and with his or her own sense of self. _____

The EFT therapist would then take this client into Step 7 enactments where he would encapsulate fears and needs, contact his longings, and ask for his needs to be met. Let us now look at Step 5 process—the deepening, distilling, and disclosing process with a blaming partner.

Example: Client Statement

Colin has become reengaged and told his partner, Harriet, "I feel it when you hurt, I want you to reach for me. I did a rotten job of taking care of you when you got sick. I tried to minimize everything because I got so scared." Harriet who has been diagnosed with chronic fatigue, says to her spouse:

"Well, things are better. You try to listen and accommodate to me." (to the therapist) "He is nicer. He does share more. But the pressure—the pressure to have a kid—is still there. And I still don't think he really sees my hurt, how miserable and lonely I have been the last two years. Perhaps I am just too pathetic. But" (to her partner) "I gave up everything to move here and be with you and got let down. But I am a big girl, independent. I can cope by myself. You promised to cook supper the other night, then when you don't—get home late, well, it seems like a really big thing to me. Maybe I am just an angry person. I put myself in this situation—decided to come here. I have a chip on my shoulder." (She swallows and fights back her tears.)

Exercise 13:

The EFT therapist might make which of the following statements to begin to focus in on, deepen, and distill Harriet's remarks? (All but two of those given below.)

a. "Can you name the main emotion that you feel here and then put it into an 'I' statement to your spouse?" _____

b. "Can you help me, Harriet? I think I hear that part of you says that you should be able to cope alone, and not be so hurt when you feel alone, but part of you is still dealing with feeling let down and abandoned in this relationship?" _____

c. "It's hard for you to think of becoming a mother when you are not sure you can depend on Colin? You need to know that he is there for you?" _____

d. "You got let down—you lost lots when you moved here to be with Colin and you felt let down by him. And little things like him breaking a promise to make supper brings that up for you?" _____

e. "What happens for you, Harriet, when you say, 'I don't think he sees me...I got let down'?" _____

f. "You ask yourself if you are just an angry person, but you talk of being hurt and lonely." _____

g. "Could you help me? What is 'pathetic'? Is that like 'sad' and 'small,' not 'big' and 'independent'?" _____

h. "All your hurt, all that feeling of Colin not being there for you, of you feeling abandoned—all that came up when he disappointed you around the supper?" _____

i. (Focus on the action tendency) "So when all this hurt came up, were you able to tell him, or did he see the 'chip on the shoulder' more?" (This could lead into how her fear of feeling/showing her hurt sparks off the couple's negative cycle.) _____

j. "The anger and the talk about you should be independent is there, but there is also so much hurt, and feeling that, perhaps...perhaps when you need Colin, you will find yourself alone like before?" _____

k. "What happens to you, Harriet, as you say this? I notice you swallow, there are tears, but it's hard for you to just let them show?" _____

l. "Can we put the feelings aside? On a scale of 1 to 10, how important is it that he didn't make supper?" _____

Example: Client Statement

"Yes. Yes, I gave subtle signals about the hurt. It's so pathetic to be so hurt. I try to swallow it, but, there you are, alone again—it's too much."

Exercise 14:

Write out at least six ways that you would deepen and distill (perhaps put in the frame of attachment fears, losses, and needs) Harriet's statement in the example above.

Exercise 15:

Now see if you can write out two responses, using specific interventions, reflection and evocative responding to each of the client statements given below.

a. "I have been able to tell him, under all that criticalness was a lot of hurt and feelings of being all by myself for so long, and bringing up the kids alone, but, I am not even sure how to really talk about that—even now when he is more open, like he is now."

_____

b. "Once you have been let down like I have, well, even when things improve there is a kind of reluctance. You might think of taking a few risks and getting closer, but..."

_____

EFT therapists heighten emotions through techniques such as repetition and the use of imagery, with the intended outcome of deepening the client's engagement in his/her emotions. The goal is to intensify each partner's engagement with and exploration of key attachment emotional experiences. The therapist attempts to help the client add "color" and "shape" to emotional experience so it becomes tangible and can then be grasped and dealt with. People use shorthand labels for complex feelings; the EFT therapist focuses in and walks around with the client in shorthand phrases or labels and attempts to distill the core attachment experience referred to by such phrases.

Example: Client Statement

Sue says: "I was less lonely when I lived alone in the house on Temple Street. Then I didn't expect anything. It was easier to live with. None of this now-you-see-me–now-you-don't stuff."

Exercise 16:

Check the ways that, as an EFT therapist, you might expand and intensify the Step 5 statement in the example above:

1. Repeat key phrases, as: "It's easier to be physically alone than to hope for—expect—closeness and then you have him disappear, as in 'now you see me, now you don't.'"

_____

2. Focus in on a poignant phrase or image—"Now you see me, now you don't"—that captures a partner's experience of relationship distress and develop it by unpacking it, especially using evocative images whenever possible. _____

3. Stay at the unclear edge of an experience and focus on it, using evocative questions and responses to develop it as: "'Now you see me, now you don't'—what is that? Can you help me understand that picture? Is it that he seems like he will be with me, but then he is gone?" _____

4. Evocatively focus on and develop the different elements of the emotion, with questions, evocative responding, and conjectures, as below. _____
    a. "So when do you feel most alone, when is it hardest?" (focusing on the cue for the sense of aloneness/abandonment)
    b. "So how do you feel as you say this right now, that somehow it is like he is not with you ? Where do you feel it in your body?" (focusing on the bodily felt sense)
    c. "So what do you tell yourself when you feel this way?" (focusing on the reappraisal/ meaning making)
    d. "What do you do/want to do when you feel this way?" (focusing on the action tendency)
    e. "So is that the time when you start to grasp for him, try to get his attention, have him become clearer, in the hope that he will respond so you can see him?" (focusing on the consequence/context of experience; link to how the client responds to the other partner. A sense of being alone cues this client to attack and helps maintain the negative cycle with her husband.) _____

5. State the pain in the statement in more vivid obvious terms, a heightening reflection/ conjecture as: "It hurts to hope for closeness, to expect it, and then to have it disappear in a flash—it is there and then it is gone." _____

6. Validate to heighten emotion/deepen engagement: "It must be so hard to expect and have the hope dashed, to see what you long for and have it gone, out of reach." _____

7. Label the client's experience—"You feel loss"—and encourage ventilation to create catharsis. _____

Exercise 17:

Write out one response you might make to Sue's statement (you can use some of the responses given above if you wish) and what you think/hope the client might say next.

_____

_____

Exercise 18:

A withdrawn husband says—in response to his wife commenting that she still might decide to leave him, even though they are getting along better—"There is nothing I can do." Write out at least three responses using one validating reflection and one evocative responding to expand and heighten this remark.

_____

_____

The therapist uses interpretation or conjecture to go just one step ahead of a partner in the elaboration of the nature of an emotional response or the meaning of an experience for the self and how this self responds to the other partner. The therapist uses the framework of the core emotions and of the attachment context to expand or make sense of an experience. Interpretations are always respectful and tentative and are best if kept simple. Even with interpretation, the aim is to engage the client in the experience rather than simply label the experience.

Exercise 19:

A partner says: "I am not sure how I feel. I feel squirmy, uncomfortable." (covers her face and addresses her partner) "Stop looking at me, okay! I think we have to go now."

Write out how you would phrase a conjecture to bring this emotion into the session and clarify it and then compare your version with the answer key in the back.

_____

_____

Which of the six core emotions—joy, surprise, sadness/loss/anguish, rage/anger, fear, and shame—do you think this client is feeling? _____

Exercise 20:

A partner says: "Are you joking? You want me to open up to you at those times. That is wild. I don't think so. Even if I could, it wouldn't go anywhere. I'd get hammered." (very quietly) "I couldn't do it."

Write out how you would phrase a conjecture to bring this emotion into the session and then again compare your version with the one in the answer key.

_____

_____

Which of the six emotions do you think this is client feeling? _____

Example: Client Statement

Sarah: (to her spouse) "You said, in this angry voice, 'For God's sake, don't even think about getting pregnant.'" (she weeps) "And I felt hurt then. You know we can't have another baby and that I did want another one. You know that."

Therapist: "Did you tell him about the hurt feelings?"

Sarah: "No. I shut down. I just went away. Until now. (this is 4 weeks later)

Therapist: "You couldn't tell him about the hurt feelings?"

Sarah: "I can't." (She then launches into a long blaming list of his flaws.)

Therapist: "What would have happened if you had just turned to him and told him you were hurt?"

Sarah: (gasps and weeps) "I don't know. That would be worse—it will be much worse then."

Exercise 21:

Write out a conjecture that you could make to Sarah now using one of the core emotions.

_____

_____

Exercise 22:

Conjectures also link emotional realities to relational moves and patterns. The client, Sarah, says: "It was too much—terrifying." Write out an interpretation that now links her fear to her responses to her spouse.

_____

_____

Exercise 23:

Sarah's partner, Sam, says: "Then she refuses to speak to me, only talks to me about chores and arrangements. So then I get very frustrated. Suddenly I have no wife, but I try to stay calm, even though the door is closed. I try to stay reasonable and talk to her about what is wrong." Write a conjecture linking this partner's emotional experience to his likely responses to his spouse.

_____

_____

Exercise 24:

The last word of the 3 Ds set out at the beginning of this chapter is disclose. Disclosure in enactments is part of the process of restructuring interactions in EFT. It is also a process that deepens and clarifies the experience of emotion. Can you write out how you would set up an enactment, how you would help Sarah disclose to her spouse her emotions as expressed in the answer section in Exercise 21 above.

_____

_____

Exercise 25:

Take the following client statements and write four responses to each one showing how you would intervene to expand and deepen the client's experience using all the interventions referred to above, such as evocative responding, interpretation, and heightening.

(No sample answers are given for this exercise. If you have EFT colleagues, you may want to discuss and evaluate your responses with them.)

a. Morag, the withdrawer in her relationship says: "Well, he is friendlier. We are better. But, there is a, well, a kind of 'let's just wait and see' feeling, if you know what I mean. Better safe than sorry."

b. Peter, the demanding husband says: "It is unpleasant for me when she goes into this distancing thing. I get kind of frazzled" (shakes his hands in the air) "you know. It is not the way marriage is supposed to be."

c. Amy, the withdrawer who is beginning to risk, says: "I don't know how to talk about my needs. Kind of used to putting them to one side. Trying to be a good wife and mother. But then, that doesn't seem to be going so well—not making it on that list am I? Boo-hoo-hoo." (she giggles)

Exercise 25 – part 2:

In Step 5 of EFT, as engagement with underlying core emotions deepens, attachment theory tell us to expect that the process of therapy will extend to an existential level that addresses working models as to the nature of others, the connection to others, and the value of the self. Attachment theory speaks of lack of connection as trauma, isolation as unbearable, and to how the self is defined in interactions with loved ones. Part of the deepening and distilling process is including this existential level in validations and conjectures at this point in therapy. Check the responses that make up these kinds of conjectures in the examples below:

a. "As you say this, Jane, as you shake your head and whisper, 'I just can't let myself feel it, say it, must zone out,' I get the sense that this is a life and death matter for you. Something tells you that you must move away. Perhaps, in another place, it saved your life, being able to move away and 'zone out.' It feels like you must do it, seems like there is no other way, yes?" _____

b. "You speak of feeling upset, but this seems bigger than just upset, yes?" _____

c. "As you say this—as you say, 'I don't know how to let him in,' I get the sense that this really is foreign territory for you. It's like no one has ever been there for you—never. You never have let anyone in, there never has been anyone to really comfort and hold you?" _____

d. "You have never really had anyone to comfort and reassure you, someone who you know keeps you in mind, values you, sees you as precious. You have always had to fight to try to prove to you and everyone else that you were worthy." _____

e. "This discomfort in your chest, is this like a sadness, a grief?" _____

f. "You have never been able to just rest in someone's hands and let them hold you up? You have always had to be on guard, ready to fight. There was no safe place for you, and you long for this?" _____

Exercise 26:

In Step 5, as part of the deepening process the therapist can also self-disclose as a way of leading the client to touch and process a difficult experience. Check the self-disclosures below that fit with the EFT model.

a. "I think it is best if you try again to use softened startup as you tell him your concerns. I might react negatively to your comments as framed." _____

b. "I just get this sense that this is very hard for you right now. As I hear you describe your pain, I too begin to feel sad and a little overwhelmed. This is so hard." _____

c. "You are somehow feeling ashamed, like you should not be afraid of risking with him? I know that for me there are times when I feel afraid of reaching out to my partner, even though I am strong and capable." _____

Exercise 27:

Take any of the chapters on EFT on the EFT Web site or from the reference list in the back of this book and look in the clinical excerpts and case examples. Take one excerpt and discuss the therapist responses from the point of view of Stage 5 processes (that attempt to deepen, distill, and disclose emotion) with a colleague. You can also take the therapist responses and ask yourself what intervention the therapist is using—what is the apparent effect of a particular intervention and how could you improve on it—or offer another alternative intervention.

Exercise 28:

The goal of Step 5 is for clients to reach a poignant, felt, and congruently expressed statement of their underlying primary emotions—usually sadness, fear, and shame—and to connect them to their problematic ways of responding to their spouse. Can you think of a time in your life when you were finally able to formulate your painful emotions to an attachment figure in a way that distilled your experience of this relationship? If so, try to write this down. If not, perhaps you can think of what you might have liked to say to a loved one? Include what you were afraid of in this relationship. The most common fears are

- Fear of being abandoned and alone
- Fear of being unacceptable, unlovable, or unworthy of care and rejected
- Fear of being overwhelmed and helpless, going crazy, losing any coherent sense of self

Exercise 29:

What was it that you needed in that relationship, given that awareness of hurt and pain tells us what we need? If this is hard to formulate, perhaps you can check one or more of the attachment longings/needs listed below:

- The need to know you exist for another, they see and recognize you.
- The need to know you are precious, you count for another.
- The desire to be held and comforted when vulnerable.
- The desire for reassurance, that the other will respond when needed.

STEP 6: FACILITATING ACCEPTANCE

In Step 5, the "observing partner" witnesses the "experiencing partner" express and process his/her emotional experience. These disclosures present new information and, more importantly, a "new way of being" to the other. In Step 6, the therapist helps the observing partner hear and accept these disclosures (the fears and hurts of the other) and then respond. Acceptance involves "letting in" and acknowledging both the experience of the other and the other's confiding. Acceptance involves a shift in perception—"seeing" the other in a different light. Acceptance involves empathically allowing oneself to "feel moved" by the other's experience. So, for example, a spouse who is seen as "distant and cold" by her husband begins to reveal deep shame and fear of feeling exposed. She links this vulnerability to her "distant" stance. Her spouse shakes his head and says, "You have been cold for years. I don't understand what this is all about. I'm not sure I believe what you are saying." The task of the therapist is to help the non-accepting spouse hear, feel, and respond to the disclosures. The therapist first helps unfold the observing partner's reactions and then assists this partner in encountering the other partner through an enactment.

When, in Step 5, the therapist supports and validates the experiencing partner's disclosures, the witnessing partner is often left with a great deal of internal dissonance. The therapist must be mindful about the alliance with each partner and work to repair any rifts by exploring, validating, and processing each partner's reactions. The therapist must be able to support the experiencing partner's disclosures and in turn to support, validate, and process the witnessing partner's reactions.

Following the disclosure of the experiencing partner's underlying feelings, the therapist will typically begin Step 6 by engaging the "observing partner" with a simple question such as: "What happens for you when he says...?" The question should elicit the observing partner's reactions to the disclosures. Basically, there are two possible responses: acceptance or non-acceptance. If the "observing partner" is accepting, the therapist will highlight and reinforce the acceptance and then ask the accepting partner to turn and share the acceptance with the other partner. Validating, reflecting, and heightening are common interventions here. Most importantly, acceptance must be enacted, because the contact creates a powerful reinforcing event.

If the observing partner is not accepting (either being reluctant to accept or rejecting), then the therapist must help this partner process these reactions. Reflecting, validating, evocative responding, heightening, empathic conjectures, and reframing are all used to process non-accepting responses. In addition, the therapist may use enactments to highlight, own, and make more explicit any non-accepting responses. Clearly and explicitly owning a stance of non-acceptance often results in a shift to more acceptance.

The EFT therapist does not see the reluctance to accept as "resistance" but as confusion resulting from viewing their partner out of the realm of their usual experience. The experiencing partner's act of disclosing, itself, presents the observing partner with a new experience of the other. The therapist's empathy for the non-accepting spouse is a key element at this stage in the process. The therapist views the non-accepting spouse's reactions from the viewpoint that their confiding partner has suddenly become a stranger, one whom he doesn't know. The observing partner often needs help to "digest" and shift perception to "accept" the new experience and new person.

As the observing partner experiences the other's disclosures, internal "models" of the other are challenged and expanded. While the observing partner may experience the other as perhaps unavailable or blaming, by the conclusion of Step 5 the observing partner is now confronted with a "more engaged" or "softer" partner. As the disclosing partner's behavior changes, the observing partner may have trouble making the shift. It is usually a substantial risk to accept new behavior from a partner. The observing partner lets his/her guard down with the potential of having the rug pulled out from under. The therapist may need to hold the focus on the new image of other, unfold the experience, and validate the responses many times before the observing partner can feel safe enough to hear the disclosures, assimilate the information, and allow their model of the other to change. So one might hear the EFT therapist say, "It's hard for you to take this in. It seems strange. It doesn't fit with your experience. Is that how it is for you?"

In terms of actual time spent, Step 6 may be the briefest step in EFT, but the process provides an essential step toward creating stable change. In a typical pursue/withdraw pattern, the more withdrawn partner usually enters step 5 first, resulting in the processing of the pursuing partner's responses in Step 6. This first time through in Step 6 with the pursuing partner usually takes longer than the second time through with the withdrawn partner. Acceptance generally happens more easily the second time through because the withdrawer is already more open and engaged when the pursuer begins to confide.

Key Moves in the Process of Acceptance

This section deals with a typical therapist/client process when the observing partner is not accepting or receptive. The process starts when the "experiencing" partner discloses underlying experience and the observing partner ignores, dismisses, discounts, or rejects the experiencing partner's disclosures. The following are some of the key therapist moves in facilitating acceptance:

- The therapist validates the observing partner's present experience and difficulty accepting, while supporting the new view of the experiencing partner.

Therapist: "It's so hard to see her as fearful when all this time you have seen her as 'removed.'" (reflecting, validating)

- The therapist reflects back and repeats the disclosures of new emotional experience and the "new view" of the other. The therapist maintains the focus on this new image of the partner, while blocking avoidance and facilitating the observing partner's hearing, seeing, and feeling the partner's message.

Therapist: "When she says, 'I cringe when you are angry, I'm shaken after we argue, I'm scared of your disapproval, and I'm afraid you won't like what you see,' I guess that's hard for you to take in. What's that like for you to hear that?" (reflecting, validating)

- The therapist heightens and unfolds the observing partner's experience of the new responses and disclosures of the other partner.

Therapist: "What's it like for you to hear her say she cringes?" "What happens inside when you hear that?"

Husband: "I feel nothing. I feel cold."

Therapist: "Can you help me? What does cold feel like exactly? (pause) Where do you feel cold in your body? (pause) How does what she said set off the spark of coldness in you? (pause) What do you do when you feel cold?"(pause) (evocative responding, heightening)

- The therapist ties non-accepting responses to negative cycle and attachment experiences.

Therapist: "You've had years of experiencing her as 'remote and distant'; saying she 'cringes' isn't what you expected—this isn't how you've seen her all these years. You never felt that you moved her or that you matter. When she didn't respond, you always took it as her not caring and being unmoved, leaving you out in the cold. So you turned up the heat and knocked on her door trying harder to get a response." (validating, conjecturing, reframing)

- The therapist gently challenges old models of other and of relationship by highlighting the new view of the other with its attachment implications.

Therapist: "It's hard to imagine that when she distances she is cringing and protecting herself, feeling scared of your disapproval. You've seen her as remote and not caring about you. It's hard to imagine that she is protecting herself and that, for her, making contact is likely to expose her to feeling dreadful and not good enough. I guess that's not the way you've seen her." (validating, conjecturing, reframing)

- The therapist helps the observing partner own her sense of self in the non-accepting position or own her sense of self as shifting into a more accepting position.

Therapist: "Let me see if I understand. You're having a hard time seeing her this way? You're confused? It's hard to believe that she is afraid? You're even not quite sure how to respond to her? Is this how you experience it? Do I have it right?" (validating, conjecturing)

- The therapist creates an interaction for the observing partner to either enact and own reluctance and non-acceptance or to enact and highlight newly accepted experience.

Therapist: "Can you tell her what it is like for you to hear her say she is afraid and for you not to know how to respond?" (enactment)

Exercise 30:

Case Example: Responding to non-acceptance.

A withdrawn husband diagnosed as having bipolar disorder has, in previous sessions, confessed a past affair to his wife, and she has reacted with intense hurt and anger. During sessions when she has become "emotional," he has become cold, stoic, and "numbed out," leaving her feeling that she can't reach him and that he doesn't care. The therapist explores the husband's underlying experience, and the husband expresses that whenever the wife is upset and angry he numbs out and loses all feeling and withdraws. He discloses how hard it is for him when he experiences her disappointment, how he experiences his own hurt and anger and then he numbs out. The therapist asks him to enact his underlying experience by telling his wife how scary her being angry, emotional, and disappointed in him is and that what he has done for years is to "numb out" and protect himself. The husband cries as he relates his feelings. The therapist asks the observing wife, "What's it like seeing him talk this way?" She responds tearfully saying, "I've never heard this before." (turning toward husband) "I am really very touched and I feel like reaching for you and hugging you, but I also feel so angry with what you did, I still feel like I don't want to touch you. I still feel like slapping you." Tearfully laughing and crying in the same moment, she blurts out, "I'm a mess. I'm completely mixed up. I don't know how to respond to you."

Check the answers below that you think are typical EFT therapist responses to the non-accepting reactions of the partner: (more than one correct answer)

a. "This is very hard for you. You've never heard these feelings and are very touched by his pain, but your own feelings of betrayal and pain are so strong you can't reach for him. You're pulled in two directions. Which feeling is strongest for you now?" _____

b. "When you hear his pain, the alarms go off in your head—'don't reach for him, you can't trust him. He'll hurt you again.' There is no safe place for you; part of you wants to reach for him and the other part says don't be a fool, he'll hurt you again. That's hard." _____

c. "Do you see how by refusing to accept his softer feelings when he expresses them you turn him away and make his withdrawal all the more solid? It would be better if you could let him in and validate his feelings." _____

d. "No wonder this is difficult for you. Your experience of him has always been that he is cold and stoic when you are upset and now you see his softer side. That's very different. It is quite a difference in your experience of him. Yes?" _____

e. "Can you tell him, 'I'm stuck—I don't know how to respond to you? I want to reach for you but part of me says, "don't, he'll let you down and betray you again."'?" _____

f. "Can you tell him, 'Right now, I'm too angry to hear your pain? I want to reach for you but I can't. I have to protect myself.'?" _____

g. "He shuts down and pulls away and 'numbs' out because he is so sensitive to how you see him. The ironic thing is that in some ways it is because he cares so much about how you feel that he pulls away. But it is hard to feel his caring when you still feel betrayed." _____

The "observing partner" will likely ignore, discount, or dismiss the disclosure upon first hearing of new emotional experience. When this occurs, the therapist must slow down the process, refocus, and present again the new view of the experiencing partner. In a sense, the therapist "holds up" the new view of the partner and asks the observing partner to take another look and to take time to hear, see, feel, and respond. In the following exercises, you will be developing your skills in working with non-accepting responses.

Case Example 2:

A withdrawn wife, Jody, discloses in Step 5 through an enactment to her husband, Len, that she wants to feel closer but that she feels afraid to talk to him, that she can never say anything right. She expresses that she feels overwhelmed by their conflict and the demands of their young children so she crawls into her shell, clams up for days, and ends up feeling alone and isolated. She ends the enactment saying she would like to feel closer but she can't stand his demanding voice. Beginning Step 6, the therapist asks Len, "What's it like when you hear Jody say that she feels afraid, that she can't say anything right, and ends up shutting down and feeling alone for days?" Len responds by saying, "I don't know what the problem is. And it seems to me that Jody is crabby all the time. If she wants to talk she should just speak up nicely."

In the exercises below, compare your answer to the suggested answers in the back of the book.

Exercise 31: Validating and Refocusing

Write a brief statement validating Len's (observing partner's) initial reactions and then refocus on Jody's disclosures:

_____

_____

Exercise 32: Unfolding the Non-Accepting Reaction

The therapist may focus on the word "scared," saying to the Len, "Could you come back here a minute and, Len, could you help me? What's it like to hear Jody say how scared she is, that she feels like she can't ever say anything right?" The husband then responds by saying, "I don't know. I guess I feel stuck. I feel bad for her, but I don't know what to do. She says she feels scared, but she won't talk. I'm at a complete loss as to what to do." Write a brief statement using evocative responding and heightening to unfold and heighten the husband's experience of feeling "stuck."

_____

_____

Exercise 33: Linking Non-Accepting Responses
to the Couple's Negative Cycle and Attachment Concerns

When Jody says that she is scared because of never getting it right with Len, he has "no clue" as to how to approach her without making matters worse and having her "get crabby or withdraw." Len expresses that he feels "stuck," not knowing how to approach her. Tie Len's non-accepting responses to the couple's negative cycle and attachment experiences. Try including validating, empathic conjecture, and reframing.

_____

_____

Exercise 34: Challenging Old Models of Other

Len says that Jody is "unreachable" and "not there." He says that he feels like "a little kid groveling for attention." Think of ways to gently challenge Len's old models of Jody. Try highlighting the new view of her with its attachment implications and possibilities. Identify the type of interventions you used, before checking the answer. Typically, challenging old models includes evocative responding, empathic conjecture, and validation. Consider using these interventions in your answer.

_____

_____

Exercise 35: Consolidate Position and Create an Enactment

Help Len, the observing partner, own his difficulty of accepting the new view of Jody, by creating an enactment (enact present position).

_____

_____

While the above process has been stretched out and divided into pieces, it is more fluid and integrated in actual practice. Usually, at the completion of Step 6 the therapist will return to the experiencing partner and process his/her own experience of the accepting or non-accepting responses of their observing partner. It is also important to keep in mind that Steps 5 and 6 may be visited several times with each partner during change events.

*Example: Practice Processing a Non-Accepting Response in Steps 5 and 6:
Putting It All Together*

A husband, Ron, and his wife, Tammy, are separated. Both requested and agreed to work to try to save the marriage. Ron had been in individual therapy and received medications for depression and panic with little improvement. Their cycle has been identified as Ron withdrawing from any sign of conflict and Tammy being frustrated by his withdrawal and reacting to it by turning up the heat to get a response. He would react by briefly "fighting back" or sometimes shutting down in silence. Tammy expressed that Ron's leaving and "not talking about what's going on" left her feeling totally abandoned and with no options but to make herself more "self sufficient."

In Step 5, Ron's feelings of being judged and evaluated were explored and expanded. As he expressed how he felt like a "little kid" in the relationship, he drew his hands to his chest and said he felt like curling into the fetal position. He spoke about the utter panic and the sense of being paralyzed and frozen that he experienced whenever he received or anticipated disapproval in any way. Following the exploration and deepening of these feelings, the therapist asked Ron to disclose his experience to his wife, "Could you tell her what it is like when you feel her disapproval and you freeze?" Ron said to his wife, "I get paralyzed thinking you will get mad or critical. My chest gets tight and I want to get away as quickly as I can."

Step 6 begins with the therapist asking Tammy, "What's it like to hear Ron talking about how he lives in constant fear of not measuring up and of disappointing you, which keeps him in this frozen, paralyzed place?" Tammy then quickly points out that she is not the only person with whom her husband avoids conflict, pointing to his interactions with his mother and father. Ron agrees. Tammy adds that she also doesn't feel "approved of at all" and that his leaving was "the biggest dose of disapproval" she has ever experienced. With this, both partners stop talking and look at the therapist.

The therapist is now at a common and crucial point in EFT therapy, when the "observing partner" is not accepting of their partner's disclosures.

Exercise 36:

In this exercise, help the observing partner process their non-accepting experience.

1. Write a brief statement demonstrating how you might reflect and validate Tammy's non-acceptance (using validation and reflection).

   _____

   _____

2. What might you say to help Tammy unfold her reaction, her experience of Ron? (reflection, validation, empathic conjecture, and evocative responding)

   _____

   _____

3. Use empathic conjecture and reframing to tie Tammy's non-acceptance to both the negative cycle and her attachment experience.

   _____

   _____

4. Tammy responds with: "This is too overwhelming for me right now. Yes, I'm angry, and I don't really believe that he cares about me. He left me. I didn't want him to leave." Help Tammy formulate (own) her feelings and reactions and put them in an attachment context of her experience and needs.

   _____

   _____

5. Having helped Tammy explore, unfold, and formulate her experience, now help her create an enactment for her to engage Ron in a new way.

   _____

   _____

In working with the observing partner's non-accepting responses the therapist must return many times to validate and unfold his/her reactions before this partner is able to take in, hear, and accept the other partner's confiding.

In completing this chapter you will have added to your repertoire of skills: 1) of helping each partner explore, experience, and disclose underlying emotional experience in Step 5 and 2) of helping the observing partner process and accept these disclosures in Step 6. The creation of acceptance in Step 6 now sets the stage for the beginning of a new kind of contact in Step 7.

7

STEP 7 AND KEY CHANGE EVENTS: RE-ENGAGEMENT AND SOFTENING

"And the day came when the risk to remain tight in the bud was more painful than the risk it took to blossom" — Anais Nin

The steps of EFT are circular and additive. Therefore, Step 7 is discussed here in the context of Steps 5 and 6 that prepare clients for the relationship transforming risks they take in Step 7.

In Step 7, the therapist uses new emotional experience and expression to change interactional positions and restructure interactions. The processing of key change events in this step is necessary to produce a successful outcome in EFT. The completion of Step 7 for the more-withdrawing partner results in the Withdrawer Engagement Event wherein the previously more withdrawn spouse shares attachment needs and wants from a now-engaged relational position. This partner experiences and asserts a newly discovered intense desire for a safe and secure connection with the other partner.

Completion of Step 7 for the more blaming partner results in the blamer softening event wherein this partner is now able to ask for contact and comfort from a position of personal vulnerability. As this partner "softens" both partners are now able to begin interacting from positions of emotional accessibility and responsiveness, key elements in building and maintaining secure bonds. Powerful bonding events can now occur as partners *own these new positions* and walk through new positive interactional cycles in which they are emotionally accessible and responsive to each other.

For each partner, the processing of emotional experience in Step 5, and the ensuing interactional events in Step 6, prepare the soil for the further expansion and sharing of attachment fears, longings and wants in Step 7. Requests for connection are made in Step 7 from an emerging, empowered, and accessible position that pulls for the other partner to engage in the same attachment-related process. Previous processing through Step 5 with the withdrawing partner naturally evolves into a heightened awareness and expression of needs and wants in Step 7. When one truly experiences a sense of thirst, for example, such awareness leads to a clear expression of need and desire for water. The formulation and expression of needs occur within the context of each person's interactional position in the relationship. As the attachment-related affect is engaged and expanded, new meanings organized by emotion emerge into awareness. Statements made by the withdrawing partner in Step 5, for example, summarized as "I feel small and inept with you, and live in fear of you really seeing this and leaving me, so I go numb, defend, and withdraw" evolve and crystallize in Step 7 as: "I am exhausted from all of this defending and numbing out. I want to feel special to you. I want you to hold off on the criticism and quit threatening to leave me. I'm not going to leave, and I don't want to feel small in this relationship anymore." The partner is now emotionally engaged and speaking from a position of increased efficacy, defining the relationship for himself, rather than reacting to his partner's definitions. He has integrated attachment-related affect and subsequent newly emerging meaning into a new position that is emotionally accessible and responsive, rather than distant and inaccessible.

As each partner goes through Step 7 they are able to stay engaged with their immediate emotional experience and clearly ask for what they need to feel safe and connected in the relationship. These requests naturally stem from each partner's views of self and other. One spouse, for example, may share that "I am afraid that you can't love someone as disgusting as me. Who could?" Such a statement suggests a negative view of self as unlovable or deficient. Another spouse may state, "I don't think you really love me. I am not sure you ever have." Such a statement may revolve more around this partner's view of other. The EFT therapist should develop a sensitive ear to the nuances of attachment-related fears emanating from views of self and other when working through Step 7. The therapist does this by staying emotionally engaged to the immediate in-session experiencing of each partner. A sincere "not knowing" and emotionally reflecting therapeutic stance is crucial.

The type of expression promoted in this step represents a new interactional stance that is much more equal and affiliative. These requests have the quality of *a new and authentic attempt at emotional engagement*. Emotional processing creates a different context and atmosphere than, say, negotiating behavioral contracts, seeking solutions, or gaining insight into family of origin. Requests are not made as demands on the other, nor are they stated in the context of blaming the other. Requests in Step 7 emerge from new positions that arise out of a new integration of emotional experience. When a more blaming partner makes an accusation, an engaged withdrawer is now able to steadfastly hold on to a new stance without resorting to the previous negative cycle of defending and withdrawing. For example, a withdrawer may state, "Yes, I temporarily resorted to my past behavior once this week. I've learned to react that way unfortunately. But that was temporary, and I don't want you to take that as evidence that I am not trying, or that I don't care, and get so angry that I can't get close to you. I am working hard over here, and often I am doing things differently in ways that we both recognize and like, ways that bring us together. I need you to trust me in this."

In Step 7, partners are able to share specific requests in a manner that pulls the other partner toward them and maximizes the possibility that the other will be able to respond with accessibility and comfort. In short, *the attachment signals are clear*. The very nature of the requests tends to affirm the other partner's sense of being the prized one, the irreplaceable one, which has a powerful, immediate effect. From an attachment perspective these interactions are extremely confirming and compelling. Common sentiments from the listening spouse, for example, after the engaging withdrawer shares attachment needs and wants, are often similar to: "I had no idea that I mattered this much to you. You really do need me. Wow, I am not alone in this after all." Here, the withdrawers sharing echoes the others deprivation and attachment needs, which then makes it easier for the other to respond positively. The usually blaming spouse, for example, may say to her engaging partner in Step 6, "I can really relate to your aloneness. I am sad as I hear you right now. I don't want to play a part in you feeling alone. I often feel alone too. I did not know the depth of this inside you. I am sad, and yet on the other hand I am so glad that you are sharing this with me."

The process of Step 7 takes the emotional experience of Step 5 and further crystallizes emerging meanings into expanded views of self and other. These new meanings emerge from experientially processing attachment-related affect, now used to restructure the relationship. The new emotional experience of a partner in Step 5 becomes a new interactional event in Step 7—one that redefines the control and affiliation in the relationship.

Withdrawer Engagement Event Snapshot: Inez and Fernando

Inez and Fernando had some close times following the last session, and as the therapist had suggested, discussed key elements of the previous session. They also began having a date night each week and reported increased closeness. The couple delayed session 12 because Inez' mother was visiting. When the couple arrived for this session Fernando reported that he was feeling "frustrated" with the therapy process.

Fernando: "I thought we were doing really well, getting better—you know, closer. Happier. But I don't know anymore. We're on a retirement budget and these sessions are a stretch for us."

Therapist: "Sounds like you're feeling discouraged, Fernando?"

Fernando: "Well, I just wonder if we've come as far as we can."

Therapist: "Hmm. You sound a little disappointed."

Fernando: "Well, actually, I don't want to sound angry with Inez." (directs an anxious look at Inez who is looking down at her fingers) "But quite frankly, it seems to me like" (turns to Inez) "—do you really have any desire for us to get close?"

Inez: "What do you mean?"

Fernando: "Well, you know…You've been avoiding me again."

Inez: (continues to study her fingers) "I've just been busy."

Fernando: (Fernando angrily takes the cushion behind him and drops it on the floor.) "Fine then! You've been busy, and I think it's time we stopped coming for the sessions."

Therapist: "This is what it can go like between you guys, isn't it? This is kind of like the cycle starting up right here and now. It's like you're reaching for Inez, right Fernando? And when she doesn't respond you get frustrated, mad, but inside you feel…" (Therapist waits for Fernando to complete her sentence.)

Fernando: "Like she disrespects me. Yes—and mad."

Therapist: "So Inez, you're quiet today. Where are you? What's happening for you?"

Inez: "It's been rough for me. Yes, I guess I've been feeling depressed and sad."

Therapist: "You've been depressed and sad?"

Inez: "Well, my mother's visit is always hard."

Fernando: "She's really a difficult woman."

Inez: "She even follows me round the kitchen telling me I stir the sauce wrong or I'm putting too much flour in the gravy."

Therapist: "So having your Mom here's been really hard for you."

Inez: "Yes, but then Fernando's been difficult too. Snappy. Angry. And dealing with both..."

Therapist: (RISSSC manner) "Ah, so you've had lots of messages to let you know you're not worth much, you don't count?"

Inez: (nods tearfully)

Therapist: (RISSSC manner; uses Inez' words from previous sessions) "Back to that really, really painful place where you don't count. You're not enough. No one cares."

Inez: (nods, weeping)

Therapist: "So, Inez, what do you need when you get to that place, that painful place where you feel so small and defective?"

Inez: "I need for Fernando to be on my side. To stop taking his anger out on me. I am not a defective person. I work hard and I do a good job. I make good gravy too!"

Therapist: "Right. You need for Fernando to see your value and treat you like you count. Can you let Fernando know now what you need from him?"

Inez: (turns to Fernando) "I want you to support me. When I'm feeling crummy and small, I want you on my side."

Therapist: "You'd like for him to be beside you, not on the other side. So what would you like from him?"

Inez: "I want you to come and support me when I'm upset and not get angry right away. Come and give me a hug, and tell me you think I count. Like you did in here last week."

Fernando: (leans forward, looks emotional)

Therapist: "That was good for you? Here in the session when he said that you're incredibly important to him?"

Inez: (nods, weeping) "It meant a lot to me."

Fernando: "I guess I get anxious when you get quiet and withdrawn. I'm so busy worrying about me; I forget you need me there for you." (Fernando moves to sit beside her and puts his arms around his wife.)

STEP 7 GOALS

- Further process and expand the emotional experience of Step 5 to include greater awareness and ownership of attachment fears, longings, and needs.

- Facilitate experientially vivid awareness of attachment-related views of self and other.
- Integrate newly crystallized attachment fears and needs into interactions that restructure the relationship towards a more secure bond.

STEP 7 FOCUS POINTS

What is the therapist likely to see at this stage of the process moving from Steps 5 and 6 into Step 7? Listed below are the common observations and accompanying therapist actions.

What a therapist sees	What a therapist does
In turn, a withdrawing and later a more-blaming partner reiterates the emotional experience encountered in Step 5, but doesn't expand and crystallize the attachment fears, needs, and wants implicit in this experience.	In turn with each partner, aid in the further expansion and formulation of attachment-related fears, needs, and wants, and in the expression of these to the other partner.
A partner spontaneously begins to state attachment-related fears, needs, or wants to the therapist.	Redirect partner to share directly with their partner, rather than through the therapist.
A partner exits from an attachment context into a less pertinent or unfocused dialog.	Refocus the process back to attachment-related fears, needs, and wants.
The other, more-listening partner either responds to the new behavior of the experiencing partner or begins to discount this new behavior.	In both cases the therapist invites the more-experiencing spouse to continue to respond in an emotionally engaged manner, continuing to state attachment fears and associated needs and wants. The therapist often reflects and validates the listening partner's struggles with responding to the changes in their spouse. If the listening partner responds positively, the therapist reflects, heightens, and fosters this response.

CRUCIAL INTERVENTIONS IN STEP 7

Evocative Response

The therapist focuses on the client's emerging experience to aid in clarifying wishes and longings and to clarify difficulties in expressing these to the other partner. An evocative response vividly brings attachment-related affect to the forefront.

Exercise 1:

1. Which of the following is an evocative response?
    a. "You run and hide to protect yourself. It's just too scary." _____
    b. "The anger comes rushing in, overwhelming the pain and hurt." _____
    c. "You seem very sad as you say that, you look down at the floor." _____
    d. "What's it like for you right now as you share how afraid you are of being once again found as failing? What happens inside as you say this?" _____

2. Choose the evocative response from the selections below:

   a. "What happens inside when you throw your arms up, like, 'Once again, I've failed.' What's that like inside for you?" _____

   b. "The dance seems to be that he comes in angry and you meet that anger with your own." _____

   c. "I think it's great that you both are able to share how happy you are right now." _____

   d. "You guys really noticed the cycle this week, really worked hard to not fall under its spell." _____

3. Choose the best evocative response from the selections below:

   a. "Jon, just now you smiled when you said that. That's the first time we've seen a smile in some time." _____

   b. "You're speaking from anger; but my guess is that underneath that is a lot of guilt perhaps? Do you feel guilt?" _____

   c. "You seem really sad as you say that Jon. I noticed that your head dropped and you looked to the floor. What happens inside as you say that now?" _____

   d. "This makes a lot of sense in the context of your family growing up Jon. I can certainly understand why you see it that way." _____

Empathic Conjecture

In using empathic conjecture, the therapist seeks to tentatively go one step forward in a client's present experience. What often appears implicit is conjectured upon to better understand and deepen attachment-related affect. The implicit becomes explicit. In Step 7 empathic conjecture is often used to spotlight attachment-related fears associated with views of self and other, such as fears of being rejected, shamed, unlovable, or fears of finally being recognized as failing as a partner.

Exercise 2:

1. Which of the following is an empathic conjecture?

   a. "You are angry with her for not being more sensitive to your needs." _____

   b. "Help me out if I miss here, but, you seem very sad as you say this. It hurts deeply. But also, I seem to be hearing a sense of loneliness from you?" _____

   c. "Who does what at home after something like this is said?" _____

   d. "Your fear of her rejection is huge, like you said though; you show her your anger." _____

2. Choose the empathic conjecture from the selections provided below:

   a. "The cycle is up and running now isn't it?" _____

   b. "You respond with anger, but underneath is a hurt that that fuels these fights." _____

   c. "What's happening for you now as he says this Mary?" _____

   d. "I see the frustration, but I also wonder if there is a kind of sadness, a sense of loss, lurking inside?" _____

3. Choose the best empathic conjecture from the selections provided below:

    a. "You're sad, but you're angry, too, it seems to me." _____

    b. "As I see your eyes fill with tears of sadness, I hear a slight edge in your voice. It's like a part of you is also saying, 'I want this to be better. I am tired of being alone.' Is that close?" _____

    c. "Can you tell him now how you feel? Tell him right now?" _____

    d. "You said you were sad, but what else are you feeling?" _____

HEIGHTENING IN STEP 7

Heightening is used to "prime the pump" as spouses are on the edge of taking new risks and positions in the relationship. Heightening in this phase of EFT is not just focused on primary emotion, it is used to expand attachment-related fears and dreams, and thus to generate new meaning. This new meaning usually has an embedded and previously dormant *action component* that the therapist seizes upon when asking partners to ask for their attachment wants, longings, and needs to be honored and met. Heightening in this step occurs within the very specific attachment context of promoting the two change events: withdrawer engagement and blamer softening. As the withdrawing spouse engages, for example, the therapist heightens the attachment-related affect, often fear, that lies unprocessed, stubbornly blocking movement toward emotional connection with the other. "You can't stand in the face of his anger," a therapist may heighten with an engaging partner in Step 7. "A part of you says, 'He may be right. Maybe I am incompetent. Maybe there is really something wrong with me.' This fear rises up and you do anything it takes to escape. Yeah?" (She nods.) "The accusations are just so painful and overwhelming. You protect yourself by withdrawing."

Exercise 3:

1. Choose the Step 7 heightening response from the selections below:

    a. "What happens inside as you say this?" _____

    b. "Could you turn and share this with him now please?" _____

    c. "You hear his anger and you respond in anger. The cycle gets going once again and you two go at it. Inside you both are heading toward hurt and loneliness, often for days." _____

    d. "This voice inside says, 'You can't dare reach for him. He won't be there. You've never had anyone really be there. You've tried this before, don't do it! He won't be there and it will hurt too much.'" _____

2. Choose the best Step 7 heightening response from the selections below:

    a. "There's this scared part that we've talked about in here before. A part that says, 'Maybe he doesn't really love me after all. Maybe he really doesn't want to stay with me. Maybe I shouldn't risk sharing with him, letting him in, counting on him.' You begin to fear that this may in fact be the case, right?" (nods) "This fear rises up and sort of paralyzes you. So you see him here, right now, he's saying 'Risk. Please…risk. I am here.' But it's just so scary for you, this battle rages so intensely inside of you." _____

    b. "You see him here right now, and he's asking you to risk. But it's too scary for you. So you push that fear away and stay put. This ends up leaving you alone." _____

c. "Do you ever tell him when you feel overwhelmed by him? Do you ever say, 'Honey, I am feeling so alone right now?' Do you ever risk that with him when it's really hitting you hard?" _____

d. "Has there been a time where you were able to share this with him, and he was able to hear you in a way that was comforting? What was different about that specific time? My hunch is that you were able to talk to him in a nonblaming manner that probably did not push him away. I bet you were able to use 'I statements' and I bet to some degree he was able to let you know he was listening by a response of replaying what you said." _____

RESTRUCTURING INTERACTIONS IN STEP 7

Restructuring interactions are used after evocative responses and heightening interventions have clearly brought attachment-related affect to the forefront of immediate experiencing. Following the momentum built from this more-intrapsychic focus, the therapist helps partners directly turn and share attachment fears, and ask for needs and wants to be honored and met.

Exercise 4:

1. Choose the Step 7 restructuring interactions intervention from the selections below:
   a. "When he attacks you in anger, you initially stand up and attack back, from within your own anger. You guys fight for awhile, and at some point you start defending and withdrawing." _____
   b. "How were you guys able to sit and talk at home this week? What was different?" _____
   c. "This 'cycle' really attacks both of you. Has there been a time when you were able to defeat this 'cycle'?" _____
   d. "Maria, would you please turn and share this now directly with Frank, in your own words?" _____

2. Choose the best restructuring interactions intervention from the selections below:
   a. "Would you please turn and share that with him now?" _____
   b. "Would you please turn and share this with him now, in your own words?" _____
   c. "Would you please turn and share that with him now? How a part of you says, 'How could he possibly want me,' and fear really sets in. It's really scary for you. Would you please turn to him now and share this with him, in your own words." _____
   d. "What do you think she is thinking right now as you say this? How do you think she would respond if I asked her what she was thinking?" _____

CHANGE EVENTS

Step 7 is processed first with the more-withdrawn partner. This process is recognized as withdrawer engagement. The processing of Step 7 with the more-blaming spouse is titled blamer softening. The following exercises work within the specific context of each of these change events to deepen conceptual understanding and clinical application.

Please read through the following withdrawer engagement event, noting the therapist process comments and interventions supplied in brackets throughout the dialog. The withdrawer engagement event is broken into three therapist themes:

- Expanding attachment-related affect
- Sharing attachment fears/asking for needs to be honored and met
- Processing attachment-related affect and needs with each partner

These themes are circular rather than linear. The EFT therapist is free to circle back through them based on the processing needs of each particular couple. The withdrawer engagement example is followed by exercises that allow practice with your own responses.

Expanding Attachment-Related Affect

Initially the therapist seeks to reenter the withdrawing partner's experience stemming from work in Step 5. This work sets the tone and context for expanding attachment-related fears and needs that are crucial in Step 7. The therapist pays particular attention to key attachment themes and emotions discovered in Step 5, often centering on the more withdrawing partner's inner experience of self and other during the negative interactional dance or pattern. The therapist now seeks to more precisely heighten previously acknowledged attachment-related affect. This anticipates the withdrawing spouse sharing attachment fears and asking for attachment needs to be honored and met from the other spouse. The following transcript segment and exercises illustrate the expanding attachment-related affect theme of the withdrawer engagement event.

Withdrawer Engagement Example: Brief Couple Context

Rosalita and Jon have been married for 3 years, each having children from previous marriages. They presented for couples therapy because of "intense fighting" and lack of communication. In previous sessions, it became clear that Rosalita was the more pursuing partner, and Jon the more withdrawing. "I get so mad at him," Rosalita explained. "I hate it, but I do. He's so competent at work, you know, such a leader. But at home with me he just melts, runs away, acts at times like he's a baby or something." The therapist learned that Jon got nervous when the couple began to argue, and when it escalated, Jon soon learned that he was no match for Rosalita. "I can't stand and fight it out with her anymore. Her tongue is sharp, and her mind thinks so quickly. I don't know, maybe it was because she grew up with a lot of brothers and sisters and learned early to argue well, but I am no match." In Step 5, Jon began to touch his attachment-related affect, sharing that when things are not going well and a fight ensues, that "I get all sweaty in no time. It's like I almost see white. I get so tense, so afraid I guess. Being afraid sounds weird, but my heart pounds, and I have to get out of there." He went on to talk about feeling "like I am not much of a husband" and "wondering if she really still respects and loves me." The following therapy segment occurred in session number nine, Step 7 of EFT, focused initially on the more withdrawing spouse.

Jon: (withdrawer) "Yeah. That's it. It's all very frustrating." (fidgets in chair)

Therapist: "What's that? Frustrating? You fidget in your chair as you say this. Help me understand?" (Therapist notes immediate experience of client as seen in his fidgeting.

This is reflected to better understand client and to intensify immediate experience; evocative responding.)

Jon: "Well, I am trying now to not attack back, or to not run away when conflict comes around. But, it's tough to respond differently when she keeps coming at me at full speed."

Therapist: "So, you're trying to change this cycle, but it's hard to stay engaged when you're feeling attacked, yeah?"

Jon: "Yes. I get a bit shaky, you know? Kind of like, 'Wow, the heat's coming.'"

Therapist: "What's that like for you Jon? When the 'heat is coming.'" (evocative responding)

Jon: (7-second silence) "I hate it. I start thinking that I can't match her. I can't do this right. I feel like a dog on a training leash. Problem is, like the dog, I don't speak English."

Therapist: "Right. The heat is coming, and something inside says, 'Oh no. Here we go again. I am about to get corrected,' kind of like a puppy in training. And you don't even speak her language, right? There's nothing you can say—you're trapped on a leash. Is that close to what happens?" (heightening, evocative responding)

Jon: "Yes. I do feel like a puppy dog on a training leash. I just sit and take my medicine for pissing on the carpet."

Therapist: "You feel talked down to, trapped on a leash, unable to respond, like a puppy." (heightening)

Jon: (slowly, with head down) "Yeah. Like a little puppy. Small, unprotected, scolded, afraid, tensed up. That's me."

Therapist: "What is happening inside right now Jon as you say this?" (Note: There was no need to heighten any further. Therapist moved to processing current experiencing; evocative responding.)

Jon: "I feel sad. Beaten down. Like that puppy."

Therapist: (softly and slowly) "Right. Yes. You're touching that sense of feeling defeated, and sad."

Jon: (sighs heavily)

The therapist summarizes and repeats the key aspects of Jon's experience and its interpersonal consequences (e.g., that Jon hides).

Sharing Attachment Fears/Asking for Needs to be Honored and Met

The therapist has just expanded and heightened the withdrawer's attachment-related affect to a kind of "boiling point" if you will. The withdrawer is integrating the new meaning being generated into awareness as a result of this process. It's now time for the therapist to move into restructuring and shaping interactions, the interpersonal element of EFT. The therapist begins this by directing the withdrawer to share attachment fears and needs directly with the spouse.

> *Therapist: "Would you be able to begin telling Rosalita about this? Would you be able to turn to her now and begin to share with her what it's like for you to feel this way?" (restructuring interactions)*

> *Jon: (to therapist) "Whew. That won't be easy."*

> *Therapist: "I hear you. It won't be easy sharing this with her. It's kind of scary to share this with her? To open up to her like that?"*

> *Jon: (nods)*

> *Therapist: "Yeah, it's kind of scary to share this with her. She could get mad and go for you, right?" (validation, empathic conjecture)*

> *Jon: "Yes, or she could belittle me."*

> *Therapist: "Yes, she could. You're right, I am asking you to risk. And she could miss how much of a risk this is for you, she could. Could you share with her how risky and scary this is to share with her like this? Could you help her understand this in your own words right now?" (Therapist reflects Jon's fear of reaching and validates. A restructuring interaction intervention is then used to again direct an enactment.)*

> *Jon: (12 seconds of silence) "It's hard to share this with you. I am afraid that you won't understand and will get mad. When that happens it really affects me. I feel like a helpless little puppy dog. I sometimes fear that you really don't love me, or that you may leave. I know I have at times acted like that little puppy dog. I run away and hide when a disagreement occurs. But, I guess, I am just getting tired of running. And I am tired of being afraid and feeling helpless." (Note: Jon is sharing his attachment fears.) "I sometimes feel like I am just not being the husband I want to be...and that hurts me." (Jon now moves into asking for his attachment needs to be honored and met. The therapist can, if necessary, prompt this asking; for example, saying "What you want is...") "But I am tired of running away from that, and I don't want to do it anymore. I need you to respect this, honey. I don't like feeling separated or cut off from you, and that's how I feel after we fight or are mad at each other for days. I need you to try to stop attacking me so quickly and loudly. I am going to try my best here, and I want you to work with me and try your best, too."*

Processing Attachment-Related Affect and Needs with Each Partner

The therapist intervenes to reflect, validate, and support each partner, supporting the engaging partner first. If the more blaming spouse is accessible and responsive, the therapist often briefly reflects this and has this partner reach back with support to the engaging withdrawer. However, the formally withdrawn spouse has just "come towards" and the first priority is to support this person as he/she takes this new position in the relationship.

> *Therapist: (to Jon) "That was great Jon. You just really risked. What's it like to share this with her?" (By validating, the therapist supports the engaging withdrawer and also sends strong signals to other partner that this was an important and valiant risk; validation and evocative responding.)*

Jon: "It was good. I feel very good about it."

Therapist: "It feels good to open up to Rosalita and share with her like this?" (evocative responding)

Jon: "Yeah. It's risky, I mean, she could nail me, but it feels really good to get this out there and to make it concrete. I feel exhilarated."

Therapist: (to Rosalita) "What was it like for you as Jon risked and shared how scary it is for him to open up to you, and how he no longer wants to withdraw and protect? Being 'separated' from you really wreaks havoc on him. What happened inside as he shared these things?" (Attachment-related affect draws partners together to comfort. The therapist is using emotion for possible connection; reflection, evocative responding. Also note how the therapist "resets the table" so to speak, slowly repeating key attachment themes just shared, before ending by repeating an evocative response. The EFT therapist often "sandwiches" like this—evocative response, repeat key attachment themes, and repeat evocative response.)

Rosalita: "On one hand it was sad for me, because I don't want him to feel like a little puppy that has to be obedient or else. That was hard to hear, but I am not angry. On the other hand, it was really good to hear because I never hear this from him."

Therapist: "This is sort of new to you, Rosalita? You aren't used to seeing this part of Jon? The part that needs you to help him open up to you more? That no longer wants to be emotionally separated?" (Therapist helps spouse begin to integrate other partner's attachment fears and needs for accessibility and responsiveness; evocative responding, heightening.)

Rosalita: "Yes it is. I usually just see him closing down, or getting quiet. I thought he didn't care."

Therapist: (to Rosalita) "You thought he didn't care, that's why he shut down, or withdrew."

Rosalita: "Yes. Right now I feel sad for him." (looks at Jon)

Therapist: (to Rosalita) "You feel sad for him, yeah. Could you please share this with him now?" (Therapist processes with the other spouse, assessing whether she is accessible and responsive. Believing Rosalita is responsive, the therapist moves toward having her begin to meet her partner's attachment needs in the session. There are times when the more blaming partner is not yet able to be accessible and responsive. At these times the therapist would work towards validating this partner's difficulty in understanding or hearing the emerging position of the engaging partner, rather than having he/she try to respond directly to attachment fears and needs; restructuring interaction.)

Rosalita: (to Jon) "I am sad that you feel this way. I've never wanted you to feel unloved, or be afraid that I might leave you. I don't want to leave you. I didn't think you cared this much. I am used to seeing the backside of you walking away."

Therapist: (to Rosalita) "You don't often see this vulnerable part of Jon, right?"

Rosalita: (nods)

Therapist: "This part that says, 'I long to be connected with you. I long to know that I am first in your heart.'" (heightening; to Jon) "Is that okay Jon?"

Jon: (nods yes)

Therapist: (continues with Rosalita) "And yet when he shows this vulnerable part, it seems to draw you to him. It's like you immediately wanted to comfort him." (Note here that the therapist has reflected key attachment-related themes such as comfort and connection repeatedly. The therapist is actively choreographing the change event; reframing behavior in the context of attachment needs and wants.)

Rosalita: (nods)

Exercise 5: Withdrawer Engagement

1. Which of the following best describes the therapist theme expanding attachment-related affect?
   a. Initially, the therapist seeks to reenter the more blaming partner's experience stemming from work in Step 5. _____
   b. The therapist seeks to reenter the withdrawing partner's experience stemming from work done in Step 5 to more precisely heighten attachment fears, hurts, and longings. _____
   c. The therapist seeks to create a contract specifying behavioral rewards and consequences for each partner. _____
   d. The therapist focuses on past exceptions in which the couple resolved conflict. _____

2. Which of the following best illustrates a typical therapist heightening response when working from within the expanding attachment-related affect theme?
   a. "Lucinda, you mentioned that sometimes you guys don't argue and fight around this issue. What are you doing differently in those times?" _____
   b. "Lucinda, this reminds me of the conflict you had with your mom when you were a child, always wanting her approval and affection." _____
   c. "You feel so alone, so emotionally disconnected right now. It matters not how hard you try, your sense is that it's just not safe to turn to him." _____
   d. "Why don't you tell him to stop, tell him that you've had enough? Can you enforce such a boundary with him now?" _____

Example:

Jon: (withdrawer) "Yeah. That's it. It's all very frustrating." (fidgets in chair)

Therapist: "What's that? Frustrating? You fidget in your chair as you say this. Help me understand?" (Therapist notes immediate experience of client as seen in fidgeting.

This is reflected to better understand client and to intensify immediate experience; evocative responding.)

Jon: *"Well, I am trying now to not attack back, or to not run away when conflict comes around. But, it's tough to respond differently when she keeps coming at me at full speed."*

Therapist: *"So, you're trying to change this cycle, but it's hard to stay engaged when you're feeling attacked, yeah?"*

Jon: *"Yes. I get a bit shaky, you know? Kind of like, 'Wow, the heat's coming.'"*

Exercise 6:

Which choice best surmises how the therapist seeks to experientially reenter this partner's position in the cycle?

a. Therapist initially seeks to intensify immediate experiencing by using an evocative response when Jon "fidgets" in his chair. _____
b. Therapist confronts Jon and challenges his commitment and thinking. _____
c. Therapist heightens Jon's sense of reaching behavioral goals set forth in last week's contract. _____
d. Therapist purposely ignores secondary emotion and attends to primary. _____

Exercise 7:

Write an evocative response to Jon's last statement. The objective is to get Jon presently experiencing what he is describing.

_____

_____

Example:

Jon: *(7-second silence) "I hate it. I start thinking that I can't match her. I can't do this right. I feel like a dog on a training leash. Problem is, like the dog, I don't speak English."*

Exercise 8:

Write a response that first heightens Jon's statement. The goal is to expand his present experiencing. Follow that with an evocative response that checks in with him to be sure you are on track.

_____

_____

Example:

Jon: *"Yes. I do feel like a puppy dog on a training leash. I just sit and take my medicine for pissing on the carpet."*

Exercise 9:

Write a response that uses Jon's own words to continue expanding his present experiencing of his withdrawn position in the relationship.

_____

_____

Exercise 10:

Choose the heightening responses from the list below: (more than one correct answer)

a. "You're trapped on a leash. You feel like you have to just sit there and 'take your medicine,' you say. Like a dog that pissed on the carpet." _____
b. "Have you noticed your thought pattern when this happens? What do you tell yourself?" _____
c. "What do you do when you feel like a dog? What action do you take?" _____
d. "Has there been a time when you didn't feel like a dog? What was different about those times?" _____
e. "A dog on a leash. A dog on a leash that has once again messed up, once again not come through, once again come up short." _____
f. "Why don't you stand up to her? Why do you take being treated like a dog? 'Here boy, here boy!' Does that make you feel at home?" _____

Example:

Jon: *(slowly, with head down)* "Yeah. Like a little puppy. Small, unprotected, scolded, afraid, tensed up. That's me."

Therapist: *"What is happening inside right now Jon as you say this?"*

Jon: *"I feel sad. Beaten down. Like that puppy."*

Therapist: *(softly and slowly)* *"Right. Yes. You're touching that sense of feeling defeated, and sad."*

Jon: *(sighs heavily)*

Exercise 11:

1. In the therapist's first response above, what is the name of the intervention used?
   a. Heightening _____
   b. Restructuring interaction _____
   c. Reframing _____
   d. Evocative responding _____
2. In the therapist's second response above, what intervention is used?
   a. Heightening _____
   b. Evocative responding _____
   c. Finding the exception _____
   d. Restructuring interactions _____

Exercise 12:

In the vignette on page 205, circle each occurrence of primary emotion. Clients often do not use actual word labels such as "sad," etc. Be sure to circle implicit referrals or metaphors alluding to emotional states. "The sky seems so dark," for example, would be a metaphor describing sadness. Compare your response to the one provided in the Answer Section.

Exercise 13:

Which of the following best describes the goals of the expanding attachment-related affect theme?

a. Prepares the way for a concrete and specific behavioral contact between spouses. _____

b. Builds toward cycle de-escalation that is crucial for positive outcomes in EFT. _____

c. The expansion of attachment-related fears and needs poignantly reconnects the withdrawing partner to what is longed for. This empowers one to ask for attachment needs to be honored and met. _____

d. By making fears and needs explicit, the other spouse is not left guessing why her husband acts as if he is from Mars. _____

Example:

Jon: (slowly, with head down) "Yeah. Like a little puppy. Small, unprotected, scolded, afraid, tensed up. That's me."

Therapist: "What is happening inside right now Jon as you say this?"

Jon: "I feel sad. Beaten down. Like that puppy."

Therapist: (softly and slowly) "Right. Yes. You're touching that sense of feeling defeated, and sad."

Jon: (sighs heavily)

Therapist: "What would it be like to begin telling Rosalita about this? Would you be able to turn to her and share with her what it's like for you to feel this way?"

Exercise 14:

Choose the EFT restructuring interactions intervention from the list below that might be the therapist's next step in the previous example:

a. "Do you ever share this with her at home? You don't because your childhood wounds are too great." _____

b. "You'd really like to be able to share this with her, but it needs to be safe, right?" _____

c. "I'd like you to communicate clearly with her now. Be sure to use 'I' statements, and if you start blaming or speaking for her, I will stop you and we'll discuss it. Okay?" _____

d. "Would you please turn now and share with her how scary this is for you, how badly you don't want to defend and withdraw. Would you please turn to her and share this in your own words now?" _____

e. "What do you think she is thinking right now? Why don't you ask her?" _____

Exercise 15:

Write your own restructuring interactions response asking Jon to turn and share with Rosalita.

_____

_____

Example:

Therapist: "Would you be able to begin telling Rosalita about this? Would you be able to turn to her now and begin to share with her what it's like for you to feel this way?"

Jon: (to therapist) "Whew. That won't be easy."

Based on Jon's response in the above segment, the therapist wants to support Jon by validating and heightening his emerging immediate experience (slight fear). In attachment terms, Jon's fear blocks attempts at risking and asking for emotion reconnection. By expanding Jon's fear in a supporting and validating context Jon is aided toward sharing and connecting with Rosalita from within his fear, rather than the normal pattern of defending and distancing away from his fear. When fear is a factor, it's very important for the EFT therapist to aid partners in risking and comforting each other from within their fear. By processing attachment-related affect moment by moment, the EFT therapist is in tune with emerging emotion, and helps create the context for this in-session. Step 7 is the pivotal place for this to happen.

Exercise 16:

Select the response below that validates and expands Jon's immediate and burgeoning fear of turning and sharing with Rosalita before he's again asked to directly share.

a. "It's okay. Go ahead and risk. You can do it. I know you can. I've seen the strength of your family, the strength you've shown in here. You can do it." _____

b. "Right. Sharing your fear with her is really scary. And why wouldn't it be? She could belittle you, she could attack you, right? It's very scary for you to risk opening up to her like this. She means so much to you. Would you please turn to her now and tell her a little bit about how scary this is for you, this is no easy task. Would you let her in on that now please?" _____

c. "Has there ever been a time when you did share this with her? What was different about that time?" _____

d. "You see your mother in her, and you fear that you won't be good enough for her. You were never really good enough for your mom's acceptance." _____

Exercise 17:

Write your own response that validates Jon's current experience of fear, expands his fear of turning and sharing with Rosalita, and then asks him again to turn and share directly with her.

_____

_____

_____

_____

Exercise 18:

Looking at your own response above, list the EFT interventions you employed. When finished, compare and contrast your chosen interventions with typical ones listed in the answer section.

1. _____
2. _____
3. _____

Example:

Therapist: *"Would you be able to begin telling Rosalita about this? Would you be able to turn to her now and begin to share with her what it's like for you to feel this way?"*

Jon: *(to therapist) "Whew. That won't be easy."*

Therapist: *"I hear you. It won't be easy sharing this with her. It's kind of scary to share this with her? To open up to her like that?"*

Jon: *(nods)*

Therapist: *"Yeah, it's kind of scary to share this with her. She could get mad and go for you, right?"*

Jon: *"Yes, or she could belittle me."*

Therapist: *"Yes, she could. You're right, I am asking you to risk. And she could miss how much of a risk this is for you, she could. Could you share with her how risky and scary this is to share with her like this? Could you help her understand this in your own words right now?"*

Jon: *(12 seconds of silence) "It's hard to share this with you. I am afraid that you won't understand and will get mad. When that happens it really affects me. I feel like a helpless little puppy dog. I sometimes fear that you really don't love me, or that you may leave. I know I have at times acted like that little puppy dog. I run away and hide when a disagreement occurs. But, I guess, I am just getting tired of running. And I am tired of being afraid and feeling helpless. I sometimes feel like I am just not being the husband I want to be...and that hurts me. But I am tired of running away from that, and I don't want to do it anymore. I need you to respect this, honey. I don't like feeling separated or cut off from you, and that's how I feel after we fight or are mad at each other for days. I need you to try to stop attacking me so quickly and loudly. I am going to try my best here, and I want you to work with me and try your best, too."*

Therapist: *(to Jon) "That was great Jon. You just really risked. What's it like to share this with her?"*

Jon: *"It was good. I feel very good about it."*

Therapist: *"It feels good to open up to Rosalita and share with her like this?"*

Jon: *"Yeah. It's risky, I mean, she could nail me, but it feels really good to get this out there and to make it concrete. I feel exhilarated."*

Exercise 19:

Choose the best answer. In the above segment the therapist is:

a. Supporting Jon's turning and sharing with his spouse. _____
b. Inquiring about Jon's family of origin. _____
c. Using transference effectively. _____
d. Assessing for contempt in the relationship. _____
e. Supporting Jon's engaging position with validation and processing it with evocative responding. _____

Exercise 20:

Create your own responses of validation and evocative responding.

Validation: _____

_____

Evocative responding: _____

_____

The therapist now moves to process with Rosalita. The key objective here is to tap into Rosalita's experience of hearing Jon's attachment-related affect and wants/needs. The engaging withdrawer (Jon) is in a very vulnerable position, and the therapist wants to keep the atmosphere "hot." This helps *pull* for a response of accessibility and responsiveness from Rosalita.

Example:

Jon: (12 seconds of silence) "It's hard to share this with you. I am afraid that you won't understand and will get mad. When that happens it really affects me. I feel like a help-less little puppy dog. I sometimes fear that you really don't love me, or that you may leave. I know I have at times acted like that little puppy dog. I run away and hide when a disagreement occurs. But, I guess, I am just getting tired of running. And I am tired of being afraid and feeling helpless. I sometimes feel like I am just not being the husband I want to be...and that hurts me. But I am tired of running away from that, and I don't want to do it anymore. I need you to respect this, honey. I don't like feeling separated or cut off from you, and that's how I feel after we fight or are mad at each other for days. I need you to try to stop attacking me so quickly and loudly. I am going to try my best here, and I want you to work with me and try your best, too."

Exercise 21:

Jon's previous sharing of his attachment fears and needs with Rosalita is presented above. In preparation for processing with Rosalita, go back and underline all of the instances where Jon shares his primary emotion and associated metaphors. When finished, circle where Jon is stating and asking for his attachment wants/needs to be met. When finished, compare your answer to those provided in the answers section.

Exercise 22:

Based on your work in the previous question, create an evocative response to Rosalita that poignantly reflects the key elements of Jon's fears and needs.

_____

_____

Example:

Therapist: (to Rosalita) "What was it like for you as Jon risked and shared how scary it is for him to open up to you, and how he no longer wants to withdraw and protect? Being 'separated' from you really wreaks havoc on him. What happened inside as he shared these things?"

Rosalita: "On one hand it was sad for me, because I don't want him to feel like a little puppy that has to be obedient or else. That was hard to hear, but I am not angry. On the other hand, it was really good to hear because I never hear this from him."

Therapist: "This is sort of new to you, Rosalita? You aren't used to seeing this part of Jon? The part that needs you to help him open up to you more? That no longer wants to be emotionally separated?"

Rosalita: "Yes it is. I usually just see him closing down, or getting quiet. I thought he didn't care."

Therapist: (to Rosalita) "You thought he didn't care, that's why he shut down, or withdrew?"

Rosalita: "Yes. Right now I feel sad for him." (looks at Jon)

Exercise 23:

The therapist picks up on Rosalita's sadness for Jon and recognizes the compassion she is feeling for him in the moment. Choose the best restructuring interaction from the list below.

a. "You feel sad for him now, yes. When he shows this part of him, when he risks like this, it brings up a sadness and compassion in you, yeah?" (she nods) "Would you please turn to him and share this with him now, in your own words?" _____

b. "If it was safe to talk to him right now, what would you say?" _____

c. "Have you ever let him know that you feel compassion for him? How did you do that?" _____

d. "Tell him about this sadness." _____

Exercise 24:

Create your own restructuring interaction for Rosalita below.

_____

_____

Example:

Therapist: (to Rosalita) "You feel sad for him, yeah. Could you please share this with him now?"

Rosalita: (to Jon) "I am sad that you feel this way. I've never wanted you to feel unloved, or be afraid that I might leave you. I don't want to leave you. I didn't think you cared this much. I am used to seeing the backside of you walking away."

The therapist interjects to choreograph and further shape Rosalita's response by reframing it into a more focused attachment context. Reframing in the context of attachment needs and wants is used. The desire is to heighten what she is saying, and to keep the process slow and focused.

Exercise 25:

Choose the reframing in the context of attachment needs and wants intervention from the list below.

a. "Rosalita, what's it like to share this with him?"

b. "You're not used to seeing this part of Jon that is afraid of losing you, that longs for you. What you see is him withdrawing in fear and to protect, right? So this is kind of new for you. You're not used to hearing about how much you impact him, and how much he needs you."

c. "Suppose he was able to show this side of himself more this week. How do you think your response would be different?"

d. "You're able to have compassion on him right now Rosalita. You weren't able to before—your memories of your father kept you from doing that. But here you were able to do it, to respond to him."

Exercise 26:

Create your own reframing in the context of attachment needs and wants response.

_____

_____

_____

Example:

Therapist: (to Rosalita) "You don't often see this vulnerable part of Jon, right?"

Rosalita: (nods)

Therapist: "This part that says, 'I long to be connected with you. I long to know that I am first in your heart.'" (heightening; to Jon) "Is that okay, Jon?"

Jon: (nods yes)

Therapist: (continues with Rosalita) "And yet when he shows this vulnerable part, it seems to draw you to him. It's like you immediately wanted to comfort him."

Rosalita: (nods)

Exercise 27:

In the segment above the therapist is primarily:

a. Finding exceptions to the problematic cycle. _____
b. Making insights into past key attachment events that keep each spouse stuck in their defenses. _____
c. Looking to externalize the struggle between the couple. _____
d. Choreographing a new positive interactional cycle by reframing behavior in the context of attachment needs and wants. _____

Blamer Softening Event Snapshot: Inez and Fernando

When the couple arrived at session 14 they announced that they had been caught in the negative cycle that morning, but let it go in the car on the way to the session. The therapist decided to explore this incident.

Fernando had been checking his emails prior to getting ready to come for their session. The first email he read was from a former work colleague. As he read, he spiraled down into the negative mix of feelings associated with his work experience. The next email message was from Angela, and she had sent holiday photographs. He called to Inez to join him at the computer. To his irritation, Inez insisted on examining the photos in minute detail. Already tense from his first email, and now worried about being late for their appointment, he snapped at Inez, who, true to her usual form in the cycle, puffed up and shouted at him.

Fernando: "Well I got flipped into that place again. I got an email from someone at—at work. You know, it put me back there. To all the dreadful times I had at work—disrespected, dismissed, struggling so hard to show I'm not a failure."

Therapist: (RISSSC manner) "Right. So you're back in the old place—the disrespecting, the dismissing, the struggle. It's hard to feel that you're enough."

Inez: "Well why can't you talk about that then, instead of going for me?"

Fernando: "I just tried to get past it. I called you in to see Angela's holiday photos."

Inez: "Yes, but, just like you said, you were in that place again."

Therapist: "It's hard for you to let her in when you are 'flipped into that place?'"

Fernando: "I never wanted her to see me there."

Therapist: "Never wanted her to see that inside you were struggling, that it was so hard for you. Such a tough place. What would happen, Fernando, if she saw that?"

Fernando: "I wouldn't be manly, you know? She wouldn't respect me."

Therapist: "She wouldn't respect you?"

Fernando: "Look, the real truth of the matter is that if she saw me, saw how pathetic I really am—she'd probably find someone else." (Laughs bitterly.) "That's why I always came on so strong—never let them catch you with your armor off!"

Therapist: (softly) "It's hard to trust that if she saw the real Fernando, it's like a part of you says, 'If she saw the real me, there's no way she'd stay around. She'd probably head out the door.' Is that close?"

Fernando: (head down) "That's it. That's exactly it."

Therapist: "Can you turn and share this directly with her now Fernando? Would you please turn and tell her how a part of you says, 'She'll leave if you admit this. Don't you show her the real you!' Can you share that directly with her now in your own words please?"

Fernando: (smiles weakly) "Well, yes, but no. Yes, I did it again today. I did it again. I know I've done things to hurt her, and I know I can't change the past. But I want to change the future. I...I want to make things different."

Therapist: (repeats her request) "Can you let her know, Fernando just how hard it is for you, for you to let her see the guy on the inside, the inside Fernando?"

Fernando: (turns to Inez) "Inside, inside I feel..." (Fernando pauses) "It's hard."

Therapist: "It's hard to say?"

Fernando: (small voice) "Yes."

Therapist: "So hard. So hard to look at her and say..."

Fernando: "I...I..." (Fernando pauses again)

Therapist: "It sounds like this is really scary—a real risk for you, yes? It's really scary to begin to tell her how low you sometimes feel, how afraid you get that if she really sees you, she may not like what it looks like, and she may head out the door?"

Fernando: "Yes, a risk. But Inez, you've taken risks with me."

(Inez reaches out to take Fernando's hand.)

Fernando: (his voice is thick and husky) "Sorry, kid. Thank you. I feel you there. You know I feel so puny sometimes, it's so damned hard to be me sometimes. Armor. That's what I do—and yes, I see how it pushes you away."

Therapist: "So what do you need, Fernando, when you feel so small and puny?"

Fernando: "I have it right here in my hand." (He looks tenderly at his wife.) "I need for you to hold me. Comfort me like you are now."

Inez: (with tears in her eyes) "I am here, Fernando. I am here for you."

Therapist: "I see there are tears, Inez, and you look emotional. I am wondering what this is like for you?"

Inez: "I only saw him cry once in his life. When his father died."

Fernando: "Did you despise me for it?"

Inez: "No! You placed your trust in me. I am honored by it. You trusted me. It means so much. I've never felt closer to you than I do right now."

Therapist: "When you see his softer tender side like you do right now, this pulls you towards him? You say, 'I've never before felt this close to you.'"

Inez: "Yes, never like I do right now."

Therapist: "This tender side of Fernando pulls you in, and you are really here to comfort him."

Inez: "Right now I feel like I do count."

Therapist: "Right. When he lets you in and is vulnerable and shares his needs for you, then you feel like you matter to him."

Inez: "Yes, I feel important to him. And I am not alone."

Therapist: "Can you tell him that, Inez, right now?"

BLAMER SOFTENING EVENT

Research demonstrates that softenings are crucial to success in EFT (Johnson & Greenberg, 1988). Softening events fuel creation of secure relationships where both partners are emotionally accessible and responsive. In secure relationships spouses ask for attachment fears to be soothed, and attachment needs to be met. Softening events powerfully initiate the bonding process, wherein secure attachment bonds are kindled. Softenings and subsequent bonding events effectively create securely attached relationships, perhaps, for many partners, for the first time.

Once the more withdrawing spouse is "engaged" into the relationship, the therapist focuses primarily on the more blaming spouse (Steps 5 and 6). In Step 7, this culminates into the blamer softening event. The now softening partner, immersed in attachment-related affect, directly shares attachment fears with their partner, and directly asks for attachment needs and wants to be met.

The softening process often begins with the softening partner sharing attachment-related fears. These fears have often shut partners down through the years, blocking the healthy integration of emotion-generated meaning, much less the actual divulgence of these fears. The primary object is not to gain insight into these fears and blocks, rather, to experientially expand the attachment-related emotions, that organize and orient partners to what is important. When attended to and integrated, these expanded emotions propel partners to dare reach to a spouse for comfort, acceptance, and love—through fears and all.

Living in fear is exhausting and debilitating. It keeps partners alone and unseen. Attachment-related fears are often embedded in internal working models, or views of self and other. Consider these typical Step 7 statements from softening partners: "Will you be there for me if I show you this weak and fragile person that I hide from everyone? Why would you be there for me if I opened up this much with you? How can I trust you? No one has ever really been there for me."(view of self and other). "I know you are there. You are always there. It's just… It's just how could someone really love me? I mean, just look at me?" (view of self). With time the EFT therapist picks up on whether softening partners are speaking from within views of other, self, or both in Step 7. The following transcript and exercises will help in beginning to recognize the differences.

Initial research has demonstrated that an expert EFT therapist typically processes through softenings from within the following six themes (Bradley & Furrow, 2004):

1. Possible blamer reaching
2. Processing fears of reaching
3. Actual blamer reaching
4. Supporting softening blamer
5. Processing with engaged withdrawer
6. Engaged withdrawer reaching back with support

This process is one of preparing for, shaping and setting up *enactments* where partners express attachment needs and connect emotionally.

The themes above are sequential rather than linear, meaning the therapist is free to circle back through them based on the processing needs of each particular couple (see Figure 7.1). Below, the softening process is artificially broken into distinct themes to aid in conceptualization. Questions are asked from within each theme.

Summary of Couple Context

Marcus and Fresca have been married for 30 years, with three children now grown and out of the house. They are in their mid-50s with middle class socioeconomic status. Marcus has a European cultural background, while Fresca is Hispanic. Fresca reports that religion and spirituality are very important to her, while Marcus reports

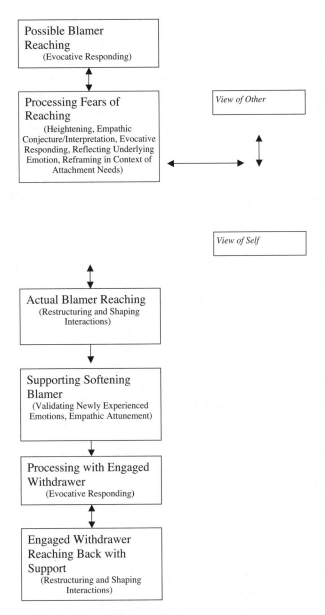

Figure 7.1   The six themes of the softening process.

that Fresca's Catholic background has impacted him positively, although he wasn't raised particularly religious. They are both second-generation Americans, and both are employed full-time. They entered couples therapy reporting ongoing marital conflict for "as long as we can remember." Fresca reported battling with an eating disorder for years, for which she had attended therapy. She also reported depression, a sense of "almost just giving up on us." Marcus reported severe anxiety, to the point at times that he could barely get up and go to work. He also reported being hospitalized for his anxiety several years ago. Each reported that they could not count on the other for emotional reassurance or trust, and that it was "too risky to go there."

Their cycle on a secondary level saw Marcus getting frustrated at Fresca and raising his voice. Fresca responded to this by trying harder to abate the growing intensity by answering more clearly or quickly. "Even then though, right at the beginning of these times, I feel myself starting to tense up. It's like, 'Oh no, he's building anger here. I've got to defuse it or he'll explode into me.'" So Fresca would try to stop the ensuing "volcano," but it rarely worked. Marcus reported that he just wanted her to pay attention to things and have her support. "Half the time she barely notices that I am asking her for help, or that I can't find something." Marcus quickly escalated into anger, criticizing and attacking Fresca. Fresca used to fight back at some point, but for the last ten or so years she has been just giving up and going silent. "He rages on for some time, but eventually he stops. I just let him go. There is no stopping him." On a primary level Fresca was very lonely. She also felt a sense of being deficient in that "I can't please him. I can't do it right. I come away feeling like an idiot over and over. That just hurts too much, so I've learned to put up the wall and shut him out."

In Step 5 of the withdrawer engagement process, Fresca touched a deep sense of wanting more in the relationship. She realized that she was not perfect, but that she was not deficient either. She was tired of walking on eggshells over his anger, and she wanted him to stop attacking her. She wasn't getting any younger, and she wanted them to be able to hold each other. Marcus was able to solemnly hear her, and stated that he wanted that too, but that he was scared. "I don't know if I know how to stop myself in my negative ways, but I want to. I can see how much this means to you, how much we mean to you" (Step 6). In Step 7, Fresca turned to Marcus and stated "I am tired of being lonely in our marriage. It doesn't have to be this way. I don't want to hurt like this anymore. I want you to work with me rather than pushing me away with your anger. I need a husband that will love me. One that will hold me when I feel alone or scared. I want you and no one else. We can do this."

When Step 5 focused more on Marcus, he felt the nagging pain and fear associated with getting older. He wasn't happy with how much he had done with his life, how much he had saved for his family financially—and he wasn't getting any younger. He reported hearing the "Tick! Tick! Tick!" of the "clock of life." "It's screaming at me, 'You've failed to make enough to support your wife and family! What good are you after all of these years?'" So when he saw bills to pay, or something broken needing replacement, he would quickly go to Fresca to ask how they could possibly owe so much, or how something else could yet again be broken. He was quickly overwhelmed, and responded in intense anger.

At a primary level Marcus felt like he had failed as a provider to his family, and that there was no time left to amend that. Marcus had always been taught by his father that the most important thing in life was financially taking care of family. When this sense of failure hit him, he felt panicked in the pit of his stomach, and had a history of panic attacks. On top of this, the couple's cycle had become so negative and rigidly set over the years that Marcus doubted whether Fresca really loved him. The therapist supported Marcus in sharing these fears with his wife. "I can't say I would blame you if you didn't love me," Marcus reported. "I haven't been very supportive, either emotionally or financially. Why would you love such a loser and wimp? I get all mad at you, when underneath I feel like such a loser."

Fresca had no idea these emotions were behind Marcus' angry attacks. "I never see this side of you," she responded. Later she reflected on her Hispanic background as being helpful to her in this specific situation: "You know my Latino heritage really places family in high esteem. I want to understand this better, and support you." The therapist helped accent how important this was to her, and how her cultural background well prepared and spurred her on to have a secure connection with Marcus, and that she desperately wanted him to feel safe in sharing with her. "In fact," she said, "these are the same kinds of fears and emotions I have. This lets me know that we are more similar than I ever knew. And that I am not alone in my pain in this relationship" (Step 6).

As the couple enters Step 7, the therapist initially moves to an inquisitive stance, wondering if Marcus is ever able to share his attachment fears with Fresca. Is he able to reach for her as and let her be his ally?

Theme One: *Possible Blamer Reaching*

The therapist often "choreographs" entrance into the softening event by asking the couple to imagine engaging with one another from a new level of vulnerability. The stage is set when the couple has reentered a recent episode in which the more blaming spouse has gotten angry, sullen, or sad, the effect of which usually shuts down hopes of mutual accessibility and responsiveness. Often, the result of this interactional sequence breaks the emotional connection between partners. "I told him I could handle it," a typical engaged partner says, "but he just kept getting angry. I wasn't withdrawing, but I wasn't going to allow him to just run over me either. I asked him what was going on, could we talk about it. He just got more angry and eventually went silent. Like we've talked about in here, at these times he won't really let me in. So I said, 'forget it.' We haven't really been 'connected' since then, and it has been 3 days."

At this point in the therapy process, the negative interactional cycle is nothing new to the couple or therapist. In Step 7, the therapist briefly reenters a recent salient episode by reflecting the behaviors and primary emotions, but then quickly follows this with an evocative inquiry that offers a new kind of relational possibility—one indirectly aimed toward the more blaming spouse. The therapist usually responds from a "first-person" stance that allows the more-blaming spouse to experientially take on this possible position. "When you get like this," a therapist may respond, "when you are so overwhelmed, so panicked, could you ever turn to her and say, 'I am so panicked right now. This fear is really welling up inside of me.'" (Note "first-person" stance.) "Would that be too hard for you? What would that be like, to let her in, to reach to her for then?" This line of inquiry allows for a "testing of the waters" so to speak, an imaginative dabble into experiencing a new way of interacting that initiates work in Step 7. This has the effect of experientially preparing the couple for what is next without creating an interpretive or skills-building context.

Example:

Earlier in the week, Marcus had learned that their house had termites and needed extensive treatment. The costs of this had sent him through the roof. On top of this, his car's engine was skipping and the mechanic suggested it was time to look for a new car. Marcus had again gone a rampage, attacking Fresca for not staying on top of when the house needed insect treatment. She had remained engaged, however, stating that she was sorry that she missed it, but that he missed it too. "I see that you're angry," Fresca had replied. "And that's okay. I am angry too. What I don't want is you going on and on at me. I want you to stop. This gets us nowhere, we both know that. Let's tackle this together. First though, what is going on for you besides the anger?" At that point

Marcus "shut down" and refused to talk. Marcus is well aware of his affect, but he is unable to take an interpersonal step and enlist his wife as an alley against the fear and loathing of himself.

"You know, you guys have come a long way," the therapist responded, as she entered Step 7 primarily focused on Marcus. "You are not fighting nearly as often, nor as intensely. Fresca, you really stood your ground when Marcus got upset this time. I think it's great how you were able to, in effect, see through his anger and not withdraw. Marcus, you were able to stop attacking when she did this. But there still seems to be one aspect missing...."

Exercise 28:

1. Check the responses an EFT therapist might make to help Marcus begin to imagine reaching to his wife in times of severe distress. The therapist wants to know if he has considered sharing with her during these times, and what that prospect is like for him. Look for responses that assess and yet invite him to experientially imagine this new way of interacting with his wife (more than one correct answer).

    a. "Could you ever turn to Fresca and share with her about how overwhelmed you feel in these times?" _____

    b. "Marcus, Fresca wants to be let in when these worries and fears invade you. This week she stood beside you and said, 'What's going on besides the anger?' On another level she is saying, 'Let me in.' Right, Fresca?" (she nods). "She's saying, 'I want to be there and help you.' What would it be like for you to try to let her in during these times?" _____

    c. "Marcus, if you used 'I' statements and Fresca assured you that she would only listen and reflect back to you, would you try communicating like that with her next time?" _____

    d. "You can't let her in because she will only make fun of you, call you a loser, remind you of how you've failed. This is what you heard all through childhood, and you're convinced that's what you would get from her." _____

    e. "Fresca didn't withdraw. My sense is she wants to be there for you, when you are overwhelmed, vulnerable, afraid and all. What would it be like to risk sharing your fears with her then? What would it be like to begin letting her in?" _____

    f. "What thoughts came into mind when Fresca asked you what was going on besides the anger?" _____

    g. Marcus, have there been times when you were able to let her in? Let's look at what was different about those times? _____

2. Continuing in the scenario above, the therapist aids the more blaming spouse in experientially imagining what an initial bid to his spouse for attachment needs to be met might look like. Choose the EFT response below that best accomplishes this.

    a. "What happens inside as you consider opening up to her during these situations?" _____

    b. "Do you ever turn to Fresca and share what's going on inside for you?" _____

    c. "The cycle between you has changed guys. Fresca, it's great how you stood your ground. It seems that you didn't let Marcus' anger push you to withdraw. Rather,

you asked him to stop the anger and include you in what was perhaps underneath and bothering him. You want him to let you in, yeah? Do you hear her right
now Marcus?" _____

    d. "Marcus, during these intense situations, do you ever think of turning to Fresca
and saying, 'You know what, Hon, I'm struggling with all of this anxiety about
this termite situation and the costs. And I am really dejected about the car. I'm
still caught in all of that, you know, all those feelings that come up for me about
money and my worth to you and the family. I am having such a hard time with it
right now.' That would have been really hard for you, yeah?" _____

Example:

*A more blaming spouse reports, "I let him have it. I did. I hate that I did. I just get so
upset with him. I just feel like he should be able to do this right! I know I am driving
him away, but at the time my anger just overruns my fear so fast." "It's easier for you
to run to your anger," the therapist responds, "than it is to risk letting him in on the
fear and pain that is going on inside of you. And so you guys get stuck here yet again,
right? (Brief summary of blamer's cycle and underlying emotion.)*

Exercise 29:

Write two of your own processing possible blamer reaching responses to the above
vignette. First, create your own brief reflection of the blamer's cycle and underlying
emotions. Second, write a brief "first-person" dialog that experientially walks the
more blaming spouse through inviting the other to come close and comfort during
overwhelming times. When finished, compare your responses with a sample response
given in the answer section.

- Response 1
  - Create a brief cycle summary with underlying emotion:

    _____

    _____

  - Create a first-person dialog inviting the other in:

    _____

    _____

- Response 2
  - Create a brief cycle summary with underlying emotion:

    _____

    _____

• Create a first-person dialog inviting the other in:

_____

_____

Theme 2: Processing Fears of Reaching

Most partners respond that they do not invite the other in mainly because it's too risky and they are afraid. They sometimes report having done this in the past, or that it is something they could try. Regardless, the EFT therapist takes them at their word and responds in a manner that moves them forward to risking this in-session. Degree of fear varies among couples, which is largely related to level and duration of distress, but there is usually some form and level of fear blocking possible attachment bids. This does not apply to any situation where distress occurs, but rather in interactions where attachment insecurities get primed and are up and running between mates. This may or may not happen in a discussion about taking out the garbage, for example. Fighting and disagreements are normal, perhaps even healthy at times.

It's the habitual negative cycle that spins out of control when attachment-related fears and insecurities are pricked that the EFT therapist doggedly hones in on. Empathic conjecture/interpretation and heightening are both used at this point. If fear has been previously recognized by the more-blaming partner as blocking in these specific situations, then heightening the attachment-related fear is in order. If fear has yet to be uncovered, the EFT therapist often uses empathic conjecture/interpretation to help the client take one step further in their experience. Insight is not the goal here. In fact, an insight-oriented interpretation at this point can shut down experiential processing, yielding more-cognitive responses such as, "Oh, I'd never connected that with my past before" or "Yes, you are right on." As opposed to this, the EFT therapist is supporting the more-blaming spouse into a deeper experiencing of attachment-related fears. Empathic conjecture/interpretation of fear is followed with heightening in order to make it more vivid and alive in the session. New meaning crystallizes from the slow processing of attachment-related affect that has previously been pushed out of awareness.

Example:

Returning to our ongoing couple scenario, Marcus states that he never really considers sharing or letting Fresca in when times get intense. "It's not safe enough for me to let her in during those situations," he reports, shaking his head demonstratively. He then talks about how she has hurt him in the past, and that he wouldn't risk showing his vulnerability by asking for anything when he's really feeling that low. "When I am that overwhelmed and low, she could really hurt me if I let her in on how I am actually feeling" he says. "I can't see doing that. The stakes are just too high." This signals the therapist to move into processing fears of reaching—fears that serve to block and shut down attachment longings for support, comfort, and reassurance. In the exercises below you will be asked to identify typical EFT responses when beginning to process fears of reaching for support. You will then practice writing your own similar responses.

Exercise 30:

Based in Marcus' responses in the above paragraph, choose the EFT responses from the list below: (more than one correct answer)

a. "I don't know, help me out here, but it sounds like you are dealing with this all alone." (Marcus nods yes) _____

b. "Have there been times when you have been able to let her in? What was different about those times?" _____

c. "Okay, I don't think you should let her in. Neither of you can handle it. It's just too much. I want each of you to promise me that you will not talk about what is really happening for either of you when these kinds of situations arise." _____

d. (slower) "It's like one part of you says, 'Well that would be pretty scary to do because suppose I did it wrong; or suppose I got aggressive like I have in the past; or suppose I just lost it and looked like a real "loser."' Right? That goes through you?" (he nods; slowly and softly) "This would just be too risky... too scary." _____

e. "It's like a part of you says, 'Oh no you don't. You're not sharing this. Not this! You could get hurt way too badly. Stop now!' Right?" (he nods) "And you run to your anger. This fear is big." _____

f. "You guys have made real progress here. But it looks like there needs to be this one more step. Fresca, you are there, standing with Marcus, asking to be let in. But Marcus, you get scared, right?" (he nods; softer) "Help me understand this fear, what happens inside when you are really overwhelmed and Fresca says, 'Hey Marcus, here I am. Please let me in. Can you hear me?' What happens?" _____

g. "This fear sounds like a regular and uninvited guest to your story. It sneaks up on you and really hampers you. Have you ever ganged up on this fear? Shown the fear who's boss?" _____

Example:

A more blaming spouse responds to the EFT therapist's imaginative inquiry (i.e., "Have you ever turned to him and...") with "I can't let him in, not then. I would never reach for him then. I just can't," shaking her head vehemently. While this partner has globally talked about her fears before, she has never shared that fear blocks her from reaching during these specific and intense situations. Based on attachment theory, the EFT therapist hypothesizes that unprocessed fear is indeed often shutting her down.

Exercise 31:

Among the selections below, select the two empathic conjecture/interpretations that best seek to help the client take one step further into her experience.

a. (softly) "It seems to me that you get to this point, when he is there wanting to understand, and you either show anger or go silent. I don't know, help me here if I am wrong, but, I am wondering if there is a part of you that really gets scared during these moments. A part that that says, 'You had better not risk this.' Is that close?" _____

b. (softly to engaged withdrawer) "It must be terribly difficult for you to want so badly for your wife to let you in when she is struggling so, only to have her get angry, or shut you out. How do you cope with this?" _____

c. (softly) "I am going out on a limb here a bit, so please help me out. I wonder if a part of you really gets scared when he is there, and you are faced with all of these things that overwhelm you. I mean at a level that perhaps you rarely allow yourself to touch. I wonder if this fear tells you that you had better not open up to him. Can you help me here?" _____

d. (softly) "It seems to me that you say you want him to be close, but then when there is a chance you sabotage it. You are withholding yourself from him. I think you are being dishonest with your husband. Let's not waste our time here. It's time to come clean like adults." _____

Example:

A more blaming spouse responds "Nooooo. I haven't let her in when I am getting that angry. I go from overwhelming shame and feelings of worthlessness to anger so fast. To show her that vulnerable stuff, that weak stuff, she'd think I was a big baby. That's not what she wants and needs from me. Who would want that?"

Exercise 32:

Write two of your own brief summary reflections and empathic conjecture/interpretations to help the client above begin to take one step further into his experience of fear that is blocking possible connection with his wife. When finished, compare your responses with the sample EFT response provided in the answers section.

1. _____

_____.

2. _____

_____.

Example:

When a more blaming partner is well aware of attachment-related fears that shut her down, the therapist moves directly to heightening these fears. Key secure attachment descriptors are often woven into the processing to further prompt the surfacing of healthy attachment wants and needs (see below "trust" and "rely"). The therapist continues to stress what is possible—the risk of reaching for comfort and security.

"No way," a more blaming partner says, "I don't reach for him. That is just too scary." "I see," the therapist responds. (slower and softer) "It's just way too scary to risk beginning to trust and rely on him. It's just not safe. A part of you says, 'Don't you dare!'"

Exercise 33:

Write one of your own heightening responses to the above scenario. Remember, the client is aware of fear, which signals the therapist to heighten rather than empathically conjecture/interpret.

_____

_____

Example:

In accord to the response you provided above, suppose the more blaming partner looks to exit processing their fear and says, "Yeah. It's too risky. But it wouldn't help anyway." "It wouldn't help anyway?" the therapist responds. "Help me understand?" "What good would it do?" the more blaming partner responds. "I mean, he'd either belittle me, or ignore me, something like that."

Exercise 34:

Choose the EFT response below that further processes the more blaming partner's fears of reaching with empathic conjecture followed by heightening.

a. "It's just too scary. You just can't bring yourself to risk." _____

b. "Help me out here, but it's like this part of you stands up and says, 'Don't you dare share how afraid or scared you are! If you show him your "underbelly" he'll belittle you, or ignore you.' Right? This part piles on and says, 'What good would it do anyway? Don't you dare do it. He won't be there. He won't care. Don't you hope for that.' It's just too scary for you let him in. The stakes are just too high, too painful."
_____

c. "You're so disgusted at him that you aren't convinced turning and sharing this with him would do any good, right? You've tried this before, and he only dismisses you. Time and time again you've risked with him and he just doesn't get it. He'll never get it." _____

d. "This is the point in the cycle where you guys never seem to be able to 'break through' and risk sharing your underlying emotion with each other. You usually choose to attack him, which covers up your fears. All he sees is your anger though, which compels him to protect and withdraw. This keeps both of you 'locked out' so to speak. Suppose I had a magic wand, and I waved this magic wand and a miracle occurred. The miracle resulted in this dilemma being solved. Suppose now that happened. What would now be different? How would you know that this dilemma between you was solved?" _____

Staying on track is also part of the processing fears of reaching theme. Sometimes when a more blaming spouse is asked if he ever considers reaching for support at home, he will report that he has reached for his spouse and that this is nothing new. This can be a way of trying to sidestep having to risk, even risking imaginatively in-session. Such responses attest to the power of the softening event. Usually the kind of reach that the therapist is talking about is not the kind the client reports. In these cases, however, the EFT therapist briefly assesses this by tracking what was said, how it was said, and how it ended. These interactions can indeed be attempts for attachment, but often lack the kind of attachment-related processing that is the key to change in softening events. In-session the therapist recreates the interaction and then intensifies it in the same manner as is being described in this chapter.

Heightening Views of Self and Other

When attachment-related fears are heightened in Step 7, they emanate from the more-blaming partner's negative views of other and/or views of self (see Figure 7.1). It is important for the therapist to recognize and attend to these distinctions. Responses centering in negative views of other usually have to do with the fear of the other partner showing contempt, criticizing, pouring shame on them, or abandoning them. Responses centering in negative views of self have more to do with an inherent sense of deficiency, worthlessness, feeling unlovable, and self-shame. As one client, speaking from a positive view of other, but a clear negative view of self, sobbed, "I know he will be there. He always is. My fear is, who would really want me? Just look at me!"

The EFT therapist starts processing fears centered in negative views of other, and for many couples this seems to be enough. But for some couples a negative view of self must be heightened and processed through as well. Note in the following exercise how the EFT therapist often uses "parts" language to separate out healthy attachment longings from the fears that block moving to get them met. At times partners will tie in attachment fears to how a parent was so condescending to them, so distant or neglectful. The therapist naturally honors such insights and memories to help shed light on and heighten the difficulty and fear of reaching to the other in the present relationship.

Exercise 35:

Choose which heightening responses address negative views of other and which address negative views of self. Write your answers at the end of each response.

1. "It's so hard for you to risk turning to her. The stakes are so high. She could really hurt you. She means more to you than anyone else, and you desperately want to reach to her, for it to be safe. But the part of you that is afraid keeps saying, 'Don't! Don't! Don't!'" _____

2. "You see him standing there, arms open. He's saying, 'Risk it honey. I'll be here for you. You can count on me.' But a part of you is saying, 'No, you can't risk it. He won't be there. No one has ever truly been there. It's too scary, too risky, it could hurt too much.' Is that close?" _____

3. "You're saying, 'I know she is there. I believe her. It's not that, it's that no one has really ever been there and cared for me.' A part of you says, 'Maybe there's something wrong with me. Maybe I am too strange, kind of unlovable.' Is that some of what goes on?" _____

4. "You're saying, 'I see you there, and I hear that you want me to risk letting you in. But I am so afraid. My parents let me down and hurt me so badly. I risked with my father and he left me all alone, crushed. I vowed that I would never let anyone hurt me that badly again. And here you are, asking me to risk with you? It scares me to death.' Am I getting it?" _____

5. "Of course this is very hard for you. Of course it's very scary. How could it not be? Bill has not been there in the past. For years you've had to go at this all alone. When you were sad, he was not there. When you were in pain, he was not there. You learned to cope without him. You gave up on your dreams for the two of you. Now, suddenly, he says that he is there, and that he wants you to let him in, after all these years. A part of you says, 'He will hurt you again. You can't count on him. Play it tight to the chest, play it safe.' Right?" _____

6. "Bill is here asking you to reach for him, to count on him, to let him in. But no one has really ever cared that much for you. No one has ever really cherished you just because you are who you are. Your mom died at an early age, and you two weren't close. Your dad drank and abused you. That's what men have done to you for most of your life, right? And so now as Bill stands here wanting you to share your heart with him, to risk sharing your fears and longings with him, you find it very hard to believe that he really wants you, that he really loves you. It's so scary for you to let yourself even begin to believe that anyone could possibly love you wholeheartedly. Am I hearing you?" _____

Example:

Marcus stated that he never turns to Fresca and shows his "soft side." "No," he reported, "I only get aggressive with her." The therapist heightened based on a possible negative view of other: "So, what you're saying to Fresca is, (slowly) 'Fresca, when these fears come up for me, when I start to feel caught in all of this stuff about that I don't feel somehow in control of my life, or that I haven't been able to do some things in my life that I wanted, I still feel somehow out of control around money, it still scares me—when I am struggling with all of these feelings, it's still really hard for me to reach for you. I am just not sure if you'll reject me, or get angry at me, or call me weak.' Yeah?"

Exercise 36:

Write two of your own responses below that similarly heighten Marcus' fears/negative view of other.

1. _____

   _____

2. _____

   _____

Example:

"Yes," Marcus responds, as he nods in agreement. "I am scared that she will see me as wimpy...small. Who wants that? My mother always told me that I'd never be able to make any woman truly happy." (he cries) "I sometimes think I am just so sick, so

weird, somehow wired differently than others. Fresca tries, she really does, but I don't know why she really cares at all."

Exercise 37:

Using the transcript above, use "parts language" (i.e., "One part of you says...but another part says...") to: (a) briefly reflect Marcus' fears/negative view of other; (b) heighten his fears/negative view of self. Try to incorporate "first-person dialog" as part of this heightening. Seek to bring the attachment fears and longings to a "boiling point"; (c) finish with an evocative response (i.e., "Is this close?"). When completed, compare your responses with one provided in the answer section.

- Briefly reflect fears/negative view of other (use parts language)

  _____

- Heighten fears/negative view of self (use parts language and first-person dialog)

  _____

- A brief evocative response

  _____

The more blaming spouse needs to deeply experience attachment-related fears in the session—in other words they need to become real and alive. This process has to reach a "boiling point" so to speak before moving forward. The duration of this, of course, varies among couples. If sufficient heightening is not accomplished, the softening may take on a more cognitive emphasis, which pulls them out of immediate emotional experiencing.

To this point the softening spouse has only spoken directly to the therapist, which is not sufficient in EFT. In fact, this only clarifies what needs to be shared and asked for from the other, now-engaged partner. In preparation for this, the therapist briefly summarizes work just completed in the processing fears of reaching theme to set up a possible softening enactment.

As demonstrated in the list below, the words used and the tone taken vary among couples. For some couples, perhaps less distressed ones, it is not as scary to share and open themselves up during softening events. For others, the process proves very difficult and requires more heightening and more processing.

Exercise 38:

Which of the following are typical therapist responses summarizing fears of reaching before initiating a softening enactment?

a. "So, to even consider turning to Fresca and saying, 'Honey, I am just so scared right now. I am overwhelmed, I need a hug, a little reassurance. I am really doubting myself.' That is really scary for you. This fear sort of paralyzes you, it keeps you alone in your doubts and fears, yeah?" _____

b. "You never show him this part of you, this part that says, 'Don't you dare open up to him again. You'll get stabbed in the heart. It just hurts too much to risk.' You never let him in when this part raises its head. You never say, 'I am really scared right now that you can't be trusted. Could you please reassure me now?' You never say that, right? Because that is just too scary, too…precise…too…on the money?" _____

c. "If we're going to be truthful here, you have to be honest with her. The fact is you don't trust her. You're not convinced that she has changed. You are being just selfish enough to not give her the chance to hurt you again, is that it?" _____

d. "She has asked for your forgiveness many, many times. She has done as much as she can to prove to you that she is trustworthy. And yet, you stay here, unflinching. Unforgiving. What will it take from her for you to honestly forgive her? I can't make you do it, and neither can she. You have to take the risk." _____

e. "So this is very dangerous territory for you, yeah? You see that she is here, right now, wanting you to come out and be with her. A part of you sees that and for the most part believes that. But there is this other part that really protects you, and it is screaming, 'No one has ever loved you. No one ever will. The only safe game in town is to hide, whether in anger or silence.' Right? So this indeed is dangerous territory."

_____

f. "Has there ever been a time where you have been able to open up to him during these episodes? What was different about those times? How did you do that?" _____

g. "Bill, I'd like for you to play her father for a minute. Elisa, look at him now. He is not the way he was before, he is your father, there to accept you and hold you. Do you see that in your father's eyes now? Bill, what did you feel as Elisa was doing this?" _____

h. "This week, Lucinda, you noticed at one point when the cycle was starting to happen that you felt afraid that Juan may leave again. But this time you didn't attack him, or go silent. This time you said, 'Honey, I am getting scared that you might leave me. The rational side of me knows that we are just arguing, but there is another part of me, a bigger part, that is scared. Could we stop arguing for now and could you reassure me?' How was that for you, to risk reaching from within your fear?" _____

Exercise 39:

In the space provided below, try out your own summarization of the work just completed in this therapist theme as illustrated above (i.e., "So to even consider turning to Fresca and saying…is just so scary…").

_____

_____

_____

_____

_____

Theme 3: Actual Blamer Reaching

The process of a softening spouse turning towards their partner and reaching for accessibility and assurance amidst their attachment fears and longings is in many ways the capstone of EFT. The therapist gently directs the now softening blamer to listen to and *enact* attachment needs and longings and to reach directly to her partner for comfort and assurance. This is one of the simplest directives the EFT therapist makes, but it is also one of the most intense, both for the couple and therapist. Having heightened the attachment-related affect, the therapist gently asks the softening partner to turn and share this with his spouse using a restructuring and reshaping interactions intervention. It often starts with having the softening partner share directly with the other how scary it is to envision openly turning to the other. Typical wording of the intervention could include: "Marcus, would you please turn now, and share this with Fresca, in your own words," or "Marcus, could you begin now to tell Fresca how scary it is to even think of turning to her during these times, would you please share this with her now." This intervention is short, direct, and to the point. The groundwork has been laid, the time to risk and reach is now. Often, the softening spouse then needs time to integrate newly emerging meaning brought into awareness from the processing of attachment-related affect before beginning to directly address their partner. Initial research shows an average of 8 to 16 seconds of silence is common, authenticating the intensity of the moment. The therapist respectfully stays out of the way unless this spouse gets stuck and asks for aid.

The "softening reach" is actually worded within each couple's own language and rhythms. It doesn't, for example, come off as dry as our academic description of "asking for attachment needs and wants to be met." It must be affectively charged for the message to come across experientially. In real-world language the softening reach often begins with the seemingly small yet transforming step of directly facing one's spouse and revealing, "It's so scary to think of turning to you and letting you in," or "I am really afraid to share this with you. I don't ever show this part of me." In these cases the therapist aids the softening spouse to articulate attachment needs and wants with their partners, which usually follows the immersion into and sharing of one's attachment-related affect. In other, perhaps less distressed couples, the softening reach may move directly into the articulation of attachment needs and wants more fluidly, such as "I need you to be there and help me with these fears, with these doubts. I've carried these with me my whole life, and it's terribly hard to share them with you. But I want to let you in…and for us to face this together." If the softening reach is not affectively charged and, for example, seems very cognitive in nature, the EFT therapist often returns to further heighten views of other and/or self.

Exercise 40:

From the list below choose the EFT responses typically used in the actual blamer reaching theme (more than one correct answer).

a. "Could you please turn to him and share with him how scary it is to reach out to him in these situations—in your own words?" _____

b. "Could you tell her, please?" _____

c. "If you were to reach out to him, what do you think he would think and say?" _____

d. "You've shared with me how afraid and paralyzed you get by this fear. But it's one thing to tell me, and quite another to tell her. Would you please, just now, turn and share this with her?" _____

e. (to engaged spouse) "What do you think is going through her mind as she considers reaching out to you?" _____

f. "Could you turn to her now and tell her how much you desperately need and want her to be there for you now, in your own words please?" _____

g. "I'd like for you to turn to him now and risk letting him in. Will you please now, in your own words, share with him what it's like for you to even consider turning to him when you are so afraid, and how he can help you in this." _____

h. "Yes, you're very clear that you desperately need him to help you with your fear of him leaving, and the painful self-doubts about you in fact being deficient and undesirable. Will you please turn to him now and just start to share this with him? He's there, and he's said that he's willing, if only you'll risk. Look at him, do you see him? He's inviting you. Please, share with him now about your fears and needs." _____

i. "You talked about wanting him to just hold you and comfort you. Do you ever just ask him for that?" (client shakes head no) "Could you please turn and ask him for what you need now?" _____

Example:

"So, to even consider turning to Fresca and saying, 'Honey, I am just so scared right now. I am overwhelmed. I am struggling with these frightful doubts about whether you really love me. I need a hug, a little reassurance. I am really doubting myself.' That is really scary for you. This fear sort of paralyzes you...it keeps you alone in your doubts and fears, yeah?" "Oh yeah," Marcus replies, looking down. "That would be huge."

Exercise 41:

Practice writing some of your own similar blamer reaching reflections below.

1. _____

     _____ .

2. _____

     _____ .

Theme 4: Supporting Softening Blamer

The therapist stands behind and supports the blamer as they risk, as the following example shows. Marcus gathered himself, turned directly to Fresca and slowly shared, "This is really hard for me. I really doubt myself and I doubt that you will even want me if I show this weak and scared part of me to you. If there's any way....I'd just love for you to grab my hand, or hug me sometimes when I am afraid or acting stupid because of all of this junk. I'd love your reassurance. But it's so scary to ask you for it, to even do this right now is all new territory for me. And I am scared right now that you'll laugh at me, or think, 'Who is this weak man I married?'" Fresca warmly replied, "I love it when you show this part of you to me, Marcus. If you ask I will do all I can to comfort you."

The therapist first moves to "shore-up" the softening blamer's new interactional stance just taken in the relationship with support, which emphasizes the importance of the relational step just risked. The therapist briefly reflects with an attachment-related affect and present focus. (Therapist, softly) "I think that was great Marcus. You really risked. You opened up and shared with Fresca what you need and how scary that is. Borrowing your own words, that was 'huge.'"

The therapist then aids the softening partner in processing their own internal responses to the softening reach with an evocative response intervention. "What was it like for you Marcus, to turn and say that to Fresca? What's happening inside now?" This helps the softening partner organize arising new meaning stemming from the attachment focused interaction. (Again, this demonstrates the inextricable interactional systemic, and intrapsychic experiential focus of EFT.)

Exercise 42:

From the list below choose the EFT supporting softening blamer responses:

a. "That was really something there, Marcus. You really did it. You jumped out there and risked. What was that like for you?" _____

b. "I want to recognize what Marcus just did. Marcus, I think you really risked here, you really risked with Fresca. You asked her in. How was that inside for you?" _____

c. "Marcus, what you just did really was different from the way you learned to interact growing up. You would never have said that to your members of your family. You're really starting to stand on your own two feet." _____

d. "What could Fresca do to help you do this more? What would you like from her to help set the stage for you?" _____

e. "You just opened up to her, Marcus. You let her in on your fears. You asked her to come stand with you. How was that for you? What's happening inside now?" _____

f. "Fresca, what was it like to hear this from Marcus?" _____

Exercise 43:

Create two supporting softening blamer responses below.

1. _____

2. _____

The therapist then briefly reflects the softening partner's response, anticipating moving to getting clear support from the other. "It was scary, but... it felt really good," Marcus replied. "It felt good to finally come clean with her about my insecurities and fears." "It feels good to open up to her like that," the therapist reflects, and then turns toward the other.

Theme 5: Processing with Engaged Withdrawer

The softening event continues as the therapist turns to process the softening reach with the other spouse. The specific focus is the immediate affective response of the engaged partner to the softening partner's reach from within attachment fears and needs. Again, the softening reach pulls for comforting responses. The objective here is to help the engaged spouse clarify and organize immediate emotional processing into a direct response of accessibility, responsiveness, safety, and comfort to the softening spouse. The therapist carefully creates the context by slowly reflecting the salient attachment themes of the softening reach, followed by an evocative response intervention. "Fresca," the therapist slowly says, "Marcus just shared how afraid he gets, scared that you will see him as weak, or somehow lacking. And how he desperately longs for you to accept and comfort him…to be there for him regardless. He really risked sharing this with you just now. What happened inside as he let you in like this?" (Therapist taps hand just above her own heart as she says this.)

Exercise 44:

From the list below choose the EFT processing with engaged withdrawer evocative responses:

a. "Fresca, has he opened up like this with your before?" _____

b. "Marcus, what did Fresca do that helped you risk and share like this?" _____

c. "What was it like for you Fresca, as Marcus shared with you how afraid he gets, how this fear grips him and tells him that you'll look down on him as somehow weak. What happened inside as he showed this part to you just now?" _____

d. "What happened inside, Fresca, as Marcus just risked sharing with you how much he desperately craves your acceptance and reassurance. It's like you have this balm of healing that he longs for, but a part of him is so afraid to ask for it. What was it like inside hearing this?" _____

e. "Fresca, can you now accept what Marcus just said? Remember, this is about accepting the differences between you. You accept that his needs are different than yours. You don't have to agree with what he said, but it's important that you each accept your individual differences in needs and perspectives. Can you state back to him his needs now from a stance of acceptance rather than blame or defensiveness?" _____

Exercise 45:

Write two of your own processing with engaged withdrawer evocative responses below.

1. _____

_____ .

2. _____

_____ .

Example:

"It was great," Fresca replies. "I don't see him as weak. In fact, when he shows me his heart like this, I want to be with him. I want to comfort him." The therapist then reflects Fresca's response, often with a sense of intrigue, framed such as "Let me see if I get this. When he opens up and shows you these parts of him that are afraid and uncertain, when he says, 'I need your acceptance and comfort,' this actually pulls you toward him?" This reflective/questioning response is important because it keeps the

process flow going naturally towards asking this spouse to now reach directly back to their partner with support.

Exercise 46:

From the list below choose the EFT reflective/questioning responses within processing with engaged withdrawer.

a. "When you hear him open up it actually pulls you toward comforting him?" _____

b. "Am I hearing this right? When in fact he shows you his fears, you want to then come and comfort him?" _____

c. "Are you able to accept that he gets afraid and feels weak?" _____

d. "What have you done in the past that has worked when he says these things?" _____

e. "Wow. I find this incredibly interesting. When he dares to show you his fear and his vital need for your reassurance and comfort, things that he fears will send you packing, it actually moves you toward comforting him?" _____

f. "Fresca, what do you think Marcus thinks is going on in your head right now? What do you think he thinks you will say?" _____

Exercise 47:

Write two of your own reflective/questioning responses within processing with engaged withdrawer.

1. _____

2. _____

Theme 6: Engaged Withdrawer Reaching back with Support

The final step in the softening event involves unfolding the processing momentum built thus far. The softening reach has now been briefly processed intrapsychically with the engaged spouse, and the therapist moves to the interpersonal, reaching back to help the engaged spouse support the softening partner. "Yes!" Fresca says adamantly. "It makes me feel close to him. Like I can come be with him. I have something special to offer him." The therapist responds with a restructuring interactions intervention such as, "Would you please tell him this in your own words right now? How when he risks like this and lets you in, that this makes you want to be with him even more? Would you please turn and directly share that with him now in your own words?"

Exercise 48:

Write two of your own engaged withdrawer reaching back with support responses below.

1. _____

   _____

2. _____

    _____

FINAL THOUGHTS

The number of softening events varies among couples. Perhaps due to level and duration of distress, some couples seem to need to process through multiple softenings over several sessions, while others move into EFT Steps 8 and 9 after one completed softening event.

Softening events start the bonding event process. After completion of Step 7, both spouses are accessible and responsive, able to share and let the other in. They are able to ask for comfort, reassurance, for fears to be soothed and attachment needs to be met. The softening process is powerful, and sets off further positive bonding interactions and cycles.

8

STEPS 8 AND 9: CONSOLIDATION

After the enactments and bonding of Step 7, the couple moves toward the final two steps before termination of therapy. In Step 8, the therapist supports the emergence of new solutions to past problems. In Step 9, new, more responsive positions are consolidated and new relational narratives created.

As the weeks progressed, Inez and Fernando increasingly improved at identifying and interrupting the negative cycle. When they caught themselves beginning a cycle, they would stop and sort out their primary emotions, rather than getting caught in the cycle and their defensive secondary emotions. The therapist helped the couple reprocess difficult incidents, linking them to the cycle and helping them to access, share, and respond to primary emotions and attachment needs. She also supported and validated the couple's progress. The couple started coming every second or third week, and after session 18, decided to wait four weeks before returning to their next session. At session 19, they said that the four weeks had been the closest month of their lives; things were going extremely well between them. Moreover, Inez had joined a fitness center and was feeling much healthier and trimmer, and Fernando, who had been trying to lose weight for some time, had now lost 15 pounds.

Fernando: "But ironically we got into a fight an hour before we came here."

Inez: "I just thought, 'Let's wait and talk about it with Jane.' He told me I need to lose weight." *(She begins to tear.)* "It hurts because I have been trying and I can see the difference."

Fernando: "I didn't just say it like that! I asked you not to buy peanuts. I can't resist them. I told you, I'd like your support in losing weight and you could use to lose a few pounds too."

Inez: "Well last time I lost 10 pounds you told me I was fat. I thought, 'Why bother?' and gave up. You'd never find me attractive anyway."

Therapist: "You worry he won't find you attractive?"

Inez: "I am not attractive to him. I know for a fact. Once he told me: 'Never gain weight, I won't find you attractive, this is simply a fact.' And we haven't had sex for years."

Fernando: (flushes, looks down at his hands)

Therapist: "So Fer..."

Inez: "No!! Wait! I have to say something. It's not all his fault! I pushed him away for years when I was in menopause."

Therapist: "Aha. So Inez, you want to help Fernando here?"

Inez: "Yes! I know how that would upset him, if he thought I was blaming him for us never having sex, and that wouldn't be fair." (turns to Fernando) "I wanted to be sure you understood. I know I was at fault too."

Therapist: "But what's on your mind today is about feeling closer and yet fearing that you guys have maybe lost the physical part?"

Inez: (looks tearful again) "I never forgot what he told me."

Fernando: "What can I ever say that will counteract that? You say some stupid things when you're in your twenties. For me today, attraction is about whether I get whacked over the head, not listened to or ordered around; then sure, that's not attractive to me."

Inez: "Well that's not happening these days is it?"

Fernando: "No. And I want you to know how much it meant to me, just now, when you said it wasn't all my fault that our sex life went down the tubes."

Therapist: "That was a tricky moment back there?"

Fernando: "It would have been. Could have felt like a whack—that's when I would get into my wobbly place."

Therapist: "So what I'm getting today is that you are understanding each other's vulnerable places and helping each other out more, is that right?"

(Fernando and Inez both nod their heads.)

Therapist: "And it sounds that, although you can still get into a fight, somehow it's at a different level than it was before?"

Fernando: "I'm trusting Inez more now too; trusting she does value me." (turns to his wife) "And you know, kid, that can be a real turn-on for me."

Inez: (reaches out and touches Fernando's knee)

Therapist: "That feels good to hear, Inez?"

Inez: (nods, tearing again) "I'd like for us to be close again."

The session continued with the therapist facilitating a discussion of their sexual relationship. She also reflected how engaged she felt Inez had become. For example, at the beginning of this session she was able to speak up and talk about how hurt and angry she was by Fernando's comment. The couple also discussed housework, a problem for them both since Fernando's retirement and Inez' depression. They worked out a solution for working together in the house, and in their final session with Jane, they proudly announced that, to their daughter Angela's amazement, they had cleared years of junk from the basement without a single episode of conflict. Time was spent in the 20th session describing the journey that the couple had made together in therapy. The therapist validated the courage and strength each possessed to endure the times that seemed almost unbearable. The couple booked a session with Jane for three months ahead, but they cancelled this session two weeks before it was scheduled. Soon thereafter Jane received a card from Inez and Fernando, thanking her for her help and telling her that things in their relationship were going very well.

After 18 sessions, Inez and Fernando are now able to discuss the difficult issue of the loss of their sexual relationship without engaging their negative cycle. The couple avoids the pull of the cycle as tender issues of physical appearance and intimacy are discussed. The couple is effective in discussing these issues as the increasing security in their relationship makes them less reactive to past problems and both discover that in facing these challenges together they find more room for trust and closeness in their relationship. As these steps conclude the couple leaves therapy with a new story of their relationship, one that is founded on a sense of safety and awareness of a secure base in their relationship.

The goals of Steps 8 and 9 include helping couples find new solutions to long-standing issues in their relationship and helping partners consolidate the gains they achieved in therapy. In Step 8, the therapist supports the couple as they discuss issues of concern in an atmosphere of safety given the changes the couple has made in their relationship. In Step 9, the therapist's goals include identifying and supporting the healthy patterns of interaction and helping the couple articulate a shared narrative that characterizes the progress the couple has made in gaining a more secure relationship. The therapist reinforces and supports the success of the couple in enacting secure patterns characterized by increased accessibility and responsiveness. The couple's story provides a reference point for their reflection on the ways they have found to leave the "problematic cycle" and take risks to connect in new ways around issues that pulled them apart in the past.

KEY MOVES IN THE PROCESS

In Steps 8 and 9, the therapist is likely to observe several key shifts that occur in the couple's process. As these moves occur the therapist assists the couple to maintain the new patterns of relating they have developed.

First, a therapist may see one partner open up new opportunities for resolving problems in the relationship. A previously withdrawn partner now may feel safe enough to discuss an issue that has been avoided. The couple is generally better able to address the issues in their relationship and display lower reactivity as a result of the greater security between them. The therapist responds by providing support to the partner initiating the concern, recognizing that this partner may be taking a risk by moving into a more engaged position. The therapist also works with the other partner to facilitate a response furthering the couple's solidification of a more-accessible and responsive pattern.

At this stage, partners often sense more freedom to revisit their concerns and raise long-standing issues that may be difficult to be resolve. The therapist promotes exploration and discussion of these issues and encourages the couple to create their own solution. As security builds in their relationship, there are greater resources for exploration and creative efforts at problem solving even in the midst of working through difficult issues.

As couples grow in their confidence in the changes in their relationship, they will describe ways in which they are engaging in new patterns in their relationship, both inside and outside therapy. The therapist helps the couple stay on track and promotes a more-secure bond through highlighting the couple's healthy patterns and encouraging them to continue taking steps toward greater security in the relationship.

As termination approaches, couples indicate that they no longer need therapy. They are clear about the changes they need to make in their relationship and what they have accomplished. The therapist responds to the couple's initiative by validating the couple's strengths and encouraging them to continue their commitment to emotional engagement and maintaining a secure bond.

STEP 8

In Step 8[1], the focus of sessions is often more pragmatic. Consider the following session where Bob and Sharon return to a discussion of financial concerns and their impact on the couple's relationship. Initially, Bob and Sharon's discussions regarding bills and savings would trigger their cycle in which Bob would criticize and blame Sharon for mismanaging their finances, and Sharon would either withdraw in self-blame or fight back by being critical of Bob's availability to the family. Through the previous EFT steps, the spouses began a new cycle of supporting one another. Sharon began to talk about her fears of being rejected by Bob because of the shame she felt. Similarly Bob softened, identifying that his need to control Sharon was based in his fear that she would reject him or leave him. The security they experience in their relationship is evident in the more responsive and accessible positions they take in their relationship. In this context, Sharon returns to the financial issue.

> *Sharon: "One of our bills was past due last month. It was on the counter when Bob came in. We didn't talk about it. He just opened it and left it on the table."*

> *Bob: "Yeah, I didn't know what to say. It just seemed best to keep quiet."*

> *Sharon: "So I figure that it really bothered him, but he didn't want to break the peace so he kept it to himself. Still, I felt the tension but left it alone cause I knew we would be talking to you." (Bob stares at the floor) "I wish he had said something to me."*

> *Therapist: "What's it like for you, Bob, when you hear Sharon say she wants to hear from you? Wants to know your frustration?"*

> *Bob: "I don't know. I mean, I believe her, but it's hard for me to believe she wants my anger. Things have been good, and it's just a late notice. Why spoil what we have worked so hard to accomplish with a picky comment? I should be bigger than that— you know let it go, because we have something better."*

> *Therapist: "Sure, it makes sense that you would want to protect your relationship from the return of the cycle that stole so much from both of you. And you figure you should be able to manage this anger, be a bigger man. But being bigger means you have to pull back, pull away."*

> *Bob: "I suppose that's it. It's hard 'cause I don't want to hurt Sharon, but we need to do better handling the money."*

> *Therapist: "You don't want to hurt Sharon? Yes?"*

---

[1] Note: The task for the therapist is to support the couple's dialogue as a source of contact and intimacy. The therapist allows the couple to discover their own solutions for difficult issues that may be longstanding in the couple's relationship. The EFT therapist does not change his or her focus on promoting emotional engagement even when the focus of the session is directed toward content rather than process issues.

Bob: (looking at Sharon) "I don't want to hurt you, and I don't want to go back to the way things were. I just don't know what to say."

Therapist: "What's it like for you to hear Bob say he doesn't want to hurt you? That he doesn't want things to go back to the way they were?"

Sharon: "Yes, I don't want it to go that way either. I am scared, too. When I saw the bill I felt this pit in my stomach. I could hear his rage—my fear—I started to cry. It's been so sweet lately, and I just couldn't handle thinking that we were going to lose it?"

Therapist: "Lose it?"

Sharon: "The softness, the closeness, the sense that we are together."

Therapist: (softly) "Can you tell him—can you tell Bob about that fearful part that worries that you might lose the closeness, the softness, the togetherness you have. Can you tell him?"

Sharon: (in tears) "I am sorry about the bill. It's my fault. I am afraid. I don't want to go back to the way things were. I want what we have now. I don't want to lose what we have."

Bob: "I know. It's okay." (Reaching out to touch her. She sobs.) "I found the bill and I was frustrated, but not like before. I just did not know if I started to talk about it if you would feel attacked and then disappear. The cycle. I was afraid that we'd go right back, you know. I don't want that. I want you to know that I am here for you. We can figure out the money situation. Just tell me next time. Let me know."

Therapist: (silence, then softly) "So when you both turn toward each other and let the other know that you care, things will be okay. A past due notice doesn't mean that the cycle takes over. When you show your fears about going backwards, you actually move forward. You both show that you are concerned—new possibilities emerge. Like you Bob, inviting Sharon to talk with you about the late notice. Does it seem different to you?"

Bob: "Yes, I am more concerned about her than the late notice. I mean it still matters, but I am thinking about her first."

Therapist: "How about you Sharon? Can you tell him what feels different?"

Sharon: "I feel responsible for the bill, but not like before. When we first started, the late notice meant that I was a bad person in his eyes, and now it's regrettable and still a problem, but it doesn't have to come between us. That's the way I feel now, more secure. I can make a mistake and maybe it's okay."

STEP 9

The final step of the EFT process focuses on the integration of more-secure patterns into the everyday interaction of the couple. The primary goal is to identify and promote healthy patterns of interaction, most commonly those that are characterized by partner responsiveness and accessibility. This is typically summarized in story or narrative form, where the couple is able to put in context the changes that they have made and the new understanding of their relationship. There are three important elements in this narrative. These include:

- Differences between how they once acted toward one another and how they act now.
- Understanding of emotions underlying each partner's actions in the cycle.
- Ways the couple has found to exit their cycle and connect to one another.

The goal for the couple is the development of a coherent narrative that brings together each partner's past and current experiences of the relationship. Achieving a shared story about their relationship further enables the couple to appreciate what they have experienced and the strength of their commitment. The coherence of a couple's narrative is a common indicator of attachment security in attachment research (Hesse, 1999).

Consolidation brings together a couple's processing of emotional experience and their hopes, needs, and goals into a coherent meaning-filled account. This process enables the experience to be more fully integrated into the life of the individual and the couple (Greenberg & Angus, 2004). The couple's story provides a way for the partners to make sense of his or her experience by tying together the emotional themes of their journey into a clear denouement of secure connection. The therapist should remain mindful of the common characteristics of a secure marital attachment narrative (Dickstein, 2004) while helping the couple construct this story.

The couple's narrative should include five distinct parts:

1. An awareness and understanding of the couple's ability to handle negative affect.
2. A clear expression of the value they both place on their relationship and specific attachment-related experiences.
3. Minimal engagement in defensiveness while discussing negative aspects or problem areas in their relationship.
4. Ability to reflect on how they each contributed to the changes in the relationship.
5. Ability to reflect on the personal growth that has resulted from the relationship.

These markers provide a therapist with the means to assess the security of the couple's relationship in narrative terms.

Steps to assisting a couple in constructing a couple narrative:

1. Help couple review changes in their relationship—what has changed?

"So when you look back at how you handled this big decision and you did it together, what seems different? What changes have you both made to make this possible?"

2. Encourage them to include emotional experiences associated with behaviors of the past and those of the present.

"Before, you felt like you had to hide because the fear of being exposed as unworthy was too much, but now you hang in there because she is there for you, and you know that now."

3. Focus on ways that they have found to exit the cycle.

"And you see the cycle and how going on the attack will take you farther away. You step back, and ask her a question rather than fire an accusation. That's amazing that you can do that even when the heat is on."

4. Emphasize the couple's courage to take risks.

"It is sometimes hard for couples to take those risky steps. To share and to reach out to the other, especially when there has been a history of disappointments. You both show a lot of courage in being there for each other even when things get difficult."

5. Highlight the potential that these changes have brought to protecting and supporting one another in the future.

"You have both found a way to make sure the other knows that you are in this together. That's a powerful thing, especially because of times when this bond of yours is tested, like last week's situation. But you have this history, this bond you have shared and that says there is another way, another option, another opportunity to be there for each other rather than against each other."

TERMINATION

Upon reaching Step 9, the couple moves toward termination. The EFT therapist should address a number of common issues at the close of treatment. For some couples, the end of therapy prompts concern about what may happen to their relationship once they discontinue regular therapy appointments. Using evocative responding, the EFT therapist helps each partner explore and share these fears. It is helpful in this sharing to facilitate how the couple can address these concerns on an ongoing basis.

Some couples fear a relapse into their old cycle. Using validation, a therapist can normalize their concern and remind the couple of the ways they have exited the cycle in the past. The therapist should focus the couple on the ways that they can respond to one another to head off the escalation leading to the start of the cycle.

At termination, the therapist can promote the couple's effort to be proactive in maintaining their emotional connection. The therapist can help the couple identify and develop rituals which symbolize their connection and promote security in their relationship. These prescribed actions are called "Attachment Rituals" because they provide regular reminders of the secure connection the two partners share. William Doherty (2001) describes a marriage ritual as a joint activity that a couple repeats on a regular basis that is meaningful to both partners. These activities may be simple or elaborate and may vary from once a year to every day. Rituals are an important resource for couples in maintaining their connection to one another.

Attachment rituals help couples focus on specific actions that symbolize partners' attachment to each other. The most common rituals mark times of greeting and times of leaving. How a couple says good-bye at the start of a day or how they greet each other when they return embodies the meaning and value of the relationship to each partner. These gestures are "meaningful" exchanges that provide an unspoken language for the attachment of the couple[2].

EXAMPLES OF ATTACHMENT RITUALS

- Kissing and hugging spouse good-bye and hello
- Letter writing and leaving notes for each other

---

[2] Note: What makes this an attachment ritual is not the activity but the meaning for both members around this activity. The ritual provides a means for routinely reminding one another of the connection that they share.

- Participate in religious rituals: Praying together, attending religious events, or sharing sacred readings together
- Reading a book together
- Saying hello and asking about the other's day
- Call during the day to check in
- Spending part of a morning together in bed talking and holding each other
- Making a conversation ritual—a daily time to talk about the day and catch up with one another
- Maintain a regular date night
- Develop a hobby that both share
- Take a class together or learn a new skill together
- Finding someone in need and working together to serve or help
- Having a ceremony to renew vows

Constructing an Attachment Ritual

The therapist can begin constructing these rituals by asking the couple how they plan to maintain the connection that they have worked so hard to create. The couple can be asked to create a list of ways they can remind themselves and their partner of the importance and closeness of their relationship. The therapist may ask a couple to consider how they can express their recognition and support for their partner when she returns from work or he leaves in the morning. The therapist helps the couple identify particular patterns of behavior or symbols that communicate to both a sense of the couple's ongoing emotional connection. It is only a ritual if both partners know what the action or symbol means. Attachment rituals may include specific romantic activities like an anniversary or a weekly date, but often the power of attachment is communicated in daily routines or connection rituals that communicate each partner's significance to the other. The most powerful rituals are based on the symbols and practices that are unique to a particular couple.

Questions a therapist may use to identify an attachment ritual:

- What does your partner do on a regular basis to show he is there for you?
- When do you make time to remind yourselves of the connection you share?
- If you could not use words to tell her/him that you really cared for him/her, how would you show it?
- How would your partner know you were on his/her mind when you were away?

As a couple near termination, therapists may also want to find closure on issues outside of the relationship that have arisen in the process of therapy. Partners may confront individual issues in the process of therapy that require further resolution. The therapist may work with the client to address the issue with the other partner or extend a series of individual sessions for the partner. For example, Sean and Linda had bitter conflicts over their competing work schedules and responsibilities. As they reconnected, they were better able to differentiate their intimacy fears and needs from their work habits. Sean reorganized his priorities and his time to better accommodate the needs of their relationship. At the same time, Sean felt increasingly conflicted by his tendency to define his worth by his work. He recognized some of the insecurity that he carried into his marriage was also defining his work behavior. He asked the therapist for some additional time to explore the "cycle" in which he found himself at the office.

COMMON INTERVENTIONS USED IN STEPS 8 AND 9

As the therapist facilitates further consolidation of the couple's newly engaged patterns, the therapist will work to keep the couple on track and highlight the gains the couple has made. The therapist should identify a narrative or story of their relationship that reflects the couple they have become since overcoming their cycle. Four interventions are commonly used in Steps 8 and 9. In the examples below, note the differences in how each intervention is used in the latter stages of EFT.

Reflection and validation.

These interventions focus on highlighting the ways in which the couple enacts new patterns and responses. The therapist uses these interventions to keep the couple available and responsive as they encounter responses from one another that may prompt more defensive responses. The therapist should validate a client's experience and reflect on a husband's ability to remain engaged.

> Therapist: "I think many husbands would have found that difficult to hear, but you hung in there. When Kari said she sometimes found it hard to trust your word, you didn't go on the attack, but asked her to tell you more. You really showed her you cared about her concern."

Evocative responding.

This intervention helps the therapist slow down the process and keep partners on track. If the therapist notices that the client is flirting with taking an old position in the problematic cycle, then the she can intervene and process the partner's experience using an evocative response.

> Therapist: "Can we come back to that? I want to make sure we don't miss you Julie. It's like you were right in there and then you disappeared. He started talking about your family and it was like we lost you. Can you help me, what happened for you when John started in about your mom and sister?"

Reframing.

At this stage, a therapist will often actively reframe the new and positive actions of each partner as a change from the problematic ways of the past. Emphasis is placed on the "way we are now" as opposed to the way things were before.

> Therapist: "So when she talked about the time she needed for work and she reminded you that her first priority was to work things out to get more time with you, you could hear that. You didn't attack like in the old arguments, but showed her again that you care about her needs."

Restructuring interactions: Narratives and enactments

At this stage in the therapy process, the therapist will summarize the changes in the couple's process and invite the couple to create their own version of a "before-and-after" account of their relationship changes. This intervention helps the couple label these changes and furthers consolidation of the new patterns they have embraced.

Therapist: "And that would have triggered a big fight weeks ago, but things are different now, that's not what happened?"

Julie: "It's almost like I was waiting for him to criticize, but I put down my guard. I thought, 'We can talk about this.' I know he cares."

Therapist: "So you saw the familiar pattern from the past, but chose to trust what's new for both of you. Can you tell me what made the difference?"

Julie: "I guess I know what happens when we fight, we never get anywhere. And I thought about John saying he cares about me and us, and sometimes don't know how to show it. I just thought, 'Give him a chance. Look at what he has to say as coming from his caring side rather than the critical side.'"

Therapist: "And you trusting him this way says a lot about where you are now compared to where you have been. Can you tell him, 'I know you care. I can risk with you now.'"

Exercise 1:

Match the therapist statement with the intervention listed below:

1. "That was nice, Brant. You were able to see your tendency to react to Sally's silence by pursuing her, but you were able to go to your feelings of concern and give her the space to respond. Can you tell Sally what has changed for you in the relationship that makes it safe for you to share your feelings more? How have things changed, what's different?"

2. "It is quite amazing to watch you two handle a hot issue. It's like I am waiting for the old cycle to kick in, but you both went a different direction. You stay connected and that must take a lot of courage and trust to stay with each other even though the stakes are higher."

3. "And that is the way things used to go. You guys would get scared and overwhelmed and the music of that old dance would take over, but now you feel safer and trust your connection more. Now you can see that old dance and feel powerful enough to risk and put on this new music, the music that leads to getting close and reaching for each other. You expect a more secure relationship, a safe relationship for your future."

4. "Tom it seems like we lost you there, when Sarah started talking about your work pressures and missing you. It is like you disengaged and backed away. Can you tell her what happens for you when you hear her concerns, can you help her understand what just happened for you?"

Reframing _____
Evocative responding _____
Reflection and validation _____
Restructuring interactions _____

Exercise 2:

Read each of the following situations and then form a therapist statement for each of the following Step 8 and 9 scenarios.

Mario and Luisa are discussing their plans for changing their son to a parochial school, when Mario increases the intensity in his voice and states definitively: "We must do what is right for our son, and I think there is only one option!" The therapist senses Luisa backing away from the discussion as she disengages, staring out the window while Mario continues his justification.

1. Form an evocative response that would encourage Luisa to process her experience and to block her withdrawal from the process.

    _____

    _____

Luisa shares that she found Mario's tone threatening, as if he just wanted her to agree with him because he thought he was right. She felt her opinion did not count. Mario responds, "Oh, I didn't mean it like that. I mean I feel strongly about this and I just don't see any other way, but you are his Mama and you see his world differently than I do. I do want to know what you think, no matter how strongly I feel."

2. As the therapist, form a statement that includes a reflection and validation of the new position that Mario took in response to hearing of Luisa's experience.

    _____

    _____

Luisa responds to Mario: "I guess sometimes it is hard for me to believe, and I hide. It helps to know that you want to hear my thoughts and concerns. I like your strong voice, and sometimes I just don't know how to respond. This is an important issue and I also have strong feelings about this as well."

3. As the therapist, you want to punctuate the real change in the pattern of attack/withdraw that this couple has avoided. Now form a reframe statement to help the couple reflect on the new way that they are relating to each other and the ways in which they are building a more secure relationship.

    _____

    _____

4. At the end of the discussion, the therapist wants to further consolidate the new positions that Luisa and Mario have taken. How would you encourage the couple to create a statement that characterizes how their relationship is different after the work they have done?

    _____

    _____

Exercise 3:

1. In Steps 8 and 9, the therapist facilitates as the couple consolidates their new positions in the relationship, that have become a _____ from which to explore the world and a _____ that offers protection.
   a. Safe haven, secure base _____
   b. Stable relationship, individuated relationship _____
   c. Secure base, safe haven _____
   d. Differentiated partnership, stable connection _____

2. Consolidation in Step 8 describes the therapist's work in:
   a. Teaching couples to apply the principles of attachment theory to their relationship. _____
   b. Guiding the couple to an understanding of their intrapsychic needs and how they inform the relationship. _____
   c. Promoting a deeper emotional experience of attachment fears and longings. _____
   d. Identifying and supporting accessible and responsive patterns of interaction. _____

3. A therapist would use which of the following interventions to help a partner avoid being derailed into withdrawal by intense exchange with his partner?
   a. Evocative responding _____
   b. Empathic conjecture _____
   c. Validation and reflection _____
   d. Reframing _____

Exercise 4:

Couples at this stage of treatment may reengage long-standing differences and issues in their relationship. For couples at Step 8, determine whether these statements are true or false:

1. Old issues no longer provoke attachment insecurities and relationship battles. _____
2. The meaning of old issues changes as a result of the partner's use of more effective communication skills. _____
3. Old issues are easier to explore when a partner is more available and responsive. _____
4. Couples have a better awareness of how to exit their cycle and safely engage each other. _____
5. Couple has learned new rules for communicating emotions and fighting fair. _____
6. Couple has insight into influence of unresolved issues in their childhood. _____
7. Couples are less likely to resolve long-standing couple issues until they are at this step. _____
8. Research has shown that EFT is more effective if it includes communication training. _____

Exercise 5:

From the above example of Bob and Sharon, identify the following therapist statements by type of intervention.

> Empathic responding
> Evocative responding
> Heighten/reflection
> Reframing/evocative responding
> Restructuring interaction
> Validation/reflection

"What's it like for you, Bob, when you hear Sharon say she wants to hear from you? She wants to know your frustration?"

1. _____

"Yes, it makes sense that you would want to protect your relationship from the return of the cycle that stole so much from both of you. And you figure you should be able to manage this anger, and be a bigger man. But being bigger means you have to pull back, pull away."

2. _____

"You don't want to hurt Sharon? Yes?"

3. _____

"What's it like for you to hear Bob say he doesn't want to hurt you? That he doesn't want things to go back to the way they were?"

4. _____

(Softly) "Can you tell him, can you tell Bob about that fearful part that worries that you might lose the closeness, the softness, the togetherness you have. Can you tell him?"

5. _____

(Silence, then softly) "So when you both turn toward each other and let the other know that you are there for each other, things will be okay. A past due notice doesn't mean that the cycle takes over. When you show your fears about going backwards, you actually move forward. You both show that you are concerned and new possibilities emerge. Like you Bob, inviting Sharon to talk with you about the late notice. Does it seem different to you?"

6. _____

"How about you Sharon? Can you tell him what feels different?"

7. _____

In Chapter 7, Marcus and Fresca worked toward engaging new positions in their relationship. When they entered therapy, Fresca was depressed and discouraged. She was ready to give up on the relationship. Marcus was overwhelmed with anxiety that was often debilitating. The couple's problem cycle was driven by Marcus's increasingly angry attacks toward Fresca, who in his mind, was unable to effectively respond to his heightened concerns. Fresca responded initially to Marcus's frustration by trying to calm and contain his agitation, and then giving way to withdrawal to protect herself from his anxious attacks. Fresca finds safety in her withdrawal but cannot escape the loneliness and feelings of inadequacy experienced in her distance from Marcus.

As therapy progressed through Steps 5 to 7, Fresca was able to reengage from her withdrawn position, sharing with Marcus her experience and needs from the relationship and him. This was powerfully seen when at a pivotal point in therapy she turned to Marcus and said: "I am tired of being lonely in our marriage. It doesn't have to be this way. I don't want to hurt like this anymore. I want you to work with me rather than pushing me away with your anger. I need a husband that will love me. One who will hold me when I feel alone and scared. I want you and no one else. We can do this."

Fresca gained a deeper appreciation for the roots of Marcus' fear and anger. His greatest fear was that he had failed in his role as a provider, disappointing himself and failing to meet his father's expectations. Marcus feared he had also lost face with her and trembled at the possibility that she no longer wanted to be with him and did not respect him. His fear and anger turned to rage as he felt control and favor slipping from this one relationship that was so important to him. At this point, the therapist helped Marcus reengage his underlying fear. "I am scared that she will see me as weak, wimpy. Who wants that? My mother always told me that I'd never be able to make a woman truly happy." (he cries). "I sometimes think I am just so sick, so weird, somehow wired differently than others. Fresca tries, she really does, but I don't know why she really cares at all."

In the softening event, Marcus expresses these fears and his wish for reassurance from her. Fresca responded with warmth and concern to this invitation. She shared how she is drawn to this soft side of Marcus and the positive effect that his openness has on their relationship. In the weeks following, the couple comes to a session beaming over a successful week. Marcus received news that his promotion was postponed because of the slowing economy. Over dinner Fresca was discussing plans for a summer vacation then stopped, picking up that Marcus seemed tense and distracted. As she asked him how he was feeling, he snapped back saying sarcastically: "Sounds like you have some big ideas about vacation, hope we find the money to keep up with them." Fresca dropped her gaze, staring at the floor. The room was silent. "Sorry, hon," Marcus finally chimed in. "It was a tough day. My promotion was delayed by the front office. I know you have these plans, and I want them to happen, but I was counting on the promotion and I am concerned about money. I feel bad that I don't have the promotion, because then I could take you on the vacation of your dreams." Fresca moved toward him, touching his arm as she was saying: "I am sorry, I didn't know. That must have been difficult news to hear after all that they have promised you. It means a lot to me that you were thinking of me and our vacation, and I feel sad that the hard work you have done for the company this past year has to wait to be rewarded." As they talked, they decided to make plans for a budget vacation and a dream vacation and see what they could afford when it came time to finalize their summer plans.

Exercise 6:

Looking back on this couple's past conflicts given in the summary above, how would you describe the positions that Marcus and Fresca would take in a heated argument? Name the fixed positions and underlying emotions of each partner.

1. Fresca (position) _____
2. Fresca (primary emotions) _____
3. Marcus (position) _____
4. Marcus (primary emotions) _____

Exercise 7:

What is different about the couple's pattern now? Answer the following questions about the changes that have occurred in the couple's cycle.

1. When Marcus sees Fresca withdraw he now intuitively knows she may be experiencing: _____
2. When Fresca withdraws what does Marcus know she may need? _____
3. When Fresca senses Marcus responding with a defensive attack she now knows he may be experiencing: _____
4. When Marcus responds with angry defensiveness Fresca knows he may need: _____

Exercise 8:

In the example above, how does the couple exit the cycle? Identify one of the ways this couple has found to exit their cycle.

_____

_____

Exercise 9:

Now imagine you are the therapist working with this couple and they have recounted their success in avoiding the problematic cycle. Write a summary narrative for the couple that includes:

- Changes in the relationship
- Emotional experience with their cycle and relationship patterns now
- The ways the couple has come up with to exit their cycle
- Emphasize the couple's courage to risk
- How these changes will help them in the future.

_____

_____

_____

_____

Exercise 10:

Review the Inez and Fernando case at the beginning of this chapter. Respond to the following questions that will lead to the creation of a narrative description of the couple's new relationship pattern. What was the couple's cycle before? Name the fixed positions and underlying emotions of each partner.

1. Inez (position) _____
2. Inez (primary emotions) _____
3. Fernando (position) _____
4. Fernando (primary emotions) _____

Exercise 11:

What is different about the couple's pattern now? Answer the following questions about the changes that have occurred in the couple's cycle.

1. When Fernando experiences Inez' withdrawal he now knows she may be experiencing: _____

2. When Inez withdraws feeling criticized what does Fernando know she may need: _____

3. When Inez senses Fernando responding with a defensive attack she now knows he may be experiencing: _____

Exercise 12:

In the example above, how does the couple exit the cycle? Identify one way the couple has found to exit their cycle.

_____

_____

_____

Exercise 13:

Now imagine you are the therapist in the 20th session with this couple. They have just recounted their daughter's surprise at the cleaned out basement. How would you help them to construct a story about their relationship that includes their success in strengthening the bond that they share and avoiding the problematic cycle? Include in your narrative each of the following:

• Changes in the relationship
• Emotional experience with their old cycle and new relationship patterns
• Ways couple has come up with to exit their cycle

- Emphasize the couple's courage to risk
- Ways these changes will help them in the future

_____

_____

_____

_____

_____

_____

Exercise 14:

Describe an attachment ritual you might suggest for this couple as a way that they can remind each other of the closeness they have achieved through all their hard work?

_____

_____

_____

Exercise 15:

If in the closing session, Inez raised concerns that the old cycle would return, how would you respond to this concern? What would you say to the couple?

_____

_____

_____

Exercise 16:

Review the transcript of Fernando and Inez at the beginning of this chapter. Check all of the following indicators of termination that apply to this case. Does the therapist see?

a. Reduction in negative affect. _____

b. Increase in positive cycles of interaction. _____

c. Expression of emotions and responses to partner's emotions. _____

d. Increase in accessibility and responsiveness between partners. _____

e. Partners ask for what they need in a way that encourages partner's response. _____

f. Partners make more positive attributions about responses of partner. _____

SECTION III:

SPECIAL ISSUES AND FAMILY INTERVENTIONS

9

COMMON PROBLEMS AND IMPASSES

Impasses are common in all types of therapy and can be very frustrating for both clients and therapists. These roadblocks can erode hope, one of the most powerful forces to fuel change. Consequently, it is important to move beyond impasses as quickly as possible. This chapter will focus on the most common impasses in EFT, warning signs or indicators, causes, responses, and methods for moving through them.

COMMON IMPASSES

Impasses can occur at any phase of therapy. They appear most often during cycle de-escalation, and with completing the key Stage 2 change events, withdrawer reengagement, and blamer softening. A less common type of impasse occurs when clients fail to generalize changes from inside the therapy room to outside the therapy room.

Impasse Indicators/Warning Signs

- No change is occurring.
- Therapist feels aligned with one or against a client.
- A member of the couple does not seem engaged in the therapy.
- The therapist is losing focus and deviating into other models.
- The therapist is feeling hopeless or doubting the viability of the couple's relationship.

Common Causes of Impasses

- A weak alliance with one or both partners.
- The couple or therapist does not have an in-depth understanding of the cycle.
- The emotions that are driving the cycle have not been fully accessed, deepened, or shared.
- One or both members of the couple avoid attachment vulnerabilities because of previous attachment injuries.
- One or both members of the couple avoid attachment vulnerabilities because of attachment-related trauma.
- One or both members of the couple lack experience in being in a secure relationship and consequently do not have a personal map for what a secure relationship looks like.

- The therapist lacks experience with being in a secure relationship and consequently does not have a personal map for what a secure relationship looks like.
- The therapist does not understand the model or certain parts of the model and how it applies to what is done in the process of therapy.
- The therapist has difficulty with basic interventions such as heightening, accurate empathy, empathic conjecture, validation, restructuring enactments, or managing the general process of therapy.
- The therapist has difficulty tolerating or working with strong emotion.
- The therapist gets caught in self-doubt, or does not have a strong belief in the potential for healing and change.
- The therapist gets caught in the couple's cycle, including blaming or pathologizing one partner or becomes caught in the couple's hopelessness.

Common Client Responses to Impasses

- Become discouraged.
- Lose trust in the therapist or the therapy.
- Lose hope that the relationship is viable or that change is possible.
- Stop working in therapy.
- Fail to take risks in or outside of therapy.
- Question whether change is possible and move toward ending the relationship.
- Revert to old behavior including escalation, placating, withdrawing, criticizing, or attacking.
- Cancel therapy appointments, fail to show up for therapy, or end therapy.

Common Therapist Responses to Impasses

- Deviate from or abandon the model.
- Question the viability of the relationship and push for separation or divorce.
- Become discouraged or less energetic and fail to promote change.
- Become impatient or overly eager and push too hard.
- Pathologize or blame one or both partners.
- Blame self and become paralyzed.

Resolving Impasses

There are a number of ways to address impasses. These include making the impasse explicit, "slicing it thinner," using disquisitions, doing individual sessions, repairing the alliance, self-observation/coding and case write-ups, and peer and formal supervision.

Making the impasse explicit.

Here the therapist reflects, validates, and heightens both the emotions and the interactional elements of the impasse. The therapist comments on the process of how the couple is not moving to a different position and puts it in the context of attachment needs and the couple cycle. The reflection is from the point of view of each person's experiences and how their responses tie into the cycle.

EFT therapists never blame clients for impasses. People have often been caught in various elements of the cycle for many years without really understanding it or knowing how to change it. Whether or not the therapist and clients understand the reason for the impasse, the EFT therapist assumes there is always an inherent logic or reasonableness behind the responses that create an impasse and by patiently searching, a way through the impasse will be found. The therapist holds the impasse up to the light and presents it multiple times, at multiple levels, from multiple angles. The idea is that the couple not only identify the action tendencies, the perceptions, and the primary and secondary emotions in the cycle and how it is keeping them stuck, but they also experience each of these as a relational process through their own experiencing and the expressed experience of the partner. As the impasse and the dilemmas it presents is repeatedly processed, different elements come forth which can lead to breaking up the impasse. Change comes from experiencing fully the responses that threaten the relationship and the degree to which these responses are compelling and legitimate.

For example, Ramona and Mike and their therapist were stuck at the de-escalation stage. One day while deepening the elements of the cycle and elaborating how they were stuck in it, the therapist talked about how they both "launched missiles at each other" when they were hurting. This then led to each of them being more hurt, feeling more violated, and more alone. Soon they were deescalating. Ramona, who was the pursuer, later said to the therapist, "When you talked about how, when we are hurt, we launched missiles at each other, I saw what we were doing and how I did launch missiles. He also saw it and how it just lead to more hurt. After that whenever I felt he was being mean and I wanted to get back at him, I had an image of me launching a missile at him and him sending missiles back and I stopped."

If the impasse continues for a while, it can be helpful to talk about the fact that we are stuck, not just that they are stuck. It is important, however, to not overdo this so that clients don't panic and lose hope. The power of the therapist's confidence that there is a way to move forward cannot be overemphasized. In a very severe impasse when there is nothing else to lose, it can occasionally help to heighten the fear and desperation of the clients as a last-ditch effort to create a shift. Sometimes the fear and desperation experienced in this type of last-ditch effort can help clients take the risks needed to move forward.

For example, Maria and Toni and their therapist were stuck in not being able to create a softening and reengage. The therapist would help Toni, who typically distanced in the relationship, to come out, but then Maria would wallop him with various types of angry attacks about how he was untrustworthy and she could never trust him because of how deeply he had hurt her. He had done this by not being there for so many years while they were raising their kids. After several months of processing and working to get past this point, the therapist realized that something needed to change. She heightened the fear and desperation Maria felt at seeing her husband coming out to meet her like she had always wanted, but not being able to trust that it was safe enough to believe and engage with him. The therapist further heightened her fear by emphasizing that they had been stuck at this point for some time, the progress in therapy had come to a halt, and now without a shift, she would never have the type of connected, close relationship she longed for. As the therapist emphasized the desperateness of their situation, Maria got in touch with her fear and sadness that things might never change. The therapist had her talk with Toni about how scary it was that things might never change and about how scary it was for her to risk trusting him, which led to a softening and the impasse was broken.

"Slicing it thinner."

Here the therapist works to identify, in as much detail as possible, the very core primary emotions, perceptions, interactional strategies or action tendencies, and other aspects of the cycle that are related to the impasse. This is often done through detailed empathic reflection and conjecture around each person's position in the cycle and tying it to action tendencies and interactions, and then through heightening the primary emotional responses. Like making the impasse explicit, slicing it thinner brings about change through helping the couple fully experience what is happening around the impasse for each of them and how that translates into actions and patterns.

Slicing it thinner can involve reflecting back the cycle in great detail. The cycle is multi-layered. The surface layer is the behaviors, typically pursue, attack, withdraw, and placate. The next layer is about perceptions, typically perceptions such as how much the other cares, what the other's intentions are, and why the other is doing what they are doing. Another layer is the secondary emotions that usually get expressed (such as anger, jealousy, and frustration), and the deepest layer involves primary emotions (such as fear, hurt, and loneliness). In EFT, these primary emotions are seen as driving the cycle. When reflecting the cycle, it is very important that all three levels of the cycle (behaviors, perceptions, emotions) are connected and reflected back to the couple.

Slicing it thinner can also involve the therapist asking the client to take very small risks. The therapist will often ask the clients to back up and go to what is blocking the client from taking risks. Acceptance of the inability to take a risk and exploration of the fear of risking is the first step towards confronting fear and connecting with a partner. If clients say they can't take a risk, the therapist goes to where the clients are, makes sure they feel the therapist understands and is with them, and then asks the client to take risks from there. For example, the therapist says, "Can you tell him how lonely you feel?" and the client refuses. The therapist then says: "That is too hard for you to do?" The client then says, "A huh, I don't feel safe enough." The therapist then follows up with "Then can you tell him 'I have to protect myself—it is too scary to tell you my softer feelings'?"

Disquisitions.

Disquisitions are expanded reflections or stories that capture the distressed couple's dilemmas and hurts. Because a disquisition involves a story similar to the couple's pattern, it can be used to help the couple see more clearly and so move past the impasse. One of the advantages of disquisitions is that couples can see their situation in a different and less threatening light. The key to using disquisitions when at an impasse is making sure that the disquisition really captures the reason for the impasse, which means the therapist must have a good idea of what is happening with the couple. For example, in a case where the husband refused to acknowledge the wife's pain and loneliness, the therapist said, "For some reason you remind me of a couple I once worked with. The wife kept talking about how unhappy and lonely she was and kept asking for change. The husband had a hard time believing that she was really that upset and that they had serious problems. Funny thing about that case, the wife finally gave up on him and filed for divorce. The divorce was very painful and involved a lot of conflict and legal battling. I saw him months later and he said, 'She really was upset, I should have taken her more seriously. Now I have lost my marriage and family and everything.' For some reason you guys really remind me of that couple. I am not exactly sure why." In this case, the husband said, "I know why—that is what I am doing." Disquisitions should be used sparingly, but when used at the right time they can help move couples forward.

Attachment history.

Taking an attachment history is part of the assessment process. However, an in-depth attachment history can often provide important clues that can help in breaking through impasses. Blocks often occur because of past relational trauma including attachment injuries, major attachment violations such as child abuse, and the lack of a consistent or safe attachment relationship growing up. A careful attachment history can help the therapist and the clients understand working models of attachment and how those models may need to be updated through new, safe attachment experiences. Attachment histories can help couples find safe attachment relationships from their past that they can use as a model in building the current relationship. For example, one woman who was having a difficult time softening because she couldn't trust her husband enough identified her relationship with her grandmother as being secure and safe. After talking about her relationship with her grandmother for a bit, the therapist asked the woman what her grandmother would say about the couple's present dilemma and what she could do to change it. With much emotion the woman replied, "She'd say, 'Trust him. Try it. He's soft—he won't hurt you or take advantage.'" (Johnson, 2004, p. 315). This facilitated her softening.

If clients do not have an image of a secure attachment, the therapist may have to "seed" the attachment. Understanding a person's past allows the therapist to see the risks involved and also to see implicit needs and so say, for example, "You would never turn to him and say 'I need you, come and be with me.'" In seeding the attachment, the therapist acknowledges difficulties and also paints a picture of what a secure attachment would look like in the couple's relationship.

Alternate forms of creating emotional awareness and heightening.

Moving past impasses generally involves creating greater emotional awareness. However, people sometimes train themselves from an early age not to feel emotion, particularly vulnerable or painful emotions. They typically become either depressed and flat emotionally or they become irritable and angry. This does not mean that they don't have other emotions; it just means that they have learned to numb themselves or channel their primary emotions into secondary emotions such as resentment, anger, or jealousy. In cases where normal heightening or empathic conjecture fails to elicit deeper emotional experiencing, explicitly talking about emotions and even providing a list of basic emotions to help people learn the language of emotion can sometimes be helpful.

Therapists may also use the client's own emotional language (especially images) and practice diligent patience. People have good reasons that they cut themselves off from emotions, reasons that should be respected and understood. The therapist may find it helpful to validate that clients once needed to bypass emotion at times and that it may have "saved their life" to shut off emotion in some circumstances. Bowlby believed that defensive or non-feeling responses were always "perfectly reasonable" if one understood a person's attachment history (Bowlby, 1988). If clients can only say they feel numb or irritated, these feelings can be repeated back, explored, and eventually expanded through patient use of the basic interventions. The therapist, however, needs to be careful to not push too hard, a particularly tempting approach during an impasse.

Individual sessions.

An individual session or two can be helpful in moving beyond impasses. When an individual session is conducted with one partner, it is also offered to the other in order to create balance and avoid aligning or being perceived as aligning with one partner. In these sessions, specific emotional responses that block emotional engagement in the couple sessions are examined. These include, for example, a person's shame or fear, which make it very difficult for people to risk, or one person's threats to leave the relationship (Johnson & Greenberg, 1995). Attachment issues, past and present may be explored, perhaps through imaginary encounters with the attachment figure. For example, a client might be asked how a safe attachment figure, such as a grandmother, might view the client in her present marriage. With the help of the therapist, she might be able to construct a more compassionate, positive view of herself in her present circumstances. This type of intervention will only have power if the clients become emotionally engaged in the process (Johnson, 2004). Individual sessions can also be used when a crisis, such as a death or illness in the family, threatens to take over the couple's work.

Repairing the alliance.

If a problem in the alliance isn't the cause of the impasse, it can evolve from the impasse and help maintain the impasse. In either case, it is important to repair the alliance so that therapy can move forward. Because alliance problems cannot always easily be detected, it is important for the therapist to be particularly sensitive to this issue. More subtle breaches in the alliance can be identified through examining therapist feelings about each member of the couple, viewing a tape of therapy, asking for feedback from each member of the couple, or through presenting the case to a supervisor or colleagues and asking them for feedback.

   Repairing the alliance can be done in multiple ways. As with other aspects of impasses, the solution often lies in going back to the basic processes of therapy. It is especially helpful to walk around in the client's emotional experience through empathic reflection, empathic conjecture, and validation. Working to really understand the client's world helps the therapist gain greater empathy and helps the client know that the therapist cares, and is with him or her. Sometimes, a breach in the alliance can best be repaired through a direct therapist apology. In this case, the therapist can often say something like "I am sorry. I don't think I have really understood," or "I am sorry, I think I have pushed too hard—that is not what I want to do."

Self observation/coding and case write-ups.

Often when learning EFT, the therapist can stray from the model. It is enormously helpful to videotape sessions, observe them, and code them. If videotape is not available, audiotape can be used. When reviewing the tape, the therapist can look at the list of interventions, and code how often they are being done. Additionally, asking the following questions can be helpful:

- Am I clear about the cycle, and have I repeatedly reflected it back along with the emotions that drive it so that the couple experiences and knows the cycle?
- Am I working to access and deepen the primary emotions that drive the cycle?
- Am I walking around in the emotional lives of the clients (i.e., Do I really have an understanding of the deep, primary emotional experiences of each client?)
- Am I tying emotions into behavioral action tendencies. For example, fear leads to shutting down and shutting the other partner out—which then cues fear and rage in them?
- Am I heightening and working with fears?
- Am I having couples talk with each other (creating enactments)?
- Do I block exits from enactments when things become intense for one or both partners?
- Are my enactments timed to create emotional heightening and engagement?
- What steps am I working in?
- Is the alliance strong with each member of the couple?

- Am I keeping in mind and pointing out the strengths of the relationship and of each member of the couple?
- Are there some primary emotions that I ignore and others that I reflect or heighten? If so, is it related to my own relationships, experiences, or traumas?
- Are there times when I block exits from intense interactions or important topics and other times when I allow exits? If so, what is the pattern? Is the pattern related to my own relationships, experiences, or traumas?
- How focused am I? Am I slowing down interactions and lowering my voice to heighten and intensify?
- How much support am I providing during emotionally intense processes?
- Am I using metaphors to create pictures and deepen experiences?
- What is the emotional tone in the session when I get stuck?

Writing up the session for the file can be a valuable learning tool. It is often a time of reflection where the therapist can process the theory and interventions used in the session along with progress that was made and new understandings that were gained. Students of EFT have found the Training Note Form (see Appendix G) helpful in writing up session notes. The sheet is only intended as a guide for training, since different therapy contexts and agencies require different types of case notes. The other side of this form can also be used for taking notes in session. The form attaches to a clipboard with the backside up, and the therapist writes down key metaphors, phrases, and emotions used in the session by each member of the couple. A simple yellow pad of paper with a line drawn down the middle can also be used for in-session notes. The advantage of taking notes in-session is that it highlights for the therapist and the clients key metaphors, phrases, and emotions that are used in session. These can then become part of the case file and can be reviewed before the next session.

Supervision.

Getting together with other EFT therapists for peer consultation and supervision can be extraordinarily helpful. There are a number of such informal groups in areas where EFT is practiced. A common format is to meet two hours a month and share videotapes (with client-written permission) and experiences regarding EFT cases and learning EFT. EFT trainers (a list can be found at www.eft.ca) can conduct both in-person and long-distance supervision and consultation.

To make supervision as effective as possible, it is helpful to write out the case in detail. Therapists should write out the emotional cycle, and the emotions that you have been heightening and working with, along with the places you feel you may be getting stuck.

De-Escalation Impasses

When the couple doesn't deescalate, they continue to fight, argue, and react to each other, often both in and out of session. When an impasse occurs during de-escalation, both the couple and the therapist can easily lose hope in the therapy's effectiveness, draining both therapist and client energy from the change process. An impasse at this point in therapy is often related to the therapist's inability to control the session, effectively engage and sooth one or both partners, or clearly identify the cycle and access the primary emotions that are driving it. Client blocks include intense anger, hurt, fear, difficulty seeing and experiencing the cycle, and being caught in a deeply engrained cycle that may have been present and reinforced for years. Attachment trauma may also block de-escalation because trauma survivors may have difficulties with affect regulation, and have an intense fear of being hurt, violated, or abandoned.

Exercise 1:

1. De-escalation impasses are often caused by:
   a. Deep-seated psychopathology in one or both members of the couple. _____
   b. A lack of softening in one or both partners. _____
   c. Failure to identify the cycle and access the underlying emotions. _____
   d. Failure to engage the pursuer. _____
   e. All of the above _____

2. De-escalation impasses usual involve:
   a. The couple remaining in their rigid, reactive attack–defend cycle. _____
   b. The couple being too busy to work on their marriage. _____
   c. The couple having too many children. _____
   d. The couple having family of origin problems. _____
   e. All of the above _____

3. In a de-escalation impasse it is generally helpful to:
   a. Reframe actions such as attacking or withdrawing as being because the partner cares so much, needs and is impacted so intensely by the other. _____
   b. Use metaphors to capture and crystallize each person's experience in the cycle. _____
   c. Work to improve the alliance with both partners. _____
   d. Work to access and have the clients express primary emotions that are driving the cycle. _____
   e. All of the above _____

4. In getting a couple to de-escalate, it is usually helpful to:
   a. Allow and even encourage them to fight so that they get the emotions out so the therapist can work with and deepen them. _____
   b. Keep things light and happy in session through the use of humor so they don't fight and will experience the relationship differently. _____
   c. Focus on using the basic interventions of empathy reflection, empathic conjecture, evocative questioning, validation, etc., to help them experience all levels of the cycle, especially the primary emotions. _____
   d. Warn them that if they don't stop this pattern, their relationship is doomed. _____
   e. All of the above _____

5. In getting a couple to de-escalate, it is helpful to:
   a. Teach each partner about the other partner's primary emotions. _____
   b. Assign the couple to do some type of ordeal that will help them give up the escalating pattern of conflict. _____
   c. Do emotionally oriented reflective listening exercises. _____
   d. Examine the strength of your alliance with each partner and work to deepen it. _____
   e. All of the above _____

Example:

Ruben and Natasha are stuck in de-escalation. Ruben works a great deal and is rarely home. When he is home, he doesn't talk much unless they are in an argument, at which time they both yell. Natasha works a part-time job and is the primary caretaker for their two daughters. She has become more and more angry with Ruben's absences and his excuses. The therapist has identified the cycle and has reflected it back, but the couple continues to argue and fight, often in session. One day they came in and started into their usual pattern:

Natasha: "You worked late every night this last week and I've had it. Don't tell me that you are going to change because you always say that and you never do. I can't believe anything you say these days. How can we have a marriage when you are never around and I can't believe anything you say?"

Ruben: "I am sick and tired of you complaining. All you do is complain. Maybe if you didn't complain so much, I would come home more."

Natasha: "Oh, so you are blaming it on me are you? You say you are going to come home and you work every night and through the weekend and you blame it on me? Well, one of these days, you are not going to have me to come home to if you don't change."

Exercise 2:

1. What are likely to be the primary emotions for Natasha?

   _____

   _____

2. What are likely to be the primary emotions for Ruben?

   _____

   _____

Exercise 3:

1. Which of the following interventions would probably *not* help slow down the interaction?
   a. Evocative responding _____
   b. Reflecting the cycle _____
   c. Empathic conjecture _____
   d. Reframing _____
   e. Enactment _____

2. What type of intervention might help make the impasse explicit?
   a. Evocative responding _____
   b. Reflecting the cycle _____
   c. Empathic conjecture _____
   d. Reframing _____
   e. Enactment _____

Exercise 4:

1. Write a sentence or two that might help make the impasse explicit. Compare your answer with the example given in the answer section.

   _____

   _____

   _____

2. How could the therapist set up an interaction to help make client responses that contribute to the impasse explicit and deepen them?

   _____

   _____

   _____

Withdrawer Reengagement Impasse

Here the withdrawer continues to avoid engagement, either in or out of session, and continues to find it too dangerous to be aware of or access his own emotions or engage with the other member of the couple. The withdrawer may continue to placate and/or stay unaware of emotional experience of the self or the partner. At this point, the therapist may be tempted to label the withdrawer, abandon the model, or give up on the relationship. The blamer may become more frustrated and firm in the view that the withdrawn partner doesn't care or isn't capable of being loving and engaged.

Exercise 5:

1. An impasse involving withdrawer reengagement is most often caused by:
   a. The withdrawer deep down being afraid of opening up and engaging. _____
   b. The withdrawer deep down being ambivalent or conflicted. _____
   c. The pursuer being angry. _____
   d. The pursuer withdrawing. _____
   e. All of the above _____

2. A withdrawer reengagement impasse usually involves:
   a. The withdrawer engaging actively in the therapy process except when the pursuer is attacking. _____
   b. The withdrawer not engaging actively or sharing emotions regularly in or out of therapy. _____
   c. The withdrawer becoming a purser. _____
   d. The withdrawer not actively engaging or sharing emotions outside of therapy, but being open and actively sharing within the safety of the therapy room. _____
   e. All of the above _____

3. When the impasse involves the withdrawer not reengaging, it is generally helpful to:
   a. Mimic the pursuer to illustrate the cycle to the withdrawer. _____
   b. Do a genogram on the withdrawer's family to determine intergenerational patterns of withdrawing. _____
   c. Work to strengthen the alliance with the withdrawer and use the basic interventions to try to access fears or hurts that may be underlying his failure to engage. _____
   d. Encouraging the client to do thought exercises three times a day where the client imagines being open and engaged. _____
   e. All of the above _____

4. When working with an intransigent withdrawer impasse, it may be helpful to:
   a. Meet with the withdrawer individually to see if there is something related to the impasse that is not coming out in the couple's session. _____
   b. Do an attachment history to highlight safe attachment relationships, identify attachment injuries, and examine attachment models and experiences. _____
   c. Do a disquisition about a previous client who could not risk engaging and so he pushed his wife away and was left all alone. _____
   d. Watch a tape of the couple's session and look for patterns, missed opportunities, alliance issues, and times where the withdrawer may begin to engage. _____
   e. All of the above _____

5. When working with a withdrawer impasse, it may be helpful to:
   a. Do a careful assessment for depression and if found refer the client for medication. _____
   b. Let the couple know that the withdrawer has been so damaged by previous attachment traumas that it is not likely that there can ever be healthy engagement. _____
   c. Work to make the therapy room as safe as possible in order to access and explore underlying emotions in the cycle and ensure the couple remains deescalated. _____
   d. Do individual therapy until the cause of the withdrawing can be found and healed. _____
   e. All of the above _____

Example:

Jose and Rosita met, fell in love very quickly, and got married 6 months later. They are in their 5th year of marriage. Jose is an auto mechanic, and Rosita is a schoolteacher who has been teacher of the year twice in the last 7 years. Rosita is earning about twice as much as Jose. Jose withdraws and Rosita has been pursuing him with anger and blame. Much of the last five years have been characterized by angry confrontations followed by Jose leaving for several hours. She does not know where he goes, and fears he is seeing another woman. He promises he is not seeing anyone, and that he just goes for long walks, drives in the car, or sometimes goes back to work. After eight sessions of EFT, they are starting to see their cycle and are fairly de-escalated, but Jose is not reengaged in the relationship.

Exercise 6:

1. What types of fears might be holding him back?

   _____

   _____

2. If he is afraid of her anger, what are five ways to reflect this fear in order to deepen it?

   a. _____

   b. _____

   c. _____

   d. _____

   e. _____

Softening Impasse

The most common impasse in EFT occurs when the therapist is trying to get the pursuing, blaming partner to soften and reengage. In this type of impasse, the withdrawer is engaged, at least during the sessions, but the other partner continues to blame, criticize, or engage in behaviors that are experienced by the formerly withdrawn partner as dangerous, thus preventing safe emotional connection. Again the therapist may be tempted to label the partner doing the blaming, abandon the model, or give up on the hope for change. The continued blaming may reinforce the withdrawer's fears, and the blamer may feel misunderstood, alone, abandoned, and afraid to engage. Fears of being abandoned, rejected, and hurt, often block blamers from softening, opening up, and engaging. Trauma in attachment relationships or lack of having experienced a safe attachment relationship can make it more difficult and risky to trust and engage.

Exercise 7:

1. Softening impasses are usually caused by:
   a. Personality disorders. _____
   b. Fear of being hurt again. _____
   c. The therapist accessing too much emotion too early in the therapy. _____
   d. The withdrawer being fully engaged and present, which creates fear in the pursing partner. _____
   e. All of the above _____

2. Softening impasses usually involve:
   a. The couple remaining in their rigid, reactive attack/defend cycle. _____
   b. The withdrawer being present and engaged and the pursuer continuing to blame, criticize, and attack as if no change had occurred. _____
   c. The pursuing partner having family of origin problems that must be resolved to move forward. _____
   d. Poor communication skills training. _____
   e. All of the above _____

3. In a softening impasse it is generally helpful to:
   a. Do individual therapy with the pursuer until there is a change. _____
   b. Let the pursuing partner know that he or she is responsible for the impasse and that no change will occur unless he or she stops pursuing. _____
   c. Slice the emotions and action tendencies thinner so that the both members of the couple and the therapist gain an experiential understanding of the block. _____
   d. Do a role-play where the therapist attacks the pursuer so that the pursuer knows how the partner feels. _____
   e. All of the above _____

4. In a softening impasse it is generally not helpful to:
   a. Make the impasse explicit. _____
   b. Seek out supervision or review tapes of the session. _____
   c. Evaluate the alliance and work to strengthen it if it is weak. _____
   d. Heighten underlying emotions in the pursuer in order to help the pursuer soften through touching his or her vulnerability in the presence of the partner. _____
   e. All of the above are helpful. _____

5. In moving beyond a softening impasse, it is sometimes helpful to:
   a. Encourage the pursuer to blame and criticize more to get the emotions out. _____
   b. Challenge the irrational aspects of the internal working model of the pursuer. _____
   c. Do family-of-origin work and teach basic listening skills. _____
   d. Do an attachment history to identify and work though attachment-related injuries and traumas in current or past relationships. _____
   e. All of the above _____

Example:

After 16 sessions of EFT, Jose is beginning to come out and be more present and engaged. The difficulty now is in getting Rosita to soften. She says she is having a hard time believing that his change is really real, that he sincerely wants to be there, and is actually afraid of her rather than simply uncaring.

Exercise 8:

1. What might be the underlying emotions that could be preventing her from softening?

   _____

   _____

2. How would you describe the cycle for Jose and Rosita at this point in therapy? Feel free to fill in details that are needed to complete a description of the cycle.

   _____

   _____

   _____

Exercise 9:

Write out the negative cycle for all of your couple therapy cases each week in your case notes for at least a month. Focus on describing all the key features of the cycle and how they are related. As you write, as yourself the following questions:

- Is the cycle clear to my clients and to me in terms of behaviors/responses?
- Do I really understand the secondary responses/emotions that are driving the action tendencies and perceptions in each partner?
- Am I accessing, reflecting back, and validating the primary emotions that are driving the cycle?
- Am I walking around in the emotions of my clients? Do I really know them intimately?

Exercise 10:

1. In trying to get Rosita to soften, you do an individual session with both Rosita and Jose. What types of interventions and topics would you focus on in your individual session with Rosita?

   _____

   _____

   _____

2. What types of topics and interventions would you focus on in your individual session with Jose?

_____

_____

3. Write a possible disquisition for Jose and Rosita designed to help her soften and reach for him.

_____

_____

_____

Generalizing Impasse

A less common impasse involves the couple making changes in session but having those changes not stick when they leave the therapy room so that when they come back to therapy, they are in the same place they were at the beginning of the previous session. This can occur at any stage of therapy, but is more likely to occur during de-escalation or while creating a softening. Generalizing impasses can be caused by a wide variety of problems including the failure of the couple to see and experience the cycle as a cycle, having been trapped in and traumatized by the cycle for many years, trauma in previous attachment relationships, a fundamental belief that the other person doesn't care, competing attachments such as an emotional or sexual affair, an ongoing addiction, or violence that has not been identified and stopped. Although these types of blocks can be difficult to get past, with hard work, patience, and the use of basic EFT theory and skills, they can often be identified, treated, and removed as barriers to success.

Exercise 11:

1. Generalized impasses are often caused by:
   a. Competing attachments _____
   b. Failure to correctly identify Axis I or II disorders _____
   c. The birth order mix of the couple _____
   d. A lack of passion in the marriage _____
   e. All of the above _____
2. Generalizing impasses usually involve:
   a. The couple hating each other. _____
   b. The couple making progress in session but not taking risks outside so the progress does not generalize to the relationship outside of the therapy room. _____
   c. The couple generalizing the problems they are experiencing from being caught in the cycle to the character of the other partner. _____
   d. The couple having difficulty accessing or even being aware of their general emotional state. _____
   e. All of the above _____

3. With a generalizing impasse, it is usually helpful to:
    a. Assign reflective listening homework so they practice the skills they are learning inside therapy to the outside world. _____
    b. Carefully assess for things such as competing attachments, addictions, or violence that may have been missed in the initial assessment. _____
    c. Do a genogram to look for an intergenerational pattern of failure to generalize. _____
    d. Assess for internal splits in one or both partners. _____
    e. All of the above _____

4. With a generalizing impasse, it is usually not helpful to:
    a. Do an individual session to better assess for things like hidden violence, addictions, or affairs. _____
    b. Work to heighten primary affect to clarify their way of interacting outside of therapy sessions. _____
    c. Assign them to make a chart of how often they fail to connect outside of the therapy. _____
    d. Carefully assess all levels of the cycle that occur outside the session. _____
    e. All of the above are helpful to do with a generalizing impasse. _____

5. In moving beyond a generalization impasse, it is sometimes helpful to:
    a. Encourage them to engage in the negative cycle more intensely outside of the therapy room so that they will gain a greater emotional understanding of how destructive it is. _____
    b. Work to help each partner experience the other person as caring (assuming this is an issue and the other person really does care). _____
    c. Assign them to practice doing kind behaviors for each other outside of therapy. _____
    d. Assign them to spend time each day expressing their emotions to each other. _____
    e. All of the above _____

Example:

Eric and Natasha had been married for 10 years when they came into therapy. He was an immigrant from Ireland, and she is an African American who was raised in Mississippi. Both of their families were against the marriage, in part because they were marrying a person outside of their race. They had two children early in the marriage soon after Eric graduated from medical school. They moved from Mississippi to California shortly after having their second child to escape unsupportive and racist attitudes about their marriage. They had a lot of debt from medical school and struggled financially for years. They began fighting more frequently and intensely after they moved. Natasha wanted to get professional help, but Eric didn't feel they could afford it with their massive school debts. Finally Natasha told him that if something didn't change, she was going back to Mississippi with the kids because she was tired, and the fighting wasn't good for the children. In working with this couple, the therapist identified a fairly classic pursue/distance pattern, with Eric distancing and Natasha pursing. After 17 sessions of intense work, Eric and Natasha were fairly de-escalated in session, but reported that outside of therapy there were still frequent fights.

Exercise 12:

1. What might some of the underlying emotions be around the impasse?

    _____

    _____

2. In this case, the therapist wondered if there was something that was missed in the assessment that could be related to the impasse. What types of things would be helpful to reassess for?

    _____

    _____

    _____

FINAL THOUGHTS

It is important to remember that the EFT model provides a map for change, but every couple is different and unique. The therapist must learn about the uniqueness of each couple and the process of change with each and every couple, which is always somewhat different. In some ways, every couple also brings out different elements of the therapist's training and experiences. These may provide important clues in understanding client, client therapist, and therapist processes. It is critical for the therapist to pay attention to all of these levels of process and to be open to the uniqueness of every individual and every relationship.

10

WOUNDS AND TRAUMAS: FORGIVENESS AND HEALING

This chapter will deal with healing relationship wounds—wounds that cause impasses in couples therapy—and using the creation of a more secure bond to promote health and resilience in wounded traumatized partners. EFT is well suited to help partners cope with traumas within the relationship as well as personal violations of connection or traumatic stress affecting an individual partner's life. EFT proves useful in this regard because, as a model, it deals with emotions and the regulation and integration of emotion, and secondly because it takes an attachment perspective. Trauma intensifies the need for protective attachments and often also destroys the ability to trust that creates the basis of such attachments (Johnson, 2002). This chapter also, when addressing relationship wounds, takes EFT into the area of forgiveness, a growing area in the field of couples' therapy.

GENERAL INFORMATION ON POSTTRAUMATIC STRESS

Exercise 1:

1. Posttraumatic stress, characterized by terror and helplessness, first became recognized as a formal diagnosis/disorder by the American Psychiatric Association in:

   a. Long ago, in 1914. _____

   b. Relatively recently, in 1980. _____

   c. In 1975. _____

2. The first therapists, like Kardiner, who studied PTSD in the first World War, found the strongest protection against terror and helplessness was:

   a. Personal hardiness and optimism _____

   b. Self-esteem and differentiation _____

   c. Religious belief _____

   d. The degree of relatedness: the bond between fighting men _____

3. The main symptoms of PTSD, which has been called an anxiety disorder, and a disorder of dissociation, are:

   a. Intrusive reexperiencing: flashbacks, intrusive thoughts, and emotional responses. _____

   b. Numbing and avoidance: detachment, restricted affect. _____

c. Hyperarousal: irritability, hypervigilance, sleep disorders. _____
d. Negative sense of self-shame. _____
e. Inability to regulate anger and anxiety. _____
f. Somatization and sexual dysfunction. _____
g. Loss of schemas about the meaning of life, hope for the future. _____

Exercise 2:

The symptom listed above that is the most difficult to treat AND best predicts distress in survivors' relationships and is associated with major depression is: _____

Exercise 3:

1. Traumas that appear to lead to Complex PTSD with many debilitating symptoms are usually:
    a. The result of natural disasters where death was imminent. _____
    b. The result of early childhood traumas. _____
    c. The result of abuse inflicted by attachment figures: violations of human connection.
        _____

2. There is general agreement that recovery from trauma involves:
    a. The creation of a clear integrated narrative of trauma and its consequences. A coherent sense of meaning is formulated. _____
    b. The tolerance, regulation, and integration of emotion. _____
    c. An exit from shame and self-blame into respect for the self. _____
    d. A corrective experience of relatedness, the ability to trust others and feel supported and connected. _____

3. A more secure attachment will logically impact the effects of chronic fear and traumatic stress in the following ways:
    a. Promotes cognitive insight into the unreasonable nature of stress reactions. _____
    b. Offers a safe haven—a sanctuary—that soothes and comforts, tranquilizes the nervous system. _____
    c. Promotes affect regulation and integration. _____
    d. Promotes respect for, confidence in, and integration of self. _____
    e. Offers an antidote for isolation and helplessness. _____
    f. Promotes trust in and attunement to others. _____
    g. Promotes the processing and integration of trauma cues/responses through confidence and support.

"Emotional attachment is probably the primary protection against feelings of helplessness and meaninglessness." (Van der Kolk, McFarlane & Weisaeth, 1996, p. 24)

RELATIONAL TRAUMAS AND WOUNDS—ATTACHMENT INJURIES

Attachment injuries are defined as relationship traumas or wounds that leave the relationship unsafe and limit emotional engagement. They appear frequently in therapy as complaints of abandonment or betrayal at a key moment of need and vulnerability. Attachment injuries arise very compellingly at moments of potential risk, especially in the second stage of EFT, where partners are asked to reach for the other, confide needs and fears, and put themselves in the hands of the other.

Attachment theory has been called a theory of trauma because it emphasizes the extreme emotional adversity of isolation and separation at moments of vulnerability. Attachment injuries frequently take the form of abandonments in transitions and crises when the need for support and comfort from the spouse is high. Common situations may include miscarriage, life-threatening medical diagnoses, the death of a parent, or immigration to a foreign country. The expectation that the spouse will be "there" for the person is violated and the subsequent lack of trust prevents the creation of a more secure bond in Stage 2 of EFT. Attempts to heal this injury and forge some kind of forgiveness have failed in the past and compounded the general distress in the relationship. The other spouse frequently has attempted to discount, deny, or dismiss the injury, thereby compounding it. These events are not general hurts; they are compelling wounds that shatter attachment assumptions about the dependability of the spouse. The significance and impact of these events can be hard to understand without the general framework of attachment. Wounded partners use phrases like, "My hurt just didn't matter to him," or "You let me drown," or "I promised myself, never again—never again—would I let myself need you." Injured partners have intrusive memories and flashbacks of these events, and often alternate between numbing associated feelings and becoming hyperaroused and accusatory. Subtle echoes of the original wound or any emotional risk can evoke extreme fight or flight responses. The EFT therapist's role is to create forgiveness and reconciliation around these wounds so that trust can be re-established and the emotional reconnection that occurs in change events in Stage 2 of EFT can be completed. Preliminary research tells us that if the EFT therapist works with and resolves these injuries then the couple is able to create a powerful forgiveness event and go on to create a more secure bond.

Exercise 4:

1. Attachment injuries can be most accurately described in the following terms:
   a. They are potential bonding scenarios, where attachment needs are tangible, that turn into a nightmare of finding oneself alone, helpless, and desperate. _____
   b. They are instances of general hurt and a reflection of a general lack of trust. _____
   c. They are disappointments and are the primary cause of marital distress. _____
   d. They are specific events that shatter attachment assumptions and plunge a vulnerable spouse into isolation and helplessness. _____
   e. They are moments of abandonment, where a spouse fails to respond at a moment of urgent need._____
   f. They are not defined by a set of content features, but by their attachment significance. _____
   g. These injuries shatter a basic sense of trust and block relationship repair. _____

2. When these events arise in the therapy process, they will remind the therapist of the symptoms of posttraumatic stress in the following ways:

   a. The injured spouse reports flashbacks or intrusive memories and ruminates on the injurious event. They cannot "let it go." _____

   b. The injured spouse appears disorganized. She or he flips between clinging to and distancing the other, since the other is paradoxically both the potential solution to and source of fear. _____

   c. The injured spouse, especially when there is a potentially risky engagement with the other, numbs out and avoids the risk. _____

   d. The injured spouse avoids any situation where he or she is "in the hands" of the other. _____

   e. The injured spouse shows exaggerated sensitivity and hypervigilance for any further signs of abandonment and betrayal. _____

3. Identify the attachment injury statements below:

   a. "You are always saying hurtful things. You just brush me off. I feel hopeless." _____

   b. "And then, as I told you the diagnosis—the 'sentence'—you got all cold. You just stepped away and said, 'Oh don't panic. It will be okay.' And then you ignored me, focused on all the details of the tests and how to arrange them. I was alone." _____

   c. "You drove me to the hospital. I was in labor. And you left me there. I asked you to hold me, but you didn't. You asked how long it would be and then you left, to finalize that so-important deal. And I had the baby by myself. Something shut down in me that night. And we have never been able to talk about it. Something is still bitter—hopeless. I gave up on us." _____

   d. "'Never again,' I said. Not after that time when our little one was so ill—never again would I count on you. And I never have." (Becomes very still, quiet, and distant.) "I thought he was dying." (Voice becomes hard and fast.) "But we have worked together. We made it—sort of." _____

4. The first two steps in the resolution of these injuries are:

   a. The therapist reflects the negative cycle and its attachment significance. _____

   b. The therapist creates an enactment where the injured person tells the other how hurt he/she is. _____

   c. The therapist helps a partner stay in touch with a compelling emotional reaction that captures a relationship trauma and begin to articulate its impact and its attachment significance. _____

   d. The therapist confronts the partner about their betrayal of the injured spouse. _____

   e. The therapist helps the other partner hear and acknowledge the injured partner's pain and see it in attachment terms—as a reflection of the injured partner's need for caring. _____

5. The next two steps in the resolution of attachment injuries are:

   a. The therapist discusses the rewards of striving for forgiveness to both. _____

   b. The therapist coaches the offending spouse in how to make an apology. _____

c. The therapist helps the injured one move to a complete, clear, and integrated expression of his or her loss and pain. _____

d. The therapist relates the injury to deeper childhood wounds. _____

e. The therapist supports the other spouse to stay engaged, own responsibility, and express regret, remorse, and grief. _____

6. The final two steps of the process of forgiveness and reconciliation and healing the attachment injury are:

a. The creation of a contract to make sure similar injuries do not occur. _____

b. The therapist slowly, step by step, structures an enactment where the injured spouse can ask for comfort and caring—the caring that was needed at the time of the injury. _____

c. The couple agree to forgive each other and to make amends. _____

d. The therapist helps the injuring spouse to respond lovingly. This creates an antidote event. The therapist helps the couple construct a new narrative of the event. _____

7. The important outcomes of this process are:

a. That the relationship is defined as a potential safe haven. _____

b. That basic trust is restored between the spouses. _____

c. That the injury is better understood and forgiven. _____

d. That the impasse is overcome and partners can complete the EFT process. _____

e. That positive cycles of bonding and connection can then occur. _____

f. That a clear coherent narrative of the injury is integrated into the relationship context and is owned and accepted by both partners. _____

8. Forgiveness is clarified by the attachment-injury concept in the following ways:

a. Helps us understand the nature of the negative events that call for forgiveness. _____

b. Integrates forgiveness and injury into a broader theory of marriage and love. _____

c. Helps us outline the critical elements in the forgiveness process. _____

d. Helps us understand how to translate forgiveness into reconciliation. _____

e. Allows for the outlining of the key interventions in the interpersonal process of forgiveness. _____

In the first two steps of injury resolution where the therapist is distilling the pain of the injury and placing it in an attachment frame and helping the other partner hear this pain, the therapist might use all the key EFT interventions, such as reflection, evocative responding, heightening, reframing, and creating enactments.

Exercise 5:

Take the example given in Exercise 4, No 3 above, "You drove me to the hospital…" and write out five responses you might make to this statement that will distill this pain and the impact of this event and place it in an attachment frame. For example, the therapist might say, "You were alone and scared. He wasn't there. And after all these years there is still something 'bitter,' something that comes up whenever you need to count on him, something hopeless? What happens to you right now as you talk about this?"

1. _____

2. _____

3. _____

4. _____

5. _____

Exercise 6:

The partner says: "I am so tired of hearing about this. It never changes. I am sorry you were alone. You KNOW I never meant for that to happen. I am convicted and condemned here. It's like I committed a crime and must be punished. You are unreasonable about this. You were fine—nurses were there." Write 5 possible therapist responses to this statement.

1. _____

2. _____

3. _____

4. _____

5. _____

Exercise 7:

Find two colleagues and role-play the above scenario with you as the therapist for 15 minutes. If possible videotape the role play and watch it. Stop and discuss: ask the "partners" what impact your interventions had. Decide together which one was most effective.

Exercise 8:

In the middle two steps of the forgiveness process, the therapist helps to formulate a complete, emotionally engaged expression of the injury. Using your imagination and expanding on the injured partner's statement above, formulate a synopsis you might offer to her that includes the following elements:

The loss that occurred that day, how the resulting "hopelessness" felt and expressed itself, what attachment assumptions were shattered, how she then protected herself and the cycle that evolved between the couple, when these feelings come up now, what longings and needs she had to "shut down," the core attachment message that emerged out of this drama (hint: the "deal" mattered the most to him), and she still longs for what—what does she need to hear from him? Imagine yourself saying this using a RISSSC manner.

Exercise 9:

In the middle two steps, the therapist supports the other spouse to own responsibility, express remorse. Imagine stating the synopsis you have just put together and the injured wife agreeing with it and weeping and stating how much she needed him that night and still needs him, and imagine that he begins to really let this in and struggle with it. He begins to see her vulnerability, not an accusation.

He says: "Oh, I didn't understand. I always see you as so strong—oh, dear…" Give three interventions you might offer to help him hear her words and emotionally respond to them. For example, the therapist might say, "This is new for you, to see your wife as vulnerable, as desperate for your support and caring?"

1. _____

2. _____

3. _____

Exercise 10:

Formulate the ideal dialogue that would occur in the final enactment that provides an antidote bonding event for this couple.

WORKING WITH TRAUMATIZED PARTNERS

"A deep sense of belonging results in the 'taming of fear.'" (Becker, 1973)

The core assumption in working with traumatized partners, whether this trauma involves a policeman who has been wounded, a solider fresh from combat, a chronically ill partner, or a sexual abuse survivor with a history of self-mutilation, is that the lack of a safe haven, a secure attachment, perpetuates the effects of trauma and prevents healing. The effects of trauma also often prevent the creation of secure attachment and exacerbate relationship distress. A secure attachment relationship is the natural healing arena for the wounds of trauma. EFT finds that in traumas, such as sexual abuse inflicted by an attachment figure, that violate the human connection (Herman, 1992, p. 54), the creation of a more secure bond is the only route to real healing. Couples' therapy that focuses on emotion regulation and integration and on the creation of such secure emotional engagement can then be a primary intervention.

This section of the workbook also addresses the issue of using EFT with different kinds of couples where partners have significant intrapsychic problems. Anxiety disorders such as PTSD and clinical depression are frequently found in distressed couples, so it is very relevant to consider EFT with depressed and anxious partners. The creation of a more secure attachment can generally be viewed as a way of addressing individual problems and enhancing individual coping and health.

This workbook offers only a brief glimpse into adapting EFT to the fragmented world of the trauma survivor and to depressed partners. The reader is then encouraged to read other EFT literature that deals with these topics in more depth. The reader is also encouraged to read basic trauma literature in order to be able to provide a clear psychoeducational framework for clients. A reference list is offered at the end of this chapter.

Exercise 11:

How is relationship repair different for traumatized couples? (check all correct answers.)

1. Negative cycles and absorbing states of negative emotion are often more complex and more tenacious. _____

2. Distrust is higher in the survivor. _____

3. The nontraumatized partner may show signs of secondary PTSD from living in the shadow of the trauma, and so need additional support. _____

4. The alliance with the survivor is often more fragile and must be more actively monitored. The therapist is more explicitly collaborative and transparent, able to be seen. _____

5. Emotional storms, crises, and relapses must be expected and weathered. _____

6. Assessment must focus on possible violence and substance abuse and any risk of self-harm. _____

7. Emotion must be more actively contained at times; for example, flashbacks may occur as emotions are heightened in a session. _____

8. A psychoeducational component on trauma is necessary. _____

9. In Step 2 the effects of trauma and how it is coped with are included in the description of the negative interactional cycle. _____

10. Shame is a key part of complex PTSD and must be actively addressed. Survivors do not feel entitled to caring and often blame themselves for the traumatic abuse. _____

11. The destination is different and more unique to each couple. For example, sexual expression may be more limited even at the end of therapy. _____

12. Couple interventions must be coordinated with other therapies. _____

13. Therapy takes longer. Integration of new steps often takes longer. _____

14. Risks must be sliced thinner, defenses validated. _____

15. It is rare for PTSD to appear alone. It is often laced with depression, somatization, and negative coping responses, such as self-mutilation. Therapist must explicitly ask about how the person copes, so assessment is exceptionally thorough. _____

16. The therapist needs to take more care of his/her own needs for support and nurturing to work with the intense distress of trauma survivors. _____

Exercise 12:

Consider and write out what your own main anxiety is about working with survivors in couples' therapy. Also state which one of the above issues strikes you as most worrying or as needing the most awareness from you.

_____

_____

_____

_____

Exercise 13:

1. How is emotion contained; for example, in a flashback that occurs in a session? (For an example, see the excerpt in JMFT, 1998, 24, p. 24.)
    a. As in regular EFT, the therapist slowly tracks, reflects, and organizes the strong emotions/images as they occur. _____
    b. The therapist validates, normalizes, and explicates strong emotional responses. _____
    c. The therapist coaches the client in affect regulation skills. _____
    d. The therapist can use grounding techniques, talking a client through a flashback and reflecting present realities, as in, "Can you feel your back against the chair, feet on the floor. Can you breathe slowly. This is what happened..." _____

2. How does the EFT therapist deal with recurring shame and self-blame responses? (Self-blame mediates adjustment in CAS survivors)
    a. The therapist normalizes self-blame as often being the only coping mechanism open to the survivor and seeming preferable to complete helplessness. _____
    b. The therapist frames self-blame as an alternative to the loss of an abusing or abandoning attachment figure and so experiencing isolation. _____
    c. The therapist tracks the impact of self-blame and the hiding stance that goes with shame on the present relationship. _____
    d. The therapist actively uses his/her acceptance and empathy to counter self-blame. _____
    e. The therapist uses the compassion and acceptance of the other spouse in enactments to counter the survivor's self-blame. _____
    f. The therapist mainly works on extensive insight into the survivor's past and the creation of his or her model of self. _____

Case Example:

Jane: (very quiet) "So I get mad. If he's in the office, I know I can reach him. I must be able to reach him. But he goes out and he forgets to turn his cell phone on, like Wednesday when he played golf and I couldn't reach him. And I have asked him and asked him." (begins to cry very quietly)

Ed: (to the therapist) "Well, I do carry the phone with me most of the time, you know, but if I am out of the office it is hard to respond sometimes. It feels a bit unfair—like pressure." (To Jane) "You know I didn't go on that fishing trip 'cause of this kind of thing—'cause of you."

Jane: "You didn't want to go anyway. You don't like fishing." (He shrugs and looks away.)

Therapist: "Jane, last week you were telling Ed some of the details of the rape, things that are very, very hard to talk about, things that you hadn't really told him before." (Jane nods) "I remember you mentioning that during the rape you kept passing out, and that was completely terrifying for you. You were bleeding and your body was going away on you—you were totally helpless."

Jane: "Yes, I remember." (weeps)

Therapist: "You also said that you still have dreams of this—of drifting in and out of consciousness and of seeing the phone, just out of reach. You tried to reach for it each time you came to, but your body wouldn't respond—you couldn't reach it. And you were thinking, 'If I could call Ed—if I could just call him and he would come and help me,' yes?"

Jane: (nods vigorously) "I couldn't reach it. I couldn't get to it—I couldn't get Ed."

Therapist: "Right, and you were bleeding, dying. So now when you can't reach him, that same panic comes up and takes you over, yes? Is that right?"

Jane: (looking down; very quietly) "He doesn't have the phone on—I can't get to him." (looks up at therapist) "I've told him I feel so alone, I feel so abandoned." (Changes her voice; looks away) "So I get mad and won't talk to him when he comes home." (turns to Ed) "You blame me—you find the phone inconvenient. You won't even turn the phone on for me—if I was having a baby you would have it on, or miss the whole birth."

Ed: "It's not the same. I don't intend to upset you, and then you get so mad. And then you have even threatened to commit suicide, so..." (throws up his hands)

Jane: "Why not? I give up. It's such a struggle. I can't get through to you. And I feel even more alone, like when you said, afterwards, in the hospital that you didn't even believe I was raped!!"

Exercise 14:

The therapist could go in many directions here, see this dramatic dialogue in many ways and focus on many different aspects of it. What is your first impulse in terms of a response? Where would you hope to go?

_____

_____

_____

Exercise 15:

With this couple in this session the EFT therapist is likely to:

a. Move to contain this loaded topic and help couple negotiate, increase their "skills," and make a contract regarding the phone. _____

b. Help Ed talk about his limits and support the partners being more independent and having "boundaries" preventing future power struggles. _____

c. Frame the process of interaction in terms of attachment needs and fears and validate Jane's experience (without blaming Ed). _____

Exercise 16:

Write out the text of the answer you have chosen above. What would you say?

_____

_____

Case example continues: Jane: "When I call and realize that his phone isn't on, my body goes into overdrive—my face gets red hot, my temples pound—I am on alert."

Therapist: "Panic comes for you. You are alone, and so vulnerable. It is unbearable. This is one of the times you have spoken about when the only escape route you can find is to think of suicide—ending the panic."

Jane: "Yes." (looks up, dries her eyes; turns to Ed calmly) "But how can I help you understand that I don't want to restrict you." (Therapist echoes all of the above.)

Ed: "I didn't understand. I didn't understand this. I don't want you to feel so panicked."

Exercise 17:

As an EFT therapist give three responses you might make at this point:

1. _____

2. _____

3. _____

Exercise 18:

At the end of Stage 2 of EFT, what kind of corrective emotional dialogue does the therapist want to help Ed and Jane structure? What will it look like? Write out the ideal dialogue/set of responses. Begin with the therapist structuring it, as in "Can you tell her/him…"

_____

_____

_____

_____

Exercise 19:

The fact that Ed, in a moment of doubt after questioning by the police, accused Jane of wanting sex with the rapist was an attachment injury—a moment that continues to define the relationship as dangerous. How might you frame this injury and its impact on the relationship to the couple (how might Ed found himself doing this—how would Jane have heard it, how does it constrain their present interactions?):

_____

_____

_____

_____

Depression often co-occurs with problems dealing with traumatic stress and also with relationship distress. Couples' therapy is also emerging as a potent intervention for depressed, maritally distressed partners. A partner's criticism is related to more frequent relapse into depression and a partner's compassion and support predict more rapid recovery from depression. (See discussion and references in Johnson & Denton, 2002).

Exercise 20:

The EFT therapist views depression as:

1. A natural integral part of intense separation distress in an attachment relationship. _____

2. A natural response to loss and lack of connection. _____
3. A response to the sense of failure and unworthiness/inadequacy that often occurs in a distressed relationship. _____
4. A response to self-criticism where the self is viewed as weak and dependent for needing others and being vulnerable to them. _____
5. A natural response to a sense of helplessness in sudden crises or transitions, such as the birth of a child, where attachment needs arise and are, in fact, not met. _____
6. A personal response that is best understood in the context of a cycle of interactions with key attachment figures, rather than in an "in the head" variable. _____

Exercise 21:

The EFT therapist will then naturally put a partner's depression in the context of _____ and _____.

Exercise 22:

1. In the first stage of EFT, depressive responses are placed in the context of:
    a. Models of self and how they were formed in childhood. _____
    b. Negative interactional cycles, such as desperate pursuit and hopeless distancing. _____
    c. Unmet attachment needs and fears. _____
    d. Self-defeating patterns of cognition. _____

2. In the second stage of EFT, depressive responses evolve into:
    a. More explicit heightened emotional responses of grief or deprivation. _____
    b. The ability to rationalize and replace dysfunctional cognitions. _____
    c. Clear statements of longing and the assertion of needs to the spouse. _____
    d. Fears of abandonment, rejection, and aloneness, the unworthiness of self, that can be processed and dealt with. _____
    e. Acknowledgments of helplessness and vulnerability that can be legitimized and explored in the session. _____
    f. Emotional signals that pull the spouse closer and result in antidote events that empower the depressed partner and create a new connection with the other. _____

3. By the end of the EFT process, the changes (expressed below in client statements) that will logically impact depression as we understand it are:
    a. "I do not feel immature or crazy anymore. I just know how much I need to concentrate on my communication skills." _____
    b. "I have more of a sense of how scared and lost I was—we both were—and how alone I felt. It's easier to name it. I can talk about it now." _____
    c. "I just used to see it that I was failing all the time, and she was always reminding me of that. Now I see she was trying to tell me how much she needed me. I feel valued, special." _____
    d. "I feel much closer, more connected to him. I can go to him when things get rough—we are a team." _____
    e. "Even when we get stuck in a fight, I don't get into that sense of helplessness. I know we can connect, even when things go wrong." _____
    f. "Before, I used to just shut down and hide. I didn't want anyone to see me, how small I felt. Now she is beside me. I can accept me more." _____

Case Example:

Sam and Melissa are very distressed in their relationship. Sam is a demanding critical pursuer who becomes depressed and even suicidal when Melissa shuts down and shuts him out for periods of time to deal with her feelings of being overwhelmed and controlled. Sam believes that if Melissa loved him, she would know how much support and reassurance he needs since this is the only close relationship he has ever had or been able to count on. It does not then occur to him to ask for his needs to be met. Melissa becomes tired of Sam's "pushiness," especially around sex and physical affection, and recent threats that he will harm himself if she is not more "loving, as a wife should be." Sam's doctor has referred him to couples' therapy because his depression appears to be growing and medication does not seem to be stemming the tide. When Melissa says in the session that she does love Sam, he expresses cynical doubt.

Exercise 23:

Write a therapist statement placing the "dark cloud" of Sam's depression in the context of normal attachment needs and the negative cycle that Sam and Melissa have developed in their relationship.

_____

_____

_____

This chapter has briefly considered how EFT can be used with traumatized and depressed clients and how a new, more secure bond, created in EFT sessions, can lead to a healing relationship for depressed and traumatized partners. Relationship traumas, attachment injuries, and the process of forgiveness and reconciliation have also been outlined.

The following additional readings are suggested on the topics of trauma and the treatment of trauma, depression, and couples' therapy and forgiveness. This list is separate from and in addition to the EFT-related readings given at the back of this book.

TRAUMA READINGS

Allen, J. G. (2001). *Traumatic relationships and serious mental disorders.* New York: Wiley.

Courtois, C. (1988). *Healing the incest wound.* New York: Basic Books.

Foa, E., et al. (1999). Expert guidelines for post-traumatic stress disorder: A guide for patients and families. *Journal of Clinical Psychiatry, 60*(suppl. 16), 69–76.

Foa, E. B., & Rothbaum, B. O. (1998). *Treating the trauma of rape.* New York: Guilford.

Herman, J. L. (1992). *Trauma and recovery.* New York: Basic Books.

Matsakis, A. (1998). *Trust after trauma: A guide to relationships for survivors and those who love them.* Oakland, CA: New Harbinger.

McCann, I. L., & Pearlman, L. A. (1990). *Psychological trauma and the adult survivor.* New York: Brunner/Mazel.

Miller, D. (1994). *Women who hurt themselves.* New York: Basic Books.

Pennebaker, J. W. (1990). *Opening up: The healing power of confiding in others.* New York: Avon.

Van der Kolk, B., McFarlane, A., & Weisaeth, L. (1996). *Traumatic stress.* New York: Guilford.

Williams, M., & Somer, J. (1994). *Handbook of post traumatic therapy.* Westport, CT: Greenwood.

FORGIVENESS READINGS

Abrams Spring, J. A. (1997). *After the affair.* New York: Harper Perennial.

McCullough, M., Pargament, & Thoresen, C. (Eds.). *Forgiveness: Theory, research and practice.* New York: Guilford.

Worthington, E., & DiBlasio, F. (1990). Promoting forgiveness within the fractured relationship. *Psychotherapy*, 27, 219–223.

Worthington, E., & Drinkard, D. T. (2000). Promoting reconciliation through psychoeducational and therapeutic interventions. *Journal of Marriage & Family Therapy*, 26, 93–101.

Worthington, E. L. (Ed.). (1998). *Dimensions of forgiveness: Psychological research and theological perspectives*. Philadelphia: Templeton Foundation Press.

READINGS ON DEPRESSION AND RELATIONSHIPS

Beach, S. R. (Ed.). (2001). *Marital and family processes in depression*. Washington, DC: American Psychological Association.

Dozier, M., Stovali, K., & Albus, K. (1999). Attachment and psychopathology in adulthood. In J. Cassidy & P. Shaver (Eds.), *Handbook of attachment* (pp. 497–519). New York: Guilford.

Johnson, S. M. & Denton, W. (2002). Emotionally focused couples therapy: Creating connection. In A. S. Gurman (Ed.) *The Clinical Handbook of Couple Therapy*, (Third Ed.), (pp. 221–250). New York: Guilford.

Joiner, T., & Coyne, J. C. (Eds.). *The interactional nature of depression*. Washington, DC: American Psychological Association.

Snyder, D. K., & Whisman, M. A. (Eds.). (2003). *Treating difficult couples*. New York: Guilford.

Teichman, Y., & Teichman, M. (1990). Interpersonal views of depression. *Family Psychology*, 3, 349–367.

Since depression and anxiety often arise at key transitions and the couples therapist often sees new parents who are struggling with these problems and marital distress, the two readings below are also useful.

Cowan, C. P., & Cowan, P. A. (1992). *When partners become parents*. Mahwah, NJ: Erlbaum.

Feeney, J., et al. (2001). *Becoming parents*. New York: Cambridge University Press.

11

EMOTIONALLY FOCUSED FAMILY THERAPY (EFFT)

Emotionally focused family therapy reflects a new movement in family therapy with a primary emphasis on nurturance and connection between family members in contrast to past models that focused more on the dimensions of power and control. EFFT frames the emotional experiences between family members within a context of attachment theory (Johnson, 1996, 2004) and works to create and maintain secure bonds. Secure attachment is generally understood as the degree of confidence a family member has that other family members will provide support, comfort, and protection and will remain emotionally responsive and accessible. Typically the more organized, flexible, and cohesive families have secure attachment bonds, whereas the more conflicted and distant families tend to demonstrate avoidant and insecure attachments between family members (Cobb, 1996).

EFFT is a useful modality when a child or adolescent presents with symptomatic or problematic behavior, a parent or parents present with parenting problems, or when a family presents with interactional difficulties such as constant fighting or bickering. EFFT works to prevent family breakdown or the isolation of one family member. The approach can be combined with other treatment models (e.g., an autistic child in residential treatment could also be seen with her family in EFFT sessions; Efron, 2004).

WHY CHOOSE EFFT?

- EFFT focuses on the interplay between individual and interpersonal functioning; addressing both interpersonal and intrapsychic systemic issues.
- The EFFT attachment perspective focuses on secure emotional connection and felt security between family members, a factor that most impacts the family's health (Sroufe, 1988).
- EFFT focuses on a strong therapeutic alliance, which broaches the probability of productive family conversations (Diamond et al., 1999).
- EFFT allows the family to shift its focus from negative interactions about one individual member to creating strong attachment relationships between all family members.
- Preliminary evidence supports the effectiveness of EFFT (Johnson, Maddeaux, & Blouin, 1998).
- EFFT mobilizes family resources and allows for a more flexible and open system where family members are responsive and accessible and better able to effectively problem-solve.

Therapist Goals

- Modify distressing cycles of interaction that create and maintain attachment insecurity in family members
- Foster positive cycles of accessibility and responsiveness between all family members
- Promote the family unit as a secure base for children to grow in and leave from

Stages of EFFT

Assessment and de-escalation.

- Identify the negative interactional cycle and underlying feelings. The problem is framed as being the cycle and its impact on attachment issues rather than the child or the parent. The goal of reframing the problem is de-escalation.

Restructuring interaction.

- Help the family members to articulate and express the attachment emotions directly so that they are more central to the family's awareness and dialogue.
- With family members, access and reorganize emotional experience to shape new interactions, foster secure bonding, and provide for comfort, support, and protection for each family member.

Consolidation.

- Nurture and maintain secure bonding through intimate exchanges and family rituals.

Key Moves and Therapist Interventions

- Build a therapeutic alliance with each family member without invalidating, alienating, or dismissing another family member. Therapist uses validation, normalization, and empathic reflection.
- Create a secure base through focusing on attachment emotions and accompanying fears. Therapist uses empathic conjecture, exploration, and inference to expand on each client's frame of reference and access more adaptive responses.
- Create new interactions through shaping, fostering, and structuring new interactions between family members. Therapist utilizes enactment exercises within session and gives homework tasks that create new rituals or experiences for family members.

DIFFERENCES BETWEEN EFFT AND EFT

The process of therapy is the same in many ways to EFT but there are also differences between working with families as opposed to couples. Families are hierarchal, and the caretaking and nurturing roles are primarily within the parental system and children are the primary recipients. In families there are more resources for attachment needs to be met and there are less specific vulnerabilities that exist between family members than between spouses.

The interactional cycles operate on multiple levels including dyads, triads, and family groups. The format of EFFT sessions is therefore different. EFFT is formatted to include a beginning session with the entire family group followed by a series of dyads or triads including parental subsystem, sibling subsystem, identified client, mother and child, father and child, with a final session with the entire group.

The positions of pursuer/withdrawer differ in families as compared to couples. A critical, demanding pursuer is generally the parent in relation to the child. A pursuer can present as critical and forceful/authoritarian or critical and intrusive/not respectful of the child's boundaries. A withdrawer is generally the child who demonstrates either sullen, withdrawn behavior or acting out, defiant behavior. A reversal of the roles of pursue/withdraw can indicate an abdication of parental functions for a variety of reasons including neglect, depression, or addiction, or a parent may be unsure in their parenting role.

The underlying emotions are related primarily to feelings of failure for both parent and child. Children also can experience feelings of un-lovability, unworthiness, and inadequacy. Parents also may have insecure models of self and other that become triggered in their interactions with their children.

The processing of emotions is different for parents and children. Children's vulnerable feelings can be comforted and soothed by the parent. The reverse is not true. The sequencing of processing underlying emotion differs for families as compared to couples. A withdrawn child is not asked to take risks emotionally before the more-critical and pursuing parent has softened and is more accessible.

The end of EFFT is characterized by a secure and cohesive family system. Parents are accessible and attuned to the attachment needs of their children and are able to be there for their children when needed. Children are able to feel protected and safe but are also able to go out in the world with a sense of confidence in a developmentally appropriate way.

Key Theoretical Points

The family is seen through an attachment lens and family conflicts are seen as attachment dilemmas. Individual difficulties are not framed as pathologies but instead are seen as an expression of unmet attachment needs. For example, an acting-out teen is not seen as a conduct disorder but an adolescent struggling with self-direction and independent functioning and a continuing need for emotional connection with his or her parents. A conflicted adolescent's behavior oftentimes expresses the attachment dilemma of: "How can I leave you, until I know that I have you."

Attachment needs are most intense at time of transition and crisis (e.g., birth of a child, adolescence, remarriage, and sudden loss), which can prime negative interactions and individual symptomology. Attachment needs are developmentally sensitive. An infant's needs are different from that of toddler; a school-aged child's needs differ from those of an adolescent. Attachment needs can appear in ways competing and conflicting, particularly in stepfamilies, but also in intact families where couple and parental attachments collide. Children and parents can become competitors for time, attention, and emotional support, and families can develop a sense of insufficient resources.

Key Moves in the Process

The EFFT therapist works with a family in a particular way in order to help move the family from a distressed conflicted state to a more cohesive and responsive place. The therapist begins by framing the family problem in attachment terms and normalizes the family difficulties as arising out of an attachment crisis. A defiant and distant adolescent with critical and controlling parents can be understood as a family struggling with a difficult stage in family development: the emerging independence of the adolescent, the new and uncertain role of the parent, and a family coping with how to change and still be connected. The therapist then, given the attachment challenge, helps the family identify the negative interactional cycles that are creating the distress and make the cycle—not the child—the enemy. In its place, the therapist helps create new and positive interactions that promote attachment security and mobilize existent emotional resources between members. Interventions are designed to define the family as a safe haven and the cushion family members need to feel secure and connected.

The therapist helps the family identify the negative cycle and clarify the family members' positions. The family problem is framed in terms of the negative cycle.

The therapist intervenes at the level of interactional cycles and underlying emotions. The targeted cycles are those that appear related to the identified client's problems, usually the child. If a family presents with more global problems related to family functioning, the cycles identified are those related to unmet attachment needs.

After de-escalation, the therapist creates secure, responsive bonding interactions. Interventions are tailored to be sensitive to the developmental needs of the child. An adolescent's attachment needs are different from a child's because of a natural move toward autonomy that still requires parental support. An adolescent is also more capable of a mutually supportive relationship with her parent.

The therapist heightens and validates the family's strengths and reinforces family rituals that promote and encourage family connection and emotional support. The relationship between the parents becomes the focus for treatment if it presents as the primary locus of the family difficulty. EFFT then ends and couple therapy begins.

Exercise 1:

1. Emotionally focused family therapy:
   a. Focuses on attachment fears and needs, which have been found to be crucial in understanding family relationships and problems. _____
   b. Focuses on what happens between individuals but not their emotions. _____
   c. Focuses on conversational metaphor. _____
   d. Focuses on triangles in families and the detriangulization of the identified client. _____

2. The basic goal of EFFT is:
   a. Treat the identified client and alleviate his/her symptoms. _____
   b. Teach communication skills to family members. _____
   c. Modify family relationships in the direction of increased accessibility and responsiveness to create a secure base for children to grow and leave from. _____
   d. Develop individual differentiation and autonomy within the family system. _____

3. The format for EFFT sessions is:
   a. All family members are seen together for all the sessions. _____
   b. All family members are seen for the beginning and ending of therapy. The remaining of the sessions are composed of various dyads and triads within the family group. _____
   c. Family members plus all significant members of the family's system are included. _____
   d. The therapist helps the family by treating the symptomatic individual family member. _____

4. EFFT therapist skills include:
   a. Building a therapeutic alliance with all family members. _____
   b. Identify the negative interactional cycle and focus on the underlying attachment emotions and fears. _____
   c. Foster new interactions through expressing of needs and wants and creating emotional engagement. _____
   d. All of the above _____

Exercise 2:

List three examples of when attachments may compete in families:

1. _____

2. _____

3. _____

Exercise 3:

The positions of pursue/withdraw are different in families than in couples primarily because:

a. Of the parenting functions, which include caretaking, nurturing, and guidance. _____
b. There is an absence of negative interactional cycles. _____
c. There is a lack of differentiation in family systems. _____
d. There is parental neglect. _____

Family Vignette #1:

Mom and Dad, both professionals with highly demanding jobs, requested therapy for their family of three sons, Jack, age 18, Dennis, age 15, and Randy, age 13. Jack was absent for the first session because he was busy working and the parents added that he was rarely at home, spending most of his spare time with his friends. The parents began the session with the father speaking first. The father stated that there was very little cooperation in the household, the kids were not listening, and they did little to contribute to the running of the household. This meant for him that he was constantly reminding the kids to do their chores and to complete their homework. He complained there was constant bickering between the kids. The mother joined in, stating that there was a lack of enjoyable family time, with the fights at the dinner table and everybody arguing with each other. Dennis was identified as being the angriest and being physically threatening to his younger brother. He was reticent, stating he was only at the sesssion because his parents asked him to come. He saw very little wrong with the family, and stated he was feeling "fine" about his family. Randy was playful, teasing his brother and did not communicate directly about the family difficulties, instead laughing and making distracting comments to the therapist's inquiries. The parents dominated the interview, chastising the children for not contributing to the session, although mother expressed empathy for Dennis and stated that maybe everybody was picking on him. Dennis did not respond verbally to his mother's comment but physically looked like he began to relax. With the therapist's direction, the family was able to have some discussion of when they felt close to one another, which they identified as being primarily at holiday time and on special occasions.

Exercises: Building a Therapeutic Alliance

Exercise 4:

List three comments you could make that would validate these parents without invalidating the children.

1. _____

2. _____

3. _____

Exercise 5:

List three comments you could make that would validate these children without invalidating the parents.

1. _____

2. _____

3. _____

Exercises: Tracking the Cycle

Exercise 6:

How would you formulate the negative interactional cycle?

_____

_____

_____

Exercise 7:

What interventions would you use in the beginning session with this family? (more than one correct answer)

a. "This family has strengths in your ability to have fun and be close during vacations and at holiday times." _____

b. "The negative cycle has a powerful effect on everyone because it gets in the way of you feeling close as a unit and also feeling good about yourself." _____

c. "Mom and Dad, you are both are trying very hard in your roles as leaders to try and bring this family together and work as a team, to which you get resistance and a lack of cooperation from the kids. This upsets you as you want the family to work together and then you try harder. Dad, you may become louder and more forceful whereas you, Mom, find yourself saying the same things over and over again. The kids react by either fighting back or fleeing; they get into fights with each other or they leave the house or make lots of funny remarks. Everybody ends up feeling bad and not good about each other." _____

d. "I want you, Dad, to have a conversation with Dennis about how to fight more effectively and win at his fights." _____

e. "I want the family to go home tonight and make a list of chores and have a family meeting to decide who does what chore and set up a work schedule." _____

f. "I think that this family needs to have some individual work to sort out what is happening and allow you to function better as a family unit. I would suggest that Dennis see our child and adolescent therapist." _____

Exercises: Intervention to Modify Cycle

Example:

Father: "There is a lot of heaviness in our home. I need to use a harsh response because he asks for it. A simple request and he doesn't listen; the only way I can get his attention is to come down hard. And come down hard I do. It's the only way I get him to respond."

Exercise 8:

How would you intervene to begin to access this father's primary emotion and how would you frame the emotions in attachment terms?

_____

_____

_____

Example:

Dennis: (looking downcast) "It doesn't really matter." (sigh, long pause) "Whatever."

Exercise 9:

How would you begin to access this son's underlying emotions and how would you frame the emotions in attachment terms?

_____

_____

Family Vignette #2

Mom, Dad, and 18-year-old daughter, Melissa, presented for a first session. When the daughter was 15, she was hospitalized for a severe eating disorder, having weighed only 80 pounds and almost dying. The daughter was currently in individual treatment and of normal weight, although she continued to struggle with her eating. The parents had been in marital therapy for the past year and had made good progress in strengthening their marriage.

Mom began the session stating how she would like to have a better relationship with her daughter. She recognized she had made mistakes in the past with her daughter, primarily around confiding in her about her unhappiness in her marriage. The mother had realized through her own therapy that she had been a good mother and had been well-intentioned in her efforts to parent her daughter. Currently, Mom stated that she wanted to be able to offer advice to her daughter without her daughter becoming defensive. She wanted to be able to voice concerns about her schooling or her boyfriend. She felt her daughter still needed her input but she was unsure about how to communicate with her. The father said that being around his daughter was like "walking on eggshells" and that she would have angry outbursts to seemingly little provocation. He became tearful relating his concern about her and his sadness about what had happened. Melissa, in exasperated tones, said she never felt good enough for her parents and whatever she told them was never good enough. This was a long-standing pattern for her, and in the past she had lived with the constant insecurity that her parents would divorce. She constantly felt caught in the middle between her mother and father and believed it was up to her to maintain the peace in the household. While she recognized that when she was little she was close to her father, Melissa now couldn't be near him without an argument. With her mother, she felt she was a constant disappointment and that she could not confide in her for fear of hearing disapproval or judgment.

Exercises: Building a Therapeutic Alliance

Exercise 10:

List three comments you could make that would validate this mom without invalidating the other family members.

1. _____

2. _____

3. _____

Exercise 11:

List three comments you could make that would validate this dad without invalidating other family members.

1. _____

2. _____

3. _____

Exercise 12:

List three comments you could make that would validate this teenager without invalidating other family members.

1. _____

2. _____

3. _____

Exercises: Identifying the Cycle

Exercise 13:

How would you formulate the negative cycle in this family and begin to access the underlying emotions?

_____

_____

_____

Exercise 14:

Pick which would be EFFT interventions with this family in this session? (more than one correct answer)

a. "I would like to set our next meeting at lunchtime and all of us will bring our lunch, and we will eat together."

b. "Dad, I would like you to teach Melissa about how to stand up for herself and give her some lessons on assertiveness."

c. "An eating disorder can take over a family and become the ruler in how family members interact. It seems like the eating disorder has taken siege of your family."

d. "I wonder what it is like for you, Mom, when Melissa doesn't listen to your efforts to mother her?"

e. "Are there times in this family when everyone does feel connected and close?"

f. "What happens to you, Dad, when there is an explosion? What is it that you do?"

g. "Do you know what you do, Melissa, when you don't feel that you are measuring up and are disappointing your mom?"

Exercises: Interventions in Cycle

Example:

Mom: "I don't know what to do! The course she is taking I just don't understand. I think she is being influenced by her boyfriend. I mean, she talks and acts like him, using the same language. She just changed her mind at the last minute—I am not sure she thought it through at all, and I am afraid she is making a mistake. It's a lot of money."

Exercise 15:

How would you intervene to begin to access this mother's primary emotions, and how would you frame the emotions in attachment terms?

_____

_____

_____

Example:

Daughter: "I can't do anything right! Every time I bring anything to you—my grades, anything—it is never good enough! What did you say the last time I told you my marks? 'How come you got a C?' Those marks aren't important, but all I get is criticism. No wonder I don't want to tell you anything!"

Exercise 16:

How would you intervene to begin to access this daughter's primary emotions and how would you frame the emotions in attachment terms?

_____

_____

_____

SECOND STAGE EFFT: SESSION 5, MOM AND DAUGHTER

The second stage of EFFT takes place once there is de-escalation of the negative cycle and family members are then able to process their attachment emotions and fears at a deeper level. The EFFT intervenes to create new, secure bonding interactions between family members and establish the family unit as a secure base.

Mom and daughter had been seen for two sessions previously and the negative cycle, with the underlying attachment emotions had been identified. The daughter had recently decided to quit competitive dance.

Exercise 17:

After each therapist statement, identify the intervention.

Mother: "I was a little surprised last session, that you" (the therapist) "did not say anything to Melissa about what she was doing or the choices she was making. I need to be able, as her mother, to express my concern for her. I wouldn't be doing my job as a parent otherwise."

Therapist: "It's really hard for a mom not to worry. I think that is the job of moms everywhere."

1. _____

Mom: "I can't help but feel she is making a mistake, that she doesn't know what she is giving up."

Daughter: "Why can't you just trust me and let me make my own mistake? I can't tell you anything! I know from the look on your face how you feel—you make it abundantly clear!"

Mom: "But I don't know why you don't talk to me. You know I can handle it. I want you to let me know what is going on with you."

Therapist: "This is where you get caught in the cycle, because you as a mom want to do a good job parenting and protect your daughter. Melissa, you hear all this protection as disapproval and judgment, so you withdraw. Mom, you are left not knowing what is happening with Melissa, which is scarier still, plus you both don't get to have a close relationship with each other. I would expect that's what you both want—to feel closer and more able to talk to each other."

2. _____

Mom: "I want to be able to talk to Melissa, but sometimes I just don't know how. She doesn't want to talk to me."

Daughter: (rising voice) "It's not that I don't want to talk to you, but what do you expect? I just hear how I am screwing up. You think I want to hear that?"

Mom: "I am just trying to be your mom."

Therapist: "It sounds like it's really painful for you, Melissa, to go to your mom and to see disapproval. It's really important to you how your mom feels about you."

3. _____

Daughter: (starting to cry) "Of course it is important. She must know that."

Mom: "I don't know that. It seems more like you just want to get away and that you are so angry with me for the past."

Therapist: "That's so hard for you to think that Melissa is mad at you, particularly when you think of the past."

4. _____

Mom: (crying) "I don't know how I can get over the past. I thought I was such a good mom. I was so involved in Melissa's life—I did everything with her and with the eating disorder I didn't see it—I didn't see it at all."

Melissa: "I was a good liar. There was no way you could know—I covered it up."

Therapist: "This is a really painful part of your relationship. It sounds like it's really hard for you to get over what happened, and you feel so guilty as a mom that this happened to your child."

5. _____

Mom: (crying) "I don't think I can ever forgive myself. It should never have happened."

Therapist: "And you wonder how Melissa feels about it also—could you talk to her about that now?"

6. _____

Mom: (looking at Melissa) "I am so sorry that it happened."

Melissa: "You've said that before. I know that you feel that way, and I don't blame you—that's not what pisses me off!"

Therapist: "What happened in the past is not so alive for you now Melissa as it might be for your mom. When your mom feels bad about the past, you feel bad also and feel maybe a little guilty for your mom's feelings?"

7. _____

Melissa: "I want to get over the past. I feel like a big screwup when you talk about it. I want you to see what I have done and how I have got better. You don't give me any credit! You know how hard I have worked and the number of therapists I have seen— does any of that sink in!"

Mom: "I know you have worked hard, and I am not worried about your eating. I just don't know what to do."

Melissa: "You could start with not being so critical and cutting of me. I am not the little kid who was stuck in hospital and not able to eat. I have changed a lot since then."

Therapist: "I get the sense that it is more about what is happening today with your mom and the disapproval that is so hard to bear."

8. _____

Melissa: (looking at her mom) "I have been working really hard to get out of this. All my life I have been trying to please people. I would do anything for someone else and that was something that you taught me to have compassion for others—you know, even the sick squirrel on the street."

Mom: "Yes, but that is what I am afraid of—that you will get stuck there, just pleasing others and not looking after yourself."

Melissa: "I am trying to take care of myself. I need to feel good about me" (starts to cry) "and that is what is so hard."

Mom: (crying) "I want you to feel good about yourself—that's really all that I want for you. You are so beautiful and strong, and I want so much for you to see that."

Melissa: "And I am—some of the time. I am working on it. That's why I am quitting—it's not good for me, but when I try to talk to you and I see that look on your face."

Mom: "You know, I think that is when I am feeling bad about me—it's hard for me to feel the good inside."

Therapist: "It's hard for you to feel good inside, especially when you feel like you are failing or not doing it right as a mom?"

9. _____

Mom: (starting to cry) "I have always struggled with this. I never had a mom. I mean she was never there. There was no way for me to feel good, I just did things for others. I don't really know how to be a good mom. I have just been winging it, and when I don't know what to do I just lose control and say and do things I never should do and then I feel bad and the whole thing starts all over again."

Therapist: "You have tried very hard to mother Melissa without really knowing how and when things have gone wrong. It sounds like you feel such fear inside that you lose control and try to make things better by overreacting which, in the end, you regret and you end up feeling bad about yourself and your relationship with Melissa. Is that close? Is that how you feel inside?"

10. _____

Mom: "I never really thought about how I felt inside." (pause) "But yes, it's like terror."

Therapist: "'Terror.' That sounds very powerful, very scary. Kind of like when you are needed the most, you feel the least equipped, and that terrorizes you."

11. _____

Mom: (sobbing) "She is my baby and she almost died, and it was all my fault. I didn't know what to do."

Therapist: "That is so hard, to see your child so sick and to feel so responsible. You are so afraid of not getting it right and feeling so responsible. That is a heavy burden."

12. _____

Mom: (nods)

Therapist: "But I am also seeing Melissa sitting here, and she has done lots of hard work and has strength and determination. Can you look at her? Do you see that?"

13. _____

Mom: (raises her head) "Yes, I see her strength. She is amazing."

Therapist: "And I see that you are not alone—either one of you. You are here trying to work out your relationship, and you are trying to figure that out together—how to take care of yourselves and each other."

14. _____

Melissa: "And that's what you taught me, Mom, to take care of others. That is also a good thing, right?"

Mom: (looking at Melissa, smiling) "Right. And you taught me that you are growing up and that I can trust you and myself. We just need to talk to each other."

Therapist: "What you are saying is really important, Mom. It sounds like you are saying a lot about yourself and Melissa, and how you want the two of you to be. This is an important lesson and I want to make sure that Melissa understands what you are saying about the two of you. Can you tell her, right now, how you want the two of you to be in the future?"

15. _____

Mom: (looking at Melissa) "You know that your grandmother and I are not close and what I want for us is to be close. I want you to know that I will be there for you, that you can come and talk to me anytime, and you know I will try to remember just how grown up you are, and I will try to listen and not tell you how to be. I do trust you, and I want you to trust me. I am there for you."

Melissa: "I know, Mom. I do want to come to you. What do you think matters to me most? You know, I do want to talk to you. I want you to believe that I do have my head on straight, and I do know what I am doing."

Therapist: "This is really important what you are saying to each other now. This is how you want it to be and really you are doing it right now. You are talking to one another and being open and sharing. That's really nice to see."

16. _____

Exercise 18:

What is your hypothesis of the negative cycle in this dyad?

_____

_____

_____

Exercise 19:

What is Mom's primary emotion?

_____

_____

_____

Exercise 20:

What are the daughter's primary emotions?

_____

_____

_____

Exercise 21:

What is the attachment frame that the therapist uses in intervening in this dyad and restructuring their dance?

_____

_____

_____

Exercise 22:

What does the therapist do to begin to create new interactions between mother and daughter that are connecting rather than distancing?

_____

_____

_____

Exercises: Intervention

Exercise 23:

How would you continue to work with this dyad to consolidate further the positive interactional cycle? Choose all options that could apply.

a. Help mom and daughter to recognize and monitor their negative cycle. _____
b. Utilize enactment exercises to process daughter's behaviors and mom's responses in a way that creates secure, bonding interactions. _____
c. Facilitate rituals and patterns of connection for mom and daughter. _____
d. Recommend mom enter into individual therapy to understand her fear. _____

Exercise 24:

Write a response to the statement below that would heighten the primary emotion and frame it in attachment terms.

1. Mother: "When I see her going to her boyfriend, it makes me so sad. I worry about the kind of influence he has, and I worry about what is going to happen to her."

    _____

    _____

    _____

2. Mother: "I can't get it right. I say and do things I shouldn't do." (looks down) "I don't know what to do."

    _____

    _____

    _____

3. Melissa: "You can be so cutting. I know I can give it right back but you have no idea. I just go to my room and stay there. It rips me up inside. I stay there until it goes away."

    _____

    _____

    _____

4. Melissa: "I want you to respect my opinions and decisions. There are things I can figure out, and I do take things seriously. I can see that I have made mistakes in the

past and maybe it's hard for you to trust me, but I have a good head on my shoulders and I can look after myself properly."

_____

_____

_____

Case Summary

This family continued to work in therapy. The next step was to include the father and Melissa. Dyadic sessions were held with the father to open up the communication between Melissa and her dad and restructure the negative cycle. Dad was withdrawing from conflict and Melissa was being angry and explosive with her dad in order to get a reaction. In session, Melissa was relieved that she could talk openly with her father and he did not run away. Dad was reassured that he could have an open conversation with Melissa that did not escalate into conflict but brought them closer. Once this reconnection was established, the family group was reunited and sessions were held to establish a new positive pattern of accessible and responsive interactions with the entire group. Rules of engagement were established in this family with the agreement made that issues would not be fought about or ignored but everyone would talk about their feelings together. Rituals were identified that help consolidate and reinforce these gains and the family identified ways to continue to talk about and deal with their issues.

SUMMARY

Emotionally focused family therapy is an effective and powerful modality to address fractured and conflictual relationships among family members. Attachment theory guides the therapist in helping the family identify and own their negative interactional cycles and restructure the family dance to include accessible and responsive interactional patterns. The therapist utilizes the same core skills as utilized in EFT and the goals for increased closeness and secure attachment remain the same. The processes of EFFT differ in the hierarchical elements, the number of interactional patterns present, and the intensity and level of emotional engagement. EFFT is a therapeutic intervention that can be combined with other treatment options (e.g., residential treatment of the child) and works to provide a secure base for children to grow in and leave from.

12

CONFESSIONS OF AN EFT THERAPIST: A CASE OVERVIEW

"She gets this look on her face, and, I know from here on out I am relegated to the sidelines." (shakes his head slowly) *"It doesn't matter what I say or what I want—her mind is made up! My wishes are not important in this relationship. I am just like one of the kids. I can't stand it. I am just kind of...irrelevant."*

"Frank, that is SO not true! I always consider you! I always want to know what you want us to do. I can't believe you just said that." (silence; then, softer) *"Is that really how you see it?"*

Maria and Frank smiled politely yet guardedly as I initially greeted them in the foyer before our first meeting. Both were professionally dressed, not surprising considering their mutual success in the business world. Now firmly established in the mid- to upper-middle class after having graduated from college with B.S. degrees in business, things had not always been so financially rosy for either of them. "My grandparents came to this country from Mexico, and the stories they tell are amazing," reported Frank. "Stories of poverty and struggle. Hardly any skills or education, but look where the family is now. Couldn't have happened without their sacrifice." Maria's story resembled her husband's. "Our families are so similar in that. When we met in college, it was something that warmed both of our hearts to each other. You know, we were both second generation Hispanic Americans, although we each prefer 'Mexican Americans,' since that is where our grandparents are from. Our families sacrificed greatly for us to be able to go to college, to be where we are now. We are very grateful to our families."

I immediately reflected how they come from families of such strength—a source of pride for both of them. From the start, I told them that I needed them to help me understand their culture and families. "Guys, I don't have that kind of cultural story to draw from, and I can only understand what it's like to be in your family up to a point. I'd like to ask something from the start. Would you be willing to bear with me if I ask cultural questions that may seem kind of obvious to each of you, and would you be willing to correct me when I miss culturally, or otherwise, and help me understand you better?" They both nodded, "Of course we will. No problem." "Thanks," I honestly reinforced, "that will really be helpful for me. It's just so interesting, too. My apologies ahead of time if I go overboard in hearing about your cultural struggles and obvious successes." (All three laugh.)

Frank and Maria were in their 11th year of marriage with three children, boys 9 and 7 years old, and a daughter, aged 5. Early on, I noted that spirituality seemed to be very important to them, as they talked about friends from church and their pastor's sermons. "We are both active Christians," Maria reported. "I consider myself a Christian feminist. Our beliefs are very important to us. A spiritual heritage runs deeply in both of our families, and that is something else that greatly attracted us to each other. Our families are Catholic." "I'd like to ask permission for you to help me understand as we go along how important your faith is to you and your family," I responded. "A working knowledge of how that plays out in your relationship would help me." This affirmation seemed to further put them at ease. "That's really nice to hear," Maria responded. "We were both concerned that our faith might not be respected in professional therapy."

They had previously been to pastoral counseling and to the occasional marital enrichment weekends provided by their church. "The pastor was helpful, and so are the enrichment weekends," Frank reported. "But it seems like we need just a little bit more..."

SESSIONS 1 THROUGH 3: KEY ASSESSMENT THEMES

"We want to stop fighting and to communicate better," Maria and Frank reported when formulating goals. As I heard about a recent argument that represented so many others, the positions taken by each spouse and the negative interactive cycle became apparent.

"Can you take me back to a recent argument you guys had? We talk 'about' them in here, but if I were actually there, what would I see? If you had a video camera and shot the whole thing, what would I watch on the tape?" I asked. They recounted a recent negative episode in which the cycle seemed to be:

Frank attacks

Frank: *"Why did you just say that to your mom? You know that I made it crystal clear that I didn't want to go there tomorrow night! And you just told her when we'd be there!"*

Maria defends

"But honey, we had already agreed to this. They so badly want you to come."

Frank attacks further

"It doesn't matter what I say, or what I want. It just goes in one ear and out the other with you. You treat me like one of the kids."

Maria withdraws by going into her head

"I moved into another room. I go off alone and analyze in my head, 'How can I do this differently? Does he have a point? Why is he feeling this way?'"

Frank pursues

"That's it? That's all I get? It's over now?"

Maria struggles to defend

"I don't know what else to do. I am trying to make everyone happy."

Frank counters in attack/accusatory mode

"That's the point!" (raised his voice more) *"'Everyone' just includes me—it's like I am just one among many!"*

Maria further withdraws and goes silent

"His anger is too much for me, so I get out of there."

Three to 4 hours later, Frank "puts out the white flag" by coming and talking to her "in a light fashion."

There is no resolution. Apologies, yes. Resolution, no.

SESSIONS 4 THROUGH 8: UNDERLYING EMOTION IN AN ATTACHMENT CONTEXT

Therapist Reflections

I had a grasp of their negative cycle in terms of positions, patterns, and the more secondary reactive emotions. Frank usually was the more critical and demanding spouse (position), attacking from anger (secondary emotion) when fights arose, whereas Maria often found herself defending (secondary reaction) then withdrawing (position). What I didn't have a grasp on yet was the underlying, primary emotions that usually remained unseen and unspoken. My sense, based on EFT theory, was that these negative cycles and reactive emotions kept Maria and Frank often emotionally disconnected and alone.

One last thing stood out to me: this couple absolutely adored each other. While the cycle was the enemy, I felt strongly that if I could embrace them in the strength of their cultural history, faith, and love for each other they could conquer the cycle and create a new degree of intimacy with each other. In session 4, the underlying emotions and subsequent attachment context became increasingly apparent.

Frank: "I asked her to sit down and chat with me. It had been a hard day, and I just wanted to sit for minute on the couch with her. So I asked her, and she said, 'Yeah, I'll be there in a minute.' Her tone just said that she really didn't care so much about it though. So I got mad and said, 'Fine! Go talk to a friend or something when you need to talk, but don't count on me.'"

Therapist: "You really wanted to spend a little time with her, right? It had been a long day and you needed to stop for a minute and connect with her?"

Frank: "Yeah. And it pissed me off."

Therapist: "Maria, what happened when he showed his anger?"

Maria: "I just got out of there. I mean, I can't handle his anger. Like we've said in here, I just protect myself by staying away."

Therapist: "Right, right. You hear that anger and you're heading for safety."

Maria: (nods)

Therapist: "Frank, help me out here, let's go back a second. What's it like for you to reach for her, to ask her to come and sit with you, and then to feel put off."

Frank: "It's no fun."

Therapist: "It's no fun?"

Frank: "Well, I mean, it makes me feel like I am not important."

Therapist: "Yeah. So when she says, 'I'll be there in a minute,' and she isn't there in a minute, you start thinking that perhaps you're not important to her."

Frank: "Yeah." (tone softens just a hint) *"I mean, I know she's busy, but so am I, and I only want a few minutes. Aren't I worth that to her?"* (tone softens more, turns palms upward)

Therapist: "So when you ask for her to come sit with you, and you experience her putting you off, a part of you says, 'She doesn't think I'm important, or else she'd come.' Can you tell me a bit about fearing that she finds you unimportant to her?"

Frank: "Well, I try not to think about it. But, I am afraid of that. She means the world to me, and sometimes I wonder if she really needs me. I mean, she is really talented, quite the professional. Am I really someone that she wants?"

Therapist: "She means so much to you. A part of you says, 'Maybe I don't have enough to offer her,' perhaps?"

Frank: (nods)

Therapist: "That must be scary, Frank."

Frank: "Believe me, it is."

Therapist: "Maria, what's it like for you now as you hear Frank talk about a part of him fearing that he is not appealing to you, or is unimportant to you?"

Maria: "I had no idea. I had no idea this was there inside of him."

Therapist: "Right. Because what you see is his anger, right?"

Maria: (nods)

Therapist: "He doesn't often show you this part of him that is desperately afraid that you'll not want him, what he shows you is a response to this fear—his anger."

Maria: "Yes, that's exactly what I see—his anger."

Therapist: "And when you see his anger you defend for awhile, right, then protect yourself by withdrawing."

Maria: (nods)

Therapist: "In the end, help me with this guys, it seems like Frank, you end up all alone on the couch wondering if she really cares, and Maria, you end up in another place altogether in protection. Both of you are left alone and confused. Am I on track here?" (both solemnly agree)

In subsequent sessions, Maria shared how when Frank gets angry she "wilts." "I can't stand up to it," she said. "His anger shuts me down. I get afraid, not that he will hurt me, but that nothing good can come of it. I sort of get paralyzed." She then begins to feel small and inept in the face of Frank's anger. She withdraws to protect herself, and then launches into an "analyzing assault" in her own mind, rolling continuous questions such as "How can I do this differently? What am I doing wrong? Why does this happen to us?" "You know," she said, "I am this successful Christian feminist woman, and yet I can't seem to escape my husband's anger." I tracked and reflected Maria's underlying emotion of feeling overwhelmed in the face of Frank's anger:

Therapist: (to Maria) "It's as if something's wrong with you, that you aren't a good enough wife for him, that you can't make him happy. That's what courses through your veins when he gets angry?"

Maria: "Yes!" (begins to cry) *"And that's such a terrible place to be. I feel so helpless, so afraid…so inept."*

Therapist: (softly) "Right. And so alone."

Maria: "Yes. All alone."

SESSIONS 9 THROUGH 16: RESTRUCTURING EMOTIONAL BONDS

Therapist Reflections

Frank's anger coupled with her response of feeling inept stood out to me. I wanted to better understand her powerful statement "I am a Christian feminist woman who freezes in the face of her own husband's anger." These seemed to be strong images to her, ones that perhaps also stood in judgment over her. I made a note to explore that more fully when cycle de-escalation was behind us, and we faced withdrawer reengagement:

Maria's engagement highlights

Therapist: "Maria, you've talked about shrinking in the face of his anger."

Maria: "Yes, but his anger has softened considerably." (evidence of cycle de-escalation)

Therapist: "Indeed it has, as has the need to withdraw in protection on your part. Both of you are keeping the cycle at bay nicely. When you talked about the intensity of his anger and the effect that has on you, I don't think I fully understand that."

Maria: "Well, when he gets angry it's just really scary for me. I freeze. I don't like that."

Therapist: "Yes, I remember you saying something to the effect of being a Christian feminist and still being unable to deal with your own husband's anger in a manner that suited you. Could you tell me more about that?"

Maria: "I pride myself—I think we both do," (looks at Frank) "on being second generation Mexican Americans who have really done well for ourselves and our families. We come from a lot of strength, so, to show weakness in such an important relationship, the most important relationship, well, it makes me feel really inept."

Therapist: "Yes, yes, that's it, you've talked a lot about feeling inept. Like somehow you should not have this problem in your own life?"

Maria: "Yes. I believe in women being strong and supportive, and I value relationship greatly. And yet, in my own marriage, my husband gets totally frustrated with me, and I can't seem to please him."

Therapist: "You prize intimacy in your relationship very much. And yet, even though you are this strong Mexican-American woman, with all of these wonderful family traits handed down so graciously to you, and modeled to you, you still find trouble when this cycle gets going and his anger arises. If I am hearing you right, there is a part of you that kind of questions yourself. It's like this part says, 'What's wrong with you? He is so angry at you. Can't you please him?' Is that close?"

Maria: "Yes it is. When he keeps getting angry at me I feel stupid. Like only an idiot would keep making the same mistake over and over. On top of that his anger scares me, I freeze up."

Therapist: "Yes, you freeze. It's so intense, and it's coming from the person you love the most. And you say this part says to you, 'You are stupid.'"

Maria: (tears up) "Yes. I feel stupid. Inept."

Therapist: "Let me see if I am hearing you correctly, Maria. You're saying, 'I've been given this wonderful strong family heritage, my family has sacrificed for me to get a quality education, and I succeeded in that and in my profession. I am a professional woman who strongly believes and supports equality for women on all fronts.' Right?"

Maria: (nods)

Therapist: "And I am a Christian who believes that God has blessed the heck out of me, and that my life should honor him."

Maria: (nods again)

Therapist: "'And yet, here I am, unable to resolve these fights with my own husband. Unable to please him.' It's like during these times of disconnection a part of you rises up and accuses 'You are not who you say you are. You're really not strong, you're really not smart. Your own husband, the person who knows you best, is not pleased with you.' Is that some of what happens for you?"

Maria: (very softly) "Yes. These blessings can really come crashing down on me. When we fight, I just can't do it right, I just can't seem to please him. I go over this in my head over and over and over. Maybe I am not living the things I believe in."

Therapist: "Help me, Maria. What's it like for you inside to feel inept with your husband? What happens when you feel inept, when this part judges you as stupid?"

Maria: "It's awful." (sighs heavily) *"It hurts so badly. The doubts just plague me. I can't talk to him about it, because he's the one angry!"* (cries) *"I have nowhere to go. No one to go to. I just try not to think about it."*

Therapist: "There's nowhere to go. Here you are stuck in this place where the one person you want to connect and be close with, this person is also the one that scares you with his anger. That must be terribly confusing and yet scary at the same time."

Maria: "Oh, that is so it." (spontaneously turns to Frank) *"You are the one that can hold and comfort me. You are the only one I want, and yet, your anger makes you instantly go from the most precious to the most feared."* (cries)

Therapist: "You're saying, 'Frank, I get so scared of your anger, it alienates me so. You instantly go from safe and secure to dangerous and untouchable,' yeah?"

Maria: (nods)

Therapist: "And another part of me comes raining down on me saying, 'Who do you think you are? You aren't living what you believe in.' And this leaves you in a painfully alone place."

Maria: "Yes, it's awful. It's terrible. I hate being in that place. There's no help in sight when I am there."

Therapist: "Yes, the one person who can hold you, comfort you, and reassure you, seems so out of reach, so unsafe."

Maria: (nods)

Therapist: "Could you—right now, Maria—could you turn and share directly with Frank how terrible this place is, and how you need to be able to reach for him and be comforted, but he seems too unsafe? Would you please share this with him now in your own words?"

Maria: (10-second silence; turns to Frank) *"When you get angry at me, and we can't work it out, I withdraw and feel so…small. I feel like I am not a good wife."* (cries more heavily) *"If I was a good wife I'd figure all of this out. It's just terrible, Frank. I question myself as a woman, and even more deeply, I question myself as a woman before God. Your anger scares me. I get afraid of you. I need you to comfort me, and help me with these self-doubts. It's like a plague that I suffer all alone, and I don't want to suffer it all alone anymore."*

Frank: "I had no idea that my anger scared you. I had no idea. That makes me feel horrible. I am so very sorry. I am here for you. You can count on me. I will work on my anger, and I am sorry, because the last thing I want is to not be the person you can come to when you are doubting yourself and are afraid."

Frank was able to compassionately hear Maria's hurt without reacting negatively, or unduly blaming himself. "I had no idea that you felt inept, or somehow stupid in the face of my anger. I hate that—for both of us." Step 7 continued with a focus on Maria's attachment needs. She reiterated, "I need for you to work on your anger with me, so that I don't have to withdraw and protect myself from you. I need your reassurance that you love me, and that I am not inept. I so badly long for your support, Frank." Maria also battled the tendency to blame herself for these feelings because "God loves me, and I shouldn't feel inept," and "As a feminist I know that this is a two-way street and that I shouldn't just blame myself. But that knowledge also heaps blame on me when I fail." She was able to reach and ask of Frank: "I really need us both to work on this. I am tired of walking so lightly. I want this relationship to be a place where I can come and expose my deepest fears with you, and that be okay. My goodness, it scares me so to ask for this, or to put this out there like this. But this is what I want, for both of us. Please, let's face this together. Can we do this? Are you okay with it?" Frank was able to consistently reassure Maria that he deeply wanted to be able to hear and support her. "You are an incredible woman," he replied. "I want nothing more than to be there and hold you. On my end, I am afraid of my anger. I don't want to push you away." With that, the focus naturally shifted to Frank.

Therapist Reflections

Maria seemed to put a lot of pressure on herself to achieve what a "Christian feminist" woman "should." While her goals and standards seemed noble indeed, they had a tendency to overwhelm her, leaving her feeling sad and inept as a woman, wife, and professional. I was particularly interested in aiding her to begin enlisting her husband as a resource in supporting her when she became afraid that she was inept or not living up to her own standards. But before that became realistic, she needed to experience those emotions more fully in relation to her husband, and I needed to heighten and shape them within an attachment context. It came as no surprise to me that she worked right through this painful process. This led to her more deeply realizing that Frank's anger kept her away from him and the intimacy she desired. She was able to ask Frank to begin working on his anger so that she could begin trusting in him and feeling safe enough to share her attachment fears and wants. I thought it was a beautiful process of withdrawer engagement. She really was a strong Mexican-American woman, living out her Christian feminist beliefs in her marriage. I "cemented" her engagement back into the relationship by reflecting all of this to her. "I have a lot to draw from," she said. "I've been blessed."

I was also impressed by Frank. He stood beside his wife throughout the withdrawer engagement process, supporting her when she shared her fears of not living up to her standards and taking responsibility for his anger. Experiencing how scary and painful Maria found his anger affected Frank greatly and provided the motivation to change. He rarely responded defensively, but rather, stated how he loved it when she was clear about herself.

As mentioned earlier, this couple, despite all the distress, adored each other, and I never hesitated to heighten this. "When she speaks about feeling inept, my heart goes out to her," Frank said. "She is the best thing that has ever happened to me. I just want to hold her and reassure her of that." I reflected this and had him share this with her directly: "You love her throughout, don't you Frank?" I responded. "She gets down on herself, you just want to hold her and let her be herself, yeah? When she lets you in like this, you know at a deep level that you are no longer on the outside looking in. When she shares her heart and fears like this you inherently know that you are special and needed by her." He nods firmly. "Would you tell her this now in your own words, Frank? Tell her about your amazing love for her, and how when she risks letting you in it sets your world on fire."

As Frank was the more blaming partner, I thought his anger was something we definitely needed to spotlight, as it kept her away from him, and spurred on her own vicious cycle of self-doubt and judgment. What I could never have known at this point, however, was how deeply seated and painful this anger really was in Frank...

Frank's softening process highlights

"The last few weeks have been killing me," Frank reported. "We are getting along so well, it's not that. It's just that I know this anger in me scares her. I don't ever want that to happen, and I am scared that I can't always keep it in check." And with this, therapy entered Steps 5 through 7, with Frank, the more blaming spouse in this relationship.

Frank shared about how childhood was so painful for him. He reported growing up in a home where both parents were "distant" and siblings were "punishers." "My older brothers and sisters fought all the time," he said. "I was the youngest, and so I ended up getting the brunt of about everything." Frank told of how he would hide in his own home to escape the abuse of his siblings. The story provided a powerful experience to view his childhood world, and Maria herself stated later that she had never understood the degree of pain Frank lived through.

Frank shared this from a historical perspective initially, like telling a story from the past that he'd outgrown. I thought it was important to join in his childhood struggle, and to recognize how painful it must have been. "As I sit here and hear this from you Frank," I responded, "I get very sad that as a child, when you needed safety and love the most, you lived in a home where you were afraid, and physically abused by your own brothers. That's really sad, Frank. And I am sorry you had to live through that." At that moment Frank's head dropped like a rock, his chin crashing against his chest. He began to sob in a manner unlike anytime before in our sessions. As he cried heavily, Maria slid over to him and held him. It was powerful. I am not sure he had ever been heard and affirmed in this painful place. What I liked most about it, though, was how *Maria* comforted him, and he was able to find solace in her arms as he cried. At these moments I give the couple time and space to reinforce attachment cues and responses of accessibility and responsiveness. It's holy ground to me.

Therapist: (to Frank) *"So you learned early on that to survive you had to get tough, you had to produce anger in a hurry or you'd get hurt."*

Frank: "Oh yeah. I learned that an angry response was the only hope. Even then I'd get overpowered and beat up. I remember lying in my front yard, just crying after being bit by my sister. But, you see, I had to get tough, suck it up, and get angry, because if she saw me lying there crying for long, she or one of my brothers would pick on me for that. God, and now I am doing some of the same thing to my own wife!" (cries)

Therapist: "You learned early on to suck it up, get tough, or else you would be physically hurt even more. So your anger served a purpose to help you make it, to help you survive. So now, with your wife, sometimes this anger arises and you go into 'automatic mode.' And you're saying you hate it when that happens. You hate it because, as you say, 'Oh no, I am scaring my wife, pushing her away with my anger.' What happens inside, Frank, as you say this? As you recognize what is happening between you?"

Frank: "I feel so terrible. I know what it's like to be on the other end of anger, and I never want to cause that for Maria."

Therapist: "It really hurts you to really understand how your anger impacts Maria, and you want anything but that. Would you now please, turn to Maria and tell her how sorry you are for your anger in the past, and how you, of all people, resonate with being afraid and alone? Would you please let her in on how horrible this was as a child for you, and how this is the last thing on earth that you want going on between you and her."

Frank turns and shares these hurts and fears with Maria. Maria is again moved, and physically moves closer to Frank, grabbing his hand and shedding tears with him.

I usually don't spend so much time with couple's secondary anger reactions. But Frank's anger was so engrained with such a terribly painful past, and it played such a role in their relationship that it was necessary for them. We also created some coping strategies for Frank to deal with his anger before it erupted. I helped him experientially locate where in his body he felt the anger start to build. He began to learn to notice that as a kind of built-in preventive warning system. They came up with an interactional signal: Frank would raise his hand above his head, which would let Maria know that they needed to stop immediately. Frank would breathe deeply and walk away from Maria, even if it was just to a separate room, until he regained his composure. I asked them for one more step. I asked them if it would be possible for them, once Frank returned from calming down a bit, for them to hug for one minute, without saying a word. They would agree to not try to resolve any issue right then, just to allow each to feel the other's embrace. They agreed. And it worked. I hoped this ritual would let them begin risking and keeping emotional engagement even during times of distress and anger. I was also convinced that over time this increased emotional engagement would allow them to continue to build a safe and secure relationship.

As helpful as that proved to be, Frank's anger was still a secondary, learned emotional response. At this point in EFT we had achieved a first-order change. Parts of the interactional dance had changed and Maria had come out of withdrawal but the dance and music itself were still too similar to the original. The purpose of EFT is lasting, second-order change. Second-order change occurs in EFT when the relationship transforms into an emotional safe haven for both partners, evidenced by mutual accessibility and responsiveness. The time had come to expand Frank's attachment affect underlying his angry responses in his *current* relationship with Maria.

"I just feel like a child with her," Frank said in Step 5. "I can't match her 'facts' and feel less than equal to her intellect. It's like I don't count. Sometimes I hardly get considered in decisions that the family makes. Me and the kids get equal consideration." Frank went on to share that he wasn't really sure Maria needed him or really valued him. "I have a fear that I am not that important to her," he said. "But I keep that tucked away." Frank became sad when he talked about this, and it became clear that he usually spun into anger when panic or fear set in. I joined in his sadness by reflecting it and placing it in an attachment context. I asked him to share this with Maria. He solemnly confided, "I am not sure that you really value me anymore or that you think I have much to add to our family. I get angry at you, but underneath that is a fear that perhaps this is true. It scares me. And when I am alone, I realize that I am sad."

While Maria was taken aback by Frank's fear of not being as valuable to her as he once was, she was moved by his sincerity and vulnerability. "I had no idea that you felt like this," she said. "That is not how I feel at all. I hate making decisions apart from you. I don't want you to be sad." Step 6 (helping partners accept their spouse's new emotional experience) occurred rather smoothly with this couple. I often have to block the other spouse's criticism or reframe disbelief (see the latter half of chapter 6).

Maria's nurturing response propelled Frank to share his attachment-related affect even more deeply with her:

Frank: (to Maria) *"It's… terrifying to me that you may not really view me as an equal. If I am 'under' you, it's like I am a child. What kind of husband is that?"*

Therapist: *"When you start doubting whether Maria really needs you, really wants you, as a husband, not a child, a part of you feels like, help me understand, like you are not really the husband you want to be? Is that close?"*

Frank: *"Yes. If my fears are true, basically that says that I score a zero as a husband. I just can't cut it. I am a loser."*

Therapist: *"This really cuts deeply for you. When you start feeling like Maria is not considering you, or taking your opinion seriously, while you often show your anger, at a much deeper level a part of you says, 'I am not taken seriously by my own wife. I have nothing to add. I am a loser as a husband. I just can't cut it.'"*

Frank: *"Yes. I haven't just failed as a husband, I've failed as a man."* (head drops)

Therapist: *"Right. Would you please turn and share with Maria now about how scary this is for you. I don't think she sees this part of you often. Would you tell her about how sad you get, and about your deep fears of failing her as a husband?"*

Frank: (15 seconds of silence) *"When I hear a certain tone from you, it feels really belittling to me. It signals to me that I really don't count. I usually get mad, but what really is going on is this very intense…fear that I am failing once again as a husband—as a man."*

Therapist: *"When you feel like this Frank, like right now, what is it that you need from Maria? Could you ask her for what you need now?"*

Frank: (to therapist) *"I am not sure what I need from her. These are my feelings. I don't want to burden her or place my weaknesses on her plate."*

Therapist: *"Yes, you don't want to burden her, to put 'your stuff' on her back. But my sense is Frank, that Maria longs to help you with your fears, longs to reassure you when you feel like you are failing her or are sad. I think you have an incredible ally here beside you, and I'd like for you to let her in, even into these places where it is incredibly scary to do so."*

Maria: (nods affirmingly)

Frank: (to Maria) *"It would be great if you could listen to me when I start doubting myself. I need that. It's scary to ask for that, because I kind of feel weak in needing that, but…"* (breathes deeply) *"would you think I was really off the mark if I shared this with you?"*

Maria: *"No, not at all honey. I'd love it if you would share this with me. It's just the opposite of what you fear, seeing this part of you makes me love you. It tells me that you need me too. It reaffirms that I am a good wife to you."* (begins to cry)

Therapist: (to Maria) *"So, if he asked you to come be with him when he is afraid, or feeling alone, or sad, if he reaches to you, just like he did just now, you would be able to hear and comfort him?"*

Maria: *"Absolutely."* (looks to Frank) *"I would love that."*

Therapist: (to Frank) *"Do you hear her, Frank? Can you let her in? She is saying, 'Risk with me. I am here. I will listen, and I will love it when you open up all of you to me. I won't think less of you, in fact, I'll think more of you!' Can you let her in? What's happening inside as you hear her now?"*

Frank: *"I am starting to let it in. It's scary, but I want to let it in."*

Therapist: *"Could you share this with her please? Share with her what goes on inside as she says this."*

Frank: (to Maria) *"It feels great to hear you say this. I guess I always thought you would just see me as weak if I shared this with you."* (tears up) *"I need your acceptance and love, and it feels really incredible to share with you at this level and have you respond so lovingly."*

(Couple lean over and hug each other, Maria cries; 30-second silence as they hug)

Therapist: (to Frank) *"You really want her reassurance that you are the man for her."*

Frank: (nods)

Therapist: *"Her positive response is like a 'balm from heaven' to you, yeah?"*

Frank: (both partners smile) *"Yeah, it really is."*

Therapist: *"It's like, if you could count on her to reassure you and be there for you when you feel discounted and doubtful, it would just mean the world to you."*

Frank: *"It would just flood into my heart."*

Therapist: *"What's that—'flood into your heart'?"*

Frank: *"When I know that she is on my side, when we are together like this, I just want to love her so deeply, to show her in return how wonderful she is to me."*

Therapist: *"So when you reach for her, like you have in here, and she responds so lovingly, it just injects you with happiness and energy towards her, yeah? She just means so much to you. Would you tell her this now, in your own words?"*

Frank: *"You mean more to me than anyone ever has. You make me so happy. When I share like this and you respond so lovingly, you accept me as I am, my heart just melts for you."*

(Maria reaches to Frank and they hug again.)

Therapist Reflections

This was a powerful softening. Frank was able to experience his attachment fears and needs, and ask for them to be met. Maria was able to respond in a safe and responsive manner. They naturally progressed into a bonding event, in which they began to deepen and share the meaning and importance of the other. I found it particularly interesting how the softening energized Frank to turn and meet Maria's needs more intimately. A staple of EFT theory is that when safety and nurturance are established in a relationship, each partner's often untapped attachment reservoirs of deep caring for the other spring forth. I do have couples that seem to need to process through more than one softening event before being able to duplicate them outside of the therapy session and move into bonding events. But that was not the case with Frank and Maria. After this session they did have blowups, but they were able to then work through them and stay emotionally connected.

I ended session 16 by praising both partners for the attachment risks they took. I find I am often reflecting strengths and praising couples. It's inherent in such a strength-based model. But when a couple processes through change events, it is especially crucial to end the session by taking some time to praise their hard work completed in that session. I am careful to support from within an attachment context. As the couple held hands I praised Frank for how vulnerable he allowed himself to be, and how impressive it was that he was able to reach for comfort and reassurance from Maria. "You know, it's one thing to tell me that you get scared," I said to Frank. "But, it's quite another to turn and directly risk sharing that with your wife. And *then* ask her to be there for you and reassure you. That's big time." Then I turned to praise Maria from within an attachment context: "And Maria, the way you responded to him being vulnerable with you, it was *fantastic*. It's like his sharing in that way just *drew you* towards him." (Glancing over to Frank) "You're a lucky man, Frank." (Back to Maria) "And you're just crazy about him, aren't you?" Now, I knew that they were very emotionally connected right then, and moved to heighten the attachment-related affect resulting from restructuring the emotional bond. In EFT, we don't just heighten and expand affect surrounding negative cycles, we also heighten and expand affect around times of connection and intimacy. When they do it right and their world is transformed, we share their hard work and excitement.

SESSIONS 17 THROUGH 19: SOLIDIFYING AND CONSOLIDATING

"She told her mom that we were coming," Frank said. "I heard her say it, and it got to me. I thought I made it clear that I didn't want to go over that night. Once again, what I said didn't seem to matter. It was tough. I was battling my anger, boy." Oh my, I thought to myself, have they regressed back to the negative cycle? Are we back to that?

Couples still argue and fight. EFT is not magic. Frank and Maria are just normal human beings. And normal human beings argue and fight.

Okay, fine. So, what to do? Go there and emotionally process.

So, I re-entered the recent flare-up with them.

Therapist: (to Frank) *"You heard her on the phone with her mother?"*

Frank: (nods)

Therapist: "Oh, so you heard her say you'd go over to their house, but you had said earlier that you didn't want to. Is that right?"

Frank: "Yes. I was like, 'It's happening all over again! I can't believe it!'"

Therapist: "You got scared that maybe you didn't count again, maybe she didn't value you in this, right? And you know this cycle, right? You know how the steps of this dance play out. So, you're standing there, beginning to get uneasy, beginning to get a bit scared, about to go into anger. What happened next?"

Frank: "I went into my anger. I was seething. She was on the phone, so I couldn't say much, but I was mad."

Therapist: "Right, it's like, 'She's done it again. Do I really count? Am I really important to her?' These strong fears come rushing in, and you quickly run to your anger."

Frank: "Yes. It does happen fast."

Therapist: "So, what happened next?"

Frank: "Well, she got off the phone, and I went to her and told her that she once again dismissed me, and that I was mad about it."

Therapist: (to Maria) "And how did you experience this encounter at this point?"

Maria: "I could tell he was mad, but I hadn't dismissed him."

Therapist: "Right, right. Frank, my guess is that Maria didn't see your fears of being dismissed. My guess is she faced your anger. What kept you from going in and saying something like, 'Honey, I heard what you said on the phone and I am starting to question whether I am being dismissed again. I am fighting off my anger, because I don't want to get angry at you. But, when I heard you say that, all these doubts about where I stand with you came rushing in. I need some reassurance from you pretty quickly. We both know how this cycle can take off, and I don't want that.' What kept you from risking this way, and showing her what's really going on for you? Because sometimes you are able to do this, and it pays off nicely for both of you."

Frank: "Yeah, when I do share like that it does have much better results. When I do that I feel much more stable in myself too, and then when she responds to me I feel even better. Uhmm, I don't know what kept me from doing that this time."

Therapist: "Would you be able to turn now and approach her the way you wished you would have then? Could you do this now in your own words? Let her in to what is going on with you?" (Therapist immediately turns to the side and gazes at notes, getting out of the way of the couple so to speak).

Frank turned and shared with Maria his attachment-related fears and needs that he kept inside during the negative episode at home earlier in the week. Maria was able to respond in an accessible and responsive manner. The couple then discussed how talking with Maria's parents seemed to be a trigger point for them. At this stage in therapy, I intentionally let couples discuss their own unique "danger areas" amongst themselves to a great degree. It's amazing, but most of the time they come to decisions based on each partner conceding and being flexible. Couples often move into a process of serving the other, or placing the other's needs above their own in these discussions. In this session, Frank's focus turned to Maria ("It must be tough to walk this line with your mom. I know you guys are close. I love her, too. It seems kind of silly now that I used to be somehow alarmed at that.") Maria's focus naturally moved into being there for Frank ("I can see how my relationship with mom could make you feel uneasy at times, especially if I spend too much time on the phone with her when we haven't talked and touched base. You know, I am not going to let that happen anymore.")

The couple is now emotionally connected. The relationship has become a secure base for each of them. Past "danger areas" don't disappear, and the couple will still get irritated and argue occasionally. But the danger areas are now naturally addressed and tackled together because each partner addresses them from a secure relational base. They are able to define themselves and their relationship much more clearly and healthily.

FINAL THOUGHTS

This was a fascinating couple to work with in part because of their rich cultural heritage, religious beliefs, and feminist views. I felt comfortable working with them because of the constructivist nature of EFT. I didn't go in assuming that I needed to access or pursue any of these specific areas with Frank and Maria. I did go in determined to listen and honor what was important to them and their unique history. As an EFT therapist it's my job to learn and understand couples' worldviews and beliefs. I honor and use these in aiding them to restructure their relationship toward safe and secure emotional intimacy.

Unlike previous experiential approaches, which have been criticized for lacking detailed theory, EFT affords me an overall process map of restructuring couples' emotional bonds from session one onwards throughout the entire course of therapy. The intricacy yields specifications of what interventions to use and when. An early session of EFT is very different from a session 6, for example, just as a session 10 is usually different from session 16, and so forth. EFT has not been easy for me to master, but I grow more adept with each couple I see.

Working intensely with emotion is rarely boring. It has the feel of being alive and creative, very much in the moment. One has to trust the process of going into primary attachment emotion and using this emotion to move partners into a new dance.

I think every therapist has to find her own voice and style within EFT. As a male, I can confirm that one does not need to be a Susan Johnson or even a woman to be an effective EFT therapist. We all bring our own uniqueness to EFT. I'm an American southerner whose accent and metaphors often belie my roots. As a southerner, I speak more slowly than some therapists. But, despite our differences, we integrate our own personalities into the overall process that is emotionally focused therapy. I am usually an effective EFT therapist.

And you can be too.

APPENDIX A

EFT RESOURCES

BOOKS

Greenberg, L. S., & Johnson, S. M. (1988). *Emotionally focused therapy for couples.* New York: Guilford.

Johnson, S. M. (2002). *Emotionally focused couple therapy with trauma survivors: Strengthening attachment bonds.* New York: Guilford.

Johnson, S. M. (2004). *The practice of emotionally focused marital therapy: Creating connection* (2nd ed.). New York: Brunner-Routledge.

Johnson, S. M., & Greenberg, L. S. (Eds.). (1994). *The heart of the matter: Perspectives on emotion in marital therapy.* New York: Brunner/Mazel.

Johnson, S. M., & Whiffen, V. (Eds.). (2003). *Attachment processes in couples and families.* New York: Guilford.

RECENT CHAPTERS (SINCE 1995)

Most chapters contain transcripts of therapy sessions

Bradley, B., & Johnson, S. M. (2005) Emotionally focused couples therapy: An integrative contemporary approach. In M. Haraway (Ed.), *Handbook of couple therapy,* (pp. 179–193). New York: Wiley.

Bradley, B., & Johnson, S. M. (in press). Task analysis of couple and family change events. In D. Sprenkle & F. Piercy (Eds.), *Research methods in family therapy,* (2nd ed.). New York: Guilford.

Johnson, S. M. (1998). Emotionally focused interventions: Using the power of emotion. In F. Dattilio (Ed.), *Case studies in couple and family therapy: Systemic and cognitive perspectives* (pp. 450–472). New York: Guilford.

Johnson, S. M. (1999). Emotionally focused therapy: Straight to the heart. In J. Donovan (Ed.), *Short-term couple therapy* (pp. 11–42). New York: Guilford.

Johnson, S. M. (2000). Emotionally focused couples therapy: Creating a secure bond. In F. M. Dattilio (Ed.), *Comparative treatments in relationship dysfunction* (pp. 163–185). New York: Springer.

Johnson, S. M. (2001). An antidote to post-traumatic stress disorder: The creation of secure attachment. In L. Atkinson & S. Golberg (Eds.), *Attachment and psychopathology* (pp. 207–228). New York: Cambridge University Press.

Johnson, S. M. (2002). Marital problems. In D. Sprenkle (Ed.), *Effectiveness research in marriage and family therapy* (pp. 163–190). Alexandria, VA: American Association for Marriage and Family Therapy.

Johnson, S. M. (2003). Attachment theory: A guide for couples therapy. In S. M. Johnson & V. Whiffen (Eds.), *Attachment processes in couples and families,* (pp. 103–123). New York: Guilford.

Johnson, S. M. (2003). Emotionally focused couples therapy: Empiricism and art. In T. Sexton, G. Weeks, & M. Robbins (Eds.), *The handbook of family therapy* (pp. 263–280). New York: Brunner-Routledge.

Johnson, S. M. (2003). Introduction to attachment: A therapist's guide to primary relationships and their renewal. In S. M. Johnson & V. Whiffen (Eds.), *Attachment processes in couples and families,* (pp. 3–17). New York: Guilford.

Johnson, S. M. (2004). An antidote to post-traumatic stress disorder: The creation of secure attachment. In L. Atkinson & S. Goldberg (Eds.), *Attachment issues in psychopathology and intervention* (pp. 207–298). Mahwah, NJ: Erlbaum.

Johnson, S. M. (2004). Attachment theory a guide for healing couple relationships. In J. A. Simpson (Ed.), *Adult attachment* (pp. 367–387). New York: Guilford.

Johnson, S. M. (2004). Facing the dragon together: Emotionally focused couples therapy with trauma survivors. In D. Catherall (Ed.), *Handbook of stress, trauma, & the family* (pp. 493–512).

Johnson, S. M. (in press). An emotionally focused approach to infidelity. In F. Piercy (Ed.), *Handbook on treating infidelity.* Binghamton, NY: Haworth Press.

Johnson, S. M. (in press). Emotion and the repair of close relationships. In W. Pinsof & T. Patterson (Eds.), *Family psychology: The art of the science.* New York: Oxford University Press.

Johnson, S. M., & Best, M. (2002). A systematic approach to restructuring adult attachment: The EFT model of couples therapy. In P. Erdman & T. Caffery (Eds.), *Attachment and family systems: Conceptual, empirical and therapeutic relatedness* (pp. 165–192). New York: Springer.

Johnson, S. M., & Boisvert, C. (2002). Humanistic couples' and family therapy. In D. Kane (Ed.), *Humanistic psychotherapies* (pp. 309–337). Washington, DC: APA Press.

Johnson, S. M., & Denton, W. (2002). Emotionally focused couples therapy: Creating connection. In A. S. Gurman (Ed.), *The clinical handbook of couple therapy* (3rd ed., pp. 221–250). New York: Guilford.

Johnson, S. M., & Greenberg, L. S. (1995). The emotionally focused approach to problems in adult attachment. In N. S. Jacobson & A. S. Gurman (Eds.), *The clinical handbook of marital therapy* (2nd ed.). (pp. 3–26) New York: Guilford.

Johnson, S. M., & Lee, A. (2000). Emotionally focused family therapy: Children in therapy. In E. Bailey (Ed.), *Working with children in family therapy* (pp. 112–116). New York: Guilford.

Johnson, S. M., & Makinen, J. (2003). Creating a safe haven and a secure base: Couples therapy as a vital element in the treatment of post-traumatic stress disorder. In D. Snyder & M. Whisman (Eds.), *Treating difficult couples.* (pp. 308–309) New York: Guilford.

Johnson, S. M., & Sims, A. (2000). Creating secure bonds in couples therapy. In T. Levy (Ed.), *Handbook of attachment interventions* (pp. 167–191). Burlington, MA: Academic Press.

Macintosh, H., & Johnson, S. M. (in press). Emotionally focused therapy for couples facing heart disease. In E. Molinari (Ed.), *Italian handbook of clinical psychology and heart disease.* New York: Springer.

Woolley, S., & Johnson, S. M. (in press). Emotionally focused interventions. In J. Lebow (Ed.), *Handbook of clinical family therapy.* New York: Wiley.

RECENT ARTICLES

Clothier, P., Manion, I., Gordon Walker, J., & Johnson, S. M. (2002). Emotionally focused interventions for couples with chronically ill children: A two-year follow-up. *Journal of Marital & Family Therapy, 28,* 391–399.

Dessaulles, A., Johnson, S. M., & Denton, W. (2003). The treatment of clinical depression in the context of marital distress. *American Journal of Family Therapy, 31,* 345–353.

Johnson, S. (1997). The biology of love. *Family Therapy Networker,* Sept., 36–41.

Johnson, S. (1998). Listening to music: Emotion as a natural part of systems theory. Special Edition of the *Journal of Systemic Therapies, 17,* 1–17.

Johnson, S. (1998). The use of emotion in couples and family therapy. Special Edition of the *Journal of Systemic Therapies, 17,* 1–17.

Johnson, S. M. (2003). Let us keep emotion at the forefront: A reply to Roberts and Koval. *Journal of Couple & Relationship Therapy, 2*, 15–20.

Johnson, S. M. (2003). The revolution in couples therapy: A practitioner-scientist perspective. *Journal of Marital & Family Therapy, 29*, 365–385.

Johnson, S. M. (in press). Broken bonds: An emotionally focused approach to infidelity. *Journal of Couple & Family Relationship Therapy.*

Johnson, S., Hunsley, J., Greenberg, L., & Schindler, D. (1999). Emotionally focused couples therapy: Status & challenges. *Clinical Psychology: Science & Practice, 6*, 67–79.

Johnson, S., Maddeux, C., & Blouin, J. (1998). Emotionally focused family therapy for bulimia: Changing attachment patterns. *Psychotherapy: Theory, Research & Practice, 35*, 238–247.

Johnson, S., & Williams Keeler, L. (1998). Creating healing relationships for couples dealing with trauma. *Journal of Marital & Family Therapy, 24*, 25–40.

Johnson, S. M., & Lebow, J. (2000). The coming of age of couple therapy: A decade review. *Journal of Marital and Family Therapy, 26*, 9–24.

Johnson, S. M., Makinen, & Millikin, J. (2001). Attachment injuries in couples relationships: A new perspective on impasses in couple therapy. *Journal of Marital & Family Therapy, 27*, 145–156.

Johnson, S. M., & Whiffen, V. (1999). Made to measure: Attachment styles in couples therapy. *Clinical Psychology: Science & Practice, 6*, 366–381.

Knowal, J., Johnson, S. M., & Lee, A. (2003). Chronic illness in couples: A case for emotionally focused therapy. *Journal of Marital & Family Therapy, 29*, 299–310.

Makinen, J., & Johnson, S. M. (in press). An EFT approach to resolving attachment injuries in couples: Forgiveness and reconciliation. *Journal of Consulting & Clinical Psychology.*

Palmer, G., & Johnson, S. M. (2002). Becoming an emotionally focused therapist. *Journal of Couple and Relationship Therapy, 1*(3), 1–20.

Schwartz, R., & Johnson, S. M. (2000). Does family therapy have emotional intelligence? *Family Process, 39*, 29–34.

Whiffen, V., & Johnson, S. M. (1998). An attachment theory framework for the treatment of childbearing depression. *Clinical Psychology, Science & Practice, 5*, 478–492.

REFERENCES CONCERNING EMPIRICAL SUPPORT FOR THE EFFECTIVENESS OF EFT

Baucom, D., Shoham, V., Mueser, K., Daiuto, A., & Stickle, T. (1998). Empirically supported couple and family interventions for marital distress and adult mental health problems. *Journal of Consulting & Clinical Psychology, 58*, 53–88.

Dandeneau, M., & Johnson, S. (1994). Facilitating intimacy: A comparative outcome study of emotionally focused and cognitive interventions. *Journal of Marital & Family Therapy, 20*, 17–33.

Denton, W., et al. (2000). A rationalized trial of emotionally focused therapy for couples. *Journal of Marital and Family Therapy, 26*, 65–78.

Desaulles, A. (1991). *The treatment of clinical depression in the context of marital distress.* Unpublished doctoral dissertation, University of Ottawa, Canada.

Dessaulles, A., Johnson, S. M., & Denton, W. (2003). Emotion focused therapy for couples in the treatment of depression: A pilot study. *American Journal of Family Therapy, 31*, 345–353.

Goldman, A., & Greenberg, L. (1989). A comparison of systemic and emotionally focused outcome studies. *Journal of Marital & Family Therapy, 15*, 21–28.

Gordon-Walker, J., Johnson, S., Manion, I., & Cloutier, P. (1996). An emotionally focused marital intervention for couples with chronically ill children. *Journal of Consulting & Clinical Psychology, 64*, 1029–1036.

Gordon-Walker, J., Manion, I., & Clothier, P. (1998). A two-year follow-up on an emotionally focused intervention for couples with chronically ill children. *Journal of Marital & Family Therapy, 28*, 391–399.

James, P. (1991). Effects of a communication training component added to an emotionally focused couples therapy. *Journal of Marital & Family Therapy, 17*, 263–276.

Johnson, S., & Greenberg, L. (1985). Emotionally focused couples therapy: An outcome study. *Journal of Marital & Family Therapy, 11,* 313–317.

Johnson, S., & Greenberg, L. (1985). The differential effectiveness of experiential and problem solving interventions in resolving marital conflict. *Journal of Consulting & Clinical Psychology, 53,* 175–184.

Johnson, S., Hunsley, J., Greenberg, L., & Schindler, D. (1999). Emotionally focused couples therapy: Status & challenges (A meta-analysis). *Journal of Clinical Psychology: Science and Practice, 6,* 67–79.

Johnson, S., Maddeaux, C., & Blouin, J. (1998). Emotionally focused family therapy for bulimia: Changing attachment patterns. *Psychotherapy: Theory, Research & Practice, 35,* 238–247.

Johnson, S. M. (2003). The revolution in couples therapy: A practitioner-scientist perspective. *Journal of Marital & Family Therapy, 29,* 365–385.

Talitman, E., & Johnson, S. (1997). Predictors of outcome in emotionally focused marital therapy. *Journal of Marital & Family Therapy, 23,* 135–152.

RECENT ARTICLES (BY OTHER AUTHORS)

Bradley, B. (2001). An intimate look into emotionally focused therapy: An interview with Susan M. Johnson. *Marriage & Family—A Christian Journal, 4,* 117–124.

Bradley, B., & Furrow, J. L. (2004). Toward a mini-theory of the blamer softening event: Tracking the moment by moment process. *Journal of Marital & Family Therapy, 30,* 233–246.

Dankoski, M. D. (2001). Pulling on the heart strings: An emotionally focused approach to family life cycle transitions. *Journal of Marital & Family Therapy, 27,* 177–189.

Denton, W., et al. (2000). A randomized trial of emotion-focused therapy for couples at a training clinic. *Journal of Marital & Family Therapy, 26,* 65–78.

Keiley, M. (2001). Affect regulation and attachment focused treatment of a husband with OCD and his wife. *Journal of Couple & Relationship Therapy, 1,* 25–44.

Schwartz, R., & Johnson, S. M. (2000). Commentary: Does couple and family therapy have emotional intelligence? *Family Process, 39,* 29–34.

Vatcher, C., & Bogo, M. (2001). The feminist/emotionally focused therapy practice model: An integrated approach for couple therapy. *Journal of Marital & Family Therapy, 27,* 69–84.

VIDEOS/DVD

Ottawa Couple and Family Institute (Producer). (1993). *Healing broken bonds* [Motion picture]. (Available from Ottawa Couple and Family Institute, Suite 201, 1869 Carling Avenue, Ottawa, Ontario, Canada K2A 1E6)

Available on VHS and DVD, this tape shows one couple progressing through the change process in EFT, from a destructive cycle of blame/withdraw to emotional engagement and the creation of a more secure bond. Excerpts from various sessions are reenacted along with therapist commentary. Dr. Johnson presents the key interventions used in EFT. An excerpt of the first session assessment and the identification of the couple's negative cycle follows. Excerpts from sessions 8 and 12 illustrate the process of reengaging the withdrawn partner in the relationship. A key change event in EFT, softening the more hostile partner, is shown in session 14, and excerpts from sessions 15 and 17 illustrate how this change is integrated and treatment is terminated. The video runs for approximately 95 minutes and is taken from real therapy transcripts. These transcripts are illustrated by actors to protect the identity of the couple. The tape can be ordered for $130 in U.S. funds (postage included) from: Ottawa Couple and Family Institute, Suite 201, 1869 Carling Avenue, Ottawa, Ontario, Canada K2A 1E6. Phone: (613)-722-5122.

(2002). *Couples and trauma* [Motion picture].

Available on VHS and DVD, this tape shows excerpts of one couple's sessions: The husband has been diagnosed with generalized anxiety disorder and posttraumatic stress disorder. The trauma was severe childhood physical abuse. The wife has also been diagnosed with clinical depression. Excerpts include part of a change event, a "softening," for the husband and a follow-up session 9 months after treatment. There are comments at the beginning and end of the tape by Dr. Susan Johnson, the therapist on the tape. The video runs for 2 hours and 23 minutes and can be ordered for $150 in U.S. funds from the OCFI.

(2003). *A consultation in EFT: Shaping change events* [Motion picture].

Available on VHS and DVD, this tape shows a live consultation with a couple stuck in a blamer/withdrawer pattern. Dr. Johnson moves the partners into the beginning of withdrawer reengagement and blamer softening, two regular EFT change events. The couple is then able to repeat these experiences in further sessions with the referring therapist, successfully transforming their relationship. There is an introductory conversation with Dr. Johnson and Kate Ciceri, the referring therapist. The video runs for 1 hour and 22 minutes and can be ordered for $130 in U.S. funds from the OCFI.

(2005). An externship in EFT

Price: $285. Length: 12 hours and 36 minutes. The September 2004 Externship in EFT is shown with Dr. Johnson and colleagues. Presentations, discussions and live sessions can be ordered from the OCFI.

APPENDIX B

HELPING YOURSELF LEARN EFT FOR COUPLES

Having trained many gifted professionals to use EFT in clinical practice and in research projects, we suggest the following tried and tested ways to make EFT your own. All of the methods listed below can, of course, be used to learn EFFT with families.

1. Read the basic manual for EFT: Sue Johnson's book *Creating Connection* (1996, 2004).

2. Read the literature on attachment theory as a model of love – in *Creating Connection* (2nd edition, 2004) and in the chapters in Johnson & Whiffen – *Attachment Processes in Couple and Family Therapy* (2003, Guilford).

3. Therapists may benefit from reading chapters on EFT that contain excerpts of therapy (found on the Web site http://www.eft.ca). You should pay attention to what the therapist does and think about what you might have done. You can also identify the interventions used if they are not already noted in the text.

4. Working through this workbook should then focus your learning process further and help you integrate EFT with your personal style. Watching the training tapes adds to this process of integration. Tapes are listed on the Web site and can be ordered from the Institute in Ottawa.

5. Recording and watching your own sessions (do watch them more than once) until you begin to see the process in each session and how it moves and changes is invaluable. The originators of EFT learned the model using this method. You can use the note form offered in Appendix G to take notes on your sessions.

6. Watching colleagues' sessions is also a great way to learn. This can be done in a support group where colleagues help each other learn EFT. The Institute in Ottawa (ocfi@magma.ca) can often tell you about other professionals in your area with whom you can connect. There is EFT List serve.Group supervision is also part of the EFT registration process (information about this process can be found on the Web site http://www.eft.ca).

7. It is often possible to receive permission to tape your couples' sessions and then send your videos to an experienced EFT therapist for feedback. Usually this feedback is recorded on an audiotape, which can then be played with the original video for immediate feedback. This consultation process is a powerful aid to learning and is also part of EFT registration process.

8. You can register in an EFT externship and advanced externship to study EFT further and watch live EFT sessions.

9. Part of learning a model such as EFT is taking the time to consider your own attachment history and your own orientation towards emotion. Some therapists keep a notebook on how these are cued in sessions and how they work with them as part of the intervention process. It is useful to identify the kinds of responses, partners, or couples you have the hardest time dealing with, noting the impact they have on you.

The best way to learn is to let your clients teach you. You must be discovery oriented, giving yourself permission to learn from each session. You must expect to get stuck sometimes—the dance of adult love is intricate, moving, and multidimensional.

APPENDIX C

BEGINNING AN EFT COUPLE SESSION: A CHECKLIST

In the 5 minutes before the couple walk into the session, ask yourself the following:

1. Is the alliance intact with both partners?
2. What is the main negative cycle here—who does what?
3. What are the primary emotions underlying this cycle, and what are the linked attachment fears/issues?
4. Where are they in the steps of EFT? The next step is?
5. What are the pivotal incidents to be aware of that define the relationship?
6. What are the key images/definitions of self each partner uses?
7. What are the current blocks to engagement with self-emotions/other?
8. What are the highlights in the process of the last session?
9. What are the couple's strengths (to validate)?
10. What is the main goal for this session?

APPENDIX D1

UNDERSTANDING YOUR NEGATIVE CYCLE

Couples get caught in negative "cycles." A cycle is a repeating pattern of negative behaviors, thoughts, and feelings that causes distress. You react to your partner's reactions and your partner reacts to your reactions and you go round and round in a never-ending cycle. Understanding and untangling your negative cycles is a first step in climbing out of distress.

   To start understanding your negative cycles, answer the following questions. First review and think about the "When We're Not Getting Along: Feelings, Thoughts, and Behaviors" checklist to remind yourself of how you feel and interact when you are not getting along with your partner.

When my partner and I are not getting along:

I often react by (describe your behaviors)…

_____

_____

_____

My partner often reacts to me by (describe his/her behaviors)…

_____

_____

_____

When my partner reacts this way, I often feel…

_____

_____

_____

When I feel this way I, see myself as...

_____

_____

_____

When I feel this way I long for or need...

_____

_____

_____

When I react the way I do, I guess that my partner feels...

_____

_____

_____

Describe your repeating negative cycle (include how you and your partner trigger each other's feelings, thoughts, and behaviors).

_____

_____

_____

APPENDIX D2

WHEN WE'RE NOT GETTING ALONG: FEELINGS, THOUGHTS, AND BEHAVIORS

Check all the statements that reflect the way you feel or what you do when you and your partner are fighting or not getting along. Look back over the list and circle a few to indicate the most important items.

What I Do

I attack

I avoid conflict

I become cold or aloof

I blame

I clam up

I criticize

I defend

I get quiet

I leave

I withdraw

What I Feel

I feel abandoned

I feel afraid

I feel alone or lonely

I feel analyzed

I feel angry

I feel attacked

I feel blamed or criticized

I feel blank

I feel confused

I feel controlled

I feel disappointed

I feel disconnected

I feel discounted

I feel dismissed or "blown off"

I feel down or depressed

I feel empty

I feel flooded with emotion

I feel frustrated

I feel guarded

I feel guilty

I feel hopeless

I feel hurt

I feel like I don't know what I have done

I feel that I don't matter

I feel that I've failed

I feel ignored

I feel inadequate

I feel intimidated

I feel invalidated

I feel isolated

I feel like it's always my fault

I feel judged

I feel let down

I feel like clinging to my partner

I feel like getting back

I feel like protecting myself

I feel misunderstood

I feel my partner is never there for me

I feel numb

I feel overwhelmed

I feel put down

I feel rejected

I feel sad

I feel scared

I feel shut out or pushed away

I feel small or insignificant

I feel smothered

I feel unable to calm myself down

I feel unable to focus my thoughts

I feel unattractive

I feel uncared for or unwanted

I feel unimportant

I feel unlovable

I feel vulnerable

I feel worried or nervous

I have trouble putting thoughts into words

In My Body I Feel

I feel my heart speeding up

I feel pressure in my chest

I feel tense somewhere in my body

I feel tightness in my throat

I feel uneasy in my stomach

How We Interact During Conflict

____ During an argument, I become become silent, withdraw, and don't want to discuss things.

____ I often get angry and critical to get my partner to talk.

____ I often want to avoid talking about our relationship.

____ I often want to push my partner to talk about our relationship.

____ My partner often pushes an issue and won't let it drop.

____ My partner withdraws a lot and won't face an issue when I want to talk.

Other Feelings

_____

_____

_____

_____

© 2003 Douglas Tillley, LCSW-C

APPENDIX E

EFT ASSESSMENT FORM

Names of clients _____

                     Partner A   Partner B

Names of important players (e.g., children) _____

_____

Duration of relationship _____ **Marital status** _____ **Referral source** _____

Reasons for seeking therapy at this time

    Partner A _____

    Partner B _____

Stated goals for each partner

    Partner A _____

    Partner B _____

Possible attachment injury? _____

Quality of sexual connection _____

Level of commitment — Partner A

1   2   3   4   5

Low   High

Level of distress — Partner A

1   2   3   4   5

Extremely   Extremely
Unhappy   Happy

Level of commitment — Partner B

1   2   3   4   5

Low   High

Level of distress — Partner B

1   2   3   4   5

Extremely   Extremely
Unhappy   Happy

Apparent negative cycle

Attack–Defend   _____
Pursue–Distance   _____
Demand–Defend/Appease   _____
Withdraw–Withdraw   _____
Complex Traumatic   _____

Positive cycles (describe)

_____

Have partners known secure attachment? (yes/no)	**Partner A**	**Partner B**
In this relationship?	_____	_____
In previous adult relationship?	_____	_____
In family of origin?	_____	_____

Therapist sense of alliance with client? (yes/no)	**Partner A**	**Partner B**
Very easy to engage client	_____	_____
Moderately easy to engage client	_____	_____
Difficult to engage client	_____	_____
Very hard to engage client	_____	_____

Recent loss or trauma

Partner A _____

Partner B _____

Accompanying problems

Depression   _____
Anxiety/PTSD   _____
Alcohol/drug use   _____
Other psychiatric conditions   _____
Physical problems   _____

Contraindications for EFT (describe below):

_____

APPENDIX F

HOMEWORK FOR COUPLES

Steps 1 through 4

Ask the couple to write down the key points of the session at home. If they feel comfortable, they can share it with their spouse; if not, that is fine. Also ask the couple to write down the "dance" cycle that gets them stuck and how each of them moves in a way that helps the partner move into a negative stance.

When people are beginning to understand the cycle, tell them: "You will do this again. It's natural and inevitable that you will. What I ask is that you simply notice it. You may not realize you have had a cycle until it is over, or way late in the process." Tell the couple to try to be aware that they just experienced the cycle. "And if you dare," you may tell the couple, "perhaps you can even share what you think with your partner."

Ask the couple to put a pad of paper in a location where they will both see it and can use it frequently. Tell both to make entries on the pad expressing their appreciation for things the other does each day. The exercise will help the partners give positive and encouraging feedback to one another about what they like. It should increase their general level of positive behaviors.

Steps 5 through 7

Therapists may ask the couple to schedule two 15-minute talks to discuss one aspect of the process—the emotions that come up and the risks each person is taking. If the couple has trouble with the discussion, we can talk about the difficulty—the blocks and fears—that they experienced in the next session.

George Faller, a firefighter and counselor with the fire department in New York, asks partners to rate their degree of closeness each day on a scale of 1 to 10 (with 1 being distant and alone). Each must inquire and record the other's score, allowing the couple to check in with each other and helping the therapist gauge where they are when they discuss the scores in session.

Steps 8 and 9

Therapists may ask the partners to take one risk; e.g., reach for comfort from their partner at home and see what happens. If they cannot connect, then that inability may be discussed in the next session. The therapist may also ask the couple to write down their vision of the relationship one year from now. How will they use the process they have gone through? How will they use the strengths they have discovered? This process will help create a new story—a new vision for the relationship.

Introduce ritual behaviors that enhance the couple's relationship. Suggest that they find time to connect at night or at a time that works for the couple. Suggest that they share one feeling every day. Encourage the establishment of a special date night.

At Various Steps

Instruct couples to talk about specific content in a structured way. For 10 minutes, one partner talks about a specific topic while other listens. Assign content highlighted in the session. Examples include (a) talking about feelings related to depending on each other, (b) realizing how it feels to ask for help, (c) determining what it is like to be behind the wall, or (d) asking what it is like not to be known by the other partner and how would it feel to let him or her in? Tell them to stick to the 10-minute timeframe and separate talking sessions by 24 hours. Instruct the couple to not analyze, debrief, or use the sessions against each other but to wait until the next session to process the discussion. Some couples have problems with more intimate material, so start them off with more abstract content—like their vision, hopes, and dreams for the future.

APPENDIX G

EFT TRAINING NOTE FORM

EFT TRAINING NOTE FORM

Date:_____ **Session #**_____ **Length:** _____ **Clients:**_____

Therapy Stage: ☐ De-escalation   ☐ Reengagement   ☐ Consolidation

Steps Covered:

☐ 1. Alliance and assessment

☐ 2. Identify negative interaction cycle and positions in that cycle

☐ 3. Access emotions underlying interactional positions

☐ 4. Reframe the problem in terms of emotions, attachment needs, and the cycles

☐ 5. Identification with disowned needs and aspects of self and integrating into interactions

☐ 6. Promote acceptance of partner's experiences & new patterns

☐ 7. Restructure the interaction and create emotional engagement

☐ 8. New solutions to old issues

☐ 9. Consolidating new cycles of attachment

Aspect of Cycle Highlighted in Session (including action, perceptual, reactive emotion, and primary emotion levels):

Session Content Issues:

Key Emotions, Metaphors, Images, Client Phrases, and Positive Shifts in Session:

Interventions Used:

☐ Empathic reflection

☐ Validation of client realities and emotional responses

☐ Evocative responding

☐ Heighten

☐ Empathic conjecture/interpretation and inferences

☐ Track and reflect process of interaction, make positions and cycles explicit

☐ Reframe experience/interaction in terms of attachment context and cycle

☐ Restructuring and shaping interactions (enactments)

☐ Diagnostic pictures explicate

☐ Individual sessions

☐ Disquisition

Homework:

Plan for next session:

ANSWER SECTION

CHAPTER 1

Exercise 1.

1. e
2. d
3. b and d
4. h. The EFT stance is that there are common existential conditions and processes, emotion and attachment.
5. All of the above
6. b, c, d, and g. Re Answer g: The results for EFT are a significant improvement over other results reported for couples' therapy and over most results reported for individual therapy in the literature.
7. f
8. b, c, d, and f
9. f
10. b, c, and d. Re Answer a: It is impossible to prevent all occurrences of negative cycles; they will inevitably occur. But they do not have the same ability to define the relationship once partners can exit from them and secure bonding interactions also occur. Re Answer e: The experiential therapist does not pressure clients to make any choice. His or her job is to make implicit choices explicit and help clients take them with awareness and responsibility.
11. a and b
12. b. EFT stages are also differentiated into nine steps. In Stage 2 there are also two key change events: withdrawer-engagement and blamer-softening. The structure of EFT is then articulated into stages, steps within those stages, and change events in Stage 2.
13. a–c. EFT has been used extensively and successfully with depressed and traumatized partners. EFT has been found in a study of predictors of success to be particularly potent in couples where the female partner identifies the male partner as being "inexpressive." EFT has been shown to be effective with low-SES clients (Denton, Burelson, Clark, Rodriguez, & Hobbs, 2000).
14. c and e. Answer c was the most powerful predictor of success in EFT in the Johnson and Talitman (1997) study. Level of distress was found to account for only 4% of the variance in outcome 3 months after treatment termination. This is a very small percentage compared to that found in the psychotherapy literature in general, which implies that EFT can be used successfully with very distressed couples. Alliance was found to account for 20% of variance in outcome. In other studies of psychotherapy

outcome it has been found to account for 10%. Predictors noted in Answers c and e are presumed to impact outcome by influencing the level of engagement in therapy.

15. c (Johnson & Talitman, 1997).

16. b and d. Studies involve intense supervision that enhance the amount accomplished in each session.

17. a–d

18. c. (On occasion, Answer d is also valid.)

19. All but c. Answer c does not apply because, although the alliance is thought of as necessary and is a prerequisite to effective intervention, it is not sufficient.

20. All of the above

CHAPTER 2

Exercise 1.

1. a, b, c, e, and f
2. a and c. Secure interdependence and the ability to be autonomous and separate are two sides of the same coin, not dichotomies.
3. b and c
4. all but f
5. d
6. a, b, f, and g
7. c. Contempt usually occurs when protest becomes more desperate and hopeless.
8. a, c, and d
9. b and d
10. a, b, and d
11. a, b, and c. Bowlby states in the second book of his trilogy, Separation (1973), that the concept of projection is not helpful in that it directs attention away from a person's real experiences and treats him as a closed system, as little influenced by his environment.
12. a and c
13. a–c

Exercise 3.

All but h

Exercise 5.

All of the above

Exercise 7.

e

Exercise 8.

The secure wife is more likely to openly ask about the call and the relationship and be able to express concern or discomfort and ask for reassurance.

The anxious wife is more likely to accuse, to catasrophize, to demand, and to criticize or become extremely distraught in ways that annoy or alienate her spouse.

The avoidant spouse might become hostile without ever really addressing what upset her, or simply mention the message in passing but stay very distant.

The secure wife is then most likely to get reassuring feedback. The other two are likely to evoke feedback that confirms their fears.

Exercise 10.

1. b–g. Styles are explicitly interpersonal and relational and are better predictors of relationship variables than traits (Shaver & Brennen, 1992). They are predispositions but are also shaped by current relationship events. (See Johnson & Whiffen, 1999, for a general academic discussion of attachment styles/strategies/forms of engagement.)
2. a–f
3. a, b, c, d, f, and g
4. All of the above
5. All of the above. Even if they have never seen or experienced secure attachment, fearful avoidants will fight for a connection and will risk needing and wanting, if the EFT therapist cuts those risks fine enough. As Bowlby suggests, attachment needs and longings are wired in.

Exercise 11.

1. Anxious blaming pursuer
2. Dismissing avoidant husband who distances and defends
3. Fearful avoidant wife who pursues and distances
4. Husband moving out of avoidant dismissing attachment into a secure assertion of attachment needs
5. Anxious depressed husband protesting distance taken by wife
6. Wife describing secure attachment after a key change event in EFT. Attachment strategies or forms of engagement tell you how partners engage with their attachment needs and fears—their emotions and their partner—that is the basic position they take in the relationship dance. How you handle your attachment emotion is how you emotionally engage your partner in this dance.

Exercise 12.

a–e

Exercise 13.

1. Securely attached
2. Avoidantly attached
3. Anxiously attached
4. Fearful avoidantly attached

Exercise 14.

1. All but f. Childhood adversity creates sensitivities, but these can be reversed by more secure attachment experiences; secure attachment can be "earned."

2. All of the above. Think of a couple you are working with, or even your own relationship. Use attachment theory as outlined to make sense of a response, suggest a need or fear, or suggest a key move or moment that shaped the relationship or tells you what response would make a difference.

3. All but g and j. Insight into the past—a way of making coherent sense of the past—is often part of secure attachment. But in EFT, new ways to engage the spouse often "change" the past without such "insight" per se. In couples who have successfully concluded EFT and say they feel more secure, fights and cycles such as demand–withdraw still occur. But they do not take over and define the relationship and can be managed more effectively.

4. d and e. In attachment terms, marriage is more than friendship. Research suggests that only distressed couples become caught in issues of equity and profit. The Bowen perspective (reflected in Answer f) is discussed in relation to EFT in the EFT manual *Creating Connection* (2nd ed., 2004).

Exercise 15.

1–4. The man thinks on the way home of confiding in his wife and of how good it will feel to have a hug. The man comes in and asks for a hug and if they can talk about his day—he needs her support. The wife responds and the man sighs and relaxes and, as they talk and hold each other, feels calmed and soothed. After confiding in his wife, he feels better and can go and make a stressful phone call he needs to make.

Exercise 16.

1. Wife is anxiously attached, pursuing, and critical. Husband is distancing avoidant.
2. She would have been able to wait, would not have been so overwhelmed by her fears, and would not have become angry. Then she would have been able to say something like, "I guess I just got to feeling scared and a little vulnerable when I watched you with your colleague. I realize I am not quite sure of us—of how you feel about me right now. Maybe I need a little hug."

Exercise 18.

1. c–e
2. All but e and g. Acceptance is not the same as approval or endorsement.

3. b. Rogers (1961) pointed out the curious paradox: "When I accept myself as I am, then I change."

4. All of the above.

5. d. Rogers was an active therapist, as are modern-day experiential therapists.

6. All of the above.

7. a and d

8. e. It is interesting to note for EFT therapists that it seems easier to promote assertive responses by providing validation of hurts and fears and supporting the natural move toward assertion of needs to the partner than to formally "teach" and "coach" assertive behavior, even if such assertion seems to be very "out of character" at the beginning of therapy. Emotion tells us and others what we need.

Exercise 19.

1. a–c. Answer d is not an addition or departure but a feature that structural systemic and EFT interventions share.

2. All of the above. Answer d is compatible with systems theory but different from how this theory was traditionally applied in family therapy. Traditional applications left emotion out of the picture and have been accused of being impersonal and mechanistic in their focus on "external" variables only.

Exercise 20.

1. Yes. It places responses into a whole, a pattern, into context. A circular pattern of interactions and how it self-reinforces is laid out.

2 and 3. Yes. The process of interaction/communication (feedback loops) are set out as the problem. Individual responses are reframed as part of feedback loops.

4. Yes. The therapist sets up a new task, an enactment designed to change the way interactions are organized/structured. The above task can bring the husband closer to his partner and place him on a more equal, active footing.

5. Yes. Systems theorists believe that different contexts activate different parts of self. A change in one person's way of engaging pulls for a change in the other.

Exercise 21.

All but e. Certain less recent systemic approaches have focused almost exclusively on these elements, but a focus on these elements is not a large part of EFT. Traditional systemic interventions for child problems would often focus on "de-triangulating" the child from a parent and assume that the parents would then repair/enhance their own relationship. More recent systemic approaches (see Johnson & Whiffen, 2003) focus on the attachment security/nurturance between parent and child.

Exercise 22.

Experiential perspectives offer a map to emotion regulation and information processing and how to work with that in therapy. Systems theory offers a map to charting and restructuring interpersonal interactions. In a therapy where the client is in a relationship, both are needed.

Exercise 23.

All but a and g. In recent versions of attachment theory, attachment behaviors and concerns are integrated with caretaking and sexuality; previously these had been thought of as separate systems. Even so, a long-term love relationship is a complex, multilayered drama and no theory can encompass all elements of this drama. A basically secure attachment in a relationship also does not preclude conflicts and prevent that relationship from running into difficulties. Security is on a continuum and all can become anxious or avoidant when distressed.

Exercise 24.

1. Bowlby (1979)
2. Rogers (1961)
3. Minuchin and Fishman (1981)
4. Rogers (1961)

Exercise 25.

a–c

CHAPTER 3

Exercise 1.

1. a
2. d

Exercise 2. (sample answer)

"I am wondering what is going on for you right now."

"If you could put words to what your body is saying, what is it feeling?"

"It's like even your body is saying that you are shut out."

"So when you feel shut out, you turn away and close off."

"It's like your body is saying I am not available to you; I won't be ignored, made irrelevant."

These examples reflect body language, content and emotional meaning, action response, and the context and relationship cycles.

Exercise 3.

1. b
2. b
3. a

Exercise 4.

1. Despair
2. Anger
3. Shame
4. Surprise
5. Fear/anxiety
6. Anger/rage
7. Sadness/hopelessness
8. Shame
9. Joy
10. Fear/anxiety

Exercise 5.

1. Hurt/despair
2. Appraisal: danger, loss, fear
   Arousal: becomes rigid, flushes, wrings hands
   Reappraisal: I am on my own. He doesn't care.
   Action tendency: She withdraws and turns away.
3. Anger/rage
4. Appraisal: danger
   Arousal: becomes still and tightens up
   Reappraisal: I am being attacked. He's scapegoating me. I am flawed and it's my fault.
   Action tendency: She attacks.
5. Anxiety/fear
6. Appraisal: danger, loss, fear
   Arousal: She withdraws and backs away.
   Reappraisal: Something is wrong, something is going on.
   Action tendency: She pursues.
7. Frustration/anger
8. Appraisal: danger, fear
   Arousal: He tenses in anger.
   Reappraisal: Rejection. She does not want me.
   Action tendency: He withdraws and avoids her pursuit/shuts her out.

Exercise 6.

1. b
2. e
3. c
4. a

5. f
6. d

In distressed relationships, shame usually arises around a sense of being unlovable and so not entitled to or deserving of care. Fear can take a number of forms: it is usually expressed in terms of fear of rejection, fear of being found inadequate, fear of failing, and fear of abandonment and the helplessness that brings. Generally fear has more than one facet; for example, it always relates to the other person and how he/she will respond and to what this response then says about the self of the person who finds himself afraid, as in "I see that look and it tells me you are disappointed in me. I have failed again. Perhaps I can never make it. I am inadequate."

Exercise 7.

1. Fear
2. Despair, shut down, or attack

Exercise 8.

1. True. He saw tears on her face and asked her how she was feeling. The presence of tears on a partner's face brings the therapist's attention to the emotional concerns that are specific to the person or the relationship.
2. True. She felt ashamed when he asked her to change how she parented their daughter. The experience of shame may increase a partner's tendency to see her actions as increasingly inadequate and her partner as hostile and rejecting.
3. True. He felt anxious when she did not arrive home when she said, so he called her. Emotions may prompt behavior to restore an attachment bond in a relationship. So a partner seeks comfort from the other when anxious.
4. False. Emotions activate core cognitions. For example, she felt criticized because of a difference of opinion as it reminded her of her father's constant disapproval. Shame may prompt long-standing beliefs of personal inadequacy or the lack of trustworthiness in others.
5. True. Expression of emotion tends to pull complementary responses from partner. A vulnerable response may pull comfort or support, where a defensive response may prompt further attack.

Exercise 9.

1. Primary (Maybe instrumental depending if emotion is feigned.)
2. Secondary
3. Primary
4. Instrumental
5. Secondary - numbing
6. Primary

Exercise 10.

1. Shame, inadequacy, fear of rejection
2. Desperation, fear of abandonment
3. Fear of rejection/loss, hopelessness, helpless
4. Fear of rejection and grief or sadness
5. Fear of rejection/despair
6. Fear of abandonment
7. Shame, fear of inadequacy
8. Hurt, despair, grief, and hopelessness

Exercise 12.

1. b
2. a
3 d

Exercise 13.

Anger, frustration, irritation

Exercise 14.

"You're saying at some point in this he gets angry and raises his voice towards you, pushing for an answer. But you don't have one, which sounds really upsetting and frustrating. You in turn quickly get angry with him, and get right back into his face, too, with your own anger. Is that close to what happens?"

Exercise 15.

c

Exercise 16.

1. Irritation, frustration, anger
2. Numbing out, placating, defending, sinking, going cold
3. "So you can see this coming and you know what to expect. You see him as frustrated, irritable, and angry. When you respond he seems to become even angrier, so you numb out, go cold, back away, try to create some distance from his anger."
4. d

Exercise 17.

1. d
2. c
3. b
4. d

Exercise 18.

Anger; fear

Exercise 19.

1. Fear
2. Freezing
3. d
4. Defending or attacking

Exercise 20.

1. Sadness, fears of not being loved
2. Tearing a hole in my heart, questioning her love for him, panic
3. Anger
4. Dropped the ball—let her have it.

Exercise 21.

Loneliness, fear

Exercise 22.

1. c
2. a

Exercise 23. (Sample Answers)

1. "And that makes sense that you wonder what is going on and worry when you don't know where he is, and a call from him would make a difference at those times for many people."
2. "Yes, that is tough. You are working so hard to earn her trust and it makes sense that you see her request for a phone call as a sign that trust is not building in the relationship. Like the call is about control, not her concern."
3. "So you also are afraid of where this is leading, it makes sense that you would wonder about your future together after working hard to bring issues to the surface and face these things. And you are looking for something from Lisa and it's hard to know where you stand. Sometimes it feels like you might have already lost her, is that it?"
4. "Right, so you hear her pulling back and doubting, and if she is going for safety, you are, too. You sense her pulling away and you naturally pull back, too—it's too risky, especially when you fear there is little hope. She fears and pulls back, and you see this and you begin to do the same."

Exercise 24.

"So when conflicts come up, you see things he could do differently. But when he responds defensively, you try to let him know what his 'mistakes' are and how to he can improve this relationship. You learned with your family how to make your point with sharp words. Perhaps you had to do that to get people's attention."

Exercise 25.

1. b
2. d
3. c

Exercise 26.

1. "So what is happening for you as you talk about this? It's like your face is full of emotion."
2. "So, Shannon, what's happening for you as you hear Bob share his fear about being hurt?"
3. "So you're angry, but there also tears—and what would these tears say?"
4. "What happens for you Jane when you see that look on Steven's face?"
5. "And Steve, what is happening for you when you hear Jane talk about this fight?"
6. "What's it like for you, Russell, to hear these despairing words from Ceslie about your relationship? When you hear this, what happens to you?"

Exercise 27.

1. "So this feeling of sickness, is it more like fear, or hurt—maybe something else?"
2. "What happens inside of you when you are so exhausted from this argument that you have to lay down?"
3. "Sheri, what's it like for you to hear Paul talk about leaving?"
4. "So you could count on your grandfather's support and care. What do you think he would say to you now about these fears in your relationship with Karen?"
5. "What is happening in you as you say these words, as you hear your grandfather's words?"

Exercise 28.

1. "So it is like he locks you out. Closes the door and you don't have the key."
2. "It's like you have lost your voice in this relationship. You speak but he does not hear."
3. "It's frustrating and maddening to try so hard but not get through. You seem to end up in the same place you started from."
4. "So there's light at the end of the tunnel. You can see a new day, a different pattern in your relationship and you are not stuck in the darkness of not knowing what to do."
5. "So you found something that you thought you lost. Like it might never come back, and it's almost like it means even more to you because it seemed like it was gone."

Exercise 29.

1. c
2. b
3. a
4. c
5. d
6. a
7. d
8. d
9. b
10. b

Exercise 30.

d

Exercise 31.

1. "So when you pull away you're afraid that you won't be loved, that you are not good enough, not worthy, you will be rejected. That she will say, 'You just don't measure up.'"
2. "That's amazing. You felt safe and secure and it's been a long time. A long time since you felt this, like cool water after days wandering in the desert."
3. "So can you tell her that? Can you tell her what it's like when you hear the phone ring and you wonder if it is her and that irritation builds, the frustration, and the rage of being checked up on, even before you know why she called."
4. "Leslie, it's like you're hidden behind this wall where it is safe to hide, because if Manuel saw that you long for something different as well, something closer in this relationship, he might be there for you. He might want you. And then he would be disappointed because he would find out you're not good enough. So you keep up this wall and keep him safely away?"
5. "It's like work is your castle. You feel strong and in control and when Chris comes around and those feelings of insecurity grow, not feeling good enough, wondering if he really loves you as you are, you run. Run for safety."
6. "So she comes to you with questions and you feel the floodwaters rise. Like there is no room, no room to breathe, and you fight for space, fight to save yourself. You're drowning, slipping under."

Exercise 32.

1. d
2. a
3. d
4. c

Exercise 33.

1. c
2. d
3. a
4. c
5. c
6. a

Exercise 34.

1. "So you push back with your anger when Julie brings up your relationship issues. Is that it? It also sounds like you push away, because it all feels uncertain, out of control, too risky to go there, right?"

2. "It's like you hear her words, and they say she wants to know what is going on for you in this relationship, but you sense it's an attack/a threat, and so you respond by distancing. You have to keep her at a distance. It's out of control/not safe."

3. "So it seems, Julie, that as things get more intense, your questions do as well. Help me if this is not right, but it seems like part of you wants to know what he feels and another part just wants him to say everything is going to be okay."

4. "So you seek reassurance, and he pushes you away. Then you are more afraid, and look for something from him that will make you feel secure. And there is a part of you that is scared that he will give you nothing. He will leave you in the dark, all alone with just your fears."

5. "You push away when it's not safe, but it then becomes difficult to connect. You get stuck and you feel alone, it like part of you is looking and longing to be with Julie. To come together and make it safe and secure. Like a part of you wants her to know you want to be with her. But it is so hard."

6. "So Mark, you could never tell her that you need her and want to be with her. That your anger is your way of dealing with the fear and in your loneliness; you are desperate to tell her it's okay, that you want to be with her."

Exercise 35.

"It's hard for you to see this change and believe it. It's what you have been hoping for, but it's somehow hard to believe it's real. I know for some of the couples I have worked with this is one of the toughest steps. It's like a person takes all these risks coming to therapy and opening up and then they find there are even more risks, like believing that your partner has changed, that the words someone has wanted to hear are really true. And it is also hard for some people because they are still angry with all the hurt of the past, and this change does not wipe it all away. It's hard for others because there is now an expectation that my partner has changed so I have to change. It's difficult and it's scary for some to know what to do with all this change. I am not sure what it's like for you, because your situation may be different."

Exercise 36.

    1. c

    2. d

Exercise 37.

    1. "Nora, you see him as not being there for you, you see him as not understanding, as uninvolved."

    2. "Nora, you feel that you're not important to Nick so you don't look up, don't kiss him, you don't think there is any way to contact him, so you give up."

    3. "Nora, you see that he walks by without saying anything and your sense is that he isn't involved and you get angry because it feels like you can't count on him."

    4. "You feel that he isn't there and you then feel hurt, abandoned, and unimportant."

    5. "So, Nora, you are saying, 'I don't see you, can't count on you. I'm alone. You are gone. It's like 'I've lost you'. And that is full of loss and despair for you?"

Exercise 39.

    1. b

    2. d.

Exercise 40.

    1. Negative cycle

    2. Fight for safe attachment

    3. Reacting to the perceived unavailability of the attachment figure, protest, and separation distress

    4   An attempt to regulate intense fears and to protect the relationship from meltdown

Exercise 41.

    1. "…when she pushes you to talk, you want to leave or shut down. Oftentimes you do leave but sometimes you stay and sometimes you get defensive and attack back."

    2. "…when you want to talk, he gets defensive and leaves or shuts down and you get offended. This is very difficult for you when he turns away. You end up feeling invalidated or like you aren't important. And when he turns away, you feel left alone and really anxious and you want to chase him down the street. That's an awful feeling wanting to talk and make contact and feeling unable to get through. Is that how it is for you?"

    3. "…is that you are both caught in this negative cycle, where you both trigger each other. Gina, you want to talk and get to the bottom of things. But, Tim, you can't stand confrontation and want to leave when she wants to talk. Tim, you are often feeling that it is your fault and you hate upsetting her so you leave to protect yourself or sometimes you fight back. Gina, you experience Tim as being defensive and

leaving or abandoning you, so you fight to get him back by trying to get him to talk. But he often won't and you get angry and feel left and alone. Each of you reacts in a way that confirms the other's worst fears and makes the other react and then trigger your own reactions. I guess what strikes me most is that it is this cycle that is the enemy in your relationship. And this enemy leaves you both feeling very alone."

4. "...that the two of you could have a relationship where you could turn to each other when things are difficult. It is hard to imagine that the relationship would be safe enough that you could get upset and not leave or be left. That, Tim, you wouldn't feel so overwhelmed by conflict or guilt that you could stay and hear Gina. That she could understand how sensitive you are to her criticism and how alone you feel. And, Gina, that when you are feeling so unimportant and abandoned you could turn to talk to Tim and tell him what it is like for you to feel so alone. I guess it is hard for you guys to believe that your relationship can be safe and responsive the way it was long ago. I've seen a lot of couples make those changes, so it's not so hard for me to imagine."

Exercise 42.

1. b
2. d
3. (a) Making the request
   (b) Maintaining the focus
   (c) Processing responses
4. Helping the partner imagine what it would be like to make the proposed contact.
5. Simply by restating the request.

Exercise 43.

a and b

Exercise 46.

1. "...that was a big risk to say... What was it like for you to say that?" "Can you imagine coming to him at home and saying, 'I feel afraid when you get mad like this?' What would that be like?"

2. "...what is it like for you when she says...?" "What would that be like for you if she were able to come tell you when she is feeling that way?" "Can you tell her?"

CHAPTER 4

Exercise 1.

d. The response connects with Fernando's experience and does not attempt to judge, correct, or interpret him.

Exercise 2.

c. All of the other responses imply judgment of Inez or Fernando. In Answer c the therapist understands that an unidentified emotional reality produces his need to go off on his own. In the transcript, the therapist was intent upon understanding the moves in the cycle. At some point, however, she will want to explore and understand this reality.

Exercise 3.

c. This was the genuine response.

Exercise 4.

1. c. Although all of above are objectives in this stage of therapy, the prime objective is the creation of a therapeutic alliance.
2. d. Not known to be helpful in creating a therapeutic alliance.

Exercise 5.

1. b. Could be used when tracking the cycle, but is not an example of empathic attunement.
2. c. Directing, not attuning.
3. b. He seems not to understand why his wife launches into a tirade, he regrets the lack of hugs, and he withdraws to protect himself. He is tearful and probably anxious; he may possibly also be angry.
4. d. She is obviously angry and irritated. There is no indication that she is disengaged at this point. She may well feel hurt and rejected by Gerald.

Exercise 6.

1. A good response will include acknowledgment of some or all of the following: his confusion or lack of understanding of his wife's tirades; his loneliness and or sadness, the move he makes to protect himself (i.e., creeping into shell).
2. A good response will include acknowledging some or all of the following: how painful it would be to not feel seen, or to feel she does not exist in her partner's eyes; and given that experience, how understandable her anger, perhaps even how hard it is to hold in anger.

Exercise 7.

d. Stays with and reflects the experience she expressed (he wasn't there for me). Re a: Completely missed her experience; and b and c were not necessarily accurate. Answer d also provides a gateway to exploring what might have been a significant event between the couple (perhaps even an attachment injury).

Exercise 8.

a. The therapist simply reflects what he/she sees.

Exercise 9.

b. The other responses aren't reflections.

Exercise 10.

c. Affirms and legitimizes her experience ("I can understand that you feel nervous."). Answer a actually invalidates her, Answer b judges him, and Answer d is a conjecture that may not be accurate.

Exercise 11.

a. b and d go beyond validation and may be inappropriate for the assessment stage. c is not an EFT intervention.

Exercise 12.

d. Only d is a reframe.

Exercise 13.

c. Only c is catching the bullet.

Exercise 14.

1. True
2. True. This also helps them to say more about their experience.
3. False. A validation affirms and legitimizes the client's experience.
4. True. This takes the sting out of the interaction and helps create safety in the session.
5. False. Reflections are used throughout the EFT process.

Exercise 15.

1. a. Sarah is clearly very angry with Aaron.
2. b. The therapist simply reflects the difficulty she hears that Sarah has.
3. b. The therapist hopes to enter and understand her experience of Aaron's relationship with Ruth.

Exercise 16.

A good response will contain some or all of the following elements: (a) how she is anxious about her place in his life; (b) placing her anger in the context of her anxiety and his importance to her; (c) how torn he is; and (d) how painful this is for both of them.

Exercise 17.

1. True

2. True (demand–pursue/defend–withdraw, attack/attack, complex cycles, reactive or secondary cycles)

3. False. In these clients cycles are frequently more complex.

4. True

5. False. Negative interactive cycles are seen in terms of separation protest and attachment insecurity.

6. True. Pursuing spouses feel controlled by their withdrawing partner, while withdrawn partners feels controlled by their nagging spouses.

7. False. The most common pattern is a demanding spouse with a withdrawing partner.

8. False. This is another name for demand–pursue/defend–withdraw pattern.

9. True

10. True

Exercise 18.

1. c
2. d
3. c
4. c

Exercise 19.

1. d. Further assessment is needed at this point to understand if physical abuse was a pattern, and if this client was afraid of her partner.

2. b. The objective here is to further assess the issue including how the couple interact around this issue.

3. a. EFT is not necessarily contraindicated in the other instances.

Exercise 20.

1. c
2. d
3. b
4. a

Exercise 21.

1. True. EFT can be used in the context of substance abuse if the using partner(s) acknowledge the problem and seek help.

2. False. The therapist will tell the wife that holding secrets will interfere with the process of EFT, and will encourage the wife to end the affair and discuss it with her partner.

3. False. The therapist will focus the negative interactive patterns between the partners rather than on dysfunctional communication skills of one or both partners.

4. True. The therapist wants to understand who pursues for closeness.

CHAPTER 5

Exercise 1.

1. c
2. d
3. a. The couple has not changed the pattern of their mutual behavior but they are able to identify the pattern itself. This enables them to modify this pattern, thus de-escalating the conflict—recognizing it is set of actions they engage in together. De-escalation does not in and of itself constitute a systemic change that reorganizes the relationship.
4. b

Exercise 2.

1. Evocative responding
2. Reframing problem in terms of the cycle
3. Validation
4. Heightening
5. Empathic conjecture.

Exercise 3.

1. Validation
2. Evocative reflection/responding
3. Evocative reflection
4. Heightening
5. Reframing the problem as the cycle.
6. Evocative responding and tracking the cycle
7. Evocative reflection/responding
8. Tracking and validation
9. Tracking and evocative responding
10. Reframing in context of cycle
11. Empathic conjecture
12. Empathic conjecture
13. Reframing the problem in terms of the cycle
14. Restructuring with an enactment and validation
15. Reframing "catching the bullet" and validation
16. Empathic conjecture
17. Reframing and empathic conjecture
18. Tracking the cycle, empathic conjecture, validation

19. Empathic conjecture
20. Validation, empathic conjecture
21. Tracking and heightening
22. Evocative responding
23. Restructuring—creating an enactment
24. Reframing the problem in the cycle
25. Reframing and validation.

Exercise 4.   Answer:

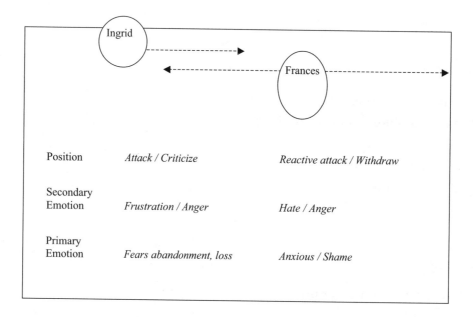

Position	*Attack / Criticize*	*Reactive attack / Withdraw*
Secondary Emotion	*Frustration / Anger*	*Hate / Anger*
Primary Emotion	*Fears abandonment, loss*	*Anxious / Shame*

Exercise 5.

1. "...give me more space and let things go now and then. Instead things have to be her way, and if I don't respond the way she wants I hear about it. It makes me want more space."
2. Frustration
3. Fear, hurt, afraid of rejection, alone, not wanted
4. Pursuer
5. "...want to spend time with me. Instead he is always looking for a way to get away from the house. He complains about never having enough time for himself and that seems like all I hear."
6. Anger, irritation, indifference
7. Frozen, overwhelmed, inadequate
8. Withdrawer

Exercise 6. (sample answers)

1. "So you are frustrated, even angry that Bob is after you about the bills, but he doesn't seem to see you, doesn't seem to hear your needs. And it makes sense that you would feel angry and hurt that he is not there for you, like the bills are more important than you. Is that it?"

2. "Bob I wonder what is going on for you as you hear Sharon? It seems like you are pulling back, like this is too much, and you can't take it, or don't want to take this. So you close off."

3. "So when these financial issues come up Sharon you hear Bob's concerns as an attack and you get angry because there seems to be no way to please him. And, Bob, when she responds you too see this as an attack and you shut down and close off and stay out of her emotional reach."

4. Hurt

5. "So it's like his concern for the money comes across as criticism and that makes you angry, but more than that you feel alone, like he has chosen money over you, like you don't mean as much, like you do not matter, and that hurts?"

6. Helplessness/fear

7. "So it's confusing, all this anger. You get lost in it all. You pull away. You are frustrated, lost, with nothing you can do. Like you feel helpless when this happens. Like things are out of control leaving you vulnerable, and that is hard for you?"

8. "So what would it be like to tell her that it is hard for you to feel like things are out of control, and that sometimes these financial issues leave you feeling vulnerable and that is a hard place for you to be?"

9. "So it is difficult to hear this, on the one hand you hear him saying that it would be different if you handled the money better, but at another level it not about the money and how you handle it. It's about you and that hurts? It's hard for him to trust you and that hurts."

Exercise 7.   Answer:

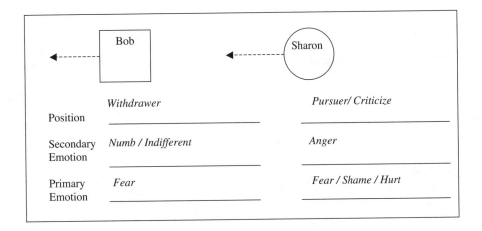

Exercise 8.   Answer:

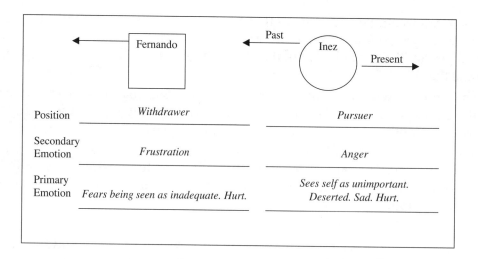

Exercise 9.

c. In the past, Inez was the pursuer but at this time in therapy she has moved to a withdrawn position. There are a few efforts made by Fernando to pursue her, but his overall position remains withdrawn and disengaged.

CHAPTER 6

Exercise 1.

For example: In response to the third withdrawer response above, the therapist might say: "So your spouse sees a 'wall,' but behind that wall you are hurting—hopeless, helpless, feeling like a failure, a big fat zero? You shut down and shut her out because you can't bear that feeling? It feels like you have lost her already? What happens to you when you hear me summarize this?" (Reflection, evocative responding, heightening, conjecture.)

Exercise 2.

The more withdrawn, less engaged partner. In a withdraw/withdraw couple, the most accessible partner.

Exercise 3.

1. All of the above
2. All of the above.

Exercise 4.

a and c

Exercise 5.

1. "You hold back. This is natural. Anything else seems foolish, immature, inviting danger?"

2. "You have a raw place. It gets touched very easily, so you are on guard, you watch and get aggressive, just in case. Always being on guard to defend that raw place must make it hard to just relax and dance with your wife?"

3. "It seems strange to you, his new desire to connect, to be with you. It is hard to trust it and begin to let him in, to talk?"

Exercise 6.

All but d, e, and h. All are evocative responding; f also includes some conjecture.

Exercise 7.

The therapist focuses on unfolding the emotionally loaded words. Interventions are mostly reflections and evocative responding: focus on the cue, body arousal, meaning, action tendency of the emotion. Validation is also used in a, and interpretation/conjecture in e. Usually an EFT therapist would implement evocative responding before moving to conjecture. Once the emotion became more specific, concrete, and owned, the therapist would help Louis to begin to disclose to his wife, as in "So can you tell her 'I shut down and go a long way away, can't bear this feeling of uncertainty, that I can't meet your expectations'?" The emotions that emerge will then be tracked, focused on, and heightened to increase engagement. In the next session, the therapist might again reflect this client's fear, which paradoxically increases as he gets closer to his spouse: that he will end up failing and disappointing his partner and that is unbearable to him.

Exercise 8.

All of the above might be used. Reflection, evocative responding, heightening, and conjecture, as well as creating an enactment, are used.

Exercise 9.

a, b, and c. Re d: The therapist might use his stated vulnerability to judgment and need to please to past relationships to validate his present sensitivity, but not in this insight-oriented way.

Exercise 10.

a–e. Fear, helplessness, vulnerability, loss, and failure, which links into shame about the self, are apparent here.

Exercise 11.

a

Exercise 12.

Answer: a, b, and c

Exercise 13.

All but a and l

Exercise 14. (sample answers)

"You try to 'swallow' the hurt, make it go away, so you can be 'independent,' but, in fact, the hurt is overwhelming, yes?" (reflection, heightening underlying emotion)

"The signals have to be 'subtle'? It's too scary to let yourself feel how hurt and alone you felt, how let down, and too scary to show that, yes?" (heightening through repletion, conjecture)

"It's hard to feel safe. You risked—you came here, put yourself in Colin's hands, and you found yourself all alone and hurting. Very risky—scary—to let yourself hope that he will be there, even if he makes mistakes sometimes. Some voice says 'there you are, he will let you down again,' yes?" (conjecture, heightening)

"It is hard to feel so small, to know you need his support, his caring...so risky...you feel so vulnerable? So hard to trust." (heightening, conjecture)

Exercise 15. (sample answers)

"What is that like for you, to have been all by yourself for so long?"

"How do you feel as you say that, as you talk of your hurt and aloneness?"

"Can you help me understand what is that, 'not being sure how to talk'?"

"Is it like, not sure of how to put it into words, or is it not sure if it's safe?"

Exercise 16.

All but 7.

Exercise 18.

"That must be so hard for you, to hear her say that and feel that there is nothing you can do to hold onto her." "What happens to you when she says that?" "What do you hear her saying?" "So what do you do then—you withdraw, perhaps?"

Exercise 19.

"You are covering your face, it is like you don't want him to see you? You feel squirmy, almost as if you feel embarrassed, somehow ashamed of what is happening right now ?"

Exercise 20.

"It would be wild for you to risk and be open to her at that moment, almost dangerous. Too dangerous? You would expect a hammering, so it would be too scary—terrifying, even—to be open at that point, yes?"

Exercise 21.

"So, you couldn't tell him you were hurt, so you had to shut down and protect yourself, for days and days? And if you did risk telling him you were hurt? There is something scary there, yes? You are afraid that he would not respond, or that—and that—then the hurt would just get worse. Is that it? It would get overwhelming?"

Exercise 22.

"So it was too hard to open up and risk telling him about your hurt—that was terrifying. So there was nothing for it but to shut down—shut the feeling down, to try to minimize it, control it? And then, as you shut down, you shut him out—you can't let him come close? When you feel vulnerable, it's still just an instant natural response for you to shut that down and shut him out, is that it?"

Exercise 23.

"So Sam, you get frustrated—the door is closed, you can't get in, you try to stay calm. But perhaps this is one of those times when your frustration takes over and you end up banging on the door, louder and louder, demanding to be let in? If she won't let you in, you have no wife. Is that it? You have lost her? So you, desperate not to lose her, bang on the door."

Exercise 24.

"So Sarah, can you tell him 'When I get hurt I am so terrified that if I tell you I hurt then you will not care, not respond, and then the hurt will get worse, it will get overwhelming, engulfing. So I have to shut down, can't risk reaching out to you.' Is that okay? Can you tell him?"

Exercise 25, Part 2.

a, c, d, and f

Exercise 26.

b and c

Exercise 30.

All but c

Exercise 31. (sample answer)

"Len, I guess I hear that you are confused by Jody saying she is afraid to talk, that she can't ever say it right. You want to be able to talk to Jody, and you try, and you wish that she could just speak up. That must be frustrating and confusing for you. You don't see her as scared, you see her as irritated and shut down, so it is hard to make sense of what she is saying. This is not the Jody you are used to." (pause) "I understand. This is not how you see her." (validating his reactions) "Could we come back to what it feels like for you to hear Jody say she feels afraid of speaking up and then feels alone and isolates herself for days?" (refocusing on the experiencing partner's disclosures)

Exercise 32. (sample answer)

Therapist in a soft, slow voice: "Len, you don't know what to do and you get no response, you get stuck, give up. Can you help me? What is this 'stuck' feeling like? What's it like, to feel stuck? (pause for response) I guess what I'm hearing is that you feel helpless. It's like you don't know how to respond, you don't know how to be with her, what to say? Help me understand what it's like for you. That must be hard. Do you feel it now? (pause for response) So, now, when Jody turns to you and says she feels she can't get it right with you and ends up feeling alone and isolated, you feel stuck again? (pause for response) You're not sure how to connect with her. It's like you're wanting to talk, not knowing how to reach her, feeling very helpless. That's hard. (pause) Can you tell me what that is like for you?" (heightening, empathic conjecture and evocative responding)

Exercise 33. (sample answer)

"It's so hard for you to hear her pain now. For so long you have seen it as you are the one who hurts, the one who asks and asks for closeness in the face of her 'distance,' and when you have wanted to talk, she shuts down and you feel more pain. Then you have gotten angry and pressed her to talk and she shuts down (linking to negative cycle) —it's very strange now to hear her say that she wants to talk but is scared to talk. Is that right? (pause) My sense is that she is scared because you are so important to her and she is afraid of disappointing you, so she shuts down. But you have seen it that she shuts down because you don't matter at all, so this is a different view of the landscape, yes? You don't see her as someone who is scared of your disapproval or rejection?" (validating, empathic conjecture, reframing)

Exercise 34. (sample answer)

Therapist in a soft, slow voice: "I understand it is hard to see Jody as wanting to connect but scared of disappointing you. That's not your experience of her. Your experience is that she holds you off, that she is irritable, angry and defensive. You don't see her as wanting to connect but afraid to. I understand. That's not your experience of her. It is strange to think of her that way." (validation) "Len, seeing her this way might be taking a big risk. I imagine that this might be scary for you—if you see her as wanting to connect and respond to that part of her that is afraid, and if she were then to push you away, that would be devastating for you,. (pause) Len, she is saying now that she wants to connect but is afraid. Can you see her as wanting to connect, but as afraid?

What's it like to think of her that way?" (evocative responding, empathic conjecture, validation)

Exercise 35. (sample answer)

"Len, could you tell Jody about this feeling—stuck and helpless. I hear you saying that you are hearing from her that she is scared of disappointing you and withdraws, but that you do want her to talk, that sometimes you are so anxious to be close and to talk to her that you get pushy and scare her away – that you end up feeling helpless and stuck. I hear her saying that she wants to connect with you but that she is scared of disappointing you and so she withdraws. Seeing her as afraid is very strange to you right now, you don't quite know what to do with that? Could you tell her that hearing that she is afraid leaves you feeling so stuck and helpless and not knowing what to do or how to approach her? Could you tell her, right now, what that's like for you?" (enactment)

Exercise 36. (sample answer)

1. "With all that you have been through and the rejection you've felt by his leaving, it is hard now to focus on and hear Ron say these things, that he is afraid—afraid of your disapproval. I realize how difficult that is to take in."

2. "Tammy, when you hear Ron say that he gets paralyzed when he thinks you might get mad and when he thinks you might disapprove, what's that like, to hear that? (pause) Do you believe him? Are you too angry or upset to hear, or too off balance? You're saying, 'No, I'm the one who is disapproved of. I'm not scary, and I'm not judgmental.' (pause) It's hard to hear that he could experience you as disapproving of him when you are also feeling so much pain and fear. What's it like that he wants you to understand his pain when you have been feeling so much pain yourself?"

3. "I guess what I am hearing here is that all these years you have been feeling Ron was distant, with you knocking on his door and him not responding and you feeling hurt and angry. All these years you were feeling that he didn't care. You saw him as distant and not caring. Now he is saying he is dreadfully afraid of doing the wrong thing and disappointing you so he withdraws. In a way his withdrawal is a measure of how sensitive he is to how you are feeling.

4. "You're saying, 'No, I can't hear this. I am not the one who left. I am not scary, not judgmental.' Part of you is massively angry and feels rejected and disapproved of by his leaving. It is so hard right now to allow yourself to hear or feel what he is saying, that he is in constant fear of disappointing you. It's too hard right now to see him that way. That would be going out on a limb – to start letting him in." "If you let him in, you risk having the limb sawed off. That's really scary. I understand you need a lot of time and more positive responses from him to feel safe and trust this new view of Ron."

5. "Tammy, it was so devastating when Ron left. It was really, really hard for you; you felt very, very disapproved of. Now, when Ron turns to you and says that your disapproval would paralyze him, you have a hard time hearing it. That's hard for you to take in. Can you tell him how hard it is to take this in? How hard it is to hear him say he felt so disapproved of that he would become paralyzed? Can you tell him what it is like to hear that?"

CHAPTER 7

Exercise 1.

   1. d
   2. a
   3. c. Note: b is more of a conjecture than an evocative response.

Exercise 2.

   1. b
   2. d
   3. b. Note: b is the best answer because the therapist uses "parts" language and a "first person dialog" that seek to reflect the client's possible emotional processing within an attachment frame.

Exercise 3.

   1. d. Note: Answer c is aimed much more at tracking the cycle and underlying emotion than it is heightening.
   2. a. Note: a is the best answer because it heightens within the context of "parts" of the client, and it heightens the interpersonal element as well.

Exercise 4.

   1. d
   2. c. Note: c is the best answer because the therapist sandwiches the restructuring interaction with a heightening of attachment fears. This serves to keep the ensuing enactment extremely focused.

Exercise 5.

   1. b
   2. c

Exercise 6.

   a

Exercise 7. (sample answer)

   "What happens for you inside Jon, when you know the 'heat is coming'?"

Exercise 8. (sample answer)

   "Right. The heat is coming, and something inside says, 'Oh no. Here we go again. I am about to get corrected,' kind of like a puppy in training. And you don't even speak her language, right? There's nothing you can say—you're trapped on a leash. Is that close to what happens?" (Heightening, evocative responding.)

Exercise 9. (sample answer)

"You feel talked down to, trapped on a leash, unable to respond, like a puppy."

Exercise 10.

a and e

Exercise 11.

1. d
2. a

Exercise 12.

Like a little puppy. Small, unprotected, scolded, afraid, tensed up. I feel sad. Beaten down.

Exercise 13.

c

Exercise 14.

d

Exercise 16.

b. Note: While Answer a encourages Jon to turn and share, it fails to validate and expand his fear, which is crucial in EFT before encouraging one to interact directly with their partner in Step 7. Fear blocks bids for attachment, and thus needs to be processed through.

Exercise 18.

Likely interventions used here are validation, heightening, and restructuring interactions.

Exercise 19.

e

Exercise 21.

Primary emotion and metaphor: afraid that you won't understand and will get mad, feel like a helpless little puppy dog, fear that you really don't love me, fear that you may leave, tired of being afraid and feeling helpless, sometimes feel like I am not being the husband I want to be and that hurts me, tired of running.

Attachment wants/needs: Don't want to run anymore, I need you to respect that I am tired of running away and don't want to anymore, I don't like feeling separated or cut off from you, I need you to try to stop attacking me so quickly and loudly, I am going to try my best, I want you to work with me and try your best too.

Exercise 23.

   a

Exercise 25.

   b

Exercise 27.

   d

Exercise 28.

1. a, b, and e. Incorrect and why: c (too skills based); d (too interpretive); f (focus on thoughts to the exclusion of emotion); g (finding an exception).

2. d. The therapist uses words as if she were the client. By taking this "first-person stance" the therapist is imaginatively walking each partner through what a secure interaction can look and feel like for them. The first-person stance more deeply involves the client. This anticipates the therapist asking the more-blaming spouse to indeed reach later in the session. They experientially "try it on" before they actually are asked to risk reaching in reality. Note: c does not anticipate Marcus reaching to his spouse. It could, however, be followed by a response akin to d, which then puts it squarely into the initiation of Step 7.

Exercise 29. (sample answer)

"I was wondering—When you start to feel really upset over this Tom, when you start getting scared that Rebecca really doesn't believe in you, or fear that she really doesn't want to see this relationship work, do you ever turn to her and say, 'Rebecca, I am starting to get really scared right now. I am having all of these doubts about whether you really care about me and whether you really want this to work. Could you just give me a little hug right now, just let me know that I am not alone here?' What would this be like for you to try this, Tom?"

Exercise 30.

a, d, e, and f. Incorrect: b (finding an exception); c (prescribing the symptom); g (externalizing).

Exercise 31.

a and c

Exercise 32. (sample answer)

So when you feel this shame about yourself, like you are just not cutting it, feeling worthless, rather than reaching for her and showing that you are hurting, you show her anger. It's like it's just too scary to show her that side of you—the side that hurts so much. Part of you says, 'She will see me as weak—a big baby'? So you hide it from her. It's safer that way. You stay alone in your pain?

Exercise 34.

b

Exercise 35.

1, 2, 4, and 5: negative view of other; 3 and 6, negative view of self.

Exercise 37. (sample answer)

"So there is a part of you that fears Fresca's possible responses if you reach out to her. She could reject you, she could shame you. But then there's this other part that wonders if you are somehow wired differently, if it's possible that someone like Fresca could really accept and love you, right? This part is about you. It says something akin to 'Your mom was right. You are not someone who a woman will love, you can't make a woman happy. If you show Fresca all of you she will be disgusted, appalled...' Am I hearing you right?" "Yes," Marcus responds with tears." (looking down) "I am afraid that she won't want me. That's the biggest fear in my life."

Exercise 38.

a, b, e, and h. Note: Answer h is an example of a couple that begins to soften at home before an occurrence in-session. When this happens the therapist "reenters" the episode with the couple, slows it down, and heightens the attachment-related affect. A more heightened and processed softening event is the goal.

Exercise 40.

All but c and e

Exercise 42.

a, b, and e. Incorrect and why: c (too insight driven); d (fails to process softening reach); f (moves to other spouse too quickly).

Exercise 44.

c and d

Exercise 46.

a, b, and e

CHAPTER 8

Exercise 1.

1. Restructuring (Focusing and complementing–creating enactment)
2. Reflection and validation (New patterns and responses)
3. Reframing
4. Evocative responding

Exercise 2. (sample answer)

1. "Okay, Mario, can we come back to that? Luisa it seems like something just happened. It's like you kind of disappeared. I am wondering what changed. What's it like for you now?"
2. "So you heard her concern, and you let her know her voice is important to you. You invited her back to the discussion and that is not always easy to do especially when her experience of your words was so different than you intended."
3. "So when you hear Mario saying he wants to hear your voice, you feel important and like your ideas matter and you matter. This helps you move toward him, and share appreciation for his strong ideas and those of your own. It's like you are working together on this rather than letting the strong ideas divide you. You are making sure the other person knows he or she is important."
4. "So you have both come a long way to changing your pattern and staying out of the cycle that was ruining the love you share. How would you say you are different? What has changed for you?"

Exercise 3.

1. c
2. d
3. a

Exercise 4.

1. True
2. False
3. True
4. True
5. False
6. False
7. True
8. False

Exercise 5.

1. Empathic responding

2. Validation/reflection
3. Reflection/heighten
4. Evocative responding
5. Restructuring interaction
6. Reframing/evocative responding
7. Restructuring interactions—creating an enactment

Exercise 6.

1. Withdrawer
2. Loneliness, sadness
3. Attacker/Pursuer
4. Fear, shame

Exercise 7.

1. Fear, sadness
2. She needs support, to be hugged, and to be reassured that she is loved.
3. Fear, shame, loss of control
4. He needs reassurance that he is wanted and respected, that he is valued.

Exercise 8.

Marcus sees Fresca's withdrawal and his angry response as a sign that they are entering the cycle. Marcus softens his angry response by acknowledging the loss of his promotion and how he has tied that to Fresca's vacation plans. Fresca in turn responds to Marcus's vulnerability and offers support and reassurance in response to the loss of the promotion.

Exercise 9. (sample answer)

"So that's amazing! You really ended that situation in a different way than you would have in the past. Marcus, you saw the cycle raising its head and you moved off your anger to your fears and concerns. That was risky, but you went for it. And Fresca, you moved toward him and let him know you understood his loss about the promotion. And as you share this, it's like you are proud of what you have done, like your relationship is stronger, and you have a creative solution for vacation. It was a risk, but you both went for it and you are learning that good things can come from that. You came together so that the promotion situation won't steal away the hopes you have for your vacation together. You both can be quite creative when you work together."

Exercise 10.

1. Withdrawer
2. Sadness, fear of abandonment, shame

3. Pursuer. Note: Fernando was initially in more of a withdrawer position, but then Inez began to withdraw from the relationship after burning out from her initial pursuit of Fernando. Fernando's anxious response to her withdrawal prompted his pursuit.

4. Shame, inadequacy, fear of rejection, and fear of losing Inez

Exercise 11.

1. Fear, sadness
2. She needs support, reassurance, and comfort.
3. Shame, fear of rejection

Exercise 12.

Inez refers to Fernando's remark from years ago, and how it hurt her. But, she softens her response by acknowledging the ways she has shut him out on her own account. Fernando responds with regret over his remark and is able to own his fears and immaturity. Fernando also shares how he was drawn closer by Inez acknowledging that part of the distance between them was a result of her own choices.

Exercise 13. (sample answer)

"So it really surprised your daughter that you could both do this. You have come along way. The cycle kept you at a distance, and there was no way you could work together without facing those patterns. There were times when the distance was so great and you seemed to be headed for separate lives. The concerns seemed to drive you apart, with Fernando pulling away from you, Inez, as you both tried to connect through the frustration you were feeling and the fears that you had that you might be unwanted and rejected in this relationship. Yet, you have been able to see the soft side of your hurts and fears and to express this to one another. You've been able to see the cycle and slow things down, seeing your partner's needs and fears and moving to support each other. Whether it's the basement or talking about your sexual relations, you are finding a way to stay connected even when dealing with issues that have been around for a while. It's risky and it's normal to find yourself in the pattern again, but you also have the experience and awareness to see the cycle and make yourself more available to the other. That is quite remarkable."

Exercise 14.

A number of rituals would be helpful. It may be helpful to suggest a ritual involving physical intimacy that builds on the hard work they have done to reconnect in this area. A meeting/greeting ritual where the couple kissed or hugged hello/good-bye would serve as a sign that they want this connection and they can stand up to the fears that used to keep them apart.

Exercise 15. (sample answer)

"Sure, that makes sense after living with this cycle for so many years, it's hard to believe that it wouldn't come back in some way. Yes, there may be times when you see the cycle start to raise its head, but you now know how to recognize it. Like when you want Fernando's attention and it's frustrating that he doesn't appear available, you also know ways to exit the cycle. You can check it out with him, letting him know what you need. You both found ways to stay connected even though you are discussing threatening issues. Now you know the feelings that escalate the cycle and getting those out and into the open will help keep the cycle from taking over. Just like when we talked about Fernando's comment about weight—that was a tough issue—but you both found a way to stay connected through it. It was scary, but you did it."

Exercise 16.

All apply.

CHAPTER 9

Exercise 1.

1. c
2. a
3. e
4. c
5. d

Exercise 2.

1. Natasha may be feeling abandoned, hurt, afraid of losing him permanently. She may use the words lonely, disrespected, betrayed, unloved.
2. Ruben may be feeling fear of failure and inadequacy, hurt, and sadness are probably primary emotions for him. He may be afraid of her anger and attacks, of being unloved, and of not being good enough or capable of meeting her needs.

Exercise 3.

1. e. Enactment. The problem with enactment is that unless they are very tightly controlled, enactments at this stage tend to simply allow couples to enact their present cycle and the secondary emotions that are being expressed with it.
2. b. Reflecting the cycle e. Enactment may work if they enact the impasse and the therapist keeps the enactment slow enough so that the clients can reflect on the impasse and not escalate.

Exercise 4. (sample answer)

1. Therapist says in a voice that becomes softer and slower through the interventions: "Natasha, if I am getting this right, it is very painful for you when he doesn't come home. You end up feeling very lonely and scared, but you don't talk about the

loneliness or the pain. You get angry, and somehow then in an attempt to get him to be with you, you complain and you criticize. Ruben, correct me if I am wrong, but when she criticizes or complains, that is not easy for you to hear—very painful, in fact—and you tend to withdraw as a way to protect yourself and get away from the problems and avoid another fight. Once you are in the fight, you try to get it over as quickly as possible because you fear that it will get out of hand. The more scared and angry she seems to be, the more desperate and angry you get and you withdraw. Is that correct? But that just feeds the cycle. Both of you are stuck in this cycle where you get hurt and are afraid and lonely and to deal with that you attack or withdraw or fight, which means that neither of you end up feeling safe or loved. You are stuck in this pattern where neither of you get your needs met, and it is very hard to move forward to rebuild the relationship, something both of you very much want to do. Is that it? Do I have it right?"

2. Therapist: "I get the idea it is very hard for you when she is so angry. It sounds to you like she's telling you that you have failed in this relationship and that you can't measure up and that you are not going to make it with her. So you clam up and avoid. Is that it?" Ruben: "Yes." Therapist: "Can you tell her 'it is hard for me when you get mad'?" Ruben: "No. I don't want to say it." Therapist: "I get the idea this is very painful, very painful to tell Natasha that you are learning you have failed with her. Perhaps you even feel sad about it." Ruben: (shakes his head yes, and starts to tear). Therapist: "Sad, yes, you do feel sad. Can you tell her about that sadness, the sadness that comes hearing you have disappointed her? Can you tell her about that sadness?" Ruben: "OK."

Exercise 5.

1. a
2. b
3. c
4. e
5. c

Exercise 6.

1. There could be many fears, including a fear of more fighting, fear of exposing himself and finding out he is unlovable or a failure for his wife, fear of being judged, fear of being vulnerable, fear of not knowing how to engage, fear of being seen as emotionally weak, fear of being misunderstood, fear of being verbally overwhelmed by her ability to talk, fear of losing her by any of the above.

2. "You are very concerned about another fight, and these fights are very painful for you, is that right?" "When you think of coming out and really opening up, you are afraid she will just attack again, it will be overwhelming, and it will just hurt more than it has." "Ah, so you don't come out in order to protect yourself. You are afraid you will be attacked yet again and it will just be like it always has been." "The fear of her anger and disapproval is so intense, so very intense, that you could never

turn to her and tell her you need her. It is very difficult for you to even touch that fear it is so strong. It is so much easier to run from it by either withdrawing or attacking. To turn to her and tell that you are overwhelmed by her disapproval and feel like a failure with her, that would be far too scary. So you just turn away or you attack and that seems less scary than showing how you feel. Is that it?" "Can you tell her about that fear, that fear that drives you to participate in the cycle that you are both caught in, that fear that makes it scary open up to her, even when you want to. Can you tell her about that fear, what it is like for you when you hear her anger and disapproval?"

Exercise 7.

1. b
2. b
3. c
4. e
5. d

Exercise 8. (sample answer)

1. She may be afraid that if she softens and becomes more vulnerable, he will abandon her again. She may feel deeply hurt and be afraid that if she opens up, she will just be hurt worse. Deep inside she may feel shame about herself and may be afraid that if he really knew her, he would not love her or respect her.

2. "If I understand this correctly, Jose, when you perceive her as being angry or attacking, you end up feeling a great deal of fear that you are going to have a fight which will get out of control, or she is going to overwhelm you with words and you will not be able to defend yourself, so you withdraw—you find ways to stay at work or you leave for hours at a time, or you tell her what she wants to hear, you placate. Is that right? Rosita, when he shuts down or leaves or placates, you don't perceive it as him being scared, instead you feel deeply rejected and afraid that he is going to leave you for someone else. In addition to feeling angry, you also end up feeling very hurt, lonely, and afraid and abandoned. You don't talk about fear or the hurt or the loneliness or the abandonment, but you do let him know you are angry and you see all his faults and start criticizing him and expressing your anger. Jose, that anger and criticism is very painful and leads you to fear more attacks, more fights that will get out of control, and so you work to avoid and withdraw even more. It seems that both of you are caught in this cycle that you are both participating in and are both victimized by. You both end up feeling a great deal of fear and hurt and aloneness. The ironic thing is that both of you want to connect and want it to be safe."

Exercise 10: (sample answer)

1. You might focus on and explore her fear of engaging, when it comes up, what it is connected to, and how she deals with her fears. You could have her imagine herself facing the fear, staring it down, and risking and having Jose be there.

2. You might focus on and explore the cycle and her primary emotions, such as fear and hurt, when he is not present. You could focus on her fear that if she engages, he will not be there. In order to help the fear come alive, you could have him remember a time when he was very scared and help him use that fear to construct an understanding of how she feels about risking opening up to him and being vulnerable with him. You frame her as needing his help and support.

3. "I once knew a couple that for some reason remind me of you two. They both desperately loved each other, but the husband was terrified of her anger and disapproval and often tried to escape it though working hard and keeping busy. The more he did this, the more the wife became lonely and hurt and afraid he was leaving her. In fact, she really saw it as leaving her and she become more and more angry. One day the husband decided that something needed to change. They loved each other a great deal, but he could see how they were both being hurt. The wife did too. Soon the husband was opening up and he really hoped she would open up and trust him again. However, she was so scared that he wasn't going to really be there, or want to be there if she opened up, that she refused to open up. It was so hard to see him as anything other than the man who had betrayed her and left her alone when she needed him. Despite his pleadings for her to open up and be close, which she had always wanted, she refused. It was too risky. It was too risky that he wouldn't be there, or he would stay there for a short time and then leave again. No matter how hard he tried and how much he pleaded for a chance to be there, she didn't risk it, even though she was desperate to be close to him. Finally he went away in sorrow that there seemed to be no way for her to give him a chance. When he did, she said 'I knew he wouldn't be there, I am so glad I didn't risk it.' I wonder why you two remind me of them?"

Exercise 11.

1. a
2. b
3. b
4. c
5. b

Exercise 12.

1. They may both be feeling hopeless. They may also be feeling afraid that if they let down their guard out of session, they would be hurt more and things would get worse. There could also be guilt over having married against their parents' wishes. They may be struggling with fears of abandonment, fears of finding out they are unlovable, or fears that the other spouse doesn't care.

2. Therapists might look for attachment injuries in this or previous relationships, experience or lack of experience in safe attachment relationships, previous traumas, possible competing attachments (such as sexual or nonsexual affairs or an intense relationship with a friend or family member), elements of the cycle that may have been missed, violence, and drug or alcohol usage. The therapist might also want to assess for alliance problems or difficulties related to cultural expectations and understandings.

CHAPTER 10

Exercise 1.

1. b
2. d
3. a–c, but d–g are associated general symptoms that often accompany PTSD.

Exercise 2.

Numbing-restricted affect and responses. Perhaps because this numbing narrows and restricts experience so that new learning cannot occur and isolates the person with PTSD.

Exercise 3.

1. c
2. All of the above
3. All but a

Exercise 4.

1. All but b and c. Re c: These injuries can be the primary cause of marital distress, or frequently, they exacerbate already existing distress and vulnerabilities and become a symbolic marker for the security of the relationship. Failed attempts to resolve the injury then compound already existing distress levels. Avoidance of vulnerability and numbing by the injured spouse also erode the couple's connection.
2. All of the above
3. All but a, which is a statement of general hurt and insecurity.
4. c and e
5. c and e
6. b and d
7. All of the above
8. All of the above

Exercise 5. (sample answer)

The synopsis might include the following elements:

"You were young and scared. You needed so desperately to know he was there, but you were alone."

"It seemed like you were less important than his deals. He didn't see how much you needed him."

"'Bitter.' This image still poisons your trust, your ability to put yourself in his hands, yes?"

"So you gave up and shut down and you ended up in a 'distant friends' marriage."

"But now you need each other, so this old music comes up, you need to know you can count on him, that you come first? All those soft feelings and needs you shut down..."

"You need to know he sees your pain and it hurts him, impacts him, that he won't walk away again?"

Exercise 10. (sample answer)

Wife: "I need to know that I am precious to you and that you will be there for me, not turn from me when I need." Husband: "I want to be there for you. You are so precious to me. I am here for you. You are not alone. Let me hold you. I don't want you to be afraid."

Exercise 11.

All of the above

Exercise 13.

1. All but c
2. All but f. EFT mostly works in the here and now.

Exercise 15.

c.

Exercise 16. (sample answer)

Therapist: "So for you, in that moment, when you need to reach for Ed and know he is there for you—in that moment, it is life and death, isn't it Jane? He was your lifeline, every time you grabbed onto consciousness—you tried to reach for the phone, for Ed, and it still feels like that? He was the only link to safety, the only way out of that terror, that helplessness."

Generally the therapist put Jane's need in the context of trauma and attachment, and then put all of this into the context of their relationship cycle. This cycle was withdraw/withdraw. Both were having "silent" panic attacks, sharing less and less, and becoming depressed. The therapist validated Ed in terms of how hard it was for him to understand. He got caught up in his own fears that he wasn't enough—special enough—for Jane. He had listened to his own jealousies and got caught in the fear that she must have "wanted" the rapist to make love to her. There had not been enough trust between them for her to tell him the whole picture so they would get stuck in the cycles of being "careful" and saying as little as possible or being angry and distant. Both were then traumatized and both were depressed. And both needed each other's help, touch, support.

Exercise 17. (sample answer)

Therapist: "So Ed, if I am hearing you right, you want Jane to know that you are there to hold and protect her, yes? You are distressed at her helplessness, her terror—you want her to reach for you. You grieve that your own fears blocked you seeing her pain and her need before. Can you tell her right now?" (He does.)

Exercise 18. (sample answer)

Therapist: "Can you tell him, Jane, 'I have to know I can reach you when this panic comes for me. I have to know you are there. You are my safety'? Can you tell him?"

Exercise 19. (sample answer)

"So, Jane, when Ed told you that you must have wanted sex with the rapist and that he would sell your house, find himself a girlfriend,' I am hearing that this stripped away your last shred of hope, that this was one of the times that you found yourself a 'shell.' You felt that you had lost you and your life and had lost Ed. And this is still alive for you. You still think about this a lot. It's like you are saying to Ed, 'You weren't there then, how do I know you will be there another time, next time? How can I trust and open up and put myself in your hands when this still hurts and aches and scares me.' Is that it? And Ed, you only see her anger then, not her hurt and fear, so you stay back and guard yourself. Nobody gets held and soothed here."

Exercise 20.

All of the above

Exercise 21.

The security of a person's attachment or lack of it; specific negative relationship cycles of interaction that create and maintain attachment fears and insecurities.

Exercise 22.

1. b and c. Bowlby did link depression to models of self and other formed in childhood. But this is not the primary focus in EFT, especially in Stage 1. Bowlby linked vulnerability to depression in adults (see the Dozier chapter in Cassidy & Shaver, 1999) to traumatic loss of attachment figures in childhood, to lack of secure attachment where the self is seen as a failure—and loss will then cue this again—and to messages from the parent that the child is unlovable and others are unloving. This conceptualization of depression fits well with Seligman's learned helplessness model, where noxious events are seen as uncontrollable.
2. All but b
3. b. Emotion is more articulated and regulated.
    c. Negative sense of self is replaced by a sense of self as needed and valued by the other.
    d. Isolation and loss are replaced by reassuring contact.
    e. A person can regulate negative emotions once he/she has a safe haven and a secure base.
    f. More secure attachment fosters a more accepting sense of self.

CHAPTER 11

Exercise 1.

   1. a
   2. c
   3. b
   4. d

Exercise 2.

When a baby is born and the couple system and the parental system compete.

When a couple disagree on parenting, and a member from the couple system aligns with the child.

In stepfamilies, when there is a perceived difference between how your children and my children are treated.

Exercise 3.

   a

Exercise 4.

"It sounds like the two of you are working very hard to be good parents and be good teachers and leaders for your children."

"It sounds like you have a very busy household and that you give a lot to your children and your family."

"The family conflict bothers you both as parents as you want the family to feel more harmonious and that you hope for a more positive environment for the children and yourselves. The fact that you arranged this meeting tells me how important this is to you."

Exercise 5.

"It sounds like the fighting has an effect on everyone and maybe in different ways. It seems to me that you kids are protesting in your own particular way."

"Sometimes when we don't have a way of talking about how we are feeling, the feelings come out in other ways and we show how we are feeling. Even Jack, the oldest, has shown us how he feels by not being able to come to this meeting tonight. Dennis, it seems that you are saying something about your own unhappiness in the fights and the angry outbursts and Randy, you too have your own way of getting everyone in the family to pay attention to you."

"It sounds like being in this family is also important to you guys in that the vacations and the holidays are good and a time for everyone to feel good and get along."

Exercise 6.

"The family is caught in a negative cycle characterized by critical comments and defensive reactions. The cycle prevents family members from working together and feeling close. Each member has their own way of responding to the cycle with Mom and Dad attempting to pull the family together through giving directions and when they don't get cooperation feeling discouraged and negative about the family and trying harder to get everyone to work together. Jack has dealt with the cycle by spending more and more time outside of the home. Dennis reacts to the cycle by being angry and acting out this anger through physical fights with his sibling. Randy deals with the cycle by making jokes and being the clown. The more you two youngest kids defend yourselves and make jokes, I guess, the more Dad doesn't feel heard as he ups the ante to get you to hear him—is that it?"

Exercise 7.

a, b, and c. Interventions are validating and tracking the cycle. Answer d is a more structural intervention and would not be used in a beginning session. Answer e is a behavioral intervention and would not be used in a beginning session. Answer f is an individual approach and would not be used in EFFT.

Exercise 8.

"It sounds like you are trying very hard to get your son's attention and when this doesn't happen you try harder. I wonder what it feels like for you when you can't get your son's attention and how that feels as a dad not to be able to get your son to respond to you. I would expect that must be very hard. Am I right?"

Exercise 9.

"You know, Dennis, when you look down like that and sigh it seems like you feel really discouraged, that maybe there is no use speaking up, that it doesn't really matter what you say. I wonder, too, if you think that maybe nobody is listening. Is that close?"

Exercise 10.

"It seems that it is very important to you to be a good mom to your daughter. You have worked hard recently to understand yourself more and understand your role as a mom. That takes a lot of courage."

"It seems like you would like to have a better relationship with Melissa, and you are trying hard to find a balance between protecting her and remaining connected to her."

"It must have been very hard to see your daughter so sick and so frail and not be able to do anything about it."

Exercise 11.

"It seems like you would like to have a better relationship with Melissa and you try very hard and are being very careful in your relationship with her in order to avoid conflict and keep the peace."

"You are feeling sad about what has happened in the past with Melissa, and it looks like it breaks your heart that she went through what she did."

"It seems like you are unsure about how to be a good dad to Melissa now, and you are trying your best to do that."

Exercise 12.

"It sounds like being a good daughter is really important for you, and you often feel like you are not doing a very good job at that."

"It sounds like you are not too sure about how to be a good daughter, and how your parents think about you is very important to you."

"For all of us, I think there is a part of us, no matter how old we get, that wants our parent's approval."

Exercise 13.

Therapist: "You know that when I hear you talk, it strikes me that, you, Mom, want so much to be a good mom to Melissa and offer advice and feedback, that oftentimes Melissa hears that as disapproval and criticism. She then defends herself, and Mom, you try harder to have Melissa hear your message. Melissa gets angrier, and Dad, you see an approaching storm and you just try to not rock the boat. All of you end up feeling disconnected and in a lot of pain. Does that fit with how you experience it?"

Exercise 14.

d, f, and g are tracking questions to identify the negative cycle. Answer e is an intervention to assess strengths and validate the family's emotional recourses. Answer c may be used by an EFFT therapist but would be more linked to the negative interactional cycle. Answers a and b would not be used by an EFFT therapist.

Exercise 15.

"It sounds like, Mom, you are very worried and concerned about your daughter and I am hearing in there that you also worry about your connection to her and wonder if you count or matter to her, whether your thoughts and opinions about what you hope and wish for your daughter get through to her, whether she hears you. Is that anywhere close to how you feel?"

Exercise 16.

"It sounds like you get frustrated and maybe even hurt when you share something with your mom. What you hear is that she does not approve. That can hurt a lot, especially when it's your mom, who is so important to you."

Exercise 17.

1. Validation, normalization
2. Reframing the problem in terms of the cycle and attachment emotions

3. Empathic conjecture

4. Empathic reflection

5. Empathic conjecture

6. Enactment

7. Empathic conjecture

8. Empathic conjecture

9. Empathic conjecture

10. Empathic conjecture

11. Reflection, heightening

12. Empathic conjecture, heightening

13. Heightening

14. Seeding secure attachment

15. Heightening, enactment

16. Validation, heightening

Exercise 18.

Mom reacts to daughter's autonomous behavior with anxiety expressed as disapproval and criticism to which the daughter reacts with anger and withdrawal (won't confide in mother.) Daughter's withdrawal feeds Mom's fear, which leads to more efforts to control and monitor her daughter's behavior, which leads to daughter withdrawing more.

Exercise 19.

Under Mom's criticism and disapproval there is fear that she will lose her daughter, that she has failed as a mom and that she is unlovable.

Exercise 20.

Under Melissa's anger and defiance there are feelings of unworthiness and of not being good enough, and the model of self as unlovable.

Exercise 21.

Mom's criticism is fed by her fear around failing as a mom and losing her daughter. Daughter's withdrawal is a reflection of how important her mom is to her in that her anger and withdrawal protect her from feeling her hurt and pain—the hurt of disappointing Mom.

Exercise 22.

Opening up the dialogue and promoting the sharing of each woman's internal emotional experiences creates new interactions. Both women are able to provide each other with support, Mom wanting daughter to take care of herself and her daughter supporting Mom's positive parenting. Structuring an enactment allows mother and daughter to solidify their new dance.

Exercise 23.

a, b, and c. Answer d would be chosen only if the dyad was not able to move beyond their negative cycle.

Exercise 24.

1. "It sounds like when you see Melissa turning away from you that feels sad and the worry sounds a lot like fear—fear that she will get hurt and maybe you will lose her and that's really scary. Is that close?"

2. "There are times when you interact with Melissa that you say things and do things which make you feel bad. It sounds like maybe you feel bad because what you say hurts her, and you feel like you are not measuring up as a good mother, which is very important to you."

3. "It sounds like you want your mom to know that when you and she fight, even though you fight back it hurts so much inside, it rips you apart and the way you get comfort is to go to your room. It feels safe there?"

4. "Good for you, Melissa. You are telling your mom pretty directly what you need from her, and your own confidence in yourself shines through. You want your mom to understand and trust this strong part of yourself. How is that, Mom, for you to hear?"

REFERENCES

Arnold, M. B. (1960). *Emotion and personality*. New York: Columbia Press.

Bertalanffy, L. (1956). *General system theory*. New York: George Braziller.

Bograd, M., & Maderos, F. (1999). Battering and couples therapy: Universal screening and selection of treatment modality. *Journal of Marital & Family Therapy*, 25(3), 291–312.

Bowlby, J. (1969). *Attachment and loss. Vol 1: Attachment*. New York: Basic Books.

Bowlby, J. (1973). *Attachment and loss. Vol 2: Separation*. New York: Basic Books.

Bowlby, J. (1979). *The making and breaking of affectional bonds*. London: Tavistock.

Bowlby, J. (1988). *A secure base*. New York: Basic Books.

Bradley, B. & Furrow, J. (2004). *Towards a mini-theory of the blamer softening event: Tracking the moment by moment process*. Journal of Marital & Family Therapy, 30, 233–246.

Brennan, K. A., Clark, C. L., & Shaver, P. R. (1998). Self-report measurement of adult attachment: An integrative overview. In J. A. Simpson & W. S. Rhodes (Eds.), *Attachment theory and close relationships* (pp. 46–76). New York: Guilford.

Cassidy, C., & Shaver, P. (1999). *Handbook of attachment: Theory research and clinical applications*. New York: Guilford.

Denton, W., Burelson, B. R., Clark, T. E., Rodriguez, C. P., & Hobbs, B. V. (2000). A randomized trial of emotionally focused therapy for couples in a training clinic. *Journal of Marital & Family Therapy*, 26, 65–78.

Dickstein, S. (2004). Marital attachment and family functioning: Use of narrative methodology. In M. W. Pratt & B. H. Fiese (Eds.), *Family stories and the life course: Across time and generations* (pp. 213–232). Mahwah, NJ: Erlbaum.

Doherty, W. J. (2001). *Take back your marriage: Sticking together in a world that pulls us apart*. New York: Guilford.

Fosha, D. (2000). *The transforming power of affect: A model for accelerated change*. New York: Basic Books.

Fraley, R. C., & Waller, N. G. (1998). Adult attachment patterns: A test of the typological model. In J. A. Simpson & W. S. Rhodes (Eds.), *Attachment theory and close relationships* (pp. 77–114). New York: Guilford.

Fridja, N. J. (1986). *The emotions*. Cambridge, England: Cambridge University Press.

Gottman, J. (1994). *What predicts divorce*. Hillsdale, NJ: Erlbaum.

Greenberg, L. S., & Angus, L. E. (2004). The contributions of emotion processes to narrative change in psychotherapy: A dialectical constructivist approach. In L. E. Angus & J. McLeod (Eds.), *The handbook of narrative and psychotherapy: Practice, theory, and research* (pp. 331–349). Thousand Oaks, CA: Sage Publications.

Greenberg, L. S., Rice, L., & Elliott, R. (1993). *Facilitating emotional change*. New York: Guilford.

Hesse, E. (1999). The adult attachment interview. In J. Cassidy & P. Shaver (Eds.), *Handbook of attachment* (pp. 395–433). New York: Guilford.

Johnson, S. M. (2002). *Emotionally focused couple therapy with trauma survivors*. New York: Guilford.

Johnson, S. M. (2004). *Creating connection: The practice of emotionally focused couple therapy* (2nd ed.). New York: Brunner-Routledge.

Johnson, S. M., & Greenberg, L. S. (Eds.). (1994). *The heart of the matter: Perspectives on emotion in marital therapy*. New York: Brunner-Mazel. Fishbane, M. (2001). Relational narratives of the self. *Family Process*, 40, 273–290.

Johnson, S.M., & Whiffin, V. E. (2003). *Attachment processes in couple and family therapy*. New York: Guilford.

Jordan, J. V., Kaplan, A. G., Miller, J. B., Stiver, I. P., & Surrey, J. L. (1991). *Women's growth in connection: Writings from the Stone Centre*. New York: Guilford.

Lazarus, R. S., & Lazarus, B. N. (1994). *Passion and reason*. New York: Oxford University Press.

Minuchin, S., & Fishman, H. C. (1981). *Family therapy techniques*. Cambridge, MA: Harvard University Press.

Roberts, L. J., & Greenberg, D. R. (2002). Observational windows to intimacy processes in marriage. In P. Noller & J. Feeney (Eds.), *Understanding marriage* (pp. 118–149). New York: Cambridge University Press.

Rogers, C. (1961). *Client centered therapy*. Boston: Houghton Mifflin.

Shaver, P., & Brennen, K. (1992). Attachment styles and the five big personality traits. Personality and *Social Psychology Bulletin, 5*, 536–545.

Spanier, G. B. (1976). Measuring dyadic adjustment: New scales for assessing the quality of marriage and similar dyads. *Journal of Marriage and the Family, 38*, 15–28.

Tomkins, S. (1962). *Affect, imagery and consciousness*. New York: Springer.

Wile, D. B. (1994). The ego-analytic approach to emotion in couples therapy. In S. M. Johnson & L. S. Greenberg (Eds.), *The heart of the matter* (pp. 27–45). New York: Brunner/Mazel.

ABOUT THE AUTHORS

Sue Johnson, Ed.D., is a professor of psychology at the University of Ottawa and is involved in the ongoing supervision of clinical students in couple and in individual therapy. She teaches graduate courses in couples' therapy, trauma interventions, and experiential individual therapy. She is also director of the Ottawa Couple and Family Institute and conducts externships in EFT in Ottawa every year. Sue also serves as research professor at Alliant University in San Diego, where she conducts EFT training every January. She is the main proponent of emotionally focused couples' therapy and emotionally focused family therapy and received the American Association of Marriage and Family Therapy Outstanding Contribution to the Field award in 2000. Sue is also a fellow of the American Psychological Association and received the Excellence in Education award from the University of Ottawa in 2003. She received the award for research in family therapy from the American Family Therapy Academy in 2005. She is married with two children.

Brent Bradley, Ph.D., is an associate professor and director of the Marriage and Family Therapy Track in the Graduate Counseling Department at Indiana Wesleyan University. He is a licensed marriage and family therapist and a clinical member of the American Association of Marriage and Family Therapy. Brent is a certified emotionally focused couples' therapist and supervisor. He is an active writer, researcher, supervisor, and national presenter. Brent offers an annual 40-hour training externship in EFT in coordination with Dr. Johnson and the Ottawa Couple and Family Institute. Other professional interests include process research on critical change elements in couple and family therapy; working models of self, other, and God, and their mutual influence in the change process; and effectively integrating spirituality and therapy.

James Furrow, Ph.D., is associate professor of marital and family therapy and program director of the Department of Marriage and Family at Fuller Graduate School of Psychology in Pasadena, California. He is a registered EFT therapist as well as an approved supervisor and clinical member of the American Association of Marital and Family Therapy. His research and clinical interests focus on the clinical application of EFT with couples and families. He conducts EFT training in graduate and post-graduate settings. James is codirector of the Center for Research on Child and Adolescent Development at Fuller where he conducts research on personal and social resources associated with positive youth development in childhood and adolescence.

Alison Lee, Ph.D., is vice president and founding member of the Ottawa Couple and Family Institute. She received her doctorate in clinical psychology from the University of Ottawa. Alison is a registered psychologist in the province of Ontario and practices at the Ottawa Couple and Family Institute.

Gail Palmer is a social worker and registered marriage and family therapist in full-time private practice. Gail is one of the founding members of the Ottawa Couple & Family Institute and an EFT trainer and an AAMFT-approved supervisor.

Doug Tilley is a marriage and family therapist practicing in the Annapolis, Maryland. He is certified as a licensed certified social worker—clinical and is designated as a clinical member and an approved supervisor by the American Association of Marriage and Family Therapy. In his practice he sees couples, families, and individuals dealing with a wide range of life dilemmas and clinical issues. Douglas is also a registered EFT therapist and trains mental health professionals in EFT in the greater Washington, D.C. area.

Scott Woolley, Ph.D., is the director of the marital and family therapy masters and doctoral programs in the California School of Professional Psychology at Alliant International University in San Diego and Irvine, California. He has a clinical specialization in couple therapy and MFT supervision and has trained mental health professionals in Finland, Hong Kong, Japan, Taiwan, Canada, and throughout the United States in couple therapy and/or supervision. Scott's primary clinical and research interests are in the areas of emotionally focused couples' therapy, marriage, observational therapy process research, cross-cultural issues, and supervision processes. He earned his M.S. in marriage and family therapy from Brigham Young University and his Ph.D. in marriage and family therapy from Texas Tech University. Scott is licensed in both Texas and California and is an AAMFT clinical member and approved supervisor.

INDEX